VISIONARY PRICING:
REFLECTIONS AND ADVANCES
IN HONOR OF DAN NIMER

ADVANCES IN BUSINESS MARKETING & PURCHASING

Series Editor: Arch G. Woodside

Recent Volumes:

ADVANCES IN BUSINESS MARKETING &
PURCHASING   VOLUME 19

VISIONARY PRICING: REFLECTIONS AND ADVANCES IN HONOR OF DAN NIMER

EDITED BY

GERALD E. SMITH

Carroll School of Management, Boston College, MA, USA

United Kingdom – North America – Japan
India – Malaysia – China

Emerald Group Publishing Limited
Howard House, Wagon Lane, Bingley BD16 1WA, UK

First edition 2012

Copyright © 2012 Emerald Group Publishing Limited

Reprints and permission service
Contact: permissions@emeraldinsight.com

British Library Cataloguing in Publication Data
A catalogue record for this book is available from the British Library

ISBN: 978-1-78052-996-7
ISSN: 1069-0964 (Series)

Certificate Number 1985
ISO 9001
ISO 14001

ISOQAR certified
Management Systems,
awarded to Emerald for
adherence to Quality
and Environmental
standards ISO 9001:2008
and 14001:2004,
respectively

INVESTOR IN PEOPLE

CONTENTS

LIST OF CONTRIBUTORS

George E. Cressman, Jr.	World Class Pricing, Inc. Woodbine, GA, USA
Chuck Davenport	Deloitte Consulting LLP Atlanta, GA, USA
Allan Gray	Vendavo, Inc. Mountain View, CA, USA
Reed K. Holden	Holden Advisors Concord, MA, USA
E. M. (Mick) Kolassa	Medical Marketing Economics, LLC Oxford, MS, USA
Michael Lucaccioni	Vendavo, Inc. Mountain View, CA, USA
Mike Marn	Mckinsey & Company, Inc. Sanibel, FL, USA
Kent B. Monroe	University of Richmond Richmond, VA, USA
Thomas Nagle	Monitor Group LLP Cambridge, MA, USA
Dan Nimer	The DNA Group, Inc. Northbrook, IL, USA
John Norkus	Deloitte Consulting LLP Chicago, IL, USA
Jamie Rapperport	Vendavo, Inc. Mountain View, CA, USA
Hermann Simon	Simon-Kucher & Partners Bonn, Germany
Michael Simonetto	Deloitte Consulting LLP Chicago, IL, USA

Navdeep S. Sodhi   Sodhi Pricing Minneapolis, MN, USA

Gerald E. Smith   Carroll School of Management Boston
                             College Chestnut Hill, MA, USA

Lisa Thompson   Monitor Group LLP Cambridge,
                             MA, USA

Takaho Ueda   Faculty of Economics Gakushuin
                             University, Tokyo, Japan

Arch G. Woodside   Carroll School of Management
                             Boston College Chestnut Hill, MA, USA

Elliott Yama   Vendavo Inc. Mountain View, CA, USA

Craig Zawada   PROS Pricing, Inc. Kimberley,
                             BC, Canada

Eugene F. Zelek, Jr.   Freeborn & Peters LLP Chicago,
                             IL, USA

ABOUT THE EDITOR

Gerald E. Smith is chair of the marketing faculty at Boston College in the Carroll Graduate School of Management, where he leads the product and brand management MBA specialization, and (teaches strategic pricing management.) His research has been cited in popular press outlets such as *The Wall Street Journal*, *The Christian Science Monitor*, *The Boston Globe*, *Across the Board*, and others, and has been published in *Journal of the Academy of Marketing Science*, *California Management Review*, *Sloan Management Review*, *Marketing Research*, *Marketing Management*, *Pricing Strategy & Practice*, *Journal of Retailing*, *Public Administration Review*, *Psychology and Marketing*, *Journal of Professional Pricing*, among others. He is a frequent speaker and corporate consultant on product management and pricing, including in leading business programs at Duke, Wharton, Columbia, Boston University, and Suffolk University.

FOREWORD TO VISIONARY PRICING

A rare and valuable combination of practical advice, theoretical modeling, and descriptive explanation of pricing decisions is the summary thought that best captures the overall contribution of *Visionary Pricing (VP)*. *VP* builds principally on Dan Nimer's great foresight that pricing cannot be the sole domain of finance or any singe functional area and in offering a paradigm shift from cost-plus pricing to customer-value-based pricing.

Above all else the chapters in *VP* instruct how to achieve mindfulness in pricing decisions by using Nimer's acumen: when working with the Client, keep it simple. Nimer advises, "Don't waste too much time overcomplicating the topic of customer value. Just ask the client this: 'Do you know how much it costs your customers NOT to be doing business with you?' Those simple words have sent me [Tom Nagle] on a never-ending quest to add value to my clients in simple, clear and powerful ways" (in chapter by Thomas Nagle and Lisa Thompson in this volume).

VP offers great depth and breadth in achieving nuanced wisdom of mindful-thinking by the world's leading pricing consultants. These consultants are bold and generous in describing the years of training necessary to achieve such wisdom. For example, in *VP* Hermann Simon explains, "I have to admit that it took me 20 years of research and consulting work to fully recognize the outstanding importance of pricing processes. Especially as the B2B-world is dominated by pricing processes rather than price optimization in the microeconomic sense." The brilliant study of pricing processes in gasoline markets by Howard and Morgenroth (1968) is illustrative of modeling with testing of the predictive validity of such pricing processes. In *VP* Kent Monroe applies Nimer's perspective in reviewing a substantial number of pricing process studies.

In *VP* Chuck Davenport, John Norkus, Michael Simonetto complement Monroe's contribution by offering how-to and why-to specifics in pricing metrics for answering Nimer's (1971, p. 50) question, "If the customer's perception of your product's value is worth considering at all (as it most certainly is), why ignore it when it comes to price, which is precisely what perceived value is measured against by the customer?"

This foreword has two objectives. Emphasizing the delivery of exceptional value in knowledge and skills in value pricing that VP delivers to the reader is the first objective. The second objective is to express gratitude to Dan Nimer for sharing his vast wisdom, the authors for advancing Nimer's contributions to mindful pricing practices, and to Gerald Smith for his leadership in accomplishing this unique volume in the *Advances in Business Marketing and Purchasing* series. Capturing such depth and breadth of knowledge and skills about pricing in one volume is a rare occurrence. For marketing executives, pricing consultants, and professors of marketing, an intellectual and practical feast awaits your reading of *VP*.

Arch G. Woodside

REFERENCES

Howard, J. A., & Morgenroth, W. M. (1968). Information processing model of executive decision. *Management Science, 14,* 416–428.

Nimer, D. A. (1971). There's more to pricing than most companies think. In I. R. Vernon & C. W. Lamb, Jr. (Eds.), *The pricing function: A pragmatic approach* (pp. 19–33). Lexington, MA: Lexington Books.

INTRODUCTION TO VISIONARY PRICING

In terms of the life cycle, pricing certainly would be considered a young and emerging discipline, only a few decades old. Even marketing is only 50 years old as a business discipline; Jerome McCarthy of Michigan State University introduced the Four P's classification (product, promotion, price, and place-distribution) in 1960. Peter Drucker's influential *The Practice of Management* hailed the twentieth century as a "marketing revolution" in 1954, but mentions pricing fewer than a dozen times, even then only in passing.

Pricing emerged as its own discipline in the 1980s with a flurry of conceptual development and innovation – value-based pricing, incremental costing, yield management pricing, pocket price waterfall, to name a few. In 1985 a small group of pricing pioneers led the inauguration of The Pricing Conference, organized by the Institute for International Research's Pricing Institute in New York, dedicated entirely to illuminating, sharing and encouraging research on pricing that would be relevant to pricing managers. At the time there were few attending the Conference who held a position with pricing in their title; most had only adjunct pricing responsibilities along with jobs in sales, marketing, operations, or finance. In the early 1990s the first pricing journal *Pricing Strategy & Practice: An International Journal* appeared, published by MCB University Press (later merged into *Journal of Product & Brand Management*, published by Emerald Group Publishing). In 1997 the first Behavioral Pricing Conference was held in Boston.

Behind this revolution was a group of pricing thought leaders actively committed to pricing's conceptual development. They were close to the practice of managerial pricing through consulting, advanced research, and price leadership in industry – and they were close to great universities of thought. They were schooled in economic theory, trained in research methods, and committed to pricing's application in real world companies, with real world managers, and real world results.

Visionary Pricing brings together the wisdom and perspective of these pricing thought leaders from North America, Europe, and Asia, who originally came together 30 years ago to encourage the development of pricing. They now assess the present and future destiny of pricing, pricing innovation, and pricing paradigms that are influencing the evolution of pricing throughout the world. Pricing has matured over the last several decades, but into what has it matured? Yet pricing still has not arrived and in many ways is still a nascent discipline. So, where is pricing going – what are the innovations today that will define pricing decades from now? Our contributing pricing luminaries include, listed alphabetically:

- George Cressman, World Class Pricing, Inc.
- Chuck Davenport, John Norkus, and Michael Simonetto, Deloitte Consulting LLP
- Allan Gray, Michael Lucaccioni, Jamie Rapperport, and Elliott Yama, Vendavo, Inc.
- Reed K. Holden, Holden Advisors
- E.M. (Mick) Kolassa, Medical Marketing Economics, Inc., University of Mississippi
- Mike Marn, McKinsey & Company
- Kent B. Monroe, University of Illinois, Urbana-Champaign and University of Richmond
- Thomas T. Nagle and Lisa Thompson, Monitor Group LLP
- Dan Nimer, The Dan Nimer Group, Inc.
- Hermann Simon, Simon-Kucher & Partners, Strategy & Marketing Consultants
- Gerald E. Smith, Carroll School of Management, Boston College
- Navdeep S. Sodhi, University of St. Thomas
- Takaho Ueda, Gakushuin University, Tokyo.
- Craig Zawada, PROS Pricing
- Eugene F. Zelek, Jr., Freeborn & Peters LLP.

We especially dedicate this volume to pricing's first pioneering thought leader, Dan Nimer. Now in his 91st year, Dan is a dear friend and influenced some of our earliest thinking in the field of pricing, spawning ideas that have grown into today's broad field of pricing theory and practice. Dan has been blessed with excellent health and even in his senior years continues a vigorous schedule to advance his thoughts on the field. This volume is intended to honor his legacy and say thank you from a group of colleagues who came together originally to encourage the development of pricing. Dan was trained in economic theory, learned pricing in the trenches of the real world of the 1950s and 1960s, and then embarked on a long career of pricing thought leadership through his involvement in pricing education at universities and public and private pricing seminars throughout the world for the latter half of the 20th century and the first decade of the 21st century.

Visionary Pricing contains four sections:

Section 1 first interviews Nimer and discusses the origins of value pricing as an influential pricing paradigm of the 21st century. Then, in "The Founding Principles and Strategies of Pricing," Gerald E. Smith of Boston College and Dan Nimer of the DNA Group, Inc., map the development of managerial pricing and identify some of pricing's most important conceptual developments, their origin, and their foundational role in the field of pricing today.

Section 2 focuses on pricing strategy and competitive advantage, presenting four research papers. In "Integrating Marketing and Operational Choices for Profit Growth" Thomas Nagle and Lisa Thompson of Monitor Group LLP advance the insightful thesis that future pricing will require integrating marketing and operational choices to achieve greater cost effectiveness. Pricing professionals are uniquely positioned to facilitate that integration and thus to become more involved in defining the profitable strategic focus for their companies. In "How Price Consulting is Coming of Age," Hermann Simon of Simon-Kucher & Partners shows the theoretical and methodological evolution of pricing into many specializations along price measurement, price model building, and structural and industry lines – with today's pricing marked by advanced integration of pricing theory and practice. In "Incorporating Competitive Strategy in Pricing Strategy," George E. Cressman, Jr., of World Class Pricing provides a comprehensive process for the strategic management of the connection between pricing and competitive strategy, especially focused on the active management of competitive interactions that significantly improve profitability. Finally, in "Emergent Pricing Strategy," Gerald E. Smith argues that the emergence of dynamic pricing and variable pricing strategies require that firms need to develop new strategic pricing skills that lead to more improvisational, innovative, and adaptive pricing strategies.

Section 3 focuses on the defining role of value in pricing, with five definitive papers on what we know about value, how to measure value, and how to manage value in the marketplace. In "Price and Customers' Perceptions of Value," Kent B. Monroe of the University of Illinois, Urbana-Champaign, and the University of Richmond provides a comprehensive assessment of what we know today about behavioral pricing – how buyers perceive price and how these perceptions influence their perceptions of value. Reed K. Holden of Holden Advisors, in "Using Case ROI^{TM} to Determine Customer and Segment Value in the Business-to-Business Environment," presents an innovative value measurement method, Case ROI, to calculate the value of new products and technologies with greater precision. In "Legal Tools That Support Value Pricing," Eugene F. Zelek, Jr., shows how the law permits value pricing to be facilitated and preserved through the use of non-price vertical restrictions and resale price setting. In "Understanding Value – Beyond Mere Metrics," E. M. (Mick) Kolassa of Medical Marketing Economics and the University of Mississippi explores the less tangible but equally or more important aspects of value that often drive decision making, aspects that don't lend themselves easily to the metrics many believe are essential to solving the pricing puzzle. Takaho Ueda of Gakushuin University in Tokyo, in "Creating Value with Sales Promotion Strategies That Avoid Price Discounting," introduces an innovative new form of sales promotion strategy that creates more value for goods and avoids price discounting using a psychological approach involving in-depth interviews, web-motivation research, and text mining – a hot topic among large companies in Japan.

Section 4 focuses on pricing capability and innovation, presenting four provocative papers on pricing capability, pricing technology, pricing analytics, and effectively managing pricing operations. In "Pricing – From *Good* to *World Class*," Craig Zawada of PROS Pricing and Mike Marn of McKinsey & Company argue that the growing complexity of pricing demands that companies take their pricing capabilities to the next level of performance – to a level of "world class." Allan Gray, Michael Lucaccioni, Jamie Rapperport, and Elliott Yama of Vendavo, Inc., in "Pricing Software: Ten Predictions for the Future," present a brief historical development of enterprise pricing software in a typical B2B corporation – with a set of predictions of future capabilities based on emerging trends. Chuck Davenport, John Norkus, and Michael Simonetto of Deloitte Consulting LLP, in "Capturing the Value of Pricing Analytics," show how to use analytics to determine where value resides within and among market segments and how to turn that analysis into an effective platform for pricing decisions. And finally, Navdeep S. Sodhi of the University of St. Thomas, in "Prepare Your Pricing Operations for Change," that argues companies should improve pricing operations before embarking on large initiatives that can affect prices, such as, mergers or acquisitions, business process redesign, new technology implementation, or large-scale reorganization.

This volume marks a seminal moment in the history of pricing, having arrived now as an emerging discipline with its own theory-driven paradigms and increasingly supportive empirical evidence. Now, as the tectonic plates of markets and organizations shift with rapid changes in digital technology and market priorities, pricing moves forward inexorably in the new century with new models, new applications, and new ways. The models of the past

30 years – many of them originating and documented by thought leaders appearing in this volume – are now integrated into the management curricula of many universities – they are becoming well established. They are the foundation that now point the way toward the innovations of the next 30 years that will define pricing in the 21st century.

Gerald E. Smith
Editor

SECTION 1
DAN NIMER

ON DAN NIMER

There must have been a time when Dan Nimer was not interested in prices, but obviously that was long ago. He was already well into his favorite subject in 1959, when as manager of budgets and sales forecasting for Zenith Sales Corp. (a division of Zenith Radio) he got his first chance to act on his conviction that pricing offers far more opportunities for managerial ingenuity than most businessmen realize. His move in 1963 to Canteen Corp., which is in the food service business, may seem surprising at first glance but fits in perfectly with another principle in the Nimer canon: that the rules of intelligent pricing, as of intelligent management in general, are sufficiently basic to apply with equal validity to radios and to hot dogs (which is what Canteen sells at Yankee Stadium).

In retrospect, it seems inevitable that Nimer's zeal in the cause of better pricing should have brought him to the lecture platform, but actually it happened by accident, he says. In 1963, he had put his name down for an Industrial Education Institute seminar on sales forecasting but at the last moment discovered he couldn't go. He wrote to IEI that he wanted at least the background material that had been offered as a feature of the seminar. When it didn't come, he called up and somehow got connected with IEI's president. By the time he had hung up, he had been asked to lecture on pricing under IEI's auspices.

Since then, Nimer has added the American Management Association, the American Marketing Association, the Bank Marketing Association, and a number of European organizations to the list of sponsors of his seminars on pricing, budgeting, marketing, and corporate planning. And as though peripatetic lecturing weren't enough, he also teaches managerial economics in the graduate program of the Industrial Management Institute at Lake Forest College and has been working for some time on a book about pricing.[1]

—Englebert Kirchner (1971)

NOTE

1. Nimer, D. A. (1971, August). There's more to pricing than most companies think. In *Innovations*. Reprinted in Vernon, I. R., & Lamb, C. W. (Eds.) (1976). *The pricing function* (pp. 19–33). Lexington, MA: Lexington Books, D.C. Heath & Co.

ONE ON ONE, PRICING WITH DAN NIMER

Gerald E. Smith and Dan Nimer

Smith: Dan, let's begin with value pricing. Where did value pricing
come from?

Nimer: Well, with me it started some time ago when I was at Zenith,
and we had television sets and portable televisions. We
started out with these little portables, then we had a bigger
table model, then we had the console models. And the
question was, they all had the same innards, but how do you
calculate the value of the difference to maintain some sort of
value/price consistency among them? And so one of the
problems was table models weren't selling very well and the
boss said, "Why don't we just cut the price of the
table models?" And I said, "You can't do that. If you do
that, you narrow the price difference between the
portable and the table model, even though the value has
remained the same, and you change the value/price difference
of the console versus the table model." So what we did
instead was, we offered a $19 free table when you bought a
table model, which enhanced the value of the table model
television and allowed us to maintain the value/price

Visionary Pricing: Reflections and Advances in Honor of Dan Nimer
Advances in Business Marketing & Purchasing, Volume 19, 5–11
Copyright © 2012 by Emerald Group Publishing Limited
All rights of reproduction in any form reserved
ISSN: 1069-0964/doi:10.1108/S1069-0964(2012)0000019006

differentials among the television models in the product line. That was my first attempt.

Smith: About what year was that?

Nimer: Golly, I would say it must be about 60 years ago. Sixty years ago, holy mackerel!

Smith: So, all of this was trying to keep the differential between different products in the product line, right?

Nimer: It was maintaining value/price differential, even though the whole concept of perceived value hadn't even entered my mind at the time. In my mind, the value was in just having one of these television sets. Because at that time there weren't very many TV stations operating and people would sit there and, you wouldn't believe this Jerry, they would sit there and look at the blank television screen waiting for the signal! There were three or four television stations in the Chicago area, for example, and you turned on your television set – it was ABC, NBC, and CBS.

Smith: Do you remember how much the models sold for?

Nimer: Well, there were three models. The console probably sold somewhere in the $395 level, then the tabletop model which came with a table that sold separately for $19, and then the portable model. Management wanted to come in at a very, very low price and they thought they could increase their sales if they dropped their price. And so I, in my rash youth, said, "Look guys, if you change the price once, then the market will not trust the prices that you set." And you're much better setting up three prices – for portable, table, console – maintaining those prices, but don't change the value differential between them because it means changing the product mix – and may involve changing the production line, which can also be expensive.

Smith: Talk more about how you create this perceived value.

Nimer: Well you know that when you introduce a really new product, something that people have never had before, you have to create perceived value before you get them to buy it. To do this you have to first *create the price* when you bring it to market that will establish the value, especially when people know little about the new product. In other words, you set your price first and then justify your price with your value

	later on. For a long, long time in the television market, it was
	the price differential that made the difference to the
	marketplace − not the value difference.
Smith:	How did you communicate this value to the customers then?
Nimer:	Well, Zenith *radio* had a fantastic reputation, Jerry. They

Smith: How did you communicate this value to the customers then?

Nimer: Well, Zenith *radio* had a fantastic reputation, Jerry. They said, "The quality goes in before the name goes on." And people remembered that brand name, and we would say, "Remember who makes the Zenith radio." Well, the Zenith television is made by the same people that make Zenith radio. And then Admiral came in with their prices below ours. The whole idea being to take market share away from us because they were priced lower, but their value − let's say they were priced 10% below us, but they were worth about 20% below us in terms of features and type of cabinetry and the like − and so they couldn't take market share away from us because we had the dominant share in television. There was Admiral at the time, and RCA, and then Motorola came in.

Smith: How did you monetize the difference in features between Zenith and Motorola for example?

Nimer: In fact, the basic circuitry and the basic technology at that time were used by every maker, but you changed it always by adding value. You remember the name Grundig-Majestic? Grundig-Majestic had the most beautiful cabinets you'd ever seen. So the people would buy the Grundig-Majestic, because it had short wave, it had more features. Well, now the Zenith television had a Grundig-Majestic cabinet, and a greater value.

Smith: So that was the basis for incremental value to buyers?

Nimer: Well, the concept of value was new ... ours is of greater value because we have more tubes than they have, or a nicer cabinet. But in every one of these cases, the value of that difference often was perceived as negligible versus competitors − negligible. There was very little difference in the value because management never discussed perceived value. So whatever *price differential* they had, that was the leading thing in the marketplace that changed market share. And so, I was assistant to the president of Zenith, a guy named Len Trusdale, and I said, "Len, I think we can sell 6 million television sets this year," because they were content

with a 15% sales increase every year, which they could
maintain very easily because the market would have taken
20% sales increase at the value/price differences they offered.
So, sure enough, I said, "Len, I think we can sell 6 million
and that should be our forecast." So he gave that to the
newspapers and the like and they said, "Trusdale Predicts
6 Million TV Sets Sold." You know how many sold, Jerry?
5,996,915 — because that's how many we produced. They
always had a backlog in the marketplace.

Smith: That's brilliant forecasting, but what else did you do to
                achieve that success?

Nimer: Well, I just felt that since it was a new market and very, very
                few people had television sets, the name that Zenith had in
                that marketplace was sufficient. In addition, we leveraged our
                distribution channel. At that time, manufacturers always
                worked through distributors. Zenith never sold directly to the
                stores; they sold through distributors, who would then sell to
                the stores. So, we had to make sure that the distributors
                themselves added value — and their value was called "Just in
                Time." We enabled our distributors to get a better turnover,
                so that the distributor itself made a higher return on its
                investment with Zenith than it did on any other television.
                So, the whole idea was, when you work through a distributor
                organization, the distributor itself has to create value to
                justify the price — the markup that he added for his
                profitability. And the manufacturer has to help the
                distributor in delivering that value — a partnership. For
                example, the distributors themselves couldn't afford to carry
                the inventory that we wanted them to carry. So Zenith
                arranged lines of credit with banks around the country and,
                as a result, Zenith almost guaranteed that those distributors
                were sound money managers. So working through that
                distributorship model, we increased our sales to maintain our
                position as number one in the marketplace.

Nimer: Another one of the things we did was we promoted "The
                quality goes in before the name goes on." Our advertising
                and promotion allowances were much greater than they were
                for Motorola or any other television sets. But, that was
                money we spent to enhance the perceived value of what we

had to offer in the marketplace, when nobody had any idea what the perceived value was. People were sitting around a television set that had nothing on the screen except a test pattern.

Smith: But why didn't Zenith just raise the prices if they could sell 6 million instead of 1 million?

Nimer: Because management was very very happy with the return they got on what they did. Jerry, if you've never had 20%, okay, you were very comfortable operating about at 16—17% market share. You were comfortable with that because you knew what your cash flow was going to be, you knew how much money you had to spend for advertising allowances.

Smith: Did you see others in the industry start to adopt what you guys were doing at Zenith?

Nimer: No they didn't, because they couldn't; they didn't have the quality and their name wasn't so broadly accepted. Once you've got brand recognition, it seems to me that the perceived value of anything owes just as much to the brand as to the product itself.

Smith: How did you manage value to ensure continued growth?

Nimer: Well, there would be very very little discounting. Instead, when we wanted to sell something — we'd provide something else for it. So in this case, for example, you got a free table with the table television model (and the table itself sold for $19, and it only costs us about $12). If we had dropped the price $19 to maintain that, it would have cost Zenith an awful lot of money. And that's a concept for every firm in the world, I think.

Smith: When you set the price for a new television — deciding whether the price should be $395 or $495 or whatever — did you do a lot of pricing research?

Nimer: Very, very little. They had a market research department, and I happened to be in there for a time, but the market research was mainly monitoring market share changes and share of market. There was nobody that really tried to measure the value of any of these televisions; that's because they never had televisions in the market before and they had no frame of reference. There was no base line to say ours is 20% better or 30% better or 15% worse.

Smith: When you look at the pricing work that you did, what were the other perspectives on pricing then?

Nimer: It was all cost plus. And even now, Jerry, you know I've traveled around the world, but most organizations regardless of geography or offerings look at pricing as a financial exercise and do not consider it a part of the marketing process that creates, communicates, and captures value. Anytime you get the owners or the people that are responsible for the profit, sitting in on the determination of value, they understand that it doesn't cost you a dollar to *communicate* a dollar's worth of value. But it does cost you a dollar to *create* a dollar's worth of value. In other words, if I make it, and I want to make it stronger or faster or something, it costs me money. I spend that money and it creates the value. But, if I spend all that money to create the value, and I really have the best product on the marketplace, but I don't have an advertising department that knows how to promote that value, that's money thrown away.

Smith: So, bottom line: value communication, and pricing organization as well.

Nimer: Yes. Because they've never given anybody the responsibility for pricing in the organization − they put pricing as a function of finance. Say they want to build something − what's the standard cost going to be? Take the standard costs − our customary markup is 20%, so you mark everything up 20% because it's easy for the accounting department to measure the difference. But finance and accounting don't understand anything about marketing.

Smith: How should companies organize for pricing?

Nimer: Pricing has become so important that management has to give pricing its own department. For example, I worked with a company that developed a pricing committee. Finance was a part of that committee − they had to know what happens to cost as volume changes, right? Advertising was a part of that committee because they had to know when to spend their promotion money and how to spend it in different media, right? So if you took every element of marketing − price, product, promotion, and place − every one of those as a separate function was represented as the voice of that discipline on the pricing committee. I worked at an international company and we created a position that became *marketing controller*. Marketing controller is somebody with one foot in marketing and one foot in finance. Because marketing doesn't trust finance — they think they keep giving the wrong numbers, and finance doesn't trust marketing because they believe they're not doing a good selling job. So, the purpose of the marketing controller was to serve as a liaison between the marketing function and finance function and it worked out extremely well.

Smith: Looking back, is there anything you would have done differently?

Nimer: I would have done it quicker. I left the corporate world and went out on my own. My goal was to make as much in the first year on my own as the president of the company I left made that year. If I had known the market that was out there — I just didn't know — because at that time 100% of companies priced based on cost, so I would have done this even earlier. Plus I had more impact on my own than I ever would have had within a company. Clare and I went all over the world — the United States, then Canada, then Britain, then Germany and Switzerland, then Sweden and Norway, then Australia and New Zealand — and we talked about pricing (I earned it and Clare spent it), and cost-based pricing, and value pricing. It was a great life and we loved it.

THE FOUNDING PRINCIPLES AND STRATEGIES OF PRICING

Gerald E. Smith and Dan Nimer

ABSTRACT

In this chapter, we follow the growth of the pricing discipline, especially through the ideas of one of the earliest of pricing's pioneers: Dan Nimer. The Nimer influence on pricing has been foundational, sewing seeds for the growth and development of various pricing fields and subfields — pricing objectives and pricing strategy, value-based pricing, costing and pricing, financial analysis of pricing, and price sensitivity. The ideas we present in this chapter originated largely with Nimer, many in his own voice. We interweave them with the ideas of other contributors to the pricing discipline to show the development of the field. Dan taught many foundational pricing concepts; they are captured in seminars and articles kept through the years. Founding pioneer to pricing, Nimer's influence will remain long into the new century as pricing enters a new phase as a strategic capability of the firm.

Visionary Pricing: Reflections and Advances in Honor of Dan Nimer
Advances in Business Marketing & Purchasing, Volume 19, 13–44
Copyright © 2012 by Emerald Group Publishing Limited
All rights of reproduction in any form reserved
ISSN: 1069-0964/doi:10.1108/S1069-0964(2012)0000019007

> *John Kenneth Galbraith and a good many other social critics keep telling us that business practices in capitalist countries bear little resemblance to the classical theory of market economics on which they are supposedly based. For anyone who has made a study of pricing, this is a difficult contention to rebut. The one factor in pricing decisions that is most often given insufficient weight, or in effect ignored altogether, is the market. Many businessmen deal with pricing as though it involved no more than a markup on costs, and remain quite unaware that with this attitude they may be doing serious damage to their and their companies' interests.* Source: Dan Nimer (1971).

Pricing has gone through breathtaking innovation over the past half century — value-based pricing, activity based costing, yield management pricing, pocket price waterfall, to new a few — with contributions coming from many neighboring disciplines — marketing, accounting, finance, psychology, and operations. Economics has always provided the theoretical foundation for pricing, yet for three quarters of the last century practitioners struggled to make economic theory practically useful to pricing. University pricing curricula were either non-existent or were mere extensions of economics curricula; they provided substantive theory and provocative insights but seemed to offer little practical relevance to graduates entering pricing-related professions. Early pricing thought leader Alfred Oxenfeldt (1973, pp. 48, 49) said: "The current pricing literature has produced few new insights or exciting new approaches that would interest most businessmen enough to change their present methods. Those executives who follow the business literature have no doubt broadened their viewpoint and become more explicit and systematic about their pricing decisions; however, few, if any, actually employ new and different goals, concepts, or techniques. The gap between pricing literature and practice may exist because the authors lack extensive personal experience with the practical problems facing executives in a highly competitive and complex business environment."

But over the next 50 years a new class of pricing thought leaders emerged — those actively engaged and committed to pricing's conceptual development: delineating pricing constructs, mapping out pricing's genomic DNA — its fields and subfields, and providing normative guidelines for pricing practitioners to price effectively — usually interpreted to mean *profitably* per the foundational assumptions of economics (Nagle, 1984), but in more recent years also broadened to price fairness (Xia & Monroe, 2010;

Xia, Kukar-Kinney, & Monroe, 2010; Maxwell, 2008; Xia, Monroe, & Cox, 2004) and price satisfaction (Xia & Monroe, 2004). These new thought leaders were close to the *practice* of pricing through consulting, advanced research, and price leadership in industry — and they were close to great universities of thought. They were schooled in economic theory, trained in research methods, and committed to pricing's application in real-world companies, with real-world managers, and real-world results.

We are now in a position to map out the conceptual topography of pricing and major areas of thought — costing for pricing, value and pricing, pricing strategy, price sensitivity, transactional price management — to clarify the theoretical foundations of these pricing disciplines, to describe how they developed and are developing. One purpose in this exercise is to formally document in one place the foundations of pricing knowledge. Another is to stimulate discussion at an overarching level about how the field is developing, and where it needs further development. And a final purpose is to recognize the contributions of those who were early pioneers of this growing field of pricing.

We especially look at the genesis of these fields through the ideas of one of the earliest of pricing's pioneers: Dan Nimer. Dan was trained in economic theory, learned pricing in the trenches of the real world of the 1950s and 1960s, and then embarked on a long career of pricing thought leadership through his involvement in pricing education at universities and public and private pricing seminars throughout the world for the latter half of the twentieth century and the first decade of the twenty-first century. The ideas that we present in this chapter originate largely with Nimer, many in his own voice. We interweave them with the work of other thought leaders in the pricing discipline to show the development of the field. Dan taught many foundational pricing concepts; they are captured in seminars and articles kept through the years. We will focus on four major areas of Nimer's seminal influence: pricing objectives and pricing strategy, value-based pricing, incremental costing and financial dimensions of pricing, and price sensitivity.

PRICING OBJECTIVES AND PRICING STRATEGY

The objective of a sound marketing strategy is to change the customer's perception of the availability of substitutes. Source: Nimer (1995).

Nimer developed early ideas and principles stressing that pricing objectives should be formalized and distinguished from pricing strategies and tactics. Contemporary Alfred Oxenfeldt (1973) similarly recommended formalized pricing objectives, and structured price setting and monitoring systems. Nimer's view is that an objective is a quantifiable goal to be achieved within a given time frame, under corporate guidelines, and with a given allocation of resources. It tells specifically what you hope to generate in terms of revenue growth, market share, profitability, and return on assets as a result of actions taken. Especially important is the business unit's corporate pricing philosophy and definition of formal pricing objectives (see Nimer 1995), meaning what exactly is pricing supposed to achieve?

Pricing Objectives

Lanzillotti's (1958) pioneering work in economics on the price decision-making of executives in 20 large American corporations laid out the parameters for early thinking about pricing objectives. He found that pricing decisions were driven by four primary objectives: (1) target return on investment, (2) stabilization of price and margin, (3) a target market share, and (4) to meet or prevent competition. As Lanzillotti (1958, p. 936) noted, the "company has a fairly well-defined pricing goal that is related to a long-range profit horizon .... The market, in effect, is regarded as a creature of the firm, and the firm has the responsibility for preserving ... and perpetuating its own position." It was clear in Lanzillotti's study that managers viewed pricing from the inside out, and not from the outside in. The firm determined pricing objectives, pricing strategies, and pricing success; if the firm strategized well, the market would follow. Nimer addressed these ideas very early and formulated managerially actionable guidelines grounded in economic theory but emanating from real-world pricing contexts. Let's examine each of Lanzillotti's pricing objectives.

Market share as a pricing objective usually is based on the assumption that if the firm lowers its price, the competitor will refrain from doing so and the market will bestow additional volume favors on the low-priced supplier. This is generally possible only under certain circumstances: (a) where the market is in fact price sensitive, with high price elasticity, that is, when a given percentage price reduction will result in a more than proportionate increase in volume; (b) where the firm has a small market share and is competing against companies with significantly larger market shares; (c) where the firm has a lower cost than its competitors — low-cost suppliers have more pricing options to come in under the price umbrella established by the high-cost producer; (d) where there is a strong and captive aftermarket in which the firm sets price to target initial market share and recover profits in the aftermarket — for example, Proctor & Gamble's Gillette and other razor blade firms giving away razors so they can get their customers to buy the blades. The key is that market share driven pricing objectives should be set thoughtfully as part of a sustainable marketing strategy. For example, it doesn't make sense to merely set a broad industry market share goal. (Research has shown that using price to maximize market share leads to suboptimal profitability)Simon, Bilstein, & Luby, 2006). But it does make sense to set market share goals to own highly strategic and profitable market segments, or to use market share as a goal to establish a large base of loyal customers, which becomes a foundation for future profitable business and sales.

Return on sales, or return on investment: These types of objectives are symptomatic of cost-plus pricing, and most corporations today use some form of cost-based pricing to set prices (One of the most frequent reasons for adopting a cost-plus approach to pricing is that it requires little knowledge of the marketplace.) Understanding the marketplace requires extensive market research and feedback from the field sales organization. Understandably, those firms who cling to cost-plus pricing also reduce their investment in these market intelligence activities as a means of improving profit. Among the many logical reasons for not establishing a return-on-sales (ROS) or return-on-investment (ROI) pricing objective are (a) the uncertainty of future costs and volume forecast accuracy, both of which strongly affect unit cost estimates; (b) return on sales and/or investment, which may be more of a measuring device than an objective; or (c) the wrong investment criteria used — rather than return on total assets, a more realistic yardstick would be return on manageable assets (ROMA), return on marketing investment (ROMI), or return on incremental investment (ROII), basically inventories and receivables net of payables. These are the only financial assets that marketing managers can influence.

Price level stability as a pricing objective implies that customers are sensitive to changes in price, and the key to pricing effectiveness is maintaining the same price over time. This pricing objective makes sense from a price fairness logic, since buyers infer price fairness based on their perception of current price relative to recent or historic prices, and based on their perception of the cost of the seller to produce or deliver the product (Xia, Monroe, & Cox, 2004). Of course, firms establish perceptions of differentiated value in the marketplace as a means of protecting their prices from price competition, hence achieving price stability (This is the true way to achieve price stability – to adjust price based on maintaining and managing *the value* of the product or service in the marketplace.) For example, Intel routinely cuts price on a wide range of microprocessors, including price drops of nearly 50 percent on its flagship products, recently for example with the Core i7 in 2010. These price cuts broaden the appeal of these established leading products by making them more competitive. But more importantly, they strategically free up price-points for Intel's new innovative product releases that appear at the same timeframe as the price reductions. Intel thus achieves price stability while simultaneously growing customer value to maintain a dominant presence in the marketplace.

(*Meeting the competition* is never an appropriate pricing objective.) To begin with, *price taking* leaves a company literally at the mercy of its competitor. What stops the competitor with the lowest cost from cutting prices until it has driven the copycats out of business? It can then recoup its losses by gobbling up their share of the market. A more insidious danger of imitative pricing is that it can become a cover for imitative product development. (If your product is indistinguishable from your competitor's, it indeed makes no sense to charge a different price for it. Neither did it make sense to develop this product in the first place. If there is nothing of unique value about it, why should anyone prefer it to what your competition offers? Whenever a company is tempted to copy another's price, it should stop and reconsider whether it really has something to sell.)

No one should have a pricing objective of duplicating the strategy of the competition. Rather one must go back to the options available within the marketing mix – product enrichment, advertising and promotion options, and changes in distribution patterns as a means of avoiding price subservience. (Today's highly segmented and dynamic markets demand the development of segmented product uniqueness as the only viable means of becoming a *price maker* rather than a *price taker*. There is only one valid pricing objective that cuts across all demarcation lines – to price the product or service being purchased according to the *perceived value* of what the customer is buying.

Price Strategies

Classic economics would suggest two ways to grow a firm's business: (1) lower price to increase volume along the product's existing demand curve and/or (2) shift the demand curve with investments in non-price marketing variables to increase volume at the same price (Fig. 1)(Pricing strategy can never be viewed in isolation; it is a part of total marketing strategy.)Nimer (1973, p. 8) defined marketing strategy as "the utilization of the elements in the marketing mix – prices, products/services offered, advertising and promotion programs, distribution channel access and support – on a relevant scale to meet the needs of the marketplace while ensuring attainment of the organization's objectives." Just as the military has the options of using its land, sea, and air power in attaining its goals, so pricing strategists must have the options of using all of the weapons available in their arsenal to achieve the firm's pricing objectives. This multifaceted strategic approach cannot be achieved if pricing responsibility is given solely to one function in the organization – to the finance group that controls costs and investments, to the sales group that controls customer relationships, or to the marketing group that controls market segmentation and communication. Pricing strategy, then, involves the utilization of price in conjunction with or as an alternative to the use of the other marketing weapons in the programs developed for attaining the firm's objectives. The importance of price stems from the fact that it is the only one of the marketing mix that is the income generator; all the others are cost generators.

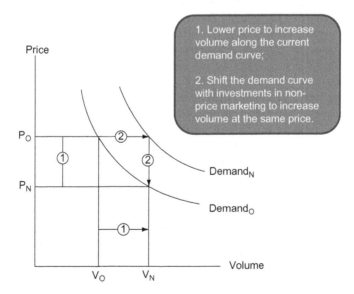

Fig. 1. Two Strategies to Grow A Business.

When we look at the elements of the traditional marketing mix – price, product, promotion, and distribution – as strategic manageable variables, the tactical options become quickly obvious:

1. Price versus Product
2. Price versus Promotion
3. Price versus Distribution

For example, as a simple pricing strategy exercise (Fig. 2), consider your product's position in the marketplace (superior, equal, or inferior) versus your competitive price position (higher price, equal price, and lower price). Suppose you have a *superior product* and a *lower price* – this is your current market reality (an *A3 market reality* in row I of Fig. 2), but you want to achieve superior product and higher price (an *A1* in "what you want" in row I of Fig. 2). Then consider strategically the investments you can make to alter customers' perceptions of the product/price relationship using product levers – product design, product performance, or product support (warranty, service). Next, suppose you have *inferior promotion* and a *lower price* – your current reality (*a C3 market reality* in row II in Fig. 2), but you want to achieve equal promotion and higher price (*a B1* in "what you want" in row II of Fig. 2). Then consider strategically the investments you can make to alter customers' perceptions of the promotion/price relationship using promotion levers – advertising share of voice, change in message strategy, or change in media strategy. Continue this for the Channel/ Price relationship, row III, and Sales/Price relationship, row IV. This helps the marketing management team consider price not in isolation, but as part of the broader mix of product and marketing strategies required to achieve the firm's objectives in the marketplace.

A U.S. firm selling steel products in Canada found itself losing business in its steel strapping product to an Asian competitor whose prices were 15 percent lower. So it dropped its prices 15 percent, only to have the Asian competitor respond with another price cut. At this point, the marketing manager of the U.S. manufacturer started having second thoughts. Taking a closer look at his problem, he realized that although steel strapping is the same everywhere, he was nevertheless not selling exactly the same thing as the Asian competitor. Because it shipped from the other side of the Pacific, the Asian company could offer only large lots, which meant that its customers had to maintain large inventories. It also offered inferior technical service. The American firm correctly concluded that it was really selling steel strapping in many different quantities, including small lots, and backed up by strong technical service. The firm reoriented its marketing

DEVELOPING PRICING OBJECTIVES, STRATEGIES, AND TACTICS

Integrating Price With Other Marketing Variables

"WHAT YOU WANT" Company Strategy	"WHAT IS" Market Reality	"WHAT CUSTOMERS THINK" Customer Perception	
		Existing	Potential
offering I. Product Strategy *incl svc*			
II. Promotion Strategy			
III. Channel/price Strategy			
IV. Sales /price Strategy			

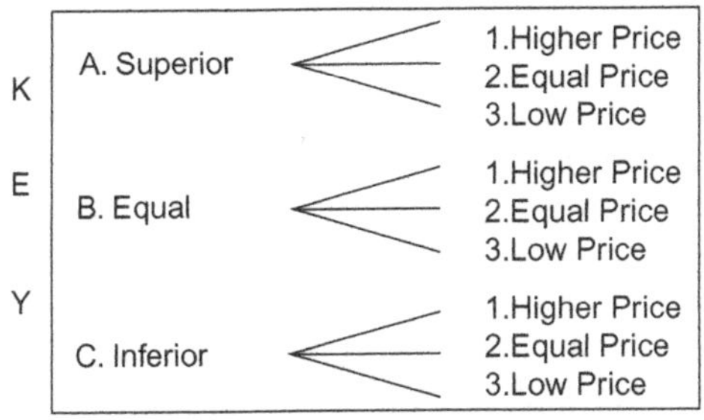

K	A. Superior	<	1.Higher Price 2.Equal Price 3.Low Price
E	B. Equal	<	1.Higher Price 2.Equal Price 3.Low Price
Y	C. Inferior	<	1.Higher Price 2.Equal Price 3.Low Price

For Product, Promotion Channel and Sales enter A, B or C for Competive Position.
For PRICE enter 1, 2 or 3 for Competitive Position. Once price set same number
used vertically for I II III And IV in each Colum

Fig. 2.   Developing Pricing Objectives, Strategies, and Tactics.

strategy to communicate these unique differentiated dimensions, put its prices back up to what they had been originally, and soon regained its profitability again.

Note that pricing levers — initiating or changing prices in the market-place — are the easiest and have the shortest lead time to implement, but they also have the shortest lead time for competitors to implement. Developing and acting on non-price levers in the current situation may take longer, but they also provide longer-term competitive protection. Similarly, if pricing managers try and exhaust their non-price options to meet a competitive threat and they don't solve the problem, they still have the alternative of a price reduction. However, once the price has been cut as the first tactic, the subsequent loss of profitability, however measured, will make it difficult, if not impossible, to get management acquiescence to additional marketing expenditures that can only erode profitability even more. Furthermore, the significance of being the low-cost supplier is that it allows the firm to invest in non-price marketing – product improvement, better advertising or promotion, enhanced distribution or delivery capabilities, or an expanded sales effort. It does not give license to use price as a key competitive tool.

In the decades since these ideas first appeared *strategic pricing* has become a central thrust for both pricing practitioners and academics. In North America, Monroe (1979) introduced his first text with a managerial pricing orientation; Nagle (1987) titled his first book *The Strategy and Tactics of Pricing*; in Europe Simon (1989) introduced his first price management text. Tellis (1986) organized the pricing literature into a taxonomy of pricing strategies, which triggered a series of empirical works validating and extending the thinking behind pricing strategy. Pricing strategy consultancies emerged in the 1980s: McKinsey in Cleveland, and Simon-Kucher and Partners in Germany; and in the 1990s: Strategic Pricing Group, which later gave birth to Holden Advisors, Medical Marketing Economics, Inc., and World Class Pricing, and then merged to become the pricing practice at Monitor Group consulting. In the 2000s, Deloitte Consulting, Accenture, Boston Consulting Group, and a variety of smaller boutique firms appeared. Countless pricing alumni from these firms have populated strategic pricing positions in industry and academia.

VALUE-BASED PRICING

> *The purpose of price is not to recover cost, but to capture the value of the "product" in the mind of the customer. Source*: Nimer (1983).

There is a simple axiom for pricing and profitability: (a) the most profitable sale begins with the best price and (b) the best price is determined in the marketplace and not by production costs. This means that pricing managers must know the prices of competitive products, and they must know the benefits the customer will realize from the product or service. The only valid pricing objective therefore is to ask customers to pay for the perceived value of what they are getting. That holds for products or services, consumer, or industrial goods. However, our thinking about perceived value has evolved over the past 50 years. Early on, perceived value was ignored as managers blindly set prices by adding a profit margin to full costs — cost-plus pricing. Nonetheless, there emerged an early school of *perceived value pricing* based on *perceptions of value* relative to price, and then a later school of value-based pricing based on the *economic value* of the product or service to the customer. Nimer was the founder of the early value pricing school, especially with his pioneering emphasis on perceived value as the primary driver of pricing strategy and pricing profitability. The model Nimer used as the basis for his theory had been known to economic theory for over a century (Jevons, 1866; Menger, 1976), but, typical of the early pricing theories, this was the first time it had been applied successfully in business practice.

The Early Perceived Value Pricing School

According to the early perceived value pricing school, perceived value is what the customer is willing to pay for the bundle of benefits offered by the supplier. To the industrial buyer, it includes not only the benefits derived from the physical product, but such extended product features as availability, quality, service, breadth of the line offered by a single supplier, technological and design service, and even the personal relationship with the suppliers sales and support representatives. The buyer of consumer goods considers such factors as social status implied by the label or the place of purchase, price/value relationships, appearance, quality, and, once again, personal relationships with the seller. The firm can affect the perceived value of your products by manipulating the non-price variables in the marketing mix — such things as advertising, sales promotion, distribution, and the nature of the product itself. Price is then used as the variable to *recover those costs* from the buyer.

For example, a half-liter bottle of *Evian mineral water* sells at retail for \$1.42, or 12.6 cents per ounce. However, a 5 ounce bottle of *Evian mineral water spray* packaged in a small bottle with fine mist spray nozzle sells for \$11.00, or \$2.20 per ounce. In other words, the Evian water spray sells for almost 18 times the price of Evian bottled mineral water packaged for drinking. What could possibly justify such a dramatic difference in price for the same identical product content? The convenience of a spray, the handy bottle it is packaged in, or the ultra-fine mist? Yes, but a more salient reason relates to the value women perceive that the product delivers. Women purchase Evian spray for skin hydration. According to Evian it "revives your makeup throughout the day, and keeps you looking fresh by replenishing that much needed moisture ... [it] removes perspiration, harmful salt or chlorine, and instantly soothes and rehydrates sun-burned or wind-chapped skin." For women, cosmetics are expensive purchases, and time spent at the beginning of the day to apply makeup is a significant investment − both economically and psychologically. The purchase of a fine mist delivers the promise of protecting that investment every day − insurance that she can avoid the time and expense of redoing makeup in the middle of the day and still look fresh for the next high-value business meeting or public occasion.

Three key insights distinguish the early perceived value school: (1) It focuses particularly on what the customer receives, or "gets" from the product or service, not limited merely to product performance but to augmented firm dimensions surrounding the product − convenience of buying from a single source, availability, personal relationships, or even social status and approval in consumer goods and some business-to-business purchasing relationships. (2) Price is viewed as a lever for the firm to recover its investment in the production of customer value − investments in product differentiation, distribution benefits, advertising, and so on. (3) Price is always judged relative to the value of the benefits the customer receives − with an emphasis on the word *relative* here, for these calculations are made in ratio form (Nimer 1975).

According to this school, the true measurement of pricing's effectiveness is a change in market share. If the company decides to *increase market share* at the expense of profits, it need only price below perceived value, meaning that the ratio of perceived value to price will increase for our product versus the similar ratios of perceived value of competitive products relative to their prices. If the company decides to *harvest its market share* and improve profitability, it will set a price above the customer's perceived value and allow competitors to move in. In cases where costs decline significantly with volume, of course, it may be possible to pick up both market share and profits through appropriate pricing strategies.

In Fig. 3 we see how perceived value calculations influence buyer decision-making, and consequently influence the firm's market share. In

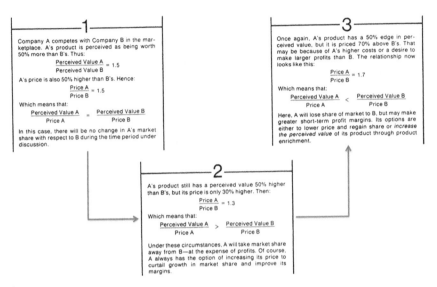

Fig. 3. Three Scenarios in Pricing by Perceived Value.

Panel 1 of Fig. 3, Company A offers 50 percent more value than Company B, for a ratio of 1.5; but A's price is also 50 percent higher than B's, so that the perceived value relative to price for A is identical to that for B. So the market is in equilibrium and there will be no change in the market shares of A and B. In Panel 2, A's perceived value remains 50 percent higher than B's, but A's price is only 30 percent higher than B's, meaning that A's product delivers a value advantage in the marketplace over B's product. Therefore, A will gain share and B will lose share. In Panel 3, A's perceived value remains 50 percent higher than B's, but now A's price is 70 percent higher than B's price, meaning that B's product delivers a value advantage over A's product. Now B will gain share and B will lose share.

An extension of this relative value logic is price/benefit analysis, a method for determining the maximum price the firm can logically be charged in a competitive situation for the value of factors not directly related to price. The method requires that the firm obtain value judgments from customers and then calculate the perceived value of the competitive alternatives. With these value calculations, we can then compare brand to brand to determine the maximum percent price premium a given brand should be able to charge in the marketplace. The analysis holds only for

Table 1. Nimer's Relative Price/Benefit Analysis.

	Smithsonian		Co. A		Co. B	
	Rating	Score	Rating	Score	Rating	Score
Attribute importance						
100 quality	100	10,000	80	8,000	70	7,000
90 promises	100	9,000	100	9,000	80	7,200
80 advising of problems	100	8,000	90	7,200	30	2,400
80 delivery	90	7,200	100	8,000	100	8,000
60 technical help	100	6,000	70	4,200	40	2,400
50 packaging	80	4,000	100	5,000	100	5,000
		44,200		41,400		32,000

competitors that are close in total perceived value. Price/benefit analysis proceeds as follows (Table 1):

1. Determine the factors or criteria (other than price) that customers consider in making a purchase decision — for example, quality, delivery, technical support, availability, and so on.
2. Ask the customer to rank these factors according to their value to the customer, and then ask the customer to rate these factors on a 100-point scale. In Table 1, you can see that quality is twice as valuable to the customer as packaging, holding to promises is 50 percent more valuable than technical help, and so on.
3. Using a 100-point scale, rate the competitive brands against the factors listed in step 2. Then multiply the value weight for each factor in step 2 by the brand rating for that factor and sum the results across all brands and factors to arrive at weighted scores for each brand.

Table 1 shows these calculations for our example product category. According to this analysis, the most our fictitious company Smithsonian could price its product is 7 percent above Brand A (44,200 ÷ 41,400 = 1.07) and 38 percent above Brand B. This tool is also diagnostically useful by pointing to areas of improvement that Smithsonian should consider, such as packaging and delivery, that would enable it to set higher prices. This analysis can be done using real customers, potential customers, or can be generated using customer-facing personnel in the firm that are familiar with customer needs and preferences.

Among pricing professionals, Nimer's price/benefit analysis from the 1970s became precedent for similar price/value models that emerged over the next two decades. Gale (1994) used a variant called *price/value modeling* in his text *Managing Customer Value*. In one example, Johnson & Johnson's new endo-surgery was priced at $3,400, compared to traditional open surgery, priced at $2,700. Gale's research found that customers perceived that endo-surgery delivered 172 percent greater quality than traditional open surgery; therefore, endo-surgery could have been priced 72 percent higher, or $4,644. Thus, at $3,400, endo-surgery was underpriced relative to the value it delivered to the marketplace; hence, endo-surgery should gain share relative to traditional open surgery, which is overpriced. The premise for this analysis is that value among market participants is in equilibrium, defined as a one-to-one relationship between perceived customer benefits and perceived price. This one-to-one relationship results in what Gale and others called a *fair value line*. During this same period, McKinsey developed its own adaptation of price/benefit modeling centered around what it termed the *value equivalence line*, similar to the fair value line. Leszinski and Marn (1997) of McKinsey's Cleveland office presented McKinsey's value mapping method in an article in *The McKinsey Quarterly* (Fig. 4). Brands along the value equilibrium line are at equilibrium − they will neither gain nor lose share. But Brand A will gain share because its ratio of perceived benefits to perceived price is greater than other brands in the marketplace; Brand E will lose share for precisely the same reason in reverse.

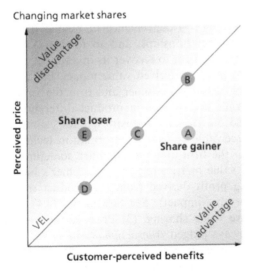

Fig. 4. McKinsey Value Map. *Source*: Leszinski and Marn (1997).

The Later Economic Value Pricing School

Meanwhile, the 1970s saw the development of a different value pricing model, a cousin to perceived value pricing and yet it had its own set of unique assumptions that were fundamentally different. Shapiro and Jackson (1978) at Harvard Business School advanced a customer-based approach in which the marketer looks at the actual utility or value of the product to the customer and compares that with the utility or value offered by competitors. Forbis and Mehta (1981), also of McKinsey's Cleveland office, followed with their notion of economic value to the customer (EVC), "defined as the relative value a given product offers to a specific customer in a particular application — that is, the maximum amount a customer should be willing to pay, assuming that he is fully informed about the product and the offerings of competitors. This will normally correspond to the purchase price of the product he is currently using, plus (or minus) any value difference between that product and the product whose EVC is at issue" (p. 36).

Again, three key insights distinguish the later economic value school: (1) It focuses specifically on the *actual monetary value, rather than the benefit/cost ratio* the customer receives from using the product or service, especially value that can be expressed in economic or monetary terms, such as cost savings, or volume or margin gains. And again this economic value is not limited merely to product performance but to all firm dimensions surrounding the product — convenience of buying from a single source, availability, personal relationships, and so forth. (2) Price is viewed not merely as a lever for the firm to recover its investment in the production of customer value, as in the perceived value model, but also as a *marker, or measure* of sharing between customer and firm the value to the customer created by the firm's investments in product differentiation, distribution, advertising, and so on. In some industries — for example, enterprise software, accounts receivable collection, information technology outsourcing, and advertising — the firm and the customer sometimes agree to track a predefined set of value metrics (e.g., the customer's incremental improvement in operating profit derived from the product or service, or operational proxies for this impact). See Sawhney (2004) for an example of enterprise software value sharing. (3) Price in the new school economic value model is always judged *transactionally* in *exchange* for the value of the benefits the customer receives — these calculations are always made in linear or subtractive form [Net Value Received = Total Economic

Value − Price], and not ratio form as in the perceived value model [Perceived Value ÷ Price].

After the introduction of Forbis and Mehta's (1981) early economic value model, many pricing strategists and practitioners adopted *actual economic value* as the conceptual foundation for their own pedagogies and philosophies. Nagle (1987), and then Nagle and Holden (1994) and Anderson and Narus (1998), and others since followed what became a well-established method for estimating value, by constructing economic value models (Fig. 5). Economic value is the price of the customer's best alternative (the reference value) plus the value of what differentiates the offering from the alternative (differentiation value). Differentiation value identifies all factors that differentiate the firm's product from the competitive reference product; these are sources or drivers of differentiation value. Smith and Nagle (2002, pp. 22−23) elaborate: "value is concerned primarily with understanding the [buyer's] system of value delivery − determining how the integration of a new product or service into the buyer's business creates incremental value and then measuring or estimating the monetary worth of this incremental value .... With economic value analysis the researcher is interested in systems of features that yield benefits and lead to monetary value outcomes." Total economic value is the sum of reference value and differentiation value; price is set to capture a portion of this total value.

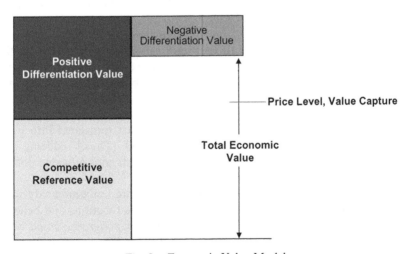

Fig. 5. Economic Value Model.

Preference-Based (Conjoint) Value School

In the meantime, a third value school in pricing emerged in the 1980s, led by Hermann Simon (1989). This school uses experimental methods, especially conjoint analysis, to calibrate the value of a product and its attributes in monetary terms (dollars, euros, yen). Conjoint analysis measures the value customers perceive in products and product features and their price sensitivity; it is especially useful in estimating the incremental price buyers are willing to pay for differences in product attributes, for comparative products comprising these product attributes, and by extrapolation to products and brands in the marketplace (Simon 1992). Dolan and Simon (1996) show an example of preference-based conjoint modeling in the auto industry in which management tested the pricing of a new product model they called *Lion*. Management decomposed the new product into five key attributes: brand, engine power, fuel consumption, environmental performance, and price. For each of these attributes, three realistic levels were chosen to test in the conjoint experiment. Respondents then chose between comparative profiles of experimentally designed hypothetical configurations of the new car model, with varying levels of the five test attributes.

Their sample calculations revealed that in making choice decisions about the new product model, brand accounted for 30 percent of the decision evaluation, engine power 28 percent, price 20 percent, fuel consumption 12 percent, and environmental performance 10 percent. In addition, respondents especially preferred German brands, were especially sensitive to prices above DM 60,000, and preferred engines above 200 horsepower. Dolan and Simon (1996, p. 58) further used *value points* derived from the conjoint analysis to calculate the incremental price test subjects were willing to pay for differences among product attributes. Their calculations were as follows: "The value difference between Lion and the established German brand is 65 value points, or in price terms, DM 10,000. Lion's value difference to the Japanese brand is 85 points; translated into price terms this would correspond to about DM 13,000. [Thus,] reducing fuel consumption by 25% from 16 to 12 liters per 100 km adds 60 value points, corresponding to about DM 9,200."

Nimer (1983) articulated the importance of using conjoint analysis to evoke market-based priority rankings to the various functions and benefits of a product, including price. Conjoint analysis, or *preference-based value modeling*, adds greater validity than *perceived value modeling* because with conjoint analysis the respondent must choose and trade off, as in any buying situation. Especially useful, it enables managers to calculate willingness to pay and perceived value, and consequently to infer price sensitivity at not only the product level, but at the product attribute level as well. Still, *perceived value modeling* has been broadly applied by marketers in many contexts because of its ease of administration. It has been useful particularly in consumer markets such as telecommunications, consumer transportation, consumer packaged goods, medical products, pharmaceuticals, and others (Gale 1994).

But perceived value is rarely the same as actual value, the focus of *economic value modeling*. Indeed, proponents of the economic value school suggest that customers' perceptions of value frequently underestimate the true, or actual, value they receive from using a product or service (see Smith & Nagle, 2005a, 2005b). Customers may not know how the product's features or benefits translate into value, or they may be unable to articulate this value to researchers − because the calculations are complex, or the buying scenarios or contingencies are difficult to pin down. Consequently, failure to use the economic value model may lead to consistent undervaluing of the product or service's benefits, and hence consistent underpricing as well. Especially in business-to-business contexts the economic value model is useful and gaining broader acceptance because it follows a more accurate process of estimating value based on the business value of the product or service measured in real profit gains and cost savings. It is interesting that, despite the development of economic value modeling at McKinsey's Cleveland office in the early 1980s, ultimately McKinsey seemed to have focused more on the conceptual development of perceived value modeling, building off the early work of Nimer, while leaving the development of economic value modeling to others.

INCREMENTAL COSTING AND FINANCIAL ANALYSIS FOR PRICING

Nothing affects price unless it affects demand or supply. The factors that influence either shift the curve or change its slope; if they don't do either, they have no relevance to the pricing decision. Source: Nimer (1995).

Over 40 years ago, Nimer (1970) estimated that nearly 80 percent of all firms in both consumer and industrial markets tend to develop prices by marking up the cost figures supplied to management by the financial division. Noble and Gruca (1999) updated this estimate at the turn of the century: 56 percent of firms they surveyed used a form of cost-plus pricing. To the degree that this practice is followed, marketing and pricing managers abdicate pricing responsibility to the finance and accounting functions of the organization. Referring back to basic economics, once the pricing decision has been made, marketing is left with the sole responsibility of *selling* the maximum quantity at that price and trying to shift the demand curve upward.

What are the consequences of indulging in this archaic practice of cost-plus pricing? First, it stresses the importance of the *cost-drives-price* relationship while ignoring the significance of the *price-drives-cost* relationship. Although it may be true that costs can determine price, it is also true that price determines cost through its impact on unit volume. The price–volume–cost–profit linkage is the relevant one to consider in the pricing decision, especially when one realizes that most cost estimates are based on standard unit volume assumptions. Second, it leads to erroneous profit projections. With cost-plus pricing, profits tend to be evaluated in terms of the *unit of sale* rather than the resulting sales volume associated with price. With costs at $50 per unit, for example, and markup at $10 per unit, profit per unit is equal to $10. Right? This is wrong because the cost structures behind these unit costs were developed based on assumed unit volume assumptions; they will be accurate only if the forecasts are precisely met. But experience indicates that this is seldom the case. As a result, actual profits usually fall short of projections, the panic button is pushed, the sales manager or person charged with generating the unit volume forecast is vilified for being an inept forecaster, and the marketing manager is chastised for adopting a poor marketing strategy.

You can see signs of cost-plus pricing especially in the marketing of new product innovations, when companies have lots of cost information and very little market information on how customers will react to prices. A good example of an underpriced innovation was that of the first stainless steel razor blade, which sold for 15.8 cents by Wilkinson Sword. At the time Wilkinson had the market to itself and could have sold just as many blades at 20 cents each, or more. The extra 4.2 cents in contribution margin could have enabled it to build its market position in preparation for competitors that inevitably would come out with their own imitator stainless blades. Almost overnight, Wilkinson accumulated a staggering order backlog. A classic case of underpricing, here the consumer thought the product worth more than the producer did.

There are of course three ways to deal with the backlog: You can ignore it and persist with anemic marketing strategies that underfund critical investments in market development and long-term differential product identity — inviting customers in the order backlog to look elsewhere for other suppliers. You can raise prices and communicate to the market that the product's demand significantly exceeds supply — raising perceptions of value and generating critical incremental profit contribution. Or you can expand production, which will drive up your costs until they have consumed the meager profit contribution provided by the low price you had set and/or force you to compromise on product quality. At least Wilkinson could have developed and marketed a very low priced razor that could be used *only* with Wilkinson blades. Eventually, Gillette and Schick came out with their own competitive blades, and Wilkinson's sales and market share shrank drastically — much more than they would have if the company had priced strategically initially and properly invested in its Wilkinson stainless steel blade franchise.

Incremental Costing

There are many subtle signals that firms are caught in this cost-plus pricing mindset, without ever being conscious of it. For example, many companies correctly authorize new ventures and/or products or services utilizing return-on-investment, or investment payback period, or hurdle rates of return as the criteria for acceptance established by management. The process simply involves dividing the total profit requirements by the unit volume forecast to arrive at a unit markup, which is then added to the projected costs. Or they simply divide the total investment by total contribution per unit, and then adjust this unit contribution (by adjusting price) to arrive at an acceptable return-on-investment or investment payback criteria. To the extent that R&D costs are included in the cost base, the resultant selling price may appear to be too high in the minds of marketing management to bring the new product to market, the project is shelved, and another competitor with more creative pricing brings the unit to the marketplace first.

Even though established competitors like Delta, United, American, or British Airways could never understand how an airline could make money

with very low per unit airfares, and therefore low unit margins, Southwest
Airlines in North America, and Ryanair in Europe, proved that maximizing volume, and adroitly managing opportunity cost by ensuring high
capacity utilization, led to superior profitability because they maximized
the total contribution across the entire customer base. Southwest's motto
exemplified this strategy of encouraging customers to make many small
inexpensive trips, as if taking an inexpensive weekend bus trip to see family
or friends: "You're now free to move about the country."

Behind these ideas was economic theory on marginal costing – which
Nimer (1973) defined for pricing as *incremental costing*. Nimer's notion of
incremental costing recommends identifying those costs that are truly relevant to pricing (costs that vary with volume, e.g., variable costs), and then
ignoring or setting aside those costs that are not relevant to pricing (fixed
costs that are already sunk and paid regardless of the pricing strategy a
firm chooses). Although a significant simplification to standard cost
accounting, incremental costing nonetheless is difficult for managers to
grasp because they have been trained to allocate fixed costs to units of
product and then set a price per unit that is profitable. We see this frequently with service firms that have very large fixed costs. Consequently,
these firms don't price their services, they cost them out and then set prices
based on those costs. Airlines have high fixed costs, but relatively low
incremental costs of serving one more customer. Banks similarly have cost
structures marked by high fixed costs and low incremental costs to serve
the next customer for many banking products.

For years, banking managers insisted that customers pay fees for each
banking product the customer utilized, such as fees on checking accounts –
the logic: customers should pay for each banking product they use. But
this ignores the greater value to the bank of the customer relationship. The
bank can generate greater *total contribution* by encouraging customers to
maintain high bank balances, thus increasing valuable deposits to sustain
greater loan activity. Still, many bankers insisted on full cost recovery in
all pricing decisions and for all service lines as a way of maintaining profit
margins as a percent of revenue, but foregoing additional profit dollars on
the additional revenues that can be generated by a pricing philosophy
based on maximizing total contribution to profit and overhead. Since over-
heads remain fixed, this approach in essence leads to maximization of
profit dollars.

In the early 1990s manufacturers of stereo speakers similarly exemplified
this unconscious cost-plus pricing mentality. Anyone who has ever purchased a stereo audio system knows that it's the speaker one must be most

careful about. If you can't afford the very best tuner or amplifier, the difference in the sound of your system may well be unnoticeable except to a stereo geek. But if you try to cut corners on the speakers, the result will be audible to the least tutored ear. However, over the years appreciably little technological improvement has gone into speakers, partly because speaker manufacturers have a long history of mistaken pricing strategies. For example, whenever they have managed to reduce the cost of their product, they promptly cut their prices accordingly – likely in the expectation of generating a larger volume of sales.

But the speaker manufacturers cannot control the price of the overall stereo system, which is what really influences the customer and therefore the volume of sales. And even if savings on speaker cost were passed along intact to the ultimate customer, they could not sufficiently affect the fairly high overall price to stimulate an appreciable increase in demand. In the absence of such an increase, most of the benefit of lower speaker prices is absorbed by stereo system producers and customers and little of it is returned to the speaker companies in the form of increased revenue. Most of these companies therefore have never been able to build up the strong financial base needed for an R&D effort that would remove the stigma of technological weakness from their products, and they remain mostly a group of precariously placed small-scale operators.

In the 1980s, McKinsey's Cleveland office introduced new innovations in costing and margins, extending Nimer's incremental costing ideas and spawning a new pricing category focused on transactional price analysis with new firms such as Vendavo and PROS Pricing, as well as existing firms like Deloitte, Monitor, and of course McKinsey. Appearing originally in *Harvard Business Review*, Marn and Rosiello (1992) showed that small incremental improvements in price had significantly greater impact on operating profit improvement than other alternative profit improvement ideas, reducing variable costs, increasing volume, or reducing fixed costs. Pricing had significant profit leverage. They then systematically measured, tracked, and analyzed product transactions across customers and selling channels to identify customer outliers – those getting inordinate price discounts and incentives, and leaks in the firm's transactional pricing incentive structure. Called the *price waterfall*, this methodology began with a product's standard list price and then tracked a variety of discount, incentive, and allowance buckets – distributor discounts, end-user discounts, on-invoice promotions, cost carrying receivables, cooperative advertising, freight costs, and off-invoice special promotions (Fig. 6).

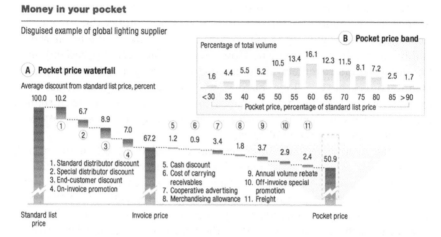

Fig. 6. McKinsey's Price Waterfall. *Source*: Marn, M. V., Roegner, E. V., & Zawada, C. C. (2003). The power of pricing. *The McKinsey Quarterly*, 1, 26–36.

Financial Analysis of Pricing

In 1968, Nimer introduced the idea of financial analysis for pricing decisions. The basis for this was incremental costing, in which the firm focuses only on those costs that are relevant to pricing – that are incremental to serving the next customer's order. In an illustrative example for a Dutch marketing consultancy, Nimer (1968, p. 5) noted the requirements for a potential price cut to be profitable.

> On the basis of 25% profit, a cut of 5% requires 18% more $ volume ... and handling 25% more merchandise. 8% requires 35% more $ volume ... and handling 45% more merchandise. 10% requires 50% more $ volume ... and handling 67% more merchandise. 12% requires 69% more $ volume ... and handling 92% more merchandise. 15% requires 112% more $ volume ... and handling 150% more merchandise. 20% requires 300% more $ volume ... and handling 400% more merchandise.

In other words, if you cut price 15 percent on $100 sales volume, it is necessary to sell $212 in volume and you must handle two-and-a-half times as much merchandise before you can make a profit of $25 to which the original $100 sales volume entitles you. Nimer discovered a mathematical formula to balance the contribution gains due to volume versus the contribution losses due to a price reduction:

$$Q_2 = Q_1 / \left(1 - \frac{\Delta P}{V/P - 1}\right)$$

Q_1 = current unit volume
Q_2 = equal dollar profit new unit volume*
ΔP = proposed percent change in price
V/P = $ variable cost (VC) as percent of $ original selling price (P)

*The new unit volume needed to hold dollars of profit constant for any given price change – percent margins will change.
Source: Nimer (1995).

His basic formulation enabled marketers to calculate the change in volume required for a price change to hold profit dollars constant. In a seminar at UCLA, Nimer (1995) extended these calculations to the development of a spreadsheet model (Table 2).

The idea of looking at the financial analytics of a price change was revolutionary and spawned other price-analytic innovations. Nagle (1987) revised and extended the Nimer formulas to make them simpler and easier to use. He inverted the focus of the calculations from variable costs to contribution margin, and then added new *breakeven sales change* formulas for three scenarios: (a) a proactive price change, (b) a price change involving changing variable costs, and (c) a reactive price change – the change in sales required to achieve break even on a constant profit basis in the wake of a competitor raising or cutting price. Smith and Nagle (1994) summarize these formulations (Fig. 7).

Monroe (2003) further expanded pricing breakeven analysis to include calculations with multiple products in the product line, calculations of breakeven elasticities, and how differences in contribution margins affect these calculations. For example, in periods of tight capacity or resource bottlenecks, leverage is achieved by emphasizing products with the highest contribution *per resource unit*. With excess capacity, profit leverage is achieved by emphasizing products with the highest contribution margin per sales dollar. "Thus, pricing and marketing strategies and tactics should be developed to shift product dollar sales mix to preserve profitability in periods of slack capacity and to obtain maximum profit leverage in periods of tight capacity" (Monroe 2003, p. 32).

Table 2. Relationship Between % Price Increases, % Unit Sales Declines and Incremental Costs Permissible % Decrease in Unit Sales with a Given % Price Increase to hold Profit Dollars Constant.

Price Increase %ΔP	Incremental Cost in Percent of Selling Price Before Price Increase (V/P)						
	50%	55%	60%	65%	70%	75%	80%
1.0%	-1.96%	-2.17%	-2.44%	-2.78%	-3.23%	-3.85%	-4.76%
2.5%	-4.76%	-5.26%	-5.88%	-6.67%	-7.69%	-9.09%	-11.11%
5.0%	**-9.09%**	**-10.00%**	**-11.11%**	**-12.50%**	**-14.29%**	**-16.67%**	**-20.00%**
7.5%	-13.04%	-14.29%	-15.79%	-17.65%	-20.00%	-23.08%	-27.27%
9.0%	-15.25%	-16.67%	-18.37%	-20.45%	-23.08%	-26.47%	-31.03%
10.0%	**-16.67%**	**-18.18%**	**-20.00%**	**-22.22%**	**-25.00%**	**-28.57%**	**-33.33%**
12.5%	-20.00%	-21.74%	-23.81%	-26.32%	-29.41%	-33.33%	-38.46%
15.0%	-23.08%	-25.00%	-27.27%	-30.00%	-33.33%	-37.50%	-42.86%
17.5%	-25.93%	-28.00%	-30.43%	-33.33%	-36.84%	-41.18%	-46.67%
18.0%	-26.47%	-28.57%	-31.03%	-33.96%	-37.50%	-41.86%	-47.37%
20.0%	-28.57%	-30.77%	-33.33%	-36.36%	-40.00%	-44.44%	-50.00%
25.0%	-33.33%	-35.71%	-38.46%	-41.67%	-45.45%	-50.00%	-55.56%

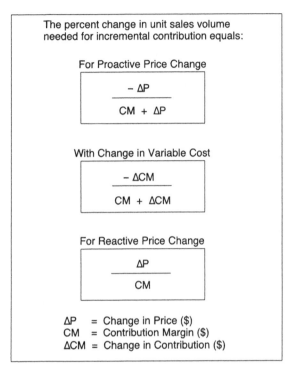

The percent change in unit sales volume
needed for incremental contribution equals:

For Proactive Price Change

$$\frac{- \Delta P}{CM + \Delta P}$$

With Change in Variable Cost

$$\frac{- \Delta CM}{CM + \Delta CM}$$

For Reactive Price Change

$$\frac{\Delta P}{CM}$$

ΔP = Change in Price ($)
CM = Contribution Margin ($)
ΔCM = Change in Contribution ($)

Fig. 7. Nagle's Breakeven Sales Change Formulas. *Source*: Smith and Nagle (1994).

PRICE SENSITIVITY

This situation might lead to the assumption that "we're overpriced." This is not *necessarily true — it may be that you are undervalued, or under-promoted, under-differentiated, or you have failed to properly segment the market or communicate your value. Try correcting all these things before you lower the price. Source:* Nimer (1985).

Key to the Nimer approach to pricing is that pricing be market oriented, that is, prices should drive costs and not the other way around. Market segmentation is essential to marketing strategy because it assumes that different buyers have different needs and hence will pay different prices for different product and service bundles. The Product/Market Matrix (Fig. 8) is an early tool Nimer used to segment markets based not only on their sales potential, but also on their profit potential as well. For example, in Fig. 8, the Finance/Insurance segment accounted for 36 percent of sales, but 26 percent of profits, while Distribution accounted for 16 percent of sales and 24 percent of profits. One true measure of whether perceived value pricing is effective is the firm's profit share versus the

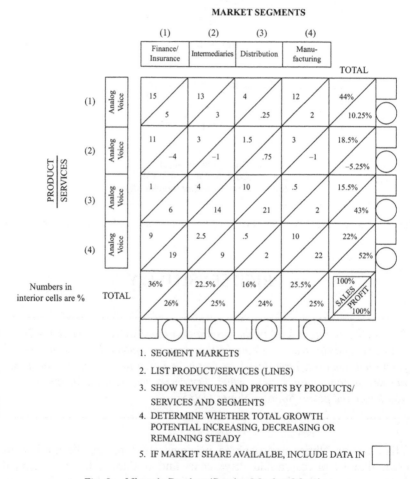

1. SEGMENT MARKETS

2. LIST PRODUCT/SERVICES (LINES)

3. SHOW REVENUES AND PROFITS BY PRODUCTS/
   SERVICES AND SEGMENTS

4. DETERMINE WHETHER TOTAL GROWTH
   POTENTIAL INCREASING, DECREASING OR
   REMAINING STEADY

5. IF MARKET SHARE AVAILALBE, INCLUDE DATA IN

Fig. 8. Nimer's Product/Service Market Matrix.

competition. Apple's iPhone, for example, captures the largest share of the industry's profit pool by far among smart phone manufacturers because it offers customers much more utility than a mere mobile phone. As a mobile Internet device, it enables customers to tap vast varieties of Internet information from anyplace where mobile infrastructure exists. Consequently, its pricing and revenue stream reflect not only standard mobile phone purchase and usage, but also customer Internet usage and the purchases of innumerable utilitarian applications, or *apps*.

Another early contribution of Nimer's pricing philosophy was to distinguish between perceived value and price sensitivity. A customer may perceive considerable value in a product or service, yet still be unable to pay for it – or be unwilling to pay for it at full price. The reason has less to do with perceived value, and more to do with the customer's price sensitivity. According to Nimer (1975), price sensitivity is a function of a number of factors, some of which include the following:

1. *Availability of substitutes* – the more substitutes available, the great the price sensitivity
2. *Frequency of purchase* – the greater the purchase frequency, the greater the price sensitivity
3. *Cost impact* – the more significant the expenditure as a part of the total budget, the greater the price sensitivity

Following Nimer's lead, Nagle expanded the number of price sensitivity factors to ten: the Unique Value Effect, the Substitute Awareness Effect, the Difficult Comparison Effect, the Total Expenditure Effect, the End-Benefit Effect, the Shared Cost Effect, the Switching Cost Effect, the Price-Quality Effect, the Fairness Effect, and the Framing Effect.

Kent Monroe especially has done extensive work on price sensitivity. Monroe (2003) noted that price sensitivity can be considered along two separate dimensions: *price awareness* refers to the ability of the buyer to remember prices; *price consciousness* denotes the buyer's sensitivity to price differentials — the differential between the buyer's internal reference price and actual price. Further, Monroe and Petroshius (1981) suggest that price sensitivity has not only a behavioral dimension but also an attitudinal component. Some buyers are innately price sensitive *attitudinally* and prefer to not spend money, and hence are prone to search carefully before parting with their money while others are more cognitive and simply search for the best long-term value for their money. Both types of buyers may search significantly, but the former person may buy the cheapest alternative, while the more cognitive person may buy another alternative that is more expensive in the short term, but is perceived as less expensive over the long term. Along similar lines, Harmer suggested that two contrasting dimensions motivate buyers: their sensitivity to getting and/or keeping *money*, and their sensitivity to getting product/service *differentiation*. The combination of these factors leads to four different customer price/value segments: Price Sensitive Buyers, Value Seeking Buyers, Loyal Buyers, and Convenience Seeking Buyers.

CONCLUSION

The Nimer influence on pricing has been foundational, sowing seeds for the growth and development of various pricing field and subfields – pricing objectives and pricing strategy, value-based pricing, costing and pricing, financial analysis of pricing, and price sensitivity. And there are others as well we can only mention due to space constraints. For example, Nimer speaks of the tendency of organizations to cede control of pricing to one functional department in the organization – usually finance, which robs pricing of its strategic integrity and marginalizes other important strategic perspectives, especially marketing. Many have called for *pricing departments* in organizations, but Nimer (1973) notes, "Pricing Committees tend to focus their attention on the pricing decision *only* rather than considering the interrelationships between [other] marketing variables .... Pricing decisions cannot be made in a vacuum, but must consider the impact on the nature of the [products and] services offered and the manner and extent to which they can be promoted." Founding pioneer to pricing, Nimer's influence will remain long into the new century as pricing enters a new growth phase as a strategic capability of the firm.

REFERENCES

Anderson, J. C, & Narus, J. A. (1998). Business marketing: Understanding what customers value. *Harvard Business Review, 76*(6), 53–61.
Dolan, R. J., & Simon, H. (1996). *Power pricing: How managing price transforms the bottom line*. New York, NY: The Free Press.
Forbis, J. L., & Mehta, N. T. (1981). Value-based strategies for industrial products. *Business Horizons, 24*(May/June), 32–42.
Gale, B. T. (1994). *Managing customer value: Creating quality and service that customers can see*. New York, NY: The Free Press.

Jevons, W. S. (1866). Brief account of a general mathematical theory of political economy. *Journal of the Royal Statistical Society London, XXIX* (June), 282–287. Read in Section F of the British Association, 1862.

Lanzillotti, R. F. (1958). Pricing objectives in large companies. *American Economic Review, 48*(5), 921–940.

Leszinski, R., & Marn, M. V. (1997). Setting value, not price. *The McKinsey Quarterly, 1*, 98–115.

Maxwell, S. (2008). *The price is wrong: Understanding what makes a price seem fair and the true cost of unfair pricing*. Hoboken, NJ: Wiley.

Menger, C. (1976). *Principles of economics*. Auburn, AL: Ludwig von Mises Institute.

Monroe, K. B. (1979). *Pricing: Making profitable decisions*. New York, NY: McGraw-Hill.

Monroe, K. B. (2003). *Pricing: Making profitable decisions* (3rd ed.). New York, NY: McGraw-Hill.

Monroe, K. B., & Petroshius, S. M. (1981). Buyers' perceptions of price: An update of the evidnece. In H. Kassarjian & T. S. Robertson (Eds.), *Perspectives in consumer behavior* (3rd ed., pp. 43–55). Glenview, IL: Scott-Foresman.

Nagle, T. T. (1984). Economic foundations for pricing. *Journal of Business, 57*(1, 2), s3–s25.

Nagle, T. T. (1987). *The strategy and tactics of pricing – A guide for profitable decision making*. Englewood Cliffs, NJ: Prentice-Hall.

Nagle, T. T., & Holden, R. K. (1994). *The strategy and tactics of pricing: A guide to profitable decision making* (2nd ed). Englewood Cliffs, NJ: Prentice-Hall.

Nimer, D. A. (1968). Prijspolitiek. *Werkbijeenkomst op 16 mei 1968 in het Mickery Theater te Loenersloot onder leiding van Daniel A. Nimer, onder auspicien van Franzen, Hey & Veltman, Adviesbureau voor Reclame en Marketing N,V.*

Nimer, D. A. (1970). About eighty percent of britain's marketing men have abdicated their pricing responsibilities. They are left with product and promotional decisions. *Marketing* (April), 24–27.

Nimer, D. A. (1971). There's more to pricing than most companies think. *Innovation* (August), 44–51.

Nimer, D. A. (1973). Is pricing bank services a marketing decision? *Bank Marketing* (January), 7–13.

Nimer, D. A. (1975, April). *Developing pricing strategies in an uncertain environment*. Presented at American Marketing Association 58th International Marketing Conference, Chicago, IL, USA.

Nimer, D. A. (1983). Untitled document. Copyright, The DNA Group, Inc.

Nimer, D. A. (1985). Preliminary draft, February 22, 1985. Untitled seminar materials.

Nimer, D. A. (1995). *Value pricing: The key to profitable growth*. Northbrook, IL: The DNA GroupPfizer/Valleylab, April 6-7, 1995.

Noble, P. M., & Gruca, T. S. (1999). Industrial pricing: Theory and managerial practice. *Marketing Science, 18*(3), 435–454.

Oxenfeldt, A. R. (1973). A decision making structure for price decisions. *Journal of Marketing, 37*(1), 48–53.

Sawhney, M. (2004). *Trilogy corporation: Customer value-based pricing*. Kellogg School of Management, Northwestern University.

Shapiro, B. P., & Jackson, B. B. (1978). Industrial pricing to meet customer needs. *Harvard Business Review* (November–December), 119–127.

Simon, H. (1989). *Price management*. Amsterdam, the Netherlands: North Holland Publishing.

Simon, H. (1992). Pricing opportunities – and how to exploit them. *Sloan Management Review* (Winter), 55–65.

Simon, H., Bilstein, F. F., & Luby, F. (2006). *Manage for profit, not for market share: A guide to greater profits in highly contested markets*. Boston, MA: Harvard Business School Press.

Smith, G. E., & Nagle, T. T. (1994). Financial analysis for profit-driven pricing. *Sloan Management Review, 35*(Spring), 71–84.

Smith, G. E., & Nagle, T. T. (2002). How much are customers willing to pay. *Marketing Research* (Winter), 20–25.

Smith, G. E., & Nagle, T. T. (2005a). Pricing the differential. *Marketing Management, May/June*, 28–33.

Smith, G. E., & Nagle, T. T. (2005b). A question of value. *Marketing Management* (July/August), 38–43.

Tellis, G. (1986). Beyond the many faces of price: An integration of pricing strategies. *Journal of Marketing, 50*(October), 146–160.

Xia, L., Kukar-Kinney, M., & Monroe, K. B. (2010). Effects of consumers' efforts on price and promotion fairness perceptions. *Journal of Retailing, 86*(1), 1–10.

Xia, L., & Monroe, K. B. (2004). Pricing partitioning on the internet. *Journal of Interactive Marketing, 18*(4), 63–73.

Xia, L., & Monroe, K. B. (2010). Is a good deal always fair? Examining the concepts of transaction value and price fairness. *Journal of Economic Psychology, 31*(December), 884–894.

Xia, L., Monroe, K. B., & Cox, J. L. (2004). The price is unfair! A conceptual framework of price fairness perceptions. *Journal of Marketing, 68*(October), 1–15.

SECTION 2
PRICING, STRATEGY, AND COMPETITIVE ADVANTAGE

INTEGRATING MARKETING AND OPERATIONAL CHOICES FOR PROFIT GROWTH

Thomas Nagle and Lisa Thompson

ABSTRACT

Differentiation and revenue growth have heretofore been the focus of marketing practice in large Western companies. That focus is unlikely to work well as growth slows in aging Western markets and volume growth comes from more price sensitive emerging markets. Successful companies will need to deliver not just better products, but better value for money. That will require integrating marketing and operational choices to achieve greater cost-effectiveness. Pricing professionals are uniquely positioned to facilitate that integration and thus to become more involved in defining a profitable strategic focus for their companies. To fulfill that role, they will need to define and target market segments that reflect not just differences in growth potential and "unmet needs," but also each segment's "strategic fit" with the firm's capabilities.

If today's largest and most profitable companies are to remain as large and profitable in the future, they will need to become more cost-competitive. In developed markets, individuals and governments are carrying record

Visionary Pricing: Reflections and Advances in Honor of Dan Nimer
Advances in Business Marketing & Purchasing, Volume 19, 47–60
Copyright © 2012 by Emerald Group Publishing Limited
All rights of reproduction in any form reserved
ISSN: 1069-0964/doi:10.1108/S1069-0964(2012)0000019008

debt burdens that presage slower growth. Competition to serve more limited demand will keep constant pressure on prices. Simultaneously, aging populations will drive up labor costs – both as a result of competition for talent and higher social taxes for health care. These trends alone will depress margins in the developed markets where large companies have historically earned most of their revenues, creating a challenge for pricing professionals.

Developing markets, although they promise strong demand growth, offer no relief from increasing competitive pressure. Indigenous competitors in Asia, India, and Brazil are developing modern operational capabilities nearly as fast as demand in those markets is growing. Embraer of Brazil now offers mid-size airplanes at lower cost than Boeing and Airbus. Indian generic drug companies are developing patented, branded pharmaceuticals. A consortium of South Korean companies is winning bids to build and operate low-cost nuclear power plants. In every case, these companies are winning share by undercutting the prices of Western competitors with products that are good enough, and getting better over time.

Companies that survive and grow despite increasingly sophisticated, low-cost competition must not only create differentiated sources of value but do so more cost-effectively than their rivals. Unfortunately, many large companies are ill-prepared for the challenge. The reason is that in large companies the drivers of profitability – revenue and cost – are managed by different people who rarely communicate, let alone collaborate, with each other. Marketers focus on driving revenue growth while viewing cost management as an operational issue beyond the scope of their responsibilities or capabilities. Similarly, operations managers focus on reducing cost per unit of output, not revenue, and so see marketers push for variety and flexibility as the enemy of efficient production and delivery (Fig. 1). With one part of the organization specialized in driving revenues and the other on reducing costs, top management imagines that they are positioning their firms for profit growth.

Such thinking fails to take into account two important interactions: the impact of marketing choices on a firm's ability to achieve a more competitive cost structure and the impact of operational choices on the firm's ability to capture profitable revenues. When revenue and costs are managed within separate silos, independent decisions create costly strategic conflicts, as summarized in Fig. 1. Following are two examples from our own experience working with clients.

	Revenue Management	Cost Management
Who Owns?	• **Marketing and Sales**	• **Operations and Finance**
Strategic Objectives?	• Add value to capture higher prices • Grow volume	• Cut variable costs of operation • Utilize existing capital (physical & IP) to increase ROI on investments

Focus of Activities	• **External**
	  – Improve offers to satisfy "unmet needs within existing target markets
	  – Accept lower margins to win share in high growth markets (e.g., China)
		•**Internal**
		  – Standardize and stream-line processes (6 Sigma)
		  – Cut overhead where ever possible
		  – Cut supply costs by "strategic sourcing"

COMMON RESULT	**New revenue more costly than existing revenue, undermining profit growth**	**Cost cuts undermine strategically important capabilities, undermining g revenue growth**

Fig. 1. Siloed Profit Management.

THE STRATEGIC COST OF SILOED MARKETING AND OPERATIONS

The marketing department at an architectural products manufacturer that annual innovation in product design enabled them to earn the highest prices in the industry, while also maintaining a large market share. They were usually the first to recognize new trends in the market, enabling them to be the first with products to meet unmet needs. As lower cost competitors eventually mimicked past innovations and won share with lower prices, the company was able to move on to the next growth market. Management's only frustration was its high costs.

Unfortunately, this company shared little information about the drivers of cost with those who created the innovations. In fact, financial management was adamant about giving sales only the "full cost" of manufacturing in order to limit excessive discounting. Our brief analysis of these "full costs" revealed that the cost of many activities, from production planning and setups to inventory of finished goods, were allocated according to formulas that simplified cost allocations despite a constantly changing mix of product SKUs. The allocated cost per unit of items with short runs (a few hours on the assembly line) was little different from that of items with long runs, despite the fact that it took as long to set up the line, fill the system with paint colors, and calibrate the equipment as it did for long runs. Moreover, short-run finished products — being lower volume — would be held in inventories much longer on average than higher volume products.

Even some very rough reallocation of costs across broad categories of products demonstrated, to the surprise of both marketing and top management, that much of the company's efforts at innovation were differentiating it into unprofitability. Increasing variety resulted in shorter production runs, larger inventories, increased waving of shipping charges for backordered items, and other "overhead" items that raised costs more than prices. Of course, marketers were doing so only because they had no visibility into the impact of different types of innovation on the real costs.

Operation choices can be equally counterproductive when operations executives have no visibility or responsibility for whatever drives profitable revenue from customers. A manufacturer of heavy equipment cut its manufacturing costs by consolidating two models of its heavy equipment into one new model that could be manufactured more efficiently. The new model included as "standard" some of the most differentiating features of its previous high-end model at a manufacturing cost equal to what had been the cost of its lower-end model. The manufacturing cost savings were huge. Unfortunately, so was the revenue loss. Previous customers for the lower end were willing to pay little more for the improved model. Meanwhile previous customers in the high-end market were unwilling to pay the same premium for what was now a much reduced set of premium options. Many bought just the now enhanced "basic product" while others bought the higher-end models of competitors who had been forced to lower their prices to compete with our client's feature-enhanced basic model. In the end, what appeared to be a smart manufacturing decision undermined the company's ability to maintain different price points for different customer segments and reduced the industry's average revenue per sale.

These two examples illustrate the risks associated with managing revenue growth and cost reduction independently. More important may be the lost opportunities. Companies that create competitive advantage to drive revenue and profit growth (as opposed to those that just lucked out by having a cheap home currency or government subsidy) often do so by creating and exploiting unexploited synergies between their revenue and cost management strategies.

Southwest Airlines and Ryan Air earned higher margins while driving share growth at the expense of their competitors by leveraging an operating model that involved turning planes faster on the ground to keep them flying for more hours each day. Key to making that strategy work was targeting markets, or in this case airports, where few congestion delays would prevent converting operating efficiency into revenue-generating flights. Apple clearly coordinated unique marketing and operational choices to create an advantaged position as a distributor of music. Even in a mature, mundane market like grocery retailing, companies have taken higher margins while achieving share growth by finding better ways to coordinate market targeting with operational choices. Tesco came to dominate convenience store retailer in Britain by creating a distribution system that reduced in-store inventories in favor of more frequent deliveries. Then, however, Tesco's marketers leveraged the system to offer more high-margin prepared foods the assortment of which changed depending upon time of day. The result: not just vastly increased revenue per store but higher margins as well.

THE PRICING FUNCTION AS THE INFORMATION INTEGRATOR

As these examples illustrate, making independent decisions to drive up revenues or drive down costs can easily create conflicts that mitigate or even eliminate the intended financial benefits, while coordinated decisions can be the key to higher margins and higher growth simultaneously. The key lies in finding a complementary "strategic fit" between whatever is essential to win some customers' business and the firm's capability to deliver those essential elements more cost-effectively than competitors can. To find such a fit, marketing decisions must take into account more than customer needs and behaviors. At a minimum, marketers need to understand their firm's unique mix of capabilities in customer acquisition, fulfillment, and distribution relative to those of competitors. At best, they need to accurately quantify the impact of marketing decisions on their firm's relative cost structure. With that knowledge, they can define customer segments for which they can leverage their firm's capabilities to create value, and earn revenue, more cost-effectively than their competitors. Competitors with different capabilities will reduce the need for head-to-head price competition by defining segments differently.

In smaller companies where sales and operations communicate routinely, creating a good "strategic fit" between marketing and operations can happen naturally. After a mid-size company's head of marketing and sales sells a big deal to a new customer or approves a new product line, she can walk into the plant and see why that work is running late or over budget. If the answer has something to do with particular aspects of that customer or product, she takes that information into account when making future marketing decisions. In similar fashion, when the head of operations negotiates directly with sales reps about the estimated cost of each job, he learns what choices exist in the market between prices and the ability to deliver particular benefits. He takes that into account when making operational investments or cutting costs.

In large companies, where marketing and operations functions are rarely even in the same building, such communication happens only when mandated by formal processes and systems. Usually, marketers in large companies make decisions with little insight into or responsibility for operational efficiency. When a company has a direct sales force, that lack of concern for cost-effectiveness carries over into the sales function. Even though sales may interact with scheduling, customer service, or shipping as advocates for their customers, they have little to no operational insight or financial incentive in large companies to redesign offers or to change the focus of their sales mix to achieve anything other than top-line revenue. On the other side, managers whose focus is operational efficiency generally lack the insight into customer needs necessary to determine the full impact of how operational changes affect the firm's ability to capture revenues.

A corporate or division-level pricing function, if managed strategically to bridge this gap, can have a huge impact on a large firm's bottom line. A strategic pricing function drives decisions to find and exploit competitive advantages, which generally require simultaneous coordination of marketing and operational decisions. Strategic pricing should not focus necessarily on raising prices, but on increasing the contribution generated by a firm's assets − both tangible and intangible. Contribution growth can be achieved with higher prices when the firm's assets are used to create defensible differentiation. But there is equally as much potential for contribution growth from using price incentives to support more efficient, lower cost operations. Southwest and RyanAir use lower prices to get customers to accept travel through secondary airports and cueing by section for quick boarding.

Tactically, a strategic pricing function can ensure that every customer negotiation is treated as a potential opportunity not just to make a sale but to define a relationship in a way that delivers value to the customer in the most cost-effective way. How marketing defines offers and how sales reps sell them can have as large an effect on a company's cost-competitiveness as any decisions made within operations. But when marketers and sales reps have little understanding of costs or incentives to minimize them, they freely offer value-added services (such as rush orders, custom packaging, longer payment terms, backup inventory) to win sales. The result is often lost operational efficiency and below average profitability, despite prices that are often above average.

Thus, one way that the pricing function can have an immediate effect on the bottom line is by identifying high-cost customer behaviors and defining pricing policies to either discourage them or to capture additional revenue that make accommodating those behaviors profitable. Once customers learn that the company will walk away from sales that are high cost to deliver unless the revenues are adequate, sales reps actually gain leverage to negotiate compromises rather than grant concessions to win deals. Rather than giving in to a lower price, the sales rep can offer discounts in return for the customer agreeing to adopt behaviors or to accept service levels that enable the firm to reduce costs.

Common examples from our experience include accepting deliveries during nights and weekends when traffic is less and trucks can complete their rounds more quickly, placing orders farther in advance of desired delivery enabling "batching" of similar orders during manufacturing, ordering and paying electronically, and agreeing to attempt to resolve service issues first via telephone support lines as an alternative to on-site customer service. If competitors have the same cost structure as your firm and do not follow these rules, they win a disproportionate share of high cost to serve customers, enabling you to develop a competitive cost advantage.

But creating a business that can sustain superior profits despite competition requires more than figuring out how to serve each customer or customer segment *cost-effectively*. It requires figuring out which market segments, and even which markets, your company has – or can create – the ability to serve more *cost-competitively*. A firm cannot achieve sustainable profit growth simply by investing resources to satisfy unmet needs in fast growing markets. Unless it can sustain margins in those markets when facing competitors, who may be copycats from developing countries, growth will prove unsustainable.

By defining segments that align with differences in operational capabilities, a firm can focus its resources where it can leverage those capabilities into competitive advantages. If a firm's strategic goal is profitable growth, then *its segmentation scheme must reflect the firm's relative ability to win and serve different customers' profitably*. The goal of the process cannot be limited to aligning offers with the needs of predefined customer segments;

it must define the segments to facilitate targeting some for growth with disproportionate profitability, while avoiding others where a high cost-to-serve is likely to drain profitability.

Consider a simple example: A firm has its manufacturing facility in St. Louis while its competitors are on each coast. Otherwise, it's manufacturing process and inputs are the same. Viewing the market as a whole, or in terms of customer-driven segments, the firm has little to no advantage in serving some customers over others. But a conversation with operations personnel reveals that plant location in fact has a large impact on the firm's ability to compete for different customers' profitably. Being located at a major rail hub enables the firm to offer lower cost, yet still quick delivery even to distant customers able to accept rail delivery from a rail freight line that passes though St. Louis. That adds value to its offer versus competitors whose delivery rates would be higher or time to deliver longer.

In this case, the most important criteria for defining a segment that the firm could target for sustainable profit growth might well be whether or not the customer's location can be served by direct rail link from St. Louis. Identifying and focusing resources to serve potential customers who meet that criteria could drive sustainable profit growth because competitors could not easily match that unique capability at as low a cost. They may have equally valuable advantages in serving differently defined segments, but could not challenge that segment without doing so less profitably. No purely customer-driven segmentation, not even one defined by product delivery preferences, would reveal this opportunity since each segment would include a mix of customers for whom the firm was cost-advantaged and cost-disadvantaged in fulfilling that preference.

To define segments that the firm can pursue with a competitive advantage, it must first find an intersection between a customer "need" and the firm's differential capability to satisfy it (Fig. 2). While traditional marketers may object to using internal capabilities to define segments, even traditional market segmentation schemes incorporate one important operational consideration: economies of scale. The only reason not to make each customer an offer that exactly aligns with that customer's needs and purchase behavior – so called "segments of one" – is the diseconomies associated with creating many custom solutions. But why should a firm limit itself to consider only scale economies when defining segments? Why not also incorporate economies related to scope, experience, and unique "assets"? Unless operational efficiency is made an explicit objective of market segmentation, the scheme will not be compatible with finding and defending unique ways to coordinate marketing and operations more profitably.

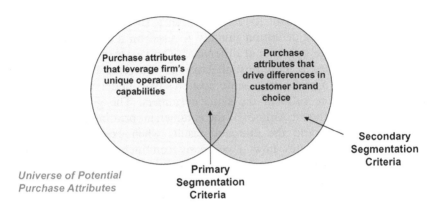

Fig. 2. Segmentation Criteria for Integrated Profit Management.

A pricing function need not necessarily, and usually does not, have the authority to set prices. But it must have the authority to define the process and the measures of performance (Nagle, Hogan, & Zale, 2010, pp. 158–166). The process must ensure that everyone with the information relating to how a marketing decision will affect operating costs, and vice versa, has one of three types of decision rights: to input, make, or ratify the decision, which may differ depending upon the type of decision (e.g., list price versus a customer-specific discount). The process should drive the organization toward increasing consistency in pricing, so that the same criteria get applied no matter who is making the decision and when it is made (Nagle et al., 2010, pp. 96–117). That will require development of common performance measures. Instead of operations viewing a deal in terms of its ability to fill capacity, sales viewing it in terms of its ability to achieve a sales objective, and finance viewing it in terms of its effect on average margins, they all need to view it in terms that lead to profitable trade-offs among those factors (Nagle et al., 2010, pp. 166–178).

BUILDING COMPETITIVE ADVANTAGE OVER TIME: THE QUAD GRAPHICS CASE

Defining the boundaries of segments to delineate and target customers that a firm can serve more cost-effectively than a competitor is key to building sustainable earning margins that are sustainable despite competition.

Initially, it may be difficult to see how such a strategy could also drive growth, since it is by definition initially focused on a niche that enables the firm to leverage operational difference. The key marketing challenge, once having defined a more cost-effective way to serve customers, is to figure out how to make that same cost-effective model work for more customers, or more sales to the same customers. The growth of Quad Graphics, the Southwest Airlines of the commercial printing industry, illustrates this process and the dramatic results when executed religiously. Quad's story illuminates how a company can increase its competitive advantage over time by continually innovating to both deepen and broaden the fit between its capabilities and its potential customer base (Fennell, 2006). From the time of its founding in 1971, Quad Graphics required that its customers be flexible about when or where a job was printed. More flexibility enabled Quad to standardize its presses, the layout of its plants, and its computer-to-press software to maximize its capital and labor productivity, increasing the profitability of a job. That initially enabled Quad to win work — and market share — by beating competitors' prices on easy-to-finish jobs. Quad initially used its higher margins to justify undercutting prices for price sensitive work.

Growth beyond the price sensitive segment required that Quad make investments that could attract higher-priced business to its low-cost model. At first, Quad could not win the higher-priced business of magazine and catalog publishers whose work required perfect color matching. Traditional publishers achieved that by having someone from the publication be on-site at the start of a job to adjust and approve the colors. The working relationships that developed between those people and particular press operators ensured customer satisfaction and strengthened customer loyalty. Quad's model of shifting jobs among printing plants and, in some cases even splitting a job across multiple plant locations, made that traditional approach impossible. Consequently, Quad's large competitors dismissed Quad as a threat to their hold on that higher quality, higher-priced segment of the market.

Quad wisely would not compromise its efficient operating model even to win higher-priced business. The company did, however, invest time and money to understand customer needs and create innovative solutions consistent with maintaining its operational cost advantage. Eventually, Quad designed and patented a method for statistical process control of color matching. Then it invested in demonstrations, guarantees, and trials to win customers' trust that the new technology could give them *even better* color control without their jobs being printed by the same people in the same location every time. Because Quad's solution was consistent with its lower cost of operation, it won business with pricing that competitors could not afford to match while still earning higher margins.

Quad's choice to change customers' behavior to fit its model, rather than compromising operational efficiency to accommodate customers' preferences, is common among companies that achieve competitive advantage that drives profitable growth. Southwest eliminated assigned seating and on-board food service, when both were an industry standard, because either could delay departures. Wal-Mart convinced people to leave the malls and shopping districts where they had been shopping and drive to a stand-alone Wal-Mart destination store where rent was cheaper and stores could be designed to facilitate the frequent, quick processing of trucks moving inventory. With the savings, they not only could earn higher profits, but could also offer lower prices and other benefits to produce a better overall experience for their targeted customers.

INTEGRATED PROFIT MANAGEMENT

As Quad, Southwest, and many other companies have shown, companies can create business models that drive profitable growth when they can find a better *strategic fit* between their efforts at revenue and cost management. They learn to choose among sources of revenue to find those that their firm can win more cost-effectively than any competitor. On the cost side, investments in new operational capabilities are driven by deep understanding of what is required to entice specific customer segments to adapt to the new model. We call marketing driven by capabilities *advantage-based marketing* and operations driven by external revenue drivers *adaptive cost management*. Figure 3 illustrates how they complement each other to drive revenue growth profitably.

Creating a system in which revenue and cost management reinforce each other does not require integrating the functions, but does require both sharing common responsibility for the same integrated result: profitability. Marketing and sales management must take ownership not only for revenue growth but also for making choices among sources of revenue that leverage the firm's operational capabilities into competitive advantage. Operational management — not just in manufacturing but in distribution, purchasing, financing, and every other function that drives a large element of cost — must define the elements of a sale that cause those costs to vary.

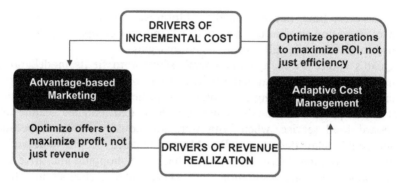

Fig. 3. Integrated Profit Management for Profitable Growth.

And top management of the entire organization must create incentives to make decisions that maximize profits, not just revenue or productivity alone.

Large companies in developed markets often have capabilities that afford them huge competitive advantages when serving particular market segments in particular ways. What they typically lack is the process to identify those segments and the most cost-effective ways to serve them. Here are three ways these marketing changes can drive competitive advantage and profit growth.

Understand what it costs to win and serve a customer. Differentiation alone is not a good marketing objective. We frequently see companies whose new, improved products and services are less profitable than the ones they replace. Product or service differentiation contribute to profit growth only if your company can produce some element of differentiation at a lower cost than a competitor can duplicate it, *and* only if customers are willing to pay a premium that exceeds the cost to offer it. Creating cost-effective differentiation requires understanding the drivers of cost in the firm's customer acquisition, production, and fulfillment processes.

Shift the focus beyond features. Differentiated product and service features are not the only legitimate dimensions of competition. The bias in market research to focus solely on feature-benefit trade-offs, rather than on understanding the entire process by which buyers make decisions, skews marketers' efforts to compete by offering more features. But a firm's unique capability to generate awareness, to induce product trial, or to gain access to channels of distribution can be leveraged to acquire customers more cost-effectively, even if there is little or no differentiation in the product or service offering. Microsoft repeatedly incorporates technologies developed by competitors into its own offers, with no feature or service improvement, but with the ability to deliver them at much lower incremental cost.

Identify costs associated with each customer segment. Statistical approaches to market segmentation obscure competitive advantage and the ability to leverage it. Market researchers typically pick a few segmentation criteria from among many to maximize statistical fit of the segments with customer needs, preferences, and attitudes. But a good statistical fit will only by chance be a good strategic fit with the firm's capabilities. Once a company selects a segmentation scheme, it restricts how it will serve the market since its offers will be designed to align with the segments. If the segmentation scheme is based purely on customer information, sales that could be delivered with cost advantage are likely to be spread across and obscured as a portion of all the segments, rather than concentrated in a subset of them that can be targeted with a cost-effective offer. By re-segmenting and targeting customers based upon the intersection of customer preferences and drivers of its own relative cost to serve, a company can define and target segments for which it can compete with a cost advantage. That cost advantage, and the resulting higher gross margins than competitors enjoy, justifies investments to win a larger share of the target segments.

THE BOTTOM LINE

When one of the authors of this chapter, Thomas Nagle, published the first edition of *The Strategy and Tactics of Pricing* in 1986, he was invited to speak at a leading business school about the role of pricing in marketing. During the question period at the end of the talk, one senior professor asked a provocative question. Noting that many of the topics in the book were the same as those in a marketing text − product development, communication, distribution, the product life cycle − he asked, "Aren't the ideas in the book just a clever repackaging of sound marketing principles?" There was silence while Thomas formulated a response. "Yes, the topics are the same," he said, "but the answers are different. In this book I have tried to describe the issues that marketers usually fail to address because they are focused on trying to drive top-line revenue rather than bottom line profitability."

As the world becomes increasingly price-competitive, successful companies will need to become ever more vigilant in targeting markets for profitability, not just volume growth. The concepts of strategic pricing are ideally suited as a guide to marketing in this new world. Creating offers that are sustainably profitable requires that marketers understand not just customer value but also their own firm's relative capabilities. To achieve this, successful firms must target not just high growth segments with unmet needs, but define unique segments whose needs they can serve more cost-competitively than anyone else. Only those companies that succeed in doing so will be able to sustain profitable growth in the face of increasing competition.

While many of us owe Dan a debt for his early advocacy of a "value-based" approach to pricing, I, Tom Nagle, feel my debt is particularly deep. While a new assistant professor at the University of Chicago, I was invited to develop a practical pricing class for the MBA program. Unfortunately, I found little in the literature beyond theory, most of little obvious practical value. Then someone suggested that I contact Dan Nimer, who fortunately lived in a Chicago suburb. Dan invited me to his home and, as we all know, Dan loves an audience. Over multiple visits, he shared freely with me his thinking and his techniques, which gave me a practical foundation upon which to build.

I, Lisa Thompson, remember meeting Dan as a wet-behind-the-ears consultant. I remember Dan teaching me my first consulting lesson: When working with the client, keep it simple. He said, "Don't waste too much time overcomplicating the topic of customer value. Just ask the client this: 'Do you know how much it costs your customers *not* to be doing business with you'?" Those simple words have sent me on a never-ending quest to add value to my clients in simple, clear and powerful ways. I hope I continue to live up to Dan's ideal of a great consultant and to use his practical advice.

REFERENCES

Fennell, J. (2006). *Ready, fire, aim*. Quad Graphics.
Nagle, T. T., Hogan, J. E., & Zale, J. (2010). *The strategy and tactics of pricing: A guide to growing more profitably*. Upper Saddle River, NJ: Prentice Hall.

HOW PRICE CONSULTING IS COMING OF AGE

Hermann Simon

ABSTRACT

This chapter describes and discusses the coming of age of price consulting from the perspective of Simon, Kucher, and Partners, today the world's leading price consultancy. Starting with modest beginnings of a predominantly theoretical and methodological nature, the field has evolved into many specializations along measurement, model building, and structural and industry lines. The current stage of development is characterized by an advanced integration of theory and practice. In spite of the big progress, large growth potentials are previewed for the future. Price consulting is today seen as a young adult who still has a lot to learn and can further contribute to the professionalization of price management.

DAN NIMER: A FIRST VIRTUAL ENCOUNTER

In January 1979, I visited Professor Philip Kotler at Northwestern University in Evanston, Illinois. At that time I was a postdoctoral fellow at MIT's Sloan School of Management. I introduced myself to Professor Kotler and

Visionary Pricing: Reflections and Advances in Honor of Dan Nimer
Advances in Business Marketing & Purchasing, Volume 19, 61–79
ISSN: 1069-0964/doi:10.1108/S1069-0964(2012)0000019009

presented my research on price elasticity and the product life cycle (Simon, 1979). I emphasized to Kotler that I was aiming to conduct pricing research that has an impact on managerial practice. Kotler replied that most marketing academics strive to do practically relevant work. But he also expressed his doubts, especially with regard to pricing which at that time was dominated by theory and microeconomics. I couldn't contradict Kotler. I myself had been educated as an economist and experienced this theoretical orientation.

But then Kotler informed me that there is one guy who actually does practically relevant work in pricing. He called him a *price consultant*. He added that this person lives in Chicago and his name is Dan Nimer. A price consultant — that was something totally new to me. That somebody could make a living from consulting on price was unheard of at that time. Shortly thereafter, I contacted Dan Nimer and he sent me an article (Nimer, 1971) which was very different from the dozens of academic pricing papers related to pricing I had read. Here was somebody who really knew and understood what the pricing concerns of practitioners were. Although I was definitely on an academic track in 1979, the virtual encounter with Dan Nimer through Philip Kotler planted the first seeds for my later interest (or one may call it my vocation) in price consulting.

Incidentally on the same trip, only one day later, I got to know Robert J. Dolan and Thomas T. Nagle, who were assistant professors at the University of Chicago. With Robert Dolan I published *Power Pricing* 17 years later (Dolan & Simon, 1996). Thomas Nagle became a leading authority in pricing and founded the Strategic Pricing Group, one of the early price consultancies. Within two days, I had made the acquaintance of three outstanding personalities who contributed to the emergence of the age of pricing. One may well say that these days marked a crossroads in my life.

PRICE CONSULTING THREE DECADES LATER

Fast forward from 1979 to 2012. Where does price consulting stand today? I cannot speak for the price consulting industry in general but would like to illustrate the rather spectacular development of this special consulting branch through the case of Simon—Kucher and Partners or Simon—Kucher for short. This firm was co-founded by myself, Eckhard Kucher, and Karl-Heinz Sebastian, my first and second doctoral students. As of 2012, Simon—Kucher has 650 employees (over 550 professionals) working out of 25 offices in 19 countries. Simon—Kucher is generally considered the global market leader in price consulting ("Simon—Kucher is world leader in giving advice to companies on how to price their products" [Ewing, 2004]; "No firm has spearheaded the professionalization of pricing more than Simon—Kucher and Partners" (Poundstone, 2010)). After a quarter century, Simon—Kucher is actually bigger in terms of professionals than the Boston Consulting Group was 25 years after its founding. According to the homepage of bcg.com, the Boston Consulting Group had 364 professionals after 25 years. Simon—Kucher had 375. This comparison alone shows the enormous growth and potential of the price consulting industry. In the following pages, I will describe important steps in the development of price consulting. Necessarily my view is strongly influenced by my experience with Simon—Kucher. Thus, I will not talk about fields such as pricing software, revenue management, or other areas that have a relation to pricing but where Simon—Kucher is not active. When we started in 1985, the world of pricing was very different from what it is today. This definitely applies to information, data, models, and methods (Ehrhardt, 2011). It applies less to decision-making processes and implementation — areas that still have huge potential for innovation and growth of price consulting.

ECONOMETRICS FOR PRICING

I already mentioned that I was educated as an economist. Demand or so-called price response functions played a major role in my studies, especially in microeconomics. But these price response functions were treated as purely theoretical concepts. Actually they were alluded to as *conjectural*, which has a connotation that they exist only in the imagination or in theory but have no practical or empirical significance. In the late 1960s and early 1970s, the first researchers started to econometrically calibrate price response functions for individual products using empirical data. The data were few and generally of poor quality, for example, the data intervals were often bimonthly or quarterly. These empirical studies attracted my interest and I started to apply econometric methods to calibrate price response functions for individual products or brands. Due to the availability of data most of my work at that time was in fast-moving consumer goods and in pharmaceuticals. Naturally my first doctoral students worked in the same field with similar methods. However, they had access to the first scanner data which made econometric methods much more meaningful.

When we founded Simon–Kucher, our vision was to use econometrics to support and improve price decisions. Econometric methods draw on historical data: for example, sales volumes, market shares, and prices of a company and its competitors are compiled and analyzed, factors influencing the sales or the market share of the product in question are estimated, and the findings are applied to the decision at hand. A fundamental assumption of the econometric approach is that effects and behavior remain rather constant over time, only then can past developments form a basis for assessing future price effects. This basic assumption of econometrics does not take into account that, in reality, the majority of decision-making situations is triggered by structural disruptions. These may come in the form of a new competitor or a shift in a competitor's behavior. Unexpected disruptions can also originate from retailers. Such situations require decisions to be made – but historical data that assume continuity and stability are of little value here. In most cases that do not involve a structural disruption, however, no major decisions are required or invoked by managers.

In terms of price elasticity – the focus of most econometric studies – there is another problem. Using econometrics, price elasticities based on market data are difficult to measure reliably. Telser, then a professor at the University of Chicago, pointed this out as early as 1962 (Telser, 1962). Telser's argument goes as follows: High price elasticities in a market allow only for minimal price differences, because the competitors are forced to align their prices. In other words, they cannot afford to maintain significant price differentials (the independent variable in the price response consequently shows a variation that is too small). With low price elasticities, the prices differ more widely, but this may not have a significant effect on the dependent variable (the market share or the sales volume) and thus the price elasticity cannot be reliably quantified (the dependent variable has too little variance).

In one of Simon–Kucher's earliest projects we applied econometric analyses to a well-known brand. The analyses were carried out by a consultant who had a PhD in statistics, was very familiar with response models, and had a sound understanding of all methodological subtleties. The results were essentially useless because the situation had changed due to the entry of generic products, a hitherto unknown category in that market.

In the several thousand price-consulting projects Simon–Kucher has conducted since the mid-1980s, econometric models and methods have been applied in less than 100 cases. Even in the relatively few projects where the method was applied, the results were not always useful. I do not want to imply that other marketing researchers and consultants haven't had different experiences with econometrics. But in Simon–Kucher's case, the expectations of econometric modeling were never fulfilled. The basic flaw is that data from the past is often not relevant for the future or the decision at hand. Our initial hope to build a price consultancy on econometric modeling did not materialize (for a deeper discussion see Simon, 2008).

EXPERT JUDGMENT

If econometrics didn't supply us with valid and practically useful price response functions, how could we generate these curves, which are indispensable to optimize prices? The answer is expert judgment. We borrowed this idea from John D. C. Little (1970) who presented the method in a seminal article and called it *decision calculus*. The expert judgment approach to determining price response functions involves asking internal or external experts familiar with the relevant market to estimate product sales or market share at different price points. The information is typically gathered during a workshop, with participants entering their responses into worksheets or directly into computers. Generally two types of sales estimates are investigated: one set assuming no price reaction on the part of the competition, the other assuming such a price reaction. Expert judgment is an inexpensive method, and is generally better than the frequently used gut feeling approaches. Its main weakness is that it relies on internal judgment and does not involve the customer.

Expert judgment has become an important and frequently used method in Simon–Kucher's consulting practice. It is mostly employed in combination with other methods such as conjoint measurement to cross-verify price elasticities. Over the years personal computers have been increasingly used for the estimations. This renders consideration of various scenarios of customer and competitive reactions to price alternatives easy.

CONJOINT MEASUREMENT

I am often asked "what is the most important aspect in pricing?" My answer is *value-to-customer*. Price and the willingness to pay are only a reflection of the value perceived by the customer. Value and price should therefore always been seen together or *conjointly*.[1] This is essentially the core and the great contribution of conjoint measurement. Conjoint measurement simultaneously measures value-to-customer and price elasticity. Instead of being asked direct questions about price and willingness to pay, the customer is required to make choices, so-called trade-offs, between various offerings, which include different levels of product attributes and price. Conjoint thus avoids the weakness of direct questioning about price, which usually sensitizes respondents to price and overestimates price elasticities.

Conjoint reveals which product attributes are particularly important to the customer and how much he or she is willing to pay for them. Conjoint measurement is undoubtedly the most important development for price consulting in the last 30 years and has proven its worth in thousands of cases. Often, conjoint measurement data forms the basis for another method that has proven successful in our consulting practice: decision support systems (discussed in the next section).

When we started to apply conjoint measurement in the 1980s, we used paper questionnaires, which were, of course, very inflexible. The introduction of adaptive conjoint and the availability of portable computers marked an important innovation. Over time all the extensions of conjoint measurement such as discrete choice modeling were integrated in our work. In the first decade, Simon–Kucher had its own market research department because the highly specialized surveys we needed were not supplied by market research vendors. In the late 1990s, we closed the department and today the data collection is outsourced. This allows us to focus on our core competency, price consulting.

DECISION SUPPORT SYSTEMS

Decision support systems for marketing were first proposed by Little (1979; for a review on applications see Wierenga et al., 1999). These systems have become very important tools for Simon–Kucher's price consulting. They offer clients a low-cost, rather risk-free method to objectively test market reactions to alternative prices and various courses of action before implementation. (See Engelke & Simon, 2008)

In price consulting, decision support systems are used to answer a large variety of questions such as the following:

• What is the relationship between price and volume, and what is the price elasticity?

- What impact will various product and price changes have on revenue and profit? How will individual customer segments react to price variations? Can segment-specific pricing measures be developed on the basis of this information?
- Which combination of product/service/price features will maximize profits?
- What is the optimal price given customers' willingness to pay, competitors' offerings, and possible competitive product or price reactions?
- What is the optimal reaction to competitors' price and other actions?
- What is the optimal product lineup?

Apart from addressing product- or service-specific issues, decision support systems can also be used to resolve conflicts between objectives. By helping to calculate the trade-off between volume, market share, and profit, these systems create a sound basis for rational strategic decision-making. Moreover, by generating quantified conclusions, they significantly contribute to more objective, cross-functional coordination, as for example between sales, marketing, production, and finance. This facilitates buy-in from decision-makers, and thereby creates the conditions necessary for a successful implementation.

Support systems for price and other decisions share some common elements and a structure (Fig. 1). The behavior of both the company's customers and of its rivals is evaluated. The system is fed with quantitative information reflecting consumer preferences and needs, the buying process, market structure, and other relevant marketing elements such as communication and distribution channels. This information is aggregated, producing

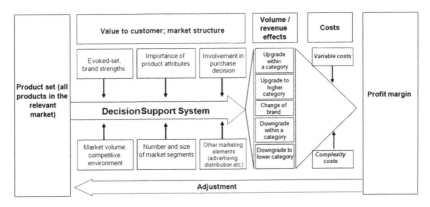

Fig. 1. Elements and Structure of a Decision Support System.

a forecast of volume and revenue based on the price and other marketing parameters entered. If costs are incorporated into the system, it can also determine profit.

The primary goal is to capture the purchase decision situation of the individual customer as realistically as possible. This requires a thorough understanding of each buyer's individual characteristics. The level of detail necessary in the information-gathering process depends on management's questions and the defined objectives for the decision support system. For example, is the price level for a whole product line to be determined? Or, is the goal to fine-tune the price levels of individual product variants within this line? In general, the finest level of segmentation determines the system's complexity, and, therefore, the quantity of information necessary to feed it.

A decision support system helps management to better estimate the consequences of product and price decisions. Does management want to maximize profit? For the short term or long term? Or does it strive to attain both adequate profit and a specific market share (a goal frequently encountered in real life)? Or does management want to increase penetration in certain customer segments? The decision support system helps select the measures that will most likely result in these and other objectives being met.

In complex and mature markets, a decision support system can be very helpful in making better decisions. Consider the automotive market. Each segment of it comprises numerous brands, models, engine derivatives, and body types. This makes it very difficult to quantify the effects of product and pricing measures on a subjective basis; complex interdependencies make it all the more necessary to employ a decision support system.

Figure 2 shows how a range of price changes (−8 percent to +8 percent) affects volume and profit of a model line of a premium car. The highest profit increase is achieved when the price is increased by 4 percent. The figure also shows, however, that the profit increase is associated with a decline in volume of 2,200 units or 13 percent.

Figure 3 summarizes the application of 600 decision support systems developed by Simon−Kucher. These decision support systems have been applied in many industries for the purpose of evaluating a broad range of decision parameters. Pricing issues occupy first place, followed by product-related issues. Frequently the system is used with respect to a combination of parameters (Note: The percentages for the main decision parameters add up to more than 100 percent, because some systems had more than one main decision parameter.) Pricing applications are dominant for two

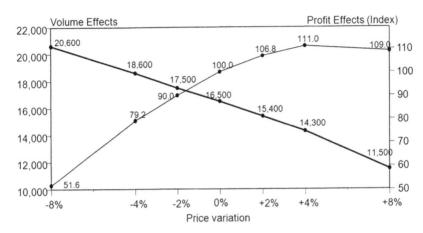

Fig. 2. Volume and Profit Effects of a Price Change in the Range of ± 8 Percent Applied to All Models of a Line.

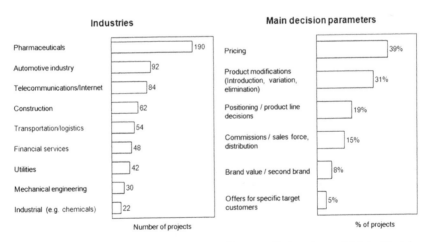

Fig. 3. Applications of Decision Support Systems: Industries and Main Decision Parameters.

reasons. First, pricing is well suited to the quantitative nature of decision support systems. Second, pricing is an enormous profit driver, making the return on investment for a pricing decision support system particularly attractive.

A prime criterion for assessing a decision support system's usefulness is the quality of its forecasts or to what extent the forecasts can predict the actual outcome. There is little research on this topic as companies are reluctant to give insight into their marketing practice (Wierenga et al., 1999). We have access to both qualitative and quantitative results for about 80 percent of systems developed by Simon–Kucher. From a scientific viewpoint, a high degree of consistency should be expected if the framework under which the decision support systems were developed and under which the strategic measures have been implemented are largely comparable. This is typical for the automotive market. For such markets, the systems regularly achieve a forecast validity of ±5 percent. Decision support systems for product innovations or for products in high-growth markets on average have a reduced level of forecast quality; however, more detailed forecasts seem implausible given the high pace at which such markets tend to evolve. Interestingly, clients usually would not even expect such high levels of forecast quality.

Another interesting finding is how the management's and the user's confidence in price decision support systems can be increased. We have noted over the years that these systems are met with considerable skepticism at first. This understandable and advisable skepticism, however, usually loses ground to a much more positive attitude in more than 90 percent of cases after some practical experience has been gained and the utility of such a system has been recognized. In order for sufficient confidence to be built, no implausible forecasts concerning volume and profit effects should be made. Such results, however, can occur if the users want to put the system to the acid test by using extreme prices. This should only be done if the database on which the system relies covers such value ranges. Drawing on our own experience, it is not advisable for the manager – as the decision-maker – to use the decision support system without the assistance of the consultant who developed the system, for only an informed and conscious use of such complex systems will lead to valid results. Ideally, the use and the updating are therefore done by an experienced expert, often the consultant who originally developed the system. Only then it is certain that for a given problem the appropriate parameters are chosen, the resulting values are correctly interpreted, and proper conclusions are drawn. This procedure is particularly advisable if the decision support system is intended for long-term use. It is wrong to assume that there is a system that solves all problems by pressing a button. The systems must be fed and interpreted with great diligence (for a deeper discussion of marketing decision support systems, see Engelke-Simon, 2007).

MULTIDIMENSIONAL PRICE STRUCTURES

Usually one thinks of a price as a one-dimensional construct. A cup of coffee costs $1.50, that's it. One-dimensional pricing is, however, a very confined concept. It does not always allow the full exploitation of customers' willingness to pay. One of the most important developments in price consulting's coming of age are increasingly complex multidimensional price structures. A milestone in Simon–Kucher's work was the introduction of the BahnCard (Railcard) in 1993 for the German Railroad Corporation (Deutsche Bahn). Before 1993, the railroad company had only offered a one-dimensional price system, tickets were priced per kilometer. The main competitor of the railroad, the automobile, has, however, an implicit two- or multidimensional price structure, consisting of fixed or semi-fixed components such as insurance and depreciation, and variable components such as gasoline. The problem for the railroad is that consumers tend to neglect the fixed components when they decide between rail and car. Thus, the one-dimensional (full cost) price structure of the railway posed a serious competitive disadvantage. We solved the problem by adopting a two-dimensional price structure, consisting of the price for the BahnCard and a reduced price per kilometer. Today the BahnCard costs €460 ($650) for the First Class and €230 ($325) for the Second Class. It gives the owner a discount of 50 percent on all tickets for the duration of 1 year. The BahnCard became a huge success and more than 5 million people have this card today. With the discount of 50 percent, the railway is highly competitive to the automobile, especially with increasing oil prices.

Price bundling is another extremely successful method for extracting customers' willingness to pay and maximizing profits. Here the customer buys a bundle of products rather than a single item. The CEO of a large bank recently stated that banks sell their customers only 2.1 products on average. This is primarily due to an ineffective approach; the number can be significantly increased through bundling. The same applies to multi-person pricing, which is particularly effective in the tourism and banking industries. Today, in about one quarter of Simon–Kucher's projects we apply multidimensional price structures. They include nonlinear pricing, price bundling, multi-person pricing, multi-product pricing, combinations of product and service prices, and multi-country arrangements. These structures can be applied in a myriad of industries; examples are telecommunications, e-commerce, and the Internet in general (Amazon's $78 offer for free shipping for a year is an interesting recent example), media, healthcare, consumer, and industrial services.

Multidimensional price structures pose complex challenges with regard to understanding, measurement, and implementation. They require very experienced consultants who need both a very solid knowledge of theory and the ability to develop practical solutions. Only by understanding the theoretical rationale for the optimality of a specific model can the consultant be sure to choose the right structure. The underlying complexities cannot be mastered by common sense, experience, or gut feeling alone. Second, with these structures it is critical to measure price elasticities and thresholds very precisely and validly. In order to capitalize on the profit potential, willingness to pay must be exploited to the full. Even a slight inaccuracy can cause strong adverse effects on profits. While big progress has been made in this area, there are still huge potentials to be exploited by sophisticated price structures. Multidimensional price structures have become an important region in Simon–Kucher's price consulting landscape.

INTERNATIONAL PRICING

It is well known that prices can differ strongly across countries. It is less obvious what companies can or should do about this phenomenon. In Simon–Kucher's consulting practice the first international pricing projects originated from the emergence of parallel imports in pharmaceuticals and the introduction of the Euro. With the disappearance of trade barriers in Europe in the early 1990s, the incentives to buy pharmaceuticals in countries where they were cheap and resell them in high price countries became very enticing. Arbitrage costs for pharmaceuticals were low, and high margins could be earned. This phenomenon was not confined to the pharmaceutical sector; however, it was most prevalent there. The introduction of the Euro in 2002 increased price transparency across countries and led to parallel imports in numerous other industries (e.g., consumer goods, cars, household appliances, many B2B sectors). Many companies reacted by introducing uniform European prices. But this uniformity is hardly ever optimal because it ignores the differences in customer behavior, trade margins, and a company's market positions in different countries. Multinational companies were forced to realign their price positions. Pricing projects, which used to be confined to one country, now became international and analytically much more complex. The allocation of price decision-making power between corporate center and country subsidiary introduced a new organizational aspect. Thus, price consulting expanded its organizational scope. On the consultant's side, multinational teams were required to cover the various markets involved. This gave a strong push to the internationalization of Simon—Kucher, because it became a necessity to have local resources for studies in key markets. Or reverse, if you were not present there, one would not get a project involving the respective country. Even today, international pricing continues to pose complex challenges for companies and attractive opportunities for consultants. A recent study found that in several sectors the Euro has not led to a narrower spread of prices. For some products (washing machines) the price differences actually increased (Deutsche Bundesbank, 2009). This is a surprising result, which shows that even after the introduction of a common currency there remains room for international price differentiation. We estimate that in the automotive industry 25 percent of the profits come from this differentiation.

PRICING PROCESSES

I have to admit that it took me 20 years of research and consulting work to fully recognize the outstanding importance of pricing processes. Especially the B2B world is dominated by pricing processes rather than price optimization in the microeconomic sense. The reason is simple: in B2B transactions most prices are negotiated. In spite of their extreme relevance in practice, pricing processes have hardly been the subject of academic research. As opposed to price optimization, pricing processes address the tricky issue of price implementation. This field encompasses everything related to price realization — from information to who is responsible for what (such as approving special conditions and discounts) to training in negotiation and price defense. Price-controlling and price- or margin-oriented incentive systems for the sales force play a critical role in this context. Figure 4 illustrates the four phases of a typical pricing process for an industrial goods company.

Reorganizing pricing processes requires an interdisciplinary approach. Aspects such as organizational structures, responsibilities of corporate functions, customer behavior, incentives, and controlling have to be included. Different functions such as marketing, sales, accounting, finance, and human resources must be involved because they may be affected by the pricing process. Based on Simon—Kucher's experience of over more than 1,000 projects, pricing process reorganization typically increases profit margins by around two percentage points, for example from 5 to 7 percent

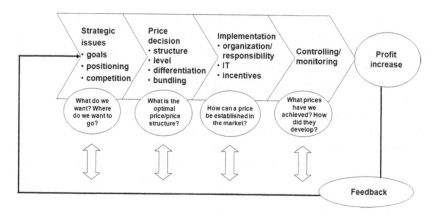

Fig. 4. A Pricing Process for an Industrial Product.

or from 10 to 12 percent of revenue. Very different factors have to be taken into account in each case. However, it is important to point out that in practice this extremely valuable approach has profited less from academic research than from the accumulation of practical experience. Pricing process reorganization is also quite taxing on the consultants because they may have to work for months on the client's site. The information comes directly from the client's employees and has to be collected in a tenuous, politically charged process. This is also an important reason why pricing processes are so difficult to access for academic researchers. Even from a consulting perspective with substantial experience in reorganizing pricing processes, generalizations are extremely difficult because these processes are highly industry and company specific.

PRICING AND THE INTERNET

In Internet 1.0 we saw many pricing innovations. A notable case was the *name-your-own-price* model, most prominently exemplified by Priceline. com. Auction mechanisms were employed on a large scale in B2C, C2C, and B2B settings, with eBay as the most popular contender. Price transparency increased dramatically through all kinds of search and price comparison engines. Internet 2.0 took pricing to new heights. Google introduced highly sophisticated pricing models such as Adwords. The pricing of digital content continues to pose a difficult challenge, because the vast majority of content is (still) offered free on the Internet. Social networks still must develop pricing systems that make them true economic successes. Groupon is one of the recent newcomers with price, or rather discount, as the core variable. Efficient payments remain a challenging issue.

All these developments have brought new opportunities for price consulting. Simon–Kucher, especially its Silicon Valley office in Mountain View, California, has worked for most contenders in the Internet space. But the coming of age of Internet marketing and pricing still lies in the future. We are at an early stage. We can expect many pricing innovations to be developed in cooperation between entrepreneurs and consultants rather than academics.

PRICING FOR BIG PROJECTS

Big projects pose one of the most difficult pricing challenges. How do you successfully negotiate prices for a power plant, an automotive supply contract which runs over five years and may have a value of several billion dollars, a global service contract for jet engines, or for large-scale IT outsourcing projects? These are not fields where the classical price response function and profit maximization according to the "marginal-cost-equals-marginal-revenue-principle" are particularly helpful. Rather both the vendor and the consultant need an extremely deep understanding of aspects such as

- the relative power between vendor and customer (and competing vendors);
- the value chain processes of the vendor's customer;
- the buying center structure on the customer's side;
- the history of transactions between vendor and customer; and
- the personalities of the key people on both sides.

At Simon–Kucher, pricing for big projects has become a focus and an area of innovation in recent years. Time and again, experience shows that executives are insufficiently prepared for their really big deals and make suboptimal decisions. The key additional value that a pricing consultant brings to the negotiation table is a neutral, quantitative view on the power balance of this particular deal. Decades of psycho-babble has led people to believe that tricks help in big deal pricing. If there is one trick, it is solid, detailed preparation of the vendor's opening offer, target price, and walk-away price.

The consultants who work on pricing for big projects have to be very experienced and senior due to two reasons. First, they must be able to both analyze very complex situations and evaluate the people who are involved in the pricing process. Second, they typically deal with top management and therefore need a strong personal standing. The stakes are very high in this arena, not only with regard to price as a determinant of the profitability of a project, but also with regard to the risk of losing a project.

The new field of behavioral economics has the potential to revolutionize economics. In 2002, Daniel Kahneman received the Nobel Prize in Economic Sciences for his original work on prospect theory, carried out with Amos Tversky. Since then numerous researchers including Richard Thaler and Dan Ariely have expanded our knowledge of seemingly "irrational" price effects. Behavioral economics found its way into price consulting at Simon-Kucher & Partners five years ago. Dr. Enrico Trevisan, partner at Simon-Kucher's Milan office, has authored a book based on his experience with applying behavioral pricing concepts, particularly in the financial services sector. Most of the findings reported by the academic researchers proved true in Simon-Kucher's practice and led to interesting new pricing concepts. Anchoring effects, product line extensions, and new temporal structures that systematically exploit the new knowledge produced significant profit improvements in several projects. A limitation of behavioral economics is that generalizations are risky. This is because the findings rely on specific experiments and are not derived from theoretical assumptions that specify the conditions under which the effects occur. One of the principles behind behavioral economics, in fact, is that decisions strictly depend on contexts. People in their everyday behavior systematically deviate from what is commonly considered as "rational," simply because they are influenced by the architecture of the choice situation in question. Applying behavioral concepts to specific price decisions therefore requires new experimentation in each project to understand the relationship between choice and frame. But over time and with more application, Simon-Kucher is optimistic about building knowledge that enables more, though cautious, generalization. The new field of behavioral pricing holds huge potential for future profit improvement.

INCREASING INDUSTRY SPECIALIZATION

While the topics treated so far have dealt primarily with the content and the methodologies of price consulting, a further development line concerns industry specialization. When I started as an academic researcher in the 1970s, I would never have imagined how varied pricing practices in different industries are. As a consequence of this insight, Simon—Kucher developed an ever increasing industry specialization. As of the early 1990s, industrial sectors became the dominant organizational dimension and the divisions are primarily organized along industry sectors. The senior people in the divisions are pronounced industry experts. Today we have pricing experts for pharmaceuticals, medical technology, banking, insurance, chemicals, building technologies, energy, engineering, automotive, technology, telecommunications, Internet, logistics, hospitality/leisure, and several other sectors. In countries where our office teams are still small the degree of specialization is naturally less pronounced. Therefore, these teams need and get support from the specialized divisions. According to our experience the clients highly value deep industry expertise of price consultants. Simon—Kucher is convinced that it has a clear competitive advantage in this regard.

QUALIFICATIONS OF PRICE CONSULTANTS

It goes without saying that price consulting requires a solid and deep understanding of the underlying theories. This applies equally to basic concepts such as price elasticity, measurement, and optimization, and to complex price structures such as nonlinear pricing, price bundling, product line, or multi-person prices. Accordingly most of Simon—Kucher's professionals graduated in business or economics, the vast majority from leading universities and colleges in the respective countries. Driven by the industry specialization we increasingly hired experts with different backgrounds. Today we employ physicians, engineers, psychologists, mathematicians, physicists, pharmacists, biotechnologists, computer scientists, and consultants from other disciplines. The reason is that we have to understand the value of our clients' offerings in order to get the price right. A physician, a pharmacist, or a biotechnologist is better prepared to analyze the true value and the competitive advantages of a new high-tech medication. Our scientists work in teams with the consultants with business backgrounds to arrive at solutions that equally observe the technical and the economic aspects of pricing. On our clients' side we often encounter scientists and engineers. They highly appreciate if a consultant from their own field is on our team. We expect that experts from various technical and scientific fields will over-proportionally grow in our work force.

SUMMARY AND CONCLUSION

Would Dan Nimer, the first price consultant I heard of through Philip
Kotler, have expected this development of price consulting? Most likely
not. Yes, price consulting is coming of age. But it is not yet there. Most
companies still price based on rules of thumb, cost-plus considerations,
and gut feelings. Therefore the growth opportunities for price consulting
are virtually unlimited. We will see a penetration of more professional pricing into industries and companies that have remained untapped. The same
applies to fast growing regions, especially the emerging markets. I know
that today few pricing projects are carried out in these fast growing economies. Relative to other consulting fields price consulting is a late comer.
The reason is obvious. Companies first have to get their fundamentals such
as product quality, supply chain, physical distribution in order before they
start to optimize their marketing instruments and especially their prices.
And sophisticated pricing requires good data, which are not always available in emerging economies.

A further growth path of price consulting results from new methods,
tools, and applications. In this regard I expect a lot from the Internet.
With regard to selling and pricing digital content and also to exploiting the
pricing potential of social networks, locational services, etc., we are at a very
early stage of development. The Internet holds unseen opportunities with
regard to behavioral data, price differentiation, addressability of segments,
and even individuals and will turn into a gold mine for sophisticated pricers.

In summary, I see price consulting today as a young adult with a great
future, a Dan Nimer at the age of 20.

NOTE

1. It was only in 2012 that I detected that the Romans had the same word for
value and price. "Pretium" in Latin means both vlaue and price.

REFERENCES

Deutsche Bundesbank (2009). *Konvergenz der Preise im Euro-Raum*. Monthly Report, March,
    pp. 39–50.
Dolan, R. J., & Simon, H. (1996). *Power pricing — How managing price transforms the bottom
    line*. New York, NY: The Free Press.

Ehrhardt, A. (2011). Then and now: 25 years of pricing history. *The Journal of Professional Pricing* (First Quarter), 28–30.

Engelke, J., & Simon, H. (2007). Decision support systems in marketing. *Journal of Business Market Management, 4*, 289–307.

Engelke, J., & Simon, H. (2008). Decision support systems in pricing. *Journal of Professional Pricing, 18*, 24–28.

Ewing, J. (2004). Hidden champions – The little-known european companies that are conquering the world. *Business Week, 26*, 42–44.

Kahneman, D. (2011). *Thinking, fast and slow*. New York, NY: Farrar Straus & Giroux.

Kahneman, D., & Tversky, A. (1979). Prospect theory: An analysis of decision under risk. *Econometrica, 47*(2), 263–291.

Little, J. D. C. (1970). Models and managers: The concept of a decision calculus. *Management Science, 16*(8), 466–485.

Little, J. D. C. (1979). Decision support systems for managers. *Journal of Marketing, 43*(3), 9–26.

Nimer, D. (1971). Nimer on pricing. *Industrial Marketing*, March, 48–55.

Poundstone, W. (2010). *Priceless: The myth of fair value*. New York, NY: Hill and Wang.

Simon, H. (1979). Dynamics of price elasticity and brand life cycles. *Journal of Marketing Research, 16*, 439–452.

Simon, H. (2008). The impact of academic research on business practice, experiences from marketing. *Journal of Business Market Management, 4*, 203–218.

Telser, L. G. (1962). The demand for branded goods as estimated from consumer panel data. *The Review of Economics and Statistics, 44*, 300–324.

Trevisan, E. (2013). *The irrational consumer: Applying behavioral economics to your business strategy*. Surrey, UK: Gower Publishing Limited.

Wierenga, B., van Bruggen, G. H., & Staelin, R. (1999). The success of marketing management support systems. *Marketing Science, 18*(3), 196–207.

INCORPORATING COMPETITIVE STRATEGY IN PRICING STRATEGY

George E. Cressman Jr.

ABSTRACT

Although critical to profitable pricing, competitive strategy is often overlooked in the pricing process. This often leads to poorly developed competitive actions with profitability suffering. This paper provides a comprehensive integrated process for the strategic management of the connection between pricing and competitive strategy. The use of the process proposed here provides active management of competitive interactions and significantly improves profitability.

INTRODUCTION

Managers often overlook the role of competitive strategy in the development of pricing strategies, yet competitive strategy plays a crucial role in achieving superior profitability. Firms that adopt value-based pricing strategies create the potential for superior profitability. But poor competitive strategy can thwart achievement of superior profitability. The objective of this paper is to introduce a systemic process for incorporating competitive

Visionary Pricing: Reflections and Advances in Honor of Dan Nimer
Advances in Business Marketing & Purchasing, Volume 19, 81–101
ISSN: 1069-0964/doi:10.1108/S1069-0964(2012)0000019010

strategy into the pricing strategy process. An underlying premise is that managers have adopted a value-based pricing strategy. A description of value-based pricing strategy is beyond the scope of this paper; the reader may refer to Nagle and Cressman (2002) and Cressman (2001a) for an introduction to value-based pricing concepts.

COMPETITIVE STRATEGY: AN INTEGRATED FRAMEWORK

Fig. 1 presents an integrated systemic view of competitive strategy useful in the development and implementation of value-based pricing strategy. This systemic view suggests three important principles:

1. Competitive strategy is closely linked to critical components of the customer management component of a value-based pricing strategy, beginning with customer selection and offering design. Decisions made in these foundational elements of pricing strategy impact competitive strategy. In addition the converse is true: the competitive actions businesses

Fig. 1.   Competitive Strategy Elements for Pricing Strategy.

take often have a significant impact on customer and offering design activities.
2. To achieve profitable results from competitive strategy, managers must actively pursue development of sources of competitive advantage, which in turn affects interactions with direct and potential competitors.
3. Because competitive tactics can dramatically impact profits, managers need a longer-term view of competitive strategy, and must carefully analyze the impact of competitive tactics on profitability.

The competitive strategy elements depicted in Fig. 1 constitute a hierarchy of activities for managers incorporating competitive strategy into pricing strategy. Successful competitive strategy is built by working from the foundation of customer targeting through tactical activities. Details of each of the hierarchy's steps are provided below.

LINKING COMPETITIVE STRATEGY TO VALUE-BASED PRICING STRATEGY

Customer Targets and Offering Design

Effective competitive strategy is tied directly to decisions firms make in targeting customers and designing offerings. Customer target selection and offering design determine the competitors the firm faces. Given the customer targets and the firm's offerings, the starting point for competitive pricing strategy is identification of the firm's competitors. Based on competitors' strategies, evolution of the seller's offering structure and sources of competitive advantage must also be planned.

Clark and Montgomery (1999) find that managers typically underestimate competition by failing to see all their competitors. Hodgkinson (1997) further suggests this can lead to allowing competitors to gain favorable positions with customers, making it difficult, even impossible, to respond. To prevent this problem, the integrated competitive strategy framework uses the customer selection (targeting) process to see competition as defined by customers. As customer targets are chosen, the management team must ask: "What competing solutions do customers have?" And: "What solution do they choose from among competing alternatives, and why?"

Note that customers choosing different competing alternatives define different customer segments. A useful way to see customer segments is to note first what solutions they choose to deal with as fundamental business objectives, and then to assess why they made that choice. This approach leads naturally to an exploration of each customer's business model and approach, and to insights into how a supplier might develop improved offering solutions. In sum, incorporating competitive strategy into the pricing process requires a target segment view. Customer target selection carries with it the competition; in turn, the identified competition defines what must be done to create offering differentiation and implies what competitive actions are appropriate.

Sources of Competitive Advantage

Mangers' choices of customer targets and offering designs further impose resource requirements on the business. The choice of the means through which these resource requirements are met creates a business design, and in turn, imposes a cost of operation on the business. The issue for managers then is to create productive ways to invest resources in delivering value to customers. This requires the development of sources of competitive advantage. Competitive advantage involves gaining more productive use of organizational resources than competitors.

Sources of competitive advantage can be described using two dimensions:

1. *Development cost*: Development cost reflects the expense required to build a source of competitive advantage.
2. *Durability*: Durability is the length of time a source of competitive advantage endures before it is matched or surpassed by competitors.

Fig. 2 summarizes types of competitive advantage using these dimensions, suggesting that as development costs increase durability follows. There are three types of sources of competitive advantage:

1. *Work process advantages*: These sources of competitive advantage are based on the work processes the firm uses to create offerings for customers. They provide advantage by utilizing fewer human resources than competitors must use. USAA, the insurance and investment firm, is a good example of a firm that achieves this type of advantage: their ability to manage customer accounts through an *expert* information system drives efficiencies in selling the entire portfolio of their offerings.
2. *Technology competencies advantages*: These sources of competitive advantage are based in the mastery of a specific set of technology

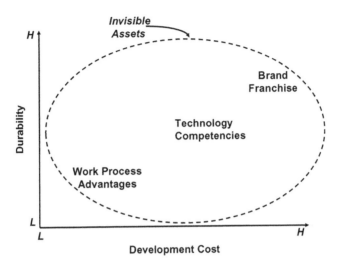

Fig. 2. Sources of Competitive Advantage.

capabilities. This results in the ability to use a specific technology platform in multiple offerings. Honda and Intel are good examples of firms deploying this type of advantage. Honda's ability to mount internal combustion engines has allowed them to enter many different equipment markets – automobiles, lawn and garden equipment, and portable generators. Intel has exploited its processing circuit design technology to the evolution of microprocessors.

3. *Brand franchise advantages*: These sources of advantage allow brand owners to bring offerings to market and gain customer preference with less marketing resources. Trials for new offerings are achieved more rapidly because of favorable brand images. Apple, Kimberly-Clark Corporation, and Proctor and Gamble are all examples of firms that have developed brand franchise advantages.

Note that sources of competitive advantage are dominated by intellectual or *invisible assets*. Itami (1987) developed the notion of invisible assets, noting they reside in the intellectual capacity of a firm. The challenge for the management team is, of course, that because invisible assets reside with individuals, they are highly mobile. This implies firms must carefully nurture the development of invisible assets, but must simultaneously engage in succession planning.

Work process advantages require the lowest development cost. In addition, work process advantages can be documented and standardized across the business. However, competitors can most easily copy work process advantages, leading to shorter durability. In contrast, brand franchises often require significant development costs, and often have much longer periods of durability.

All sources of competitive advantage, however, ultimately are reduced and often eliminated by competitive actions. The key managerial issue from a pricing strategy perspective is to understand the implications of erosion of sources of competitive advantage:

- Firms may choose to discontinue investment in the development of sources of competitive advantage. The implication is that as competitive advantage declines, offerings will become increasingly commodity-like, and firms will be required to be more price-competitive. To succeed with this choice, managers must invest in developing a low-variable cost position, allowing them to compete on price.
- Firms may choose to invest in renewing sources of competitive advantage. This choice implies the management team must plan for advantage erosion and find ways to create new sources of advantage.

Thus, the identification and development of sources of competitive advantage is a foundational component of competitive pricing strategy.

Competitor Identification

Who are the firm's competitors? Clark and Montgomery (1999) note that managers tend to underestimate the number of competitors customers consider. They suggest managers should focus more on competitors as customers define them, should periodically revisit how they define competitors, and identify potential competitors for tracking purposes.

To deal with these suggestions, Fig. 3 identifies direct and potential competitors. In this view, competitors are classified across two dimensions:

1. *Customer target overlap*: To what extent does the business target the same customers as some other firm? Note the degree of overlap is a consequence of managerial decisions on customer targets.
2. *Offering overlap*: To what extent does the business deliver the same type of offerings that some other firm delivers? Note the degree of overlap is a consequence of managerial decisions on offering design.

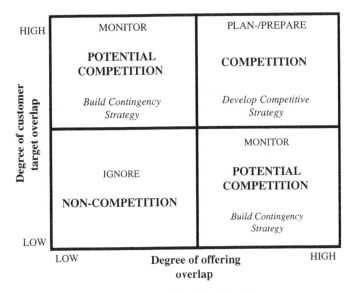

Fig. 3. Competitor Identification.

Four types of competitors are then apparent. Using the planning business as the base firm, and referring to Fig. 3, there are

1. *Noncompetitors*: In the Southwest quadrant (low–low overlap) we find noncompeting firms. These firms are pursuing a strategy that will not impact the firm's ability to achieve its objectives. There should be no planning for or response to these firms.
2. *Direct competitors*: In the Northeast quadrant (high–high overlap) are firms pursuing essentially the same strategy as the base firm. A competitive strategy must be developed for each firm in this quadrant.
3. *Potential competitors*: In the Northwest (low–high overlap) and southeast (high–low overlap) are potential competitors. While these firms are not currently a direct competitor, they could become one by developing new offerings or pursuing overlapping customer targets. A contingency competitive strategy must be developed for each firm in these quadrants.

Direct competitor analysis and strategy

For direct competitors, the use of SWOT (Strength–Weakness–Opportunities–Threats) analysis is traditionally recommended. However,

SWOT analysis does not always prove useful in developing a competitive pricing strategy because

- It does not explicitly deal with competitor intent and capabilities. A competitor with a threatening intent and the capabilities to execute its strategy is a powerful competitor – but may be overlooked in SWOT analysis. For example, although Google produces no products and sells mostly open access search capabilities and related Internet advertising, it is a real competitor for Apple computer, selling physical products and associated proprietary online libraries and *stores*.
- Strengths and weaknesses may be evaluated ignoring value delivery. A strength that cannot be converted to value delivery is an investment that may never generate a return. Likewise a weakness that does not impact value delivery may well be irrelevant.
- Opportunities are only important if the firm has the capability to capitalize on them; without capability an opportunity may only be important for a competitor.
- A threat is critical only when it impacts a firm's ability to deliver value to target customers or impacts the firm's capabilities.

These criticisms are sometimes managed in a SWOT analysis, but in my experience they are generally overlooked. An alternative evaluation approach (Fig. 4) uses the following five questions to develop an analysis for direct competitors (see Cressman, 2001b; Hamilton, Eskin, & Michaels, 1998):

1. What is this competitor's strategic intent? Consider marketing, technology, operations, finance, and general management functions.
2. What capabilities does this competitor have to support their intent? What barriers will the competitor encounter in pursuing their intent?
3. Comparing intent with barriers and capabilities, what will happen?
   a. Will the competitor succeed? If so, how will they behave?
   b. Will the competitor fail? If so, how will they behave?
4. What is the impact of this success/failure on the firm's strategic intent?
5. What actions should the firm take?

This analysis is required for all direct competitors. The analysis should be completed as part of the pricing strategy so that competitor management actions are identified and planned for.

The goal of the direct competitor analysis is to facilitate rapid response to competitor actions. Reaction speed is critical to having competitors learn the firm's actions in response to their actions. If lengthy analysis is

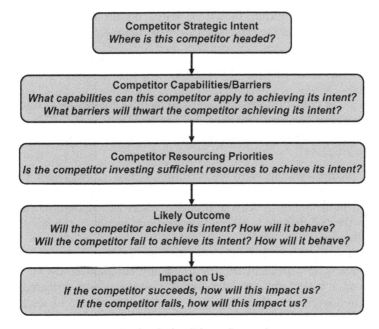

Fig. 4.   Analyzing Direct Competitors.

required after a competitor's actions, the competitor may not recognize a reaction, interpreting instead the evolution of a new series of actions.

Further, a reaction to a competitor's move must be proportional to the magnitude of the competitor's actions. As will be described below, a reaction to a competitor move can increase competitive intensity when it exceeds the level of the competitor's move.

A comprehensive competitive intelligence system is thus required. Many companies in the 1980s and early 1990s developed massive competitive intelligence systems. Unfortunately, many of these systems generated operating cost but contributed little to the refinement of business unit or corporate strategy. One reason for this outcome is that many of the competitive intelligence programs collected large amounts of data and generated many reports, much of which went unread by managers — there was just too much data and not enough information analysis for decision makers. As a result, many managers relied mostly on their own instincts when evaluating competitors, and the use of competitive intelligence systems declined.

Competitive intelligence should be based on the business unit's proposed strategy. Given the articulated strategy, managers can assess:

- How might competitors thwart our achieving our strategy?
- What early indicators signal that competitors are moving to thwart our strategy?
- What is the minimum we must know to identify competitor actions?
- What competitive intelligence do we then require?
- What market information do we need to develop the required competitive intelligence?

This requires managers to think through their strategy and consider potential competitor actions. Note this view builds on the competitor identification built in Fig. 3. This approach reduces the amount of raw data input to the competitive intelligence system and increases the relevancy of the intelligence.

Another important consideration for developing useful competitive intelligence is validation of the inputs. Many companies rely on ad hoc market data collection and impressions managers have gathered about competition over time. This approach is subject to all the biases humans apply to decision-making. Three specific biases in particular have significant impact on competitive strategy in the pricing process:

1. *Recency*: A more recent event — such as a loss of an order to a competitor with lower prices — may carry more weight in managers' minds than the longer-term competitive behavior. Managers may not consider why competitors may have made a move and whether that move can be replicated.
2. *Magnitude*: A competitive move that has a large impact on an individual business unit manager may carry more weight in that person's thinking than it should. The desire to *win* may trump smart competitive strategy and result in increased efforts to *punish* the competitor or get even.
3. *Potency*: A customer threat to give an order to a competitor with a reported lower price may be a potent threat. Business managers may react by cutting price before they have done any analysis to determine if the customer really has a lower-priced offer or can really move to a competitor. The consequence may be an increase in competitive intensity and a decline in average market prices.

Creating a useful competitive intelligence system requires attention to minimizing the effects of these biases and validating both market information and analysis. Assembly of market inputs into a central system facilitates analysis and can improve the validation effort.

Validation should first ensure the quality of inputs from the market. Source accuracy should be tested against the accuracy of past inputs from the source; this implies an on-going post-mortem process to assess market results versus source reports. Inputs should be weighted based upon confirmation from multiple sources; inputs from sole sources. For example, a competitive price cut reported by only one customer should be accepted with great caution. In addition, patterns observed in sales force reports should be regularly evaluated. Some sales personnel are more open to customer suggestions of lower competitive prices; if these sales representatives consistently report lower prices in their sales territory, they could be prone to manipulation by customers.

What information should be contained in a competitive database? Fig. 5 depicts the important information elements showing their linkage to the analysis process described above. Business unit strategy should be the basis for determining the exact information collected and the process for validating the information in the competitive database.

Planning strategy in a competitive marketplace must be highly realistic. Strategies that intend to advantage a firm will be opposed in most markets.

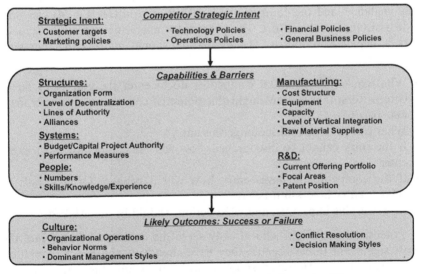

Fig. 5. Competitive Intelligence Data Base Information Elements.

In capital intense markets, attempts to increase capacity utilization beyond average industry capacity utilization often precipitate price responses from competitors. This is especially true when the industry is both capital intensive and has cost structures dominated by fixed cost. An increase in capacity utilization by one competitor means other firms have lower capacity utilization; unit costs for firms with lower capacity utilization will then increase because there is less volume to dilute the fixed costs. This unit cost increase will be immediately visible and will draw competitor attempts for redress – often in the form of a price cut. In capital-intensive businesses with high fixed costs, the business unit should always signal competitive intent to operate at the average industry capacity utilization level.

Managers must understand that their actions will always draw some form of competitive response. In fact, customers may actively encourage competitive response! For example, a customer who receives a *special* price deal may shop the price among the firm's competitors, and ask for comparable price deals from these competitors – resulting in a price war.

Potential Competitor Analysis and Strategy

Early detection of potential competitors evolving to direct competitors requires managerial vigilance. Geroski (1999) provides a framework to aid this vigilance, and the competitor identification grid (see Fig. 4) can provide assistance in this effort. The process for analyzing potential competitors is depicted in Fig. 6. The evaluation should address the following questions:

- What could this potential competitor do to enter the market of direct competitors; that is, how might this potential competitor enter our market space?
- What can be done to discourage this entry?
- If the entry cannot be discouraged, how will the competitor most likely enter?
- If the competitor achieves entry how will it behave? Or if it fails to achieve entry how will it behave?
- How will this impact us, and what actions should be undertaken?

Potential competitors who already serve the customer often create the most significant threat because they have already established a reputation with the customer. However, suppliers with similar offerings should not be overlooked, especially when they serve high-profile customers and can

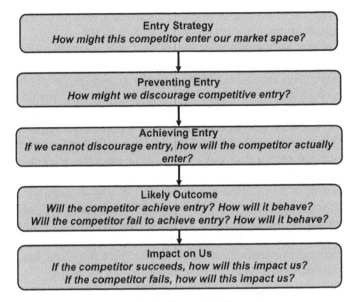

Fig. 6. Analyzing Potential Competitors.

leverage their reputation with those customers. The analysis of potential competitors is often complicated with many possible competitor actions. The scenario process (see Chermack (2011) for details on the scenario planning process) is helpful in managing this complication. In developing scenario stories, the analysis team should address four key considerations:

1. What are the multiple, different, routes a potential competitor could take to enter our market space? The objective of the scenario process is to expand the scope of considered competitor actions, thereby reducing – even possibly eliminating – surprise. Thus, the analysis team should attempt to consider widely different scenarios, although the scenarios must remain plausible.
2. After developing the scenarios, the analysis team should build a strategy to deal with the potential competitor. Scenarios are, of course, an esti-mate of what might happen in the marketplace, and it is likely no single scenario precisely describes what the potential competitor will do. Then because the potential competitor's exact actions can rarely be known with certainty, the analysis team should strive to build a robust strategy, one that spans across the scenarios and will work regardless of the poten-tial competitor's actions. When evaluating either direct or potential

competitors it is important to judge competitor actions on the basis of their impact on the firm.

3. A competitor succeeding may not be bad. For example, a competitor that pioneers a marketplace bears the cost of market development; a competitor who can quickly follow in the growth phase of the market may become much more profitable because of lower start-up expense. The Personal Digital Assistant (PDA) market provides a good example, where Blackberry devices leveraged Palm's pioneering market development investments to quickly and profitably establish a leading position.

4. A competitor failing may not be good. For example, a competitor failing in a market may perceive it has no other business options, and thus may be willing to compete at very low prices and damage the future of the market. The market for plate and sheet steel has displayed this type of behavior in the past; large integrated producers like United States Steel would face significant costs to exit the steel business, and thus have engaged in intense price wars. Similar price wars have been evident in the airline sector.

Competitive Tactics

Uncertainty complicates the task of forecasting competitive actions. In more mature markets with extended history of competitive interactions, uncertainty about competitive intent, capabilities, and tactics may be lower. But even then, in a more mature market, uncertainty about competitor strategy still may be high. As uncertainty increases, the scenario process is often useful in developing a broader view of possible competitor actions. The scenario process considers multiple different, but plausible views of competitor actions. The key to successful scenario development is to stretch managers' views of possible competitor actions while keeping the views plausible. The objective is to reduce the potential for surprise and facilitate rapid response to competitors.

When firms develop a strong market position they can anticipate two general forms of competitive response. For example, suppose a firm has developed an offering that delivers unique differential value to a set of customers, and is winning share of these customers' purchases vis-à-vis a key competitor. The competitor then may consider two possible responses:

1. The competitor may invest in developing offering components that match some of the winning firm's differentiation. The winning firm then

delivers less differential value than it did previously, and can no longer command as much price premium in the market.

2. Alternatively, the competitor may choose to not match the winning firm's differentiation, but may instead cut price on its current offerings. This may increase customer price sensitivity and force the winning firm to reduce its price.

In either case, the ability to continue to command premium prices is threatened.

The implication of this is that managers must develop competitive strategy considering not only possible competitor actions, but also the evolution of their own offerings and market capabilities. Consequently, a strong market plan should include the identification of the next four to five evolutions of the firm's offering platform, and the identification of the next two to three evolutions of the firm's sources of competitive advantage.

Cressman and Nagle (2002) propose that competitors' tactics need not always be countered; managers must weigh the long-range cost of responding. These authors provide a framework (see Fig. 7) for developing insights into profitable responses. Further, Cressman (2003) proposes that often a firm's actions drive competitive actions that can destroy profitable pricing. For example, a firm that uses a low price offer to win a competitor's loyal customer may precipitate a price war: before attempting to win a competitor's customers with a price move managers should assess the potential for the competitor to respond with a similar price move. Smith and Cressman (2008) propose guidelines for evaluating competitive responses in mature markets. While noting that in some circumstances aggressive market share growth may be appropriate, in most mature markets the goal should be profitability, not share. Instead, a winning competitive strategy in mature markets is to (1) understand target customer businesses and choose targets based on the potential to deliver differential value; (2) create offerings that deliver real value; (3) avoid price competition unless there the firm has a significant variable cost advantage; and (4) analyze competitive moves for their future impact.

An initial step in assessing how to respond to competitor tactics is to determine if customer reports of competitor moves are indeed accurate, for some customers' reports are merely games (see Yama (2004) for an excellent description of these purchasing games). For example, consider these types of customer games that lead to mistaken competitive response:

- *Creating a false sense of competition*: Customers may hint they have a number of significant competitive bids, and a supplier is priced much

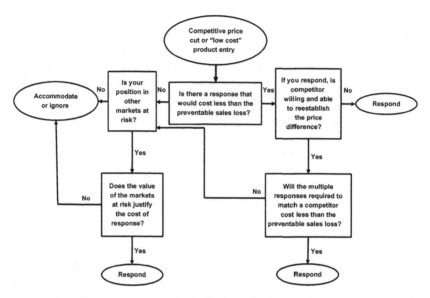

Fig. 7. Framework for Assessing Competitive Response. *Source*: Cressman and
Nagle (2002).

higher. The danger for the *high-priced* supplier is that a competitive bid
may be used to precipitate price cuts and retaliation from other suppliers. Reports of lower-priced competition must be treated with great
skepticism. First, if a customer really does have a lower competitive
offer, why are they reporting this to other competitors? Why not just
accept the lower-priced offer? An appropriate response to a reported
lower-priced offer is to say: "If you can meet your needs at a significantly lower price, then clearly it is in your best interest to accept that
offer." Customers who are gaming their suppliers may respond they
would like to keep the alleged higher priced supplier in the bidding process, tacitly acknowledging the supplier's superior value delivery; this
fact obviously should be stated.
- *Sharing deceptive competitive information*: A customer actually may have
  encouraged a lower-priced competitive offer, but the competitive offer
  may not deliver all the value that the supplier can offer; consequently,
  the customer may try to get the preferred supplier to cut price. An
  appropriate response then would be to meet the competitive price by
  removing a particularly valuable offering component. Customers who
  are gaming their suppliers will likely respond by refusing to accept the

removal of the valuable offering component, to which the supplier can respond by continuing to insist on getting paid for differential value delivery.

Using a signal detection framework, Cressman (2007) proposes a four-step analytical process to determine if customer reports of lower-priced offerings are accurate: First, ensure customer reports are gathered from more than one source: avoid relying on a lower-price report from one customer – reports of lower competitor prices from a single customer are often a customer game. Second, seek confirmation elsewhere: avoid relying on the report of lower prices from a single sales person – customers may be gaming the sales person. Determine if there is a pattern of lower prices from multiple sales people. Third, encourage market team debate: ask the marketing and sales team to debate the likelihood of a customer actually having a lower-priced offer. Finally, test customer price reports over time: evaluate customer price offer reports against what the customer has reported in the past, and the validity of those historical reports. Maintaining *log books* of customer reports and competitor reports is helpful in building this historical view.

In responding to a reported competitive price offer, managers should understand what competitive offers customers can actually use: if there are lower-priced offerings the customers cannot actually adopt, then responding with a lower price is absolutely the wrong move. Also communicate how the supplier's offering creates unique value for the customer, and why a higher price is indeed justified. Force customers to give up especially valuable offering components if they insist on a lower price.

Finally, Cressman (2007) argues that management teams evaluate a price response to a customer reporting a lower price offering by considering five useful questions (see also Cressman & Nagle, 2002):

1. Is there a potential response that would cost less than losing the sales to a lower-priced competitor?
2. What is the competitor likely to do if the report of the lower price offer is accurate and the supplier responds with a price cut?
3. What is the competitor likely to do even if it is at a cost disadvantage and the management team responds with a price cut?
4. If the reported competitor's price move *is* accurate, what actions would make the competitors price moves visible to customers who have not been given the lower price?
5. What actions would *hold a hostage for good behavior* by increasing threats in the competitor's home market or with the competitor's primary customer targets?

But what happens if customers' threats to shift an order to a competitor are real? Cressman (2005) suggests that such a threat needs to be considered in light of market issues, customer issues, and competitor issues:

- *Market issues*: First, consider *available capacity*: Does the proposed competitor have the capacity to fill the order? Second, consider *industry dynamics*: What is the proposed competitor's innovation potential? If the customer shifts to a competitor, will they lose access to the current supplier's new products/services?
- *Customer issues*: Consider switching costs: Does the customer face substantial switching costs to move to a competing supplier? What about *qualification*: Is the proposed competitor's offering qualified? And *differentiation*: Will the customer be forced to give up substantial value delivery to move to a competing alternative?
- *Competitor issues*: Finally, consider *competitor aggressiveness*: Is there evidence the proposed competitor really wants the order? And *impact on the competitor*: What will happen to the remainder of the competitor's business if they accept the order?

COMMUNICATING STRATEGIC INTENT

A key to active management of competitive interactions is public positioning of the business's intent and capabilities. Many firms hold their strategic intent as a proprietary secret. However, effective management of competitive dynamics requires informing the market of where the business will focus and how it will succeed. The intent is to encourage competitors to focus somewhere else. Assuming competitive attacks evolve, how should they be managed? Fahey (2003) provides a comprehensive process for managing competitor attacks. He suggests that scenarios can especially provide useful insights into how to forecast potential competitor actions, as discussed above.

In addition, firms must examine their own actions, assess their impact on competitive intensity, and ensure they are not sending wrong signals to the marketplace. For example, Cressman (2003, 2006) suggests that firm often unintentionally exacerbate competitive intensity by making mistaken competitive moves, sometimes leading to price wars. A series of questions to assess this potential negative impact on competition can prove useful:

- Is the business clearly focused on target customers where it can deliver differentiated value at competitive advantage?

- Have the customer targets, the firm's differentiated value, and sources of competitive advantage been communicated to the market?
- Does the firm use a disciplined approach to target customers and refrain from pursuing nontarget customers?
- Does the business avoid price competition and using price deals to try to grow market share?
- Does the firm attempt to operate at average industry capacity utilization and avoid using price to attempt to load operations in down economies?
- Does the business force customers to trade value for a lower price and avoid price concessions?

Of course, it may not always be possible to avoid a price war. Rao, Bergen, and Davis (2000) suggest a series of nonprice and price tactics to try to avoid a price war and manage successfully should a price war develop. These include *nonprice activities*, such as making competitors aware of cost advantages when they exist; focusing on differentiated value to build customer preference; and alerting customers to risks they face when adopting a lower-priced offering. They also recommend *price activities*, such as selective discounting by cutting price only on certain offerings, or developing fighting brands to flank competitors.

CONCLUSION

Managers must develop the ability to *think in time* by forecasting how their proposed competitive actions might evolve in the future. Two simple rules then can be used to judge the desirability of competitive actions:

1. *Never fight a battle you cannot win!* If a proposed competitive move puts the business at disadvantage from which there is no escape, then a different set of competitive actions should be developed.
2. *If the rules of competition don't favor the business, change the rules of competition!* Fighting a competitive battle using the competitor's ground rules is unlikely to create favorable results because the competitor will likely choose to participate in a way that favors the competitor. For example, when Nucor management realized they could not compete against large integrated steel mills, they changed the form of competition. Nucor employed new furnace technology that used scrap steel as a raw material, and thus avoided the need to invest in coke manufacture.

This allowed Nucor to achieve a low cost position that none of the integrated mills could match.

Firms can create a potentially profitable pricing strategy by delivering unique value to their target customers. The challenge, though, is to avoid giving away this profit potential through poorly conceived competitive strategy. In order to be consistently profitable, firms must actively manage how they interact with current and potential customers.

A TRIBUTE TO DAN NIMER

Dan started the effort to have managers recognize that pricing must be managed as a strategic focus of the business. I am personally indebted to Dan for helping us recognize the power of actively managing pricing practices, and salute Dan for his many contributions to the growing professionalism of pricing practitioners.

REFERENCES

Chermack, T. (2011). *Scenario planning in organizations: How to create, use and assess scenarios*. Berrett-Koehler Publishers.
Clark, B. H., & Montgomery, D. B. (1999). Managerial identification of competitors. *Journal of Marketing, 63*(3), 67–83.
Cressman, G. E., Jr. (2001a). Building business profitability: The value connection. *Chimica Oggi*, 65–68. June.
Cressman, G. E., Jr. (2001b). Building business profitability: The value connection, part three. *Chimica Oggi*, December.
Cressman, G. E., Jr. (2003). Dealing with 'dumb competitors'. *The Pricing Advisor*, 1–2. April.
Cressman, G. E., Jr. (2005). Cut your price, or your competitor gets the business. *The Journal of Professional Pricing, 14*(2). Second Quarter.
Cressman, G. E., Jr. (2006). Fixing prices. *Marketing Management*, 32–37. September/October.
Cressman, G. E., Jr. (2007). Seeing through the fog: Managing price demands. *The Journal of Professional Pricing*, 22–27. Fourth Quarter.
Cressman, G. E., Jr., & Nagle, T. T. (2002). How to manage an aggressive competitor. *Business Horizons*, 23–30. March–April.
Fahey, L. (2003). Competitor scenarios. *Strategy and Leadership, 31*(1), 32–44.
Geroski, P. A. (1999). Early warning of new rivals. *Sloan Management Review, 40*(3), 107–116.
Hamilton, R. D., III., Eskin, E. D., & Michaels, M. P. (1998). Assessing competitors: The gap between strategic intent and core capability. *Long Range Planning, 31*(3), 406–417.

Hodgkinson, G. P. (1997). Cognitive inertia in a turbulent market: The case of UK residential estate agents. *Journal of Management Studies, 34*, 921–945.

Itami, H. (1987). *Mobilizing invisible assets, cambridge.* MA: Harvard University Press.

Nagle, T. T., & Cressman, G. E. (2002). Don't just set prices, manage them. *Marketing Management, 11*(6), 29–33.

Rao, A. R., Bergen, M. E., & Davis, S. (2000). How to fight a price war. *Harvard Business Review, 78*(2), 107–116. March–April.

Smith, R. D., & Cressman, G. E., Jr. (2008). Share wars: Finding new life in mature markets. *The Journal of Professional Pricing*, 10–14. Third Quarter.

Yama, E., *"Purchasing Hardball: Playing Price,"* Business Horizons, September/October, 2004.

EMERGENT PRICING STRATEGY

Gerald E. Smith

ABSTRACT

Advances in technology, operations research, and data driven pricing and marketing are leading pricing strategy into new and untested waters — toward dynamic pricing, and variable pricing strategies, which ultimately require changes in how we view pricing strategy. The dominant view of pricing strategy is that pricing goals, objectives, and strategies should be formulated a priori, and should be consistent with marketing and corporate strategies — deliberate pricing strategy. *This chapter argues that firms need to develop new strategic pricing skills that lead to more improvisational, innovative, or adaptive pricing strategies. I call this type of price strategy-making* emergent pricing strategy. *Innovative pricing strategies that the organization judges, or* senses *to be effective, are repeated, shared, expanded, and refined into successful pricing patterns that, over time and across situations, become pricing strategy. Thus, rather than specifically designing pricing strategy to achieve a goal, here the organization acts upon a price innovation that seems to make sense for this customer, this market segment, this setting, and this situation, then interprets the outcomes, signals, and reactions that seem to flow from the pricing action, and shares and encourages adoption*

Visionary Pricing: Reflections and Advances in Honor of Dan Nimer
Advances in Business Marketing & Purchasing, Volume 19, 103–126
ISSN: 1069-0964/doi:10.1108/S1069-0964(2012)0000019011

and adaption by others in the organization. Emergent pricing strategy is particularly useful in unstable, turbulent, and complex product and market environments in which price-sensitive buyers wield significant power and influence.

For a half-century, marketing researchers and practitioners have advocated the importance of treating price as a strategic variable in the marketing mix (Dolan & Simon, 1996; Nagle & Holden, 2002; Nagle, Holden, & Zale, 2010; Monroe, 2003; Oxenfeldt, 1973; Ross, 1984; Smith & Nagle, 1994). Pricing goals, objectives, and strategies should be formulated a priori, and should be consistent with marketing and corporate strategies. Nagle et al. (2010) summarize well this notion of strategic pricing:

> Strategic pricing is the coordination of interrelated marketing, competitive, and financial decisions to set prices profitably. For most companies, strategic pricing requires more than a change in attitude; it requires a change in when, how, and who makes pricing decisions . . . Strategic pricing also requires that management take responsibility for establishing a coherent set of pricing policies and procedures, consistent with its strategic goals for the company. (Nagle and Holden 2002, p. 1)

According to this normative view, pricing strategy is formulated in advance of pricing implementation and action. Management establishes pricing objectives to direct pricing strategy and provides measurable goals with which to judge pricing's effectiveness. Pricing strategy articulates a coordinated plan with prescriptions of how functional units in the organization should act with respect to pricing − how finance should measure pricing effectiveness, how marketing should frame pricing as part of the firm's value proposition, how field sales should communicate the firm's value proposition and help customers navigate among price offerings, and how engineering, production, and service should deliver value to customers to maximize pricing's profit potential. This view is consistent with strategy researchers, who emphasize that implementation should achieve and sustain commitment to strategic purpose; it should be directed toward the organized achievement of strategic results (Andrews, 1987).

But this view of formal pricing strategy, what I call *deliberate pricing strategy*, makes assumptions about price strategy-making and pricing implementation that obfuscate other less structured or less formal ways of formulating pricing strategy. For example, formal deliberate price strategy-making implicitly assumes (1) that pricing managers are rational and well-informed information processors, consistent with behavioral economic theory (Simon, 1957, 1978); yet managers often approach pricing decisions heuristically, such as using familiar or comfortable pricing formulas, found so frequently in cost-based pricing strategies (Smith, 1995). (2) They make pricing strategies that get implemented in mature market environments that are concrete, measurable, and slowly changing, sufficiently stable to enable reliable predictions about how pricing strategies will influence market demand, customer response, and competitor reaction (Dolan & Simon, 1996; Monroe, 2003; Nagle, Hogan, & Zale, 2010).

How do we address managers in market environments that are changing, variable, difficult to measure, and challenging to discover. For them it is difficult to predict how pricing strategies will influence, or be influenced by other market forces – such as dynamic changes in customer demands – or competitor counter pricing. (3) Pricing managers consciously set out to attain specific and well-defined pricing goals and objectives, such as operating profit targets, target return on marketing or pricing investment, revenue growth targets, or market share goals (Diamantopoulos & Mathews, 1995). But some goals, such as market share or revenue growth goals, have been shown to lead to poor pricing outcomes (Simon, Bilstein, & Luby 2006), while giving the illusion that the organization is rationally pursuing profit maximization. In fact, intended goals are often poorly chosen or conflict, or they change, and form after the fact. Even then it is difficult to separate out, quantify, or measure pricing's effect versus other elements of the marketing mix. Firms in static, mature market environments hire teams of trained statisticians to measure and model pricing's effects, but one rarely finds these skillsets in firms with variable or changing market situations.

Finally, (4) the deliberate pricing strategy paradigm assumes that pricing managers approach price decision making with reasonable consensus among managers about pricing strategy; they are guided and constrained by pricing policies that are clearly articulated and consistently applied across a vast variety of customer transactions (Corey, 1991; Ross, 1984;

Smith & Nagle, 1994; Simon, 1989). But in many rapidly changing unstable market environments, achieving consensus and formulating pricing policy guidelines are much more difficult.

A foundational assumption that is especially important to the deliberate price strategy paradigm: price strategy making must be separate from pricing implementation; firms design pricing strategy, and then operationalize strategy with pricing implementation. There are feedback loops, of course, as implementation informs adjustments to pricing strategy, but price strategy making remains decoupled from pricing implementation. Organizations that consistently implement this form of pricing strategy exhibit what Smith (1995) termed a *strategic pricing orientation* – their operational pricing processes are oriented toward strategic pricing. The term "orientation" conveys more than occasional or episodic strategic pricing. It conveys a broader alignment throughout the organization, a general or lasting direction that permeates organizational thought and action over time and across situations (see also Smith & Woodside, 2009).

What about firms that successfully design more improvisational, innovative, or adaptive pricing strategies? I call this type of price strategy-making *emergent pricing strategy*. Designing emergent pricing strategy seems like an oxymoron, but the term *design* begs the question: how does a firm design, facilitate, and implement emergent pricing strategy? There are pricing situations where price strategy making and pricing action converge in time so that, in the limit, they occur simultaneously. Moorman and Miner (1998, p. 1) define such a convergence of strategy design and execution as "*improvisation* and suggest that the narrower the time gap between composing and performing (or planning and implementation), the more that act is improvisational." Improvisational, innovative, or adaptive pricing strategies that the organization judges, or *senses* to be effective are repeated, shared, expanded, and refined into successful pricing patterns that, over time and across situation, become pricing strategy. Thus, rather than specifically designing pricing strategy to achieve a goal, here the organization (1) acts upon a price point, price program, price configuration, or price idea that seems to make sense for this customer, this market segment, this setting, and situation, (2) follows through with price execution and value delivery, (3) interprets the outcomes, signals, and reactions that seem to flow from the pricing action, and (4) shares, copies, and encourages adoption and adaption by others in the organization.

Henry Mintzberg (1988, pp. 78–79) originally identified the idea of *emergent strategy* in the strategy literature in his groundbreaking *McKinsey Quarterly* essay *Crafting Strategy*:

[I]f strategies can be planned and intended, they can also be pursued and realized (or not realized, as the case may be) .... We at McGill call strategies ... that appear without clear intentions – or in spite of them – emergent strategies. Actions simply converge into patterns. They may become deliberate, of course, if the pattern is recognized and then legitimated by senior management. But that's after the fact ... strategies can form as well as be formulated.

I build on Mintzberg's ideas, and incorporate related thinking on sense-making (Weick, 2001), improvisation (Moorman & Miner, 1998), and creativity (Amabile et al., 1996). My purpose here is not to detract from the value of deliberate pricing strategy. Deliberate pricing strategy is an important and useful paradigm for designing and implementing pricing decisions. However, my field research and prior theory point to several reasons why emergent pricing strategy may be valuable and useful. First, emergent pricing strategy can be effective when the firm faces turbulent market environments that require pricing decision and pricing action in time frames and across situations that preclude advanced predictive price planning and strategizing (Moorman & Miner, 1998). Second, emergent pricing strategy focuses on the development of a new and different set of strategic pricing skills that place greater emphasis on informally adapting, innovating, improvising, and sharing. These skills include things such as how to engage in effective market *sensing* to detect the multidimensional effects of pricing actions (such as marginal changes in purchase acceleration or delay, changes in share of wallet, changes in satisfaction/dissatisfaction or loyalty), how to *scan* the market environment for weak but useful price-relevant cues, and how to *socially share* interpretations of pricing outcomes among organization members, across functional areas (finance, marketing, field sales, engineering, production), even including external pricing partners such as customers, suppliers, and channel members.

Third, emergent pricing strategy invokes a new and different form of organizational pricing idea generation and price learning – from bottom up, rather than top down. Emergent pricing strategy collapses organizational distance between price strategy making and pricing action. It requires the executive team to be close to pricing action and to pricing strategy. They engage in sensing and finding pricing patterns that work well in one situation, in one market, with one customer, in one corner of the organization, and then copy, apply, or adapt it to other situations or markets. As executives notice, share, and apply these pricing patterns throughout the organization the patterns becoming increasingly strategic to the organization — they become pricing strategy. Referring to these executive strategists, Mintzberg (1988, p. 85) noted:

> The popular view sees the strategist as a planner or as a visionary, someone sitting on a pedestal dictating brilliant strategies for everyone else to implement .... I wish to propose an additional view of the strategist — as a pattern recognizer, a learner if you will — who manages a process in which strategies (and visions) can emerge as well as be deliberately conceived .... This strategist finds strategies no less than creates them, often in patterns that form inadvertently in its own behavior.

The student of deliberate pricing strategy will see many flaws in the emergent price strategy logic. For example: How can it make sense to include outsiders, even the customer, in the firm's price setting process — a form of notoriously flawed negotiated pricing with transparent, or open pricing? This is a reasonable objection, although value-based pricing advocates precisely this idea: As customers engage in calculating the value of the product or service, their very involvement is designed to persuade the customer that the customer's level of value capture (relative to price) is compelling versus the firm's level of value capture. Another flaw: How can the firm manage various different prices to different customers for the same product or service — surely disadvantaged customers will learn of and demand equally favorable pricing? Firms that rely on more commoditized *product-driven pricing* (setting one price for the product and bundling in other services, warranties, and extras for free) may be vulnerable to this issue, but firms employing more customized *offer-driven pricing* (setting different offer prices for different value bundles) are more likely to succeed.

One more flaw: The emergent pricing model implies that pricing authority be delegated to field sales personnel, even though prior empirical research gives evidence that pricing by the sales force leads to less organizational profitability (Stephenson, Cron, & Frazier, 1979). This indeed may be an issue for sales forces trained to *sell products*, but the new model proposes that sales forces be trained to design offer bundles to meet the needs of customers – leveraging tools such as modular price menus to facilitate modular bundle building. The digital economy especially provides many more opportunities to design customized value bundles – with price and value bundle improvisation and innovation – and ultimately this kind of customization must take place at the field sales level.

CASE STUDY EXAMPLE

On June 29, 2007, Apple's original iPhone 8GB went on sale at a price of $599, a clear skim pricing strategy. Yet, only 9 weeks after product release, September 5, Apple cut price dramatically to $399, provoking a backlash from early iPhone purchasers. Two days later, September 7, Apple CEO Steve Jobs penned a personal letter to early iPhone buyers, with an apology and an explanation, and invented another price – a compensatory $100 merchandise rebate. Jobs' note to original iPhone buyers reveals hints of how Apple's iPhone pricing strategy emerged in a rapidly shifting smartphone market:

> To all iPhone customers:
> I have received hundreds of emails from iPhone customers who are upset about Apple dropping the price of iPhone by $200 two months after it went on sale. After reading every one of these emails, I have some observations and conclusions.
> First, I am sure that we are making the correct decision to lower the price of the 8GB iPhone from $599 to $399, and that now is the right time to do it. iPhone is a breakthrough product, and we have the chance to 'go for it' this holiday season. iPhone is so far ahead of the competition, and now it will be affordable by even more customers. It benefits both Apple and every iPhone user to get as many new customers as possible in the iPhone 'tent'. We strongly believe the $399 price will help us do just that this holiday season. [*Source*: Apple Computer – http://www.apple.com/hotnews/openiphoneletter/.]

What could have provoked these extraordinarily conflicting pricing actions? In 2006, as Jobs prepared to introduce iPhone at MacWorld in January 2007, he faced a key pricing challenge: Set a price point for a disruptive new product innovation that would establish the product's reference value in the marketplace, yet establish a credible market position in a highly competitive and turbulent mobile telephone market dominated by entrenched corporate icons. Three players controlled 65 percent of the mobile handset market: Nokia (38 percent), Motorola (14 percent), and Samsung (13 percent); three players controlled 73 percent of mobile carrier subscribers: AT&T (28 percent), Verizon (26 percent), and Sprint Nextel (19 percent). How should Apple price the new iPhone? Jobs' January 2007 MacWorld introduction stressed that iPhone's introductory price was based on the comparative reference prices of the iPod ($199), and an average mobile phone ($299), for a total combined reference price of $498:

So what should we price [iPhone] at? Well, what do these things normally cost? An iPod, the most popular iPod, $199 for 4 gig nano. What's a smart phone cost? ... they generally average about $299 with a two-year contract .... And so people spend $499 on this combination. What should we charge for iPhone? Cause iPhone has got a lot more than this stuff, right. It's got video. Real video. It's got what ... this beautiful gorgeous wide screen. It's got multi-touch user interface. It's got wi-fi. It's got a real browser. It's got html e-mail. It's got coverflow and on and on and on. And this stuff would normally cost hundreds of dollars. So how much more than $499 should we price iPhone? Well, we thought long and hard about it, because iPhone just does so much stuff .... Well, for a 4 gigabyte model, we're gonna price it at that same $499. No premium whatsoever. $499. And we're gonna have an 8 gigabyte model for just $599. [*Source*: http://www.european-rhetoric.com/analyses/ ikeynote-analysis-iphone/transcript-2007/.]

At $599, the iPhone 8GB was priced at a 100 percent price premium ($300) to an average mobile phone. Yet, for decades Apple had espoused a 55 percent gross margin goal for all products: "55 or die" was their motto. Based on analysts' estimates of iPhone's production cost ($265), iPhone's introductory gross margin was 56 percent. Despite Jobs' framing of iPhone's price relative to the iPod and cell phone, iPhone's initial pricing calculation looked eerily like simple cost-plus pricing. Still, Apple would receive additional payments that analysts estimated to be $18 per month, or $432 per subscriber amortized over the two-year life of an AT&T

customer contract. The January 2007 introductory price was just the beginning of iPhone's emerging pricing strategy.

On iPhone's first weekend on the market, starting June 29, 2007, it sold 270,000 units. The Apple team watched, waited, scanning and sensing iPhone's early market headway — unit sales volumes, customer price sensitivity to the very high price, competitive reactions to the January introduction, production capacity forecasts. By summer's end iPhone sales were slowing — analysts estimated to fewer than 9,000 units per day, a more precipitous drop than Apple had expected after the June 29 introduction. The three major handset manufacturers had already announced iPhone look-alike products; rumors were flying that Google was organizing an 84-company Open Handset Alliance, centered on a free and open smartphone software platform called *Android*. Smartphone category sales, only 10 percent of total mobile phone sales, were now doubling year over year, and smartphone competitors were readying for the 2007 end-of-year selling season when 30 percent of annual smartphone sales would occur. Jobs realized that January's bold $600 introductory price would now threaten the fledgling iPhone franchise as lower-priced competitors' scaled up and iPhone missed the forthcoming wave of holiday season sales — relegating iPhone to a premium-priced niche rather than mainstream product.

Still, reducing price by $200, a 33 percent price cut, to more competitively penetrate the mainstream market would dramatically reduce iPhone's gross margin, to 34 percent, far short of Apple's traditional 55 percent gross margin goal — iPhone unit sales would have to increase by 150 percent to break even on that price change. But then a pricing idea: add subscriber contract revenues ($432) to the new product price ($399), giving a 68 percent margin — the breakeven from this perspective would be only 35 percent. On September 5, the Apple team pulled the trigger and set in motion the price changes that would evolve into iPhone's new mainstream pricing strategy.

In retrospect, iPhone's pricing strategy seemed improvisational, opportunistic, adaptive, perhaps brilliant, for Apple had little idea in January 2007 how turbulent market forces would shape iPhone's original pricing strategy: setting a very high price that established the product's reference value, watching the emergent coalition of a low-price competitive platform, then sensing anemic unit sales volume, quickly adapting with a highly risky revision to pricing strategy, and finally improvising remedial price adjustments — a $100 gift certificate to ensure positive word-of-mouth from early iPhone adopters and opinion leaders. This is hardly a prescription for deliberate pricing strategy. Three years later Apple applied the same model for emergent price strategy making to the launch of the iPad as its own category of Internet device — a risky strategy with turbulent forces reminiscent to iPhone's launch. Technology experts were broadly skeptical of the iPad's prospects. One credit analyst wrote: "While it remains to be seen how much traction the iPad gets initially, management noted that it will remain nimble (pricing could change if the company is not attracting as many customers as anticipated)" (Morphy, 2010).

EMERGENT PRICING STRATEGY

Emergent pricing strategy is forming, setting, and establishing pricing strategy using pricing processes in which price action precedes interpretation, pricing goals and performance metrics emerge retrospectively as managers sense how pricing action is effective or ineffective, what seems to be working or not working in the market and in the organization. The organization makes price action strategic by identifying useful pricing innovations, ideas, and improvisations in disparate parts of the organization, and repeating, adapting, sharing, and applying these pricing innovations to other pricing situations. These innovations become strategic pricing patterns as they emerge and coalesce over time, across situations, and across organizational boundaries (Fig. 1).

Price Action, Innovation, Improvisation

The engine of emergent pricing strategy is *price action, innovation, and improvisation.* The firm acts in a way that makes sense with previous actions, and interprets retrospectively the rationale for its actions, such as a price innovation or improvisation. Rationality, goals, and preferences about the effectiveness of price innovation *emerge* from the price action itself, rather than guide the action (Choo, 1998; Daft & Weick, 1984; Weick 2001, 1995, 1979). In other words, managers see what happens; they form their own measures as they go, sometimes new and different, in response to the effects they see from price innovation. Moorman and Miner (1998) suggest that "improvisation is a strategy of emergent learning that can be employed as a substitute for planning." They found that the effectiveness of improvisation in a product planning context is especially affected by three key factors: environmental turbulence, real-time information flows

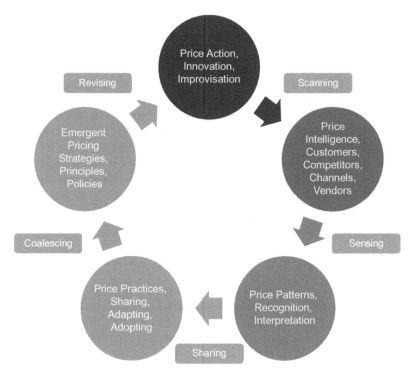

Fig. 1. Emergent Pricing Strategy.

such as face-to-face interactions or electronic communications among decision participants, and high organizational memory. When these factors
were present, improvisation had favorable effects on design effectiveness,
market effectiveness, team learning, team functioning, and sometimes
cost and time efficiency. We expect similar effects exist in pricing innovation as well.

Price Intelligence from Customers, Competitors, Channels, Vendors

Emergent pricing strategy assumes fundamentally that pricing occurs in
enacted environments in which the market landscape – customers, competitors, channel partners, and suppliers – is dynamically evolving and
changing. Smircich and Stubbart (1985, p. 725) said: "[E]nvironments are
relentlessly efficient in weeding out any organization that does not closely

align itself with environmental demands." The market topography that
provides the context for emergent price action is equivocal and confusing
(Choo, 1998; Daft & Weick, 1984; Weick, 2001). Thus, managers should
rely on informal, irregular scanning of pricing-relevant information that
enables them to detect weak but potentially important signals about
how the market is responding to price action and innovation (Daft,
Sormunen, & Parks, 1988). Effective management teams engage in high
levels of informal information gathering, boundary spanning across organizational units, and reduced communication barriers, and are constantly
in touch externally with the market and internally with supply and production resources: talking with customers, gleaning information about competitors' prices and pricing moves, following movements in supply costs or
supply futures, and so on (Thomas, Clark, & Gioia, 1993).

Price Pattern Recognition, Interpretation

We focus on how the organization *recognizes pricing patterns* within
and across customers or customer accounts, and in markets or market
segments, and how it interprets or judges the effects of these pricing patterns — because pricing patterns are the genetic structures of pricing strategy. For example, defining a discount level of 9 percent provokes a
dramatically different response than a discount level of 10 percent. Thus,
the management team searches for, identifies, defines, creates, or labels
these price patterns — where do managers see price patterns emerging and
what do they sense seems to be happening in these patterns? Where do
they see cause and effect, and what is it about the pricing pattern that is
causing the effects — and what are the effects? Mintzberg et al.'s (1976)
logic on searching for solutions is useful here: Managers can identify pricing patterns by (1) scanning organizational memory for pricing actions
they've recently or previously enacted, (2) engaging in passive search by
simply waiting for price patterns to appear, (3) engaging in active search
among existing price patterns or pricing strategies that are already established and familiar from past history, or (4) choosing familiar established
pricing patterns and strategies and adapting, modifying, or applying them
to create new pricing patterns.

Innovative pricing patterns that have the potential to enhance the firm's
pricing, value proposition, and position in the marketplace should be particularly attractive. These innovative pricing patterns may be novel pricing
ideas or solutions that are new, original, different, unusual, or unique relative to other prevailing pricing practices in the marketplace (Amabile,

1996; Andrews & Smith, 1996; Shalley, Zhou, & Oldham, 2004). Usually new and unique price-related patterns vary with the number, breadth, and diversity of pricing ideas or solutions from which to choose to address pricing problems (Amabile et al., 2005). Novel pricing solutions can apply to unique price menus, price structures such as discounts, allowances, and surcharges, scope and timing of price changes (Baker, Marn, & Zawadi, 2010), unique price metrics (like pay for usage, pay for performance, or pay for acquisition [Nagle, Hogan, & Zale, 2010; Shapiro, 2002]), unique pricing strategies (Noble & Gruca, 1999; Tellis, 1986), or unique pricing policies (Monroe, 2003; Sodhi & Sodhi, 2007).

Price Practices Sharing, Circulating, Distributing

Emergent pricing strategy requires that managers choose and share useful pricing patterns with others in the organization − they contrast and compare pricing patterns that seem to yield favorable organizational outcomes and then encourage repetition, adaption, adoption, or experimentation in other parts of the organization. These patterns thus become accepted *pricing practices*. Choosing, sharing, and encouraging adaption and adoption are carried out socially through shared interpretations of price practice effectiveness among various organization members, across functional areas, and across organizational stakeholders. These could include as well external pricing constituencies such as customers, suppliers, and channel members, and internal constituencies such as accounting, finance, marketing, sales, engineering, or production personnel. These constituencies have a voice in sensing how pricing actions and innovations affect the marketplace and the firm's value proposition in the marketplace. This sharing process may be fluid, open, disorderly, interpersonal, not linear, and ad hoc as price actions and price patterns inevitably lead to conflict and contention over differing effects on the organization's effectiveness. For example, a pricing innovation may effectively grow sales volume, a favorable outcome for the sales force and top line revenue, but also lead to deteriorating quality, production disruptions, or declining employee satisfaction.

Emerging Pricing Strategy, Pricing Principles, Policies, Rules

Finally, emerging pricing strategy involves coalescing and agreeing on price practices that work across market segments, teams, divisions, and organizational contexts. These become principles, policies, and rules that emerge into broadly accepted maxims that define and delineate pricing strategy throughout the organization. For example, Smith (1995) describes pricing practices that organizations use to signal strategic pricing principles, including accepted pricing algorithms, formulas, worksheets, calculations, benchmarks or goals, scripts, heuristics, or frequently cited "rules of thumb" (e.g., "You've got to have X% margins.").

Strategy researchers say that ideas become strategic when they are perceived to have the potential to affect the organization's ability to survive or achieve its objectives (Dutton, 1988). Firms use various ways to signal the strategic status of a price practice. One indicator is who in the organization is ultimately responsible for emergent pricing strategy. Higher ranking persons signal higher strategic pricing status. Some organizations signal the status of strategic pricing by institutionalizing the emergent pricing process: they set up pricing committees and groups, with obligations and rules (Pfeffer, 1985). Institutionalization legitimates because it implies historicity, control over a domain of strategic responsibility, and organizational validity. Some organizations create formal pricing departments to coordinate price-sharing and coalescing. These frequently consist of staff or analyst positions with no formal line authority. They assist, educate, or facilitate price interpretation, price sharing, and price evolution in strategic pricing practices, principles, and policies. These pricing managers or analysts frequently have access to and influence on key organizational leaders and are a signal of the strategic status of emergent pricing strategy.

THE REVERSE RATIONALE OF EMERGENT PRICING STRATEGY

Emergent pricing strategy is based on the theory of social psychology, and organizational researchers are increasingly assertive of the power of the emergent view of organizational decision processing. Weick (2001, pp. 27, 28) observed: "Social psychology is crucial for organizational analysis because it is the one discipline that does not fall prey to the error of assuming that large effects imply large causes. Social psychology is about *small events that enlarge* because they are embedded in amplifying causal loops, are acted into networks where they spread, become sources that are imitated." This emergent view assumes that these small events spread intermittently and fortuitously. These benefits are enhanced as managers learn how to learn, how to share patterns and practices throughout the organization, how to build and preserve organizational memory, how to encourage collaborating behaviors, and how to coalesce knowledge of successful practices into emergent pricing strategy.

Furthermore, these emergent pricing strategy ideas – of small events that enlarge – can be applied to pricing innovation and improvisation at the firm, inter-firm, or even industry level. Brandenburger and Nalebuff (1995) describe an instructive case in the U.S. auto industry in the 1990s as auto companies increasingly relied on price promotions to appeal to increasingly price-sensitive buyers. But teams of managers working together at two entirely different organizations in vastly different industries, General Motors (GM) in automobiles and Household Bank in consumer finance, came up with a new price innovation – a credit card: The new credit card allowed cardholders to apply 5 percent of their charges toward buying or leasing a new GM car, up to $500 per year, with a maximum of $3,500.

Early on GM managers interpreted this new pricing innovation as a tool to build market share by targeting prospective buyers of other competitors, like Ford. At its introduction, the new card was just one of many GM price promotion programs, but it suddenly caught on with consumers: 1.2 million accounts were opened after only 1 month; 8.7 million accounts after 2 years. GM managers realized the new card was successfully building customer loyalty and they further adjusted their broader promotional strategy by phasing out other more destructive price incentives they had previously relied on. Then as GM phased out these other destructive price incentives, it led to an unannounced, implicit price increase to non-cardholders – those considering buying a Ford, for example. This gave Ford space to raise its prices, and allowed GM, in turn, to raise its prices over time without losing customers to Ford. Management at Ford adapted their own version of a similar credit card with Citibank, then Volkswagon introduced its variation with MBNA Corporation. The net effect of one innovative pricing action in one corner of GM spawned eventual pricing relief across the entire auto industry.

VALUE-BASED PRICING AND EMERGENT PRICING STRATEGY

Note in our previous discussion that I included external constituencies among those to be included in emergent price strategy formation, such as customers, suppliers, and channel members. This seems counterintuitive to many deliberate pricing strategists who assume that the firm sets its own price and convinces or persuades the market that the value of the product or service justifies the price the firm has set. The firm assumes that it has predicted the market correctly, has set a rational price, and can now shape and control its market environment with persuasive value communication. Indeed, it is a mistake to engage the customer in price setting because it leads to counter-arguing and customer negotiation that inevitably lead to price discounting and price comparison across customers, and to eventual pricing chaos in the marketplace. This needs careful thought and explanation.

Several key assumptions of value-based pricing in business-to-business contexts overlap nicely with emergent pricing strategy. The firm (1) scans the pricing situation to identify sources and drivers of value that customers will realize from using the product, (2) then calculates the worth of these different value drivers to the customer − arriving at an estimate of total value the customer will realize, (3) then communicates this value to the customer through selling collateral, personal selling, and interactive customer consultation aided by spreadsheet or interactive models to enable customers to tailor or customize value estimates to their own environmental context, (4) chooses or designs a price offer that balances the value the customer receives with what the customer is willing to pay, and (5) tracks the value that customers realize over time relative to estimated value and refine value estimations based on actual value in use.

Throughout the entire value-based pricing process we assume fundamentally that customers must be involved in estimating value, for they must understand and perceive the value they receive − and customers are obviously involved in determining a price that they are willing to pay for that value. But the firm is not engaged in merely selling the value of the product for a given price, instead it is engaged in determining what value the customer desires, and how this balances with the price the customer can or is willing to pay. This is a consultative, collaborative process in which the seller identifies *sources of value and value drivers* − cost savings that the customer receives by using our product relative to a competitive referent product, or revenue gains or gross margin gains the customer similarly receives (Fig. 2). The seller further provides the customer with baseline *value estimations* showing the value calculations that similar customers might realize from product use. But then the selling firm engages the customer in *value customization* − an iterative process in which the customer uses models, spreadsheets, websites, and calculators to tailor, customize,

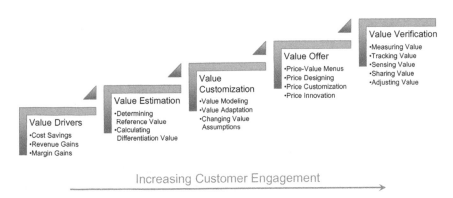

Fig. 2. Value-Based Pricing and Emergent Pricing Strategy.

and refine its estimate of the value it receives from our product. This is highly interactive, involving consultation with sales persons, field engineers, and marketing and production personnel across the customer's organization and our organization. It is important that the customer's organization understand the value it receives, and wants to receive. On the other hand, if the seller firm is engaged merely with the buyer's purchasing function, then this custom value estimation process usually fails to succeed.

Value offers involve an interactive process between buyer and seller on the price the customer pays for the value received. Astute firms have developed value-based pricing tools, skills, and resources to help facilitate this process of value-price trade-off, such as modular price menus, price structures, product and service bundles, and price policies that can be easily redesigned, adapted, tailored, and customized to meet the buyer's precise willingness to pay. This places the sales force in a new and different role, as a chief customer relationship officer in which sales persons orchestrate the entire value relationship with the client customer; they consult with, facilitate, enable, and assist customers with estimating value and finding the price offer configuration they can pay that reflects the value they receive – the focus throughout is on the customer. But this is also the location for price innovation, price customization, price designing, and price improvisation. Especially in dynamic, turbulent market environments, these tools and resources must be adaptive and require frequent innovation and improvisation.

Value verification engages the customer organization in measuring and tracking value received for price paid to ensure the customer understands accurately and perceives the actual value-price trade-off. But this process isn't done in isolation. The customer's team must sense where value delivery is succeeding, and where it is not; and adjust or adapt the value delivery model so that the customer achieves the value delivery it seeks. Successful value delivery models are shared with other divisions and groups within the customer organization to understand how to best create value not just for this buying group, but for other buying groups in the customer organization as well.

For example, in a well-known case study (Sawhney, 2004), Trilogy Software, provider of enterprise software for the automotive, communications, computer hardware, and insurance industries, instituted a new gain-sharing pricing strategy, based on value-based pricing. Although these customer industries are generally mature, the information technology dimensions are marked by rapid technological change with frequent product updates, design changes, and software versioning. Traditionally, the enterprise software market is marked by large information technology project installations usually designed with fixed schedules and precise specifications, and traditionally priced to require very large upfront investments accompanied by smaller annual maintenance contracts. By contrast, Trilogy's new "Fast Cycle Time" methodology relies on early and frequent project deliverables – occurring as often as every week, so that Trilogy's installation work can closely align and adapt to changing customer needs. This enables Trilogy to deliver key differential value by reducing the likelihood of enterprise software installations reportedly fail – up to 70 percent of installations reportedly fail – as well as facilitating faster and more accurate installations that enabled customers to achieve cost savings and time-to-market value gains.

The price Trilogy customers pay is based entirely on the level of business value that customers realize, meaning a share of the gain – *gain sharing*. As the software installation proceeds, customers pay a share of the incremental improvement in customers' operating profit derived from the software. As simple as this sounds, in fact Trilogy's pricing models are significant innovations, and require considerable adaptation, refining, and improvisation with each new customer installation. For example, these new pricing models require Trilogy and the customer to agree on how to measure Trilogy's incremental business value creation (incremental operating profit), and how to separate out Trilogy's incremental profit contribution versus other existing factors driving operating profit such as the customer's human resources, existing business processes, and technological sophistication. They also agree on a price level, that is, the level of gain sharing or incremental gain to be captured by Trilogy as price payment. Because

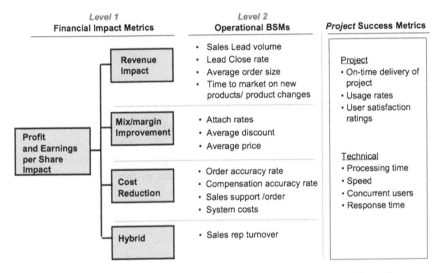

Fig. 3. Trilogy Value Tracking Metrics. *Source:* Trilogy Corporation: Customer Value Based Pricing, © 2004 Kellogg School of Management, Northwestern University. One-time permission to reproduce granted by Kellogg School of Management.

pricing and payment occur much more frequently, customers must engage in value estimation, measuring, and tracking more frequently (see Fig. 3 for examples of Trilogy's value tracking measures). Moreover, the customer's personnel involved in negotiating and tracking pricing and value now shifts from procurement to those using the technology in the IT areas of the organization. It also requires the involvement of finance and accounting, because the customer organization is treating Trilogy's price payments as a regularly recurring business expense rather than an upfront capital investment.

Although Trilogy is an example of a complex product in rapidly changing customer environments, it illustrates how involved the customer is in the value estimation and the price setting process. It also shows the level of flexible skills — such as value estimation skills, pricing innovation skills, modular price modeling skills — that Trilogy must have in place to support the selling and installation process — customer profit and loss measures and models, value estimation measures and models, operating performance measures and models, and project success tracking measures — all integrated into Trilogy's underlying support of enterprise software products and installation. This kind of dynamic pricing environment with new and unique customer installations requires pricing innovation, improvisation, and action to efficiently align the seller's value pricing model with the customer's perceived value willingness to pay.

EMERGENT PRICING IN A DYNAMIC PRICING WORLD

Emergent pricing strategy may seem unappealing to most business managers because they have been trained for decades in the ways of deliberate pricing strategy from the theories of behavioral economics; in recent decades deliberate pricing strategy has become the gold standard for efficient and effective pricing (Nagle, Hogan, & Zale, 2010). By contrast, emergent pricing seems uncontrolled, unpredictable, chaotic — risky. Yet many firms do emergent pricing all the time. We simply have never considered emergent pricing as a field of management study to understand what it is that makes emergent pricing strategy effective, and in which contexts it is likely to be most effective.

A recent study by Goldberg and Hellerstein (2011) of the Federal Reserve Bank of New York examined producer price microdata using the U.S. Bureau of Labor Statistic's product price index (PPI). They found that, contrary to previous theory developed during the early twentieth century, large firms change their prices almost twice as often as do small firms. On average prices change every 4.3 months for large product firms, every 8.5 months for small product firms, every 6 months for large service firms, and every 9 months for small service firms. Firms increase prices more often than they reduce prices. This occurs in manufacturing as well as in retailing. Other studies of consumer prices in euro-area countries found that large retail outlets change prices more frequently than do small outlets.

In addition, large firms change their prices by smaller amounts than do small firms, especially in service firms, but also significantly in product firms as well. Usually large firms change prices in the range of 1, 2.5, or less frequently 5 percent. In other words, large firms make many very small price changes, while small firms make very few larger price changes. These findings were not significantly different in the case of contract pricing, which covers roughly one third of transactions in the PPI. Industries with more differentiated goods are more likely to use contracts — for example, with transportation equipment (e.g., automobiles) 60 percent of transactions occur under contract. The price duration for goods sold under contract is 1.7 months longer, and for services sold under contract is 1 month longer than those sold under spot-market transactions. The authors conclude that contracts are more often "informal agreements that may not specify fixed prices or quantities over the period they are in effect" (Goldberg & Hellerstein 2011, p. 20). For example, when an original equipment manufacturer (OEM) in the auto industry sets up a new model's production line, it "generally commits to an overarching contract for four to eight years but then orders parts in individual purchase orders whose duration can go from several days to twelve months" (*Ibid.*, p. 21).

What explains the surprising finding that large firms change price more frequently, with small price changes, usually in the direction of price increases? One likely possibility is the returns to scale in the technology of price setting, due to fixed costs of price adjustment. It is simply more cost-effective for large firms to leverage technology to make and implement price changes throughout many thousands of stock keeping units. In fact, advances in operations research and Internet pricing have enabled firms to move increasingly toward more dynamic forms of *variable pricing structures*, due to dramatic reductions in menu cost and time required to adjust prices throughout the firm's distribution system (Monroe, 2003). For example, product firms have broadly adopted electronic coupon promotion strategies (Apple, Samsung, Sony, or Hewlett-Packard in consumer electronics). Service firms have adopted variable pricing strategies based on yield management models in airlines, cruise ships, hotels, sporting events, and health care.

These dynamic pricing strategies should enhance the firm's profitability by aligning prices more closely with what consumers are actually willing to pay, capturing more consumer surplus through higher prices and limiting the amount of inventory or capacity sold at lower prices (see Nagle & Holden, 2002). They also should motivate consumers to not delay purchases, thus enabling the firm to accelerate cash flows. Although dynamic pricing also increases buyer uncertainty about what they should be willing to pay, and when they should purchase, confusing buyers and leading to perceptions that dynamic pricing is unfair.

CONCLUSION

Advances in technology, operations research, and data driven pricing and marketing are leading pricing strategy into new and untested waters — toward dynamic pricing, and variable pricing strategies, which ultimately lead to the foundational logic underlying *emergent pricing strategy*. We are likely to find emergent pricing strategy to be particularly useful in unstable, turbulent, and complex product and market environments in which price-sensitive buyers wield significant power and influence. In practice, many firms already practice emergent pricing, and it appears that large firms may have invested in the resources and skills to enable more frequent pricing, and perhaps more effective emergent pricing as well. Our goal is to find out who does it well and what it is in their pricing that makes them successful.

TRIBUTE TO DAN NIMER

Dan and I first got to know each other in the mid-1980s when Dan was a favorite speaker at the Institute for International Research's *Pricing Conference*, later renamed *Pricex*. Dan was, and is, always beloved for his quick wit and great sense of humor. As we've worked on this book together he has come up with more ideas, jokes, humorous pricing insights, and comical anecdotes relayed through email, telephone calls, interviews, and snail mail materials. It has kept me more than amused – and extraordinarily busy too. He is a great friend, and certainly deserves the honor that is intended from all of us in this book. Thank you Dan! You are light years ahead of the rest of us – would that we all had your creative pricing DNA (pun intended) – but you do it usually with grace – and sometimes humility too, but always in a wonderfully self-deprecating way that keeps our conversations incredibly fun and lively.

REFERENCES

Andrews, K. (1987). *The concept of corporate strategy* (3rd ed.). Homewood, IL: Dow Jones Irwin.

Amabile, T. M. (1996). *Creativity and innovation in organizations*. Boston, MA: Harvard Business School Publishing (pp. 1–15), January 5, note 9-396-239.

Amabile, T. M., Conti, R., Coon, H., Lazenby, J., & Herron, M. (1996). Assessing the work environment for creativity. *Academy of Management Journal*, *39*(5), 1154–1185.

Amabile, T. M., Barsade, S. G., Mueller, J. S., & Staw, B. M. (2005). Affect and creativity at work. *Administrative Science Quarterly*, *50*, 367–403.

Andrews, J., & Smith, D. C. (1996). In search of the marketing imagination: Factors affecting the creativity of marketing programs for mature products. *Journal of Marketing Research*, *33*(2), 174–188.

Baker, W. L., Marn, M. V., & Zawada, C. C. (2010). *The price advantage* (2nd ed.). Hoboken, NJ: Wiley.

Brandenburger, A. M., & Nalebuff, B. J. (1995). The right game: Use game theory to shape strategy. *Harvard Business Review*, 57–71(July–August).

Choo, C. W. (1998). *The knowing organization: How organizations use information to construct meaning, create knowledge, and make decisions.* New York, NY: Oxford University Press.

Corey, E. R. (1991). *Industrial marketing strategy: Cases and concepts.* (pp. 311) Englewood Cliffs, NJ: Prentice-Hall.

Daft, R., Sormunen, J., & Parks, D. (1988). Chief executive scanning, environmental characteristics, and company performance: An empirical study. *Strategic Management Journal, 9*, 123–139.

Daft, R. L., & Weick, K. E. (1984). Toward a model of organizations as interpretation systems. *Academy of Management Review, 9*(2), 284–295.

Diamantopoulos, A., & Mathews, B. (1995). *Making pricing decisions: A study of managerial practice.* London, UK: Chapman & Hall.

Dolan, R. J., & Simon, H. (1996). *Power pricing: How managing price transforms the bottom line.* New York, NY: The Free Press.

Dutton, J. E. (1988). Understanding strategic agenda building and its implications for managing change. In L. R. Pondy, R. J. Boland, Jr. & H. Thomas (Eds.), *Managing ambiguity and change.* New York, NY: Wiley.

Goldberg, P. K., & Hellerstein, R. (2011). *How rigid are producer prices.* Federal Reserve Bank of New York Staff Reports, Staff Report No. 407, November 2009, Revised October 2011.

Mintzberg, H. (1988). Crafting strategy. *The McKinsey Quarterly, 3*(Summer), 71–90.

Mintzberg, H., Raisinghani, D., & Théorêt, A. (1976). The structure of 'Unstructured' decision processes. *Administrative Science Quarterly, 21*(2), 246–275.

Monroe, K. B. (2003). *Pricing: Making profitable decisions* (3rd ed.). New York, NY: McGraw-Hill.

Morphy, E. (2010). Does 'Nimble' pricing suggest iPad won't move? *MacNewsWorld*, February 9, 2010. Retrieved from http://www.ecommercetimes.com/story/wireless/69302.html

Moorman, C., & Miner, A. S. (1998). The convergence of planning and execution: Improvisation in new product development. *Journal of Marketing, 62*(3), 1–20.

Nagle, T. T., Hogan, J. E., & Zale, J. (2010). *The strategy and tactics of pricing: A guide to growing more profitability* (5th ed.). Englewood Cliffs, NJ: Prentice-Hall.

Nagle, T. T., & Holden, R. (2002). *The strategy and tactics of pricing: A guide to profitable decision making* (3rd ed.). Englewood Cliffs, NJ: Prentice-Hall.

Noble, P. M., & Gruca, T. S. (1999). Industrial pricing: Theory and managerial practice. *Marketing Science, 18*(3), 435–454.

Oxenfeldt, A. R. (1973). A decision making structure for price decisions. *Journal of Marketing, 37*(1), 48–53.

Pfeffer, J. (1985). Organizations and organization theory. In G. Lindzey & E. Aronson (Eds.), *Handbook of social psychology* (Vol. 1, pp. 379–440). New York, NY: Random House.

Ross, E. B. (1984). Making money with proactive pricing. *Harvard Business Review, 22* (November–December), 145–155.

Sawhney, M. (2004). *Trilogy corporation: Customer value-based pricing.* Evanston, IL: Kellogg School of Management, Northwestern University.

Shalley, C. E., Zhou, J., & Oldham, G. R. (2004). The effects of personal and contextual char-
    acteristics on creativity: Where should we go from here? *Journal of Management*, *30*(6),
    933–958.
Shapiro, B. P. (2002). *Performance-based pricing is more than pricing*, (pp. 1–4), February 25,
    2002, note 9-999-007. Boston, MA: Harvard Business School Publishing.
Simon, H. (1989). *Price management*. Amsterdam: North Holland Publishing Company.
Simon, H., Bilstein, F. F., & Luby, F. (2006). *Manage for profit, not for market share: A guide
    to greater profits in highly contested markets*. Boston, MA: Harvard Business Review
    Press.
Simon, H. A. (1957). A behavioral model of rational choice. In H. A. Simon (Ed.), *Models of
    man*. New York, NY: Wiley.
Simon, H. A. (1978). Rationality as process and as product of thought. *American Economic
    Review*, *68*, 1–16.
Smircich, L., & Stubbart, C. (1985). Strategic management in an enacted world. *Academy of
    Management Review*, *10*, 724–736.
Smith, G. E. (1995). Managerial pricing orientation: The process of making pricing decisions.
    Pricing Strategy and Practice, *3*(3), 28–39.
Smith, G. E., & Nagle, T. T. (1994). Financial analysis for profit-driven pricing. *Sloan Man-
    agement Review*, *35*(3), 71–84.
Smith, G. E., & Woodside, A. G. (2009). *Pricing theory and practice in managing business-to-
    business brands* (pp. 429–486). *Advances in business marketing and purchasing* (Vol. 15).
    London, UK: Emeraldpp. 429–486.
Sodhi, M. S., & Sodhi, N. S. (2007). *Six sigma pricing: Improving pricing operations to increase
    profits*. Upper Saddle River, NJ: FT Press.
Stephenson, P. R., Cron, W. L., & Frazier, G. L. (1979). Delegating pricing authority to the
    sales force: The effects on sales and profit performance. *Journal of Marketing*, *43*(2),
    21–28.
Tellis, G. J. (1986). Beyond the many faces of price: An integration of pricing strategies. *Jour-
    nal of Marketing*, *50*(4), 146–160.
Thomas, J. B., Clark, S. M., & Gioia, D. A. (1993). Strategic sensemaking and organizational
    performance: Linkages among scanning, interpretation, action, and outcomes. *Acad-
    emy of Management Journal*, *36*(2), 239–270.
Weick, K. E. (1979). Cognitive processes in organizations. In B. M. Staw (Ed.), *Research in
    organizational behavior* (Vol. 1, pp. 41–74). Greenwich, CT: JAI Press.
Weick, K. E. (1995). *Sensemaking in organizations*. Thousand Oaks, CA: Sage.
Weick, K. E. (2001). *Making sense of the organization*. Oxford, UK: Blackwell.

SECTION 3
THE DEFINING ROLE OF VALUE
IN PRICING

PRICE AND CUSTOMERS' PERCEPTIONS OF VALUE

Kent B. Monroe

ABSTRACT

This chapter summarizes the behavioral pricing research findings of price and how buyers respond to price. This includes the relationship between price and perceived value and the decision heuristics that help us understand how price influences perceptions of value and eventual product choice. Buyers also use price as an indicator of product quality, and customers' perceptions of quality, benefits, and value affect how they will respond to a purchase situation. In addition, buyers' perceptions of the sacrifice affect the purchase decision, that is the degree that consumers reflect on the amount that they would "give up" by paying the monetary price for a product may vary according to a variety of situations and conditions, such as type of product or service, or the perceived unfairness of the price, or if the buyer perceives a brand is superior to competing brands. The chapter also discusses how buyers trade off or compare the perceived gains arising from price-quality judgments versus the perceived sacrifice required to acquire the product or service, including whether buyers integrate price and other attribute information following a nonlinear (proportional) or linear (subtractive) process. It

Visionary Pricing: Reflections and Advances in Honor of Dan Nimer
Advances in Business Marketing & Purchasing, Volume 19, 129–152
Copyright © 2012 by Emerald Group Publishing Limited
All rights of reproduction in any form reserved
ISSN: 1069-0964/doi:10.1108/S1069-0964(2012)0000019012

also summarizes research on price as a multidimensional attribute, considered with additional dimensions such as warranty coverage, and warrantor reputation. Finally, the chapter examines perceived product value as being decomposed into its (1) perceived acquisition value (the expected benefit to be gained from acquiring the product less the net displeasure of paying for it) and (2) perceived transaction value (the perceived merits or fairness of the offer or deal).

Over 35 years ago Dan Nimer said that the most important pricing objective is "to ask the customer to pay for the 'perceived value' of what he is buying" (Nimer, 1975, p. 6). He then defined perceived value as "what the customer is willing to pay for the 'bundle' of benefits offered by the supplier." As usual, Dan was way ahead of the business community and sadly, his advice is still pertinent and seemingly ignored by too many business firms around the world. In this chapter, building on Dan's advice, I will summarize research that suggests some ways that pricing managers and businesses can take a value-oriented approach to their pricing.

Behavioral pricing research has provided explanations of how people form value judgments and make decisions when they do not have perfect information about alternative choices. These findings further our understanding of why buyers may be more sensitive to price increases than to price decreases, and how they respond to comparative price advertisements (e.g., regular price $65, sale price $49), coupons, rebates, and other special price promotions. The common element in these explanations is that buyers judge prices comparatively, that is, a reference price anchors their judgments. A reference price may be an external price in an advertisement or the shelf price of another product; it may also be an internal price the buyer remembers from a previous purchase, an expected price, or a belief about what would be a fair price of the product in the same market area.

It is important to understand that people seldom are good information processors and that they often take shortcuts (decision heuristics) consciously and non-consciously (Thomas & Morowitz, 2009). These shortcuts may lead to errors in judgment and choice, but they may also facilitate the choice process. For example, buyers who know that price and quality are positively related in a particular product category may correctly use price as an indicator of product quality. In other instances, however, such a shortcut may lead to errors of judgment and choice.

PRICE AND PERCEIVED VALUE

Several of these decision heuristics can help us understand how price influences perceptions of value and eventual product choice. First, the *context* of the purchase decision, including the way the offer is presented, *frames* buyers' evaluations and choices. For example, the way a sale is advertised will influence buyers' judgments about the value of the offer. Or, the sequence in which prices are observed, whether in the store, scanning a price list or menu will each influence how a specific price is encoded into working memory, represented in memory, or remembered later. For example, consider the following scenario adapted from Thaler (1985). You have been lying on the beach with a friend for most of a hot summer day. Deciding that it is time for a beer, you announce your intentions of buying one for your friend. If the only place that you can buy a beer is a short distance away at a fancy resort hotel, what do you expect you would have to pay for the beer? On the other hand, if the beer is sold in a small, run-down grocery store a short distance away in the opposite direction, what do you expect you would have to pay? Research indicates that most people expect to pay much more for the beer in the resort hotel than in the grocery store. The context of the place of purchase affects a buyer's internal reference price.

A second important variable is the *availability* of information. People tend to put more weight on information that is most readily available, even if it is contradictory. That is, information that is more easily recalled from memory either because of its recency or its impact will have a stronger effect on the purchase decision (Ofir, Raghubir, Brosh, Monroe, & Heiman, 2008).

Another important issue that has direct impact on pricing is the *anchoring* effect. The order of price presentation anchors buyers' judgments as do the low or high prices in a product line. Also, people tend to adapt to prices that are presented as the original prices. For example, real estate sellers often overprice their property, anticipating that buyers will expect to negotiate on price. But the initial high price serves as an anchor, and generally the negotiated price is higher than it would have been without this initial high anchor price. Moreover, it has been shown that a precise introductory price (e.g., $393,755) will lead to a higher eventual selling price than a round price (e.g., $395,000) (Thomas, Simon, & Kadiyali, 2010).

Finally, people often choose an alternative they *associate* with some past success, or they refuse to choose an alternative they associate with a previous failure. Price setters often fail to recognize when market conditions are favorable for a price increase, because a previous attempt to raise prices led to a sharp decline in sales. That is, people generalize from single instances of success or failure to perceived similar choice situations even when there are important differences in the choice environment.

The basic price-perceived value model suggests that buyers use price not only as a measure of sacrifice, but also as an indicator of product or service quality. That is, perceptions of quality are compared or traded off with perceived monetary sacrifice to form perceptions of value. Previous research on how buyers may combine judgments of quality and sacrifice to form perceptions of value has not clarified exactly how this trade-off may be accomplished. This model suggests that buyers use price not only as a measure of sacrifice, but also as an indicator of product or service quality. Perceived value represents a trade-off between buyers' perceptions of quality and sacrifice. We will see that buyers' knowledge of the product and of actual price-quality relationships in the market moderates the extent to which price is used to infer product quality. Hence, the degree to which buyers believe that there is a price-quality relationship influences their value perceptions and willingness to buy. Another important concept that has been developed is that it is relative price rather than actual price that is the significant price factor. Moreover, in comparing prices, buyers' judgments are influenced by the relative or perceived differences between the actual or offer price and the reference price. Using these key ideas in price perception, we now continue the development of how perceived price influences buyers' judgments of value.

Buyers' perceptions of a price derive from their interpretations of the price differences (real or implied) and from their interpretations of focal and contextual cues in the offer. Buyers make their purchase decisions in a two-step process. First, they judge the value of an offer; then they decide whether to make the purchase. It is also possible that they will postpone the purchase decision until they have more information about the offer and/or about other offers in the marketplace. Of interest here is (1) how buyers use price information and other cues to judge the value of the offer and (2) the influence this evaluation has on their purchase decisions.

Buyers evaluate prices by comparing them either to other prices available for comparison or to reference prices that are stored in memory. For example, when sellers advertise both the offered price and a (higher) comparative (regular) price, they are attempting to impose an external reference price instead of the consumers' internal reference price to be used for comparisons. To convince consumers to accept the higher price as a reference price, sellers include such words as "formerly," "regularly," and "usually" to describe the higher price. Words (semantic cues) can be used in a variety of ways to enhance consumers' perceptions that a sale is taking place and that the offer represents a savings to them.

Buyers usually have a set of prices that are acceptable for them to pay for products they purchase. If an offered price is not acceptable, buyers are likely to refrain from purchasing the product and will either search for an acceptable offer or forgo any purchase. Since prices are evaluated comparatively, the judgment of acceptability depends not only on buyers' price expectations, but also on information provided in promotions or advertisements. The perception of savings conveyed by price advertising leads to positive or favorable behavioral responses.

The evidence on how people perceive prices is based on theoretical explanations and on empirical research. The theoretical explanations offer predictions about how buyers are likely to form value perceptions and the effect these perceptions have on their purchase or information search decisions. Empirical research documents the correspondence between the theoretical explanations and buyers' behaviors.

The Price-Perceived Quality Relationship

Based on the research evidence concerning buyers' price awareness, it is clear that buyers do not use price solely as a measure of cost (sacrifice) (Monroe & Lee, 1999). Buyers also use price as an indicator of product quality. Spurred in part by business concern with product and service quality as well as recognizing the limitations of previous price-perceived quality research and conceptualizations, interest in the price-perceived quality relationship continues. Indeed, it is recognized that customers' perceptions of quality, benefits, and value comprise the reality faced by business and service organizations.

It is assumed buyers assess product or service quality by the use of cues. Products, services, or stores can be conceptualized as consisting of an array of cues that may serve as indicators of quality. Buyers are likely to use these cues so long as the cues help them predict the actual quality of the offering and as long as they have confidence that they can use and judge the cues accurately. Cues can be further classified according to whether they are part of the product, for example, ingredients, or not part of the product. *Extrinsic cues* are product-related attributes — price, brand name, packaging — but they are not part of the product. *Intrinsic cues* are also product-related attributes, but they cannot be changed without altering the physical properties of the product. Buyers rely on extrinsic cues and intrinsic cues when evaluating quality.

Some conceptual developments relating price and perceived quality include addition of the external cues of store and brand name, product warranties and guarantees, a product's country of origin, and two moderating variables: perceived product and price *differences*, and buyers' *familiarity* with the product or service. It was found that only when the perceived differences between prices or product attributes (intrinsic cues) were relatively large would significant differences in buyers' perceptions of quality occur (Krishnan, 1984; Rao & Monroe, 1988; Dodds, Monroe, & Grewal, 1991; Richardson, Dick, & Jain, 1994; Teas & Agarwal, 2000; Brucks, Zeithaml, & Naylor, 2000).

Firms may use warranties as signals of quality when buyers are uncertain about quality. That is, to signal a high-quality product, a seller should provide a warranty that provides buyers better protection against product failure. A warranty accompanying a high-quality product would be broader in the scope of its coverage and likely also longer in duration than a warranty for a low-quality product. The logic of this expectation is the seller of the low-quality product would incur prohibitive costs of fulfilling the warranty if it was as extensive in coverage and duration as that for the high-quality product. Thus, sellers offering extensive warranty coverage will attempt to provide high quality to avoid incurring high warranty costs. Research has shown that buyers would use a warranty as a cue to infer product quality when the seller was reputed to offer high-quality products, but would not use a warranty as a cue to infer product quality when the seller was reputed to offer low-quality products (Boulding & Kirmani, 1993). More recent research indicates that this particular finding applies primarily to buyers who have little knowledge or expertise to judge the relative merits of a warranty, whereas very knowledgeable buyers would have the expertise to judge the warranty on its merits and would be less likely to use firm reputation as the primary cue when evaluating quality (Srivastava & Mitra, 1998; Purohit & Srivastava, 2001).

That the combined effect of multiple extrinsic cues is stronger than the effects of individual cues is important. Indeed, other research indicates that although the effect of brand name generally is stronger than price on perceptions of quality, nevertheless the effect of brand name on quality perceptions is stronger in the presence of price information, and conversely, the effect of price on quality perceptions is stronger in the presence of brand name. These research findings support the prescription that all signals of quality must be mutually consistent and credible if they are to be effective (Miyazaki, Grewal, & Goodstein, 2005).

The Price-Perceived Monetary Sacrifice Relationship

Traditionally, price has been considered as a disincentive to purchase products and services, that is, as a negative product attribute. Further, price has been assumed to be objective information and to be encoded, remembered, and later retrieved by buyers without error. It has also been assumed that one unit of money has the same utility to a person as any other. Given these assumptions, then for any individual the disutility or pain (i.e., sacrifice) of giving up an amount of money to acquire a product or service would not vary across situations, type of product, or service. That is, money has been assumed to be fungible.

However, buyers' perceptions of the sacrifice, that is the degree that consumers reflect on the amount that they would "give up" by paying the monetary price for a product, may vary according to a variety of situations and conditions (Manning & Sprott, 2009). For example, does a buyer perceive paying $100 for a dental cleaning to be an equivalent sacrifice as paying $100 for a ticket to a concert or sporting event? Or, if the price of the product or service is perceived to be unfair, would the buyer perceive the sacrifice to be the same as when the same price for the product is perceived to be fair? Finally, if the buyer perceives a brand is superior to competing brands, would equivalent prices be perceived as representing equivalent sacrifices? Although research investigating these types of issues is not very plentiful, there is a growing body of evidence indicating that buyers may perceive equivalent prices as representing very different sacrifices. For example, consumers may "begrudge" expenditures on some products and perceived unfair prices may be judged to be more of a sacrifice than when the same prices for the same products are perceived to be fair (Cooper, 1969; Martins & Monroe, 1994).

Begrudging Expenditures
The concept of begrudging refers to the idea that for some products or services, buyers would prefer not to make the expenditure. Thus, the perceived sacrifice of paying a specific price for some products is psychologically more *painful* than others, even though the monetary outlay may be equivalent. That is, expenditures on some products are begrudged, and on

others they are not. One researcher found that expenditures on electric utilities was highly begrudged or resented, yet expenditures on other types of "necessities" were much less resented. Thus, the more buyers are reluctant or hesitant to spend money on certain products, the more likely are they to search for bargains or lower prices, and they will be more sensitive to price changes and to price differentials between alternative choices. Thus, other things remaining the same, the more that expenditures for a product or service are begrudged, the more likely is demand for such a product to be price elastic.

Perceived Price Fairness

An important point that we made earlier is that buyers' price judgments are comparative in nature. That is, to be able to judge whether a price is acceptable or fair, buyers must compare that price to a reference price. This reference price may be a previous price paid by the buyer, a previous price charged by the seller, a price paid by another buyer, or an expected price. In similar fashion, judgments of fairness from a distributive justice perspective are determined when an outcome is judged in comparison to other possible outcomes. There are two types of transaction relationships that influence buyers' perceptions of price fairness.

First, it has been shown that when buyers believe that sellers have increased prices to take advantage of an increase in demand, or a scarcity of supply, without a corresponding increase in costs, then such price increases would be perceived to be unfair. Buyers infer that the sellers have increased their benefits of engaging in a transaction, that is, profits, without a corresponding increase in investment or effort, resulting in a net gain compared to the previous transaction. On the other hand, buyers paying the higher price without a corresponding increase in benefits from the transaction have a resulting net loss relative to their previous position (Kahneman, Knetsch & Thaler, 1986; Campbell, 1999a, 2007; Cox, 2001; Bolton, Warlop, & Alba, 2003; Xia, Monroe & Cox, 2004; Xia, Kukar-Kinney & Monroe, 2010).

Second, in situations when one category of buyers receives the benefit of a lower price for an equivalent product or service but another category of buyers do not, the price-disadvantaged buyers may perceive that the price they pay is unfair. Such situations typically arise when sellers provide discounts for buyers with certain characteristics, for example, age or employment status. Further, if there is no perceived discrepancy between the investment or effort that these favored buyers make to qualify for the lower price relative to the disadvantaged buyers, then they will be receiving the same benefits as the disadvantaged buyers but incurring a smaller monetary sacrifice.

Thus, whether considering buyers' judgments of price fairness in terms of their relationships with sellers, or their lateral relationships with other buyers, a price judged as unfair can lead to lower perceptions of value and a reduction in willingness to pay (Martins, 1993; Martins & Monroe, 1994). So long as there is no perceived difference in the quality or benefits received from acquiring a product or service whose price is judged as unfair, then this reduction in perceived value must result from an increase in perceptions of monetary sacrifice. That is, a perceived disadvantaged price inequity, or a loss, increases buyers' perceptions of sacrifice, thereby decreasing their perceptions of value and willingness to buy. On the other hand, a perceived advantageous price inequity, or a gain, reduces perceptions of sacrifice, thereby increasing their perceptions of value and willingness to buy (Martins, 1995; Xia & Monroe, 2010).

Buyers will resist perceived unfair price increases more than justified price increases. Similarly, when buyers perceive that the prices they pay are higher than their comparable reference group, either in terms of ability to pay or status, then such prices are likely to be perceived to be unfair.

An important implication of an imperfect information environment is that buyers and sellers make inferences based on observed characteristics and behaviors of other sellers and buyers. Research evidence demonstrates that buyers use contextual information to infer a firm's motives. Small differences in the motive consumers inferred about a firm's pricing behavior resulted in relatively large differences in perceptions of fairness. Thus, an important prescription for pricing management is that when there are good reasons for a price, communicate these reasons publicly and widely (Campbell, 1999b; Feinberg, Krishna, & Zhang, 2002; Kukar-Kinney, Xia, & Monroe, 2007). Fairness in pricing requires just and honest treatment of all parties in a transaction including those who are indirectly involved in the transaction, for example, other buyers. Developing and following pricing policies that promote a reputation for fair treatment will enhance customer goodwill and perceived product and service value. An additional benefit of having a price structure that is perceived to be fair is that when buyers perceive prices to be fair, their upper acceptable price threshold is higher than when prices are perceived to be unfair (Maxwell, Nye, & Maxwell, 1999).

Brand Equity Effects

We have observed earlier that brand name may serve as an indicator of quality. An implication of this brand-quality relationship is that brands that are perceived to provide high quality may also receive price premiums. Another interesting advantage of a brand that has a superior or highly favorable image is that buyers likely would be willing to pay higher prices to acquire the product than for competitive brands with a less favorable image. But, a second advantage for this perceived high-quality brand is that a monetary price that is equivalent to the competitive product may be perceived to require less of an outlay or sacrifice. That is, it may be perceived to be less painful to spend a specific amount of money on a perceived high-quality brand than to spend that amount of money on a perceived lower-quality brand. Thus, not only do brands that have very favorable images have opportunities to receive above average prices, it is also likely that these higher prices are not perceived to require as much monetary sacrifice as lower-priced brands that have less favorable images.

INTEGRATING PRICE, QUALITY, AND SACRIFICE INFORMATION

When buyers use price as an indicator of cost or sacrifice, an increase in price would have the effect of reducing their perceived value for the product or service, *ceteris paribus*. On the other hand, when buyers use price as an indicator of quality or benefits, an increase in price would have the effect of increasing their perceived value for the product or service, *ceteris paribus*. Generally, buyers are not able to assess perfectly product or service quality (the ability of the product to provide satisfaction). Moreover, buyers' perceptions of monetary sacrifice for the same specific price may vary according to whether the price is perceived to be fair, the context in which the price is presented, the buyers' acceptable price range, and the extent that they are concerned about price (Monroe, 2003).

An important issue is how buyers integrate these different bits of information to determine their overall perceptions of value. Information about the product or service attributes and benefits represents positive information (i.e., what the buyer gains from acquiring the product or service). But, considering price as an indicator of cost represents negative information (i.e., what the buyer gives up (loses) when acquiring the product or service). Attempting to integrate positive and negative information simultaneously to make a value judgment is a difficult mental task for people.

Complicating the task further is the realization that price simultaneously may provide positive information relative to product quality (gain) and negative information relative to sacrifice (loss). In some situations, buyers may place relatively more weight on the positive information that price conveys, and in other situations, they may place relatively more weight on the negative information that price conveys (Erickson & Johansson, 1985; Suri & Monroe, 2003). Rarely will they view price solely as a conveyor of positive or negative information. Research has attempted to determine both how buyers perform this mental calculation and when they may be more likely to rely on the price-perceived quality relationship or when they may be more likely to rely on the price-perceived sacrifice relationship.

CONTRASTING THE PRICE-QUALITY AND PRICE-SACRIFICE JUDGMENTS

Our discussion above suggests that buyers determine perceived value by mentally trading off or comparing the perceived gains represented in their perceptions of quality or benefits to be received against the perceived loss represented in their perceptions of sacrifice required to acquire the product or service. That is, buyers integrate both the positive information relative to the perceived gain and the negative information relative to the perceived loss. While this trade-off of positive with negative information has been recognized as a difficult processing task in general, nevertheless are these two judgments equally difficult to perform, or is one of these tasks relatively more difficult to perform?

Implications of Price-Quality Trade-offs

An important point relative to this issue of information integration is that each piece of information about a product or service being evaluated is assumed to have some meaning, implication, or consequence for buyers' value judgments. Second, each of these pieces of information will have a relative degree of importance (or weight) to the buyer when making this judgment and this relative importance may vary over products and purchase context. The different influences of price on judgments of value depend on the weight people attach to the sacrifice meaning of price relative to the quality inference at the time of judgment. Indeed, there is evidence that people often weigh negative information greater than positive information of equal intensity, the negativity effect (Ahluwalia, 2002; Herr, Kardes, & Kim, 1991). Nevertheless, there are boundaries to the negativity effect, that is, where greater weighing of positive information over negative information has been shown. For example, when positive information is more diagnostic than negative information, then positive information would be weighted more than negative information (positivity effect) (Skowronski & Carlston, 1987; Skowronski & Carlston, 1989). These two effects can be distinguished using an information integration model.

$$PV = f(w_1PQ, w_2PS)$$

where
PV = perceived value of the product
PQ = perceived quality assessment
PS = perceived sacrifice assessment
w_i = relative weights for the quality and sacrifice assessments, $0 < w_i < 1$, $\Sigma w_i = 1$.

The issue of whether buyers integrate price and other attribute information following a nonlinear (proportional) or linear (subtractive) process has important implications for doing price market research and for developing pricing strategy and tactics. On the one hand, economic value analysis assumes a subtractive model in that relative economic value of a product is the customer's cost savings or revenue enhancement minus the product's price. Price market research using conjoint or multiple trade-off analysis assumes a linear model and that price as a negative attribute has disutility relative to positive utility derived from other product attributes.

As shown in the table below, depending on how the customer actually processes the price and attribute information could lead to different choices. For example, assume that in a choice situation, product A's price is $20 and a competing product B's price is $27.50. Further, assume that the customer mentally has quantified that the benefits of using A is equivalent to $60 per unit of A and $70 per unit of B.

Product	Perceived Quality (Monetary Equivalent) (1)	Price/Unit (2)	Net Value (Subtractive Model) (1) − (2)	Net Value (Proportional Model) (1) ÷ (2)
A	$60/unit	$20	$40/unit	$3/unit
B	$70/unit	$27.50	$42.50/unit	$2.55/unit

If a subtractive model is used, then the perceived net value of B is $2.50 per unit more than that of A. But, if a proportional model is used, then the performance/price ratio for A is superior to that for B. Thus, if a subtractive integration model is used, B would be judged to provide more value, while if a proportional model is used, A appears to provide more value. Given these very different conclusions, it is important to understand how customers do perform this integration of price and other attribute information as well as the relative importance they place on these attributes. Further, it is important to know the extent to which price is used as an indicator of quality and benefits as well as sacrifice.

Price-Quality Trade-offs: Price as a Negative Attribute

In some research on the price-quality-sacrifice trade-off, price has been considered only as a negative attribute or disincentive to purchase. In general, two integration models have been investigated. First, to determine the perceived value of a specific product, buyers may subtract their subjective evaluations of the perceived sacrifice of paying the price from their overall perceptions of quality. This representation assumes that buyers contrast the perceived gains to be realized based on the positive quality information against the perceived losses based on the negative sacrifice information to determine their overall value judgment for the product.

Alternatively, buyers may combine price and quality information similar to a ratio or proportional model. As developed in the above example, psychologically, this model assumes that buyers determine a quality rating per unit price. Both formulations assume that the attribute quality information is averaged to determine overall perceived quality and then compared to the perceived sacrifice represented by the product's price.

Early research implied that the subtractive model best represents the trade-offs made between perceived quality and perceived sacrifice (Hagerty, 1978). In another study, subjects received information for two different purchases for ground beef. One purchase was described by price and quality (defined either as percentage fat or percentage lean). The second purchase was described only by price or only by quality (Levin & Johnson, 1984). In the second purchase, subjects were asked to infer the appropriate (1) price when only quality information was provided or (2) quality level when only price information was given. The researchers concluded that the subtraction model best represented buyers' processing of quality and price information.

One important result from the ground beef study was that consumers' transformation of objective stimuli into subjective judgments can change as a function of the *context* in which judgments are made. That is, the quality of ground beef described as 80% lean was rated more favorably than ground beef described as 20% fat.

A second important result of the ground beef study was the finding that subjects had difficulty integrating two stimulus dimensions when high ratings on one dimension are favorable (i.e., high quality implied by a relatively high price) and when high ratings on another dimension are unfavorable (i.e., high monetary sacrifice implied by a relatively high price). This particular finding would suggest that it might be more difficult for consumers to judge the value of relatively high-priced products in a product category when they are also inferring that the high price implies high quality. Conversely, would this result imply that consumers would also find it difficult to judge value for relatively low-priced products in a category when they are also inferring that low price implies low quality? Overall, these questions imply that when quality is uncertain and buyers use price both as an indicator of a product's quality as well as an indicator of the monetary sacrifice, they face a difficult task of integrating both the positive attribute quality information with price information that provides both negative information (sacrifice) and positive information (quality).

Price-Quality Trade-offs: Price as a Multidimensional Attribute

A third research effort studying how subjects judged the risk of new products across the dimensions of warranty coverage, warrantor reputation, and price provides insight into this difficult integration process (White & Truly, 1989). Initially, subjects' perceived performance risk of a durable new product was a function of their perceived quality of the product given by the length of the warranty coverage and warrantor reputation. Prices provided both positive and negative risk information. It was expected that a positive price-perceived quality relationship would lead to a negative price-perceived performance risk relationship. That is, as perceived quality increased, perceived performance risk would decline. On the other hand, similar to the price-perceived monetary sacrifice relationship, perceived financial risk would increase as price increased (see also Grewal, Gotlieb, & Marmorstein, 1994). However, subjects resolved this more difficult information integration task by not using price to assess performance risk. Instead they integrated the warranty coverage and reputation information to form their judgments of product quality. As expected, perceived performance risk was lower for the high reputation warrantor. That is, within the current context of perceived price-quality trade-offs, perceived risk (sacrifice) was inferred to be lower when perceived quality was relatively high.

After examining the individual subject data, the researchers concluded that buyers' integration of price and quality information was not sufficiently represented by a simple subtraction process. Hence, the researchers repeated the study using an expanded price by warranty coverage design and shifted from a between-subjects design to a within-subjects design. Using a within-subjects experimental design allowed the researchers to have multiple trials per participant and have a better opportunity to examine the integration strategies used by different participants. Contrary to previous studies briefly summarized above, only 15% of the subjects used a subtractive integrative process.

This last study clearly showed that only a minority of the subjects followed a strict subtractive integration process while a larger percent of subjects used some form of a nonlinear strategy for integrating price and quality information. Perhaps the most important implication of their results is a majority of the subjects apparently relied heavily on either price information or the warranty quality information when making their judgments. Thus, another important unresolved issue is to determine when buyers will be more likely to use price primarily either as an indicator of quality or as an indicator of sacrifice.

SUMMARIZING PERCEIVED QUALITY AND MONETARY SACRIFICE

Although previous research has not been able to clarify the exact nature of the trade-off between perceived quality and perceived monetary sacrifice, there is an important implication given what we do know. The relative weights buyers attach to perceptions of quality and sacrifice apparently depends on the relative magnitude of the product's price. Generally, for a specific product category, both quality and sacrifice are perceived to be low when price is perceived to be relatively low, and to be high when price is perceived to be relatively high. At either low- or high-price ends within a product category, it is expected that perceptions of value would be more difficult to judge than at intermediary prices. Nevertheless, when evaluating a perceived low-priced product, buyers may weigh quality more heavily than sacrifice. If so, an evaluation of low quality and low sacrifice may lead to perceiving the product as low in value. Yet, when evaluating a high-priced product, buyers may weigh sacrifice more heavily than quality. If so, an evaluation of high quality and high sacrifice may lead again to perceiving the product as low in value.

While previous research on how buyers may combine judgments of quality and sacrifice to form perceptions of value has not clarified exactly how these judgments may be accomplished another perplexing question has yet to be addressed. That is, how difficult or easy is it to judge a product's quality or sacrifice based primarily on price information? Previous research has implicitly assumed that these perceptions do occur and that buyers somehow integrate their judgments to form value perceptions, regardless of whether they follow a linear (adding or subtracting), weighted averaging, or some form of nonlinear integration strategy. Moreover, if it is relatively more or less difficult to judge perceptions of sacrifice in contrast to perceptions of quality, what are the implications for how this information is integrated into value judgments? One implication of the White and Truly (1989) study is consumers may find it more difficult to evaluate sacrifice or risk than to judge quality. Generally, it has been suggested that evaluating negative information is more difficult than evaluating positive information. If so, would negatively valenced information, for example, price as a sacrifice, be accorded relatively heavier weights than positively valenced information, such as price as an indicator of quality?

DECOMPOSING PERCEIVED PRODUCT VALUE

We have suggested that buyers first *judge* the value of an offer and then *decide* whether to purchase the item. One aspect of this purchase decision is whether the buyer believes that information about the offer is sufficient to support a choice. The overall perceived value of a product being considered for purchase is its (1) *perceived acquisition value* (the expected benefit to be gained from acquiring the product less the net displeasure of paying for it) and (2) *perceived transaction value* (the perceived merits or fairness of the offer or deal).

Perceived Acquisition Value

As suggested earlier, buyers' perceptions of acquisition value represent a cognitive trade-off between the benefits they perceive in the product and the sacrifice they perceive to be required to acquire the product or service. In part, the perceived benefits of a product are related to the buyers' judgments about the product's quality. Lacking perfect information about the inherent quality of the product, many consumers tend to believe that there is a positive relationship between a product's price and its quality ("You get what you pay for"). Thus, other things remaining the same, a higher priced product would be perceived to provide more benefits because of its higher perceived quality. However, at the same time, a higher price increases buyers' perceptions of their sacrifice. Thus, within some range of prices, the perceived benefits in the product will be larger than the perceived sacrifice, and buyers will perceive that there is positive acquisition value in the product. The greater the perceived acquisition value, the greater is the likelihood that a consumer would be willing to purchase the product. However, in addition to evaluating the product's value, buyers also evaluate the offer itself.

Perceived Transaction Value

Transaction value is defined as the buyers' perceived merits of the offer or deal. By drawing on findings in behavioral decision theory, a more complete model of buyer judgment and choice can now be developed. Replacing the utility function of economics with a value function, the model uses three key propositions:

1. The value function is based on perceived gains and losses relative to a reference point.
2. The value function is assumed to be concave for gains and convex for losses, relative to the reference point.
3. People are more sensitive to the prospect of a loss than to the prospect of a gain (Kahneman & Tversky, 1979; Thaler, 1985).

The individual's current position provides a reference point. The concavity of the gain portion of the value function indicates that the function increases at a slower rate as gains become larger. However, the convexity of the loss portion of the value function at the smaller loss amounts indicates that the function increases at a faster rate initially and then later behaves like the gain function. Considering a gain or a loss of $10 from the current position the decrease in perceived value for the $10 loss will be greater than the increase in perceived value for the $10 gain. This difference in perception between losses and gains helps explain the different degrees of price sensitivity between price increases and price decreases.

Of concern in our conceptualization is how buyers evaluate a purchase situation in which the buyer gains a product but loses (gives up) the money paid for the product. It is assumed that buyers first *judge* the value of the offer and then *decide* whether to make a purchase. To explain the role of price in this process, three price concepts are used. The *perceived benefit* of the product is equivalent to the utility inherent in the *maximum price* the buyer would be willing to pay for the product. The *acquisition value* of the product is the perceived benefits of the product at this maximum price compared to the actual selling price, that is, Pmax − Pactual, which is equivalent to our initial perceived value concept. The *transaction value*, or the perceived merit of paying the actual price, is determined by comparing the buyer's reference price to the actual price, that is, Pref − Pactual. Transaction value is positive if the actual price is less than the buyer's reference price, zero if they are equal, and negative otherwise.

It should be noted that in the above conceptualization the actual selling price (Pactual) appears in both the definitions of perceived acquisition value and perceived transaction value. This dual appearance of the actual selling price has raised some problems for researchers studying the influence of transaction value and acquisition value on buyer behavior. The answer to the issue was solved by some extensive research. When researchers were able to develop measures that clearly distinguished between acquisition value and transaction value, they discovered that when transaction value was present it enhanced acquisition value, but did not directly influence buyer behavior. Thus, acquisition value was determined by the buyers' perceptions of quality or benefits to be received plus perceived transaction value which represented the comparison of the selling price to the buyers' reference price (Grewal, Monroe, & Krishnan, 1998). One important implication of the finding that perceived transaction value enhances buyers' perceived acquisition value is buyers need to feel confident that they either can determine quality prior to purchase, or they can infer quality because the various signals of quality used by the sellers are appropriate indicators of quality (Urbany, Bearden, Kaicker, & Smith-de-Borrero, 1997).

Enhancing Transaction Value

As indicated previously, the reference price may be a price internal to the buyer (e.g., an expected price, a believed fair or "just" price, or a remembered price) or it may be an external price in the purchase situation. The use of comparative price advertising or price tags to communicate the usual or regular price and a lower actual price is an attempt to provide buyers with a price frame of reference and to capitalize on transaction value by augmenting buyers' perceptions of acquisition value. Coupons or rebates are also used to enhance transaction value, but the efforts expended to redeem coupons or qualify for rebates may increase perceived sacrifice (Monroe & Chapman, 1987).

The presence of a higher reference price compared to a lower selling price suggests a "deal" or "bargain" and strengthens positive transaction value, or the perceived reduction of a sacrifice or loss (the price normally paid for the product). Since people value a reduction in a loss more than a gain of the same magnitude, by emphasizing the reduction in sacrifice (the amount paid for the product, or loss), the comparative price advertisement enhances transaction value more than a sale price-only presentation would. The reduction in the sacrifice (reduction in a loss) is perceived as an *increase* in value (i.e., an increase in transaction value).

Transaction value can have a positive or negative effect on overall per-ceived acquisition value. Positive transaction value is the perceived reduc-tion of a loss by a small gain (i.e., the original or reference price minus the savings perceived by a lower price). When the components of the offer are framed in terms of a gain and a loss, the perceived acquisition value of the offer is enhanced because positive transaction value augments acquisition value. Similarly, if a buyer perceives that a price has increased, this increase is perceived as a loss. A price increase viewed as a loss would be perceived to be larger than the same proportionate price decrease viewed as a gain. The observation we made earlier about demand being more sen-sitive to price increases than to price decreases has a theoretical as well as an empirical foundation.

Framing Price Offers and Price Changes

There are several ways that sellers can communicate price offers and price changes. For example, sellers can present a price change in monetary terms (\$ off), percentage terms (% off), or some combinations of these methods. Further, they can offer a price discount to all customers or only to a sub-set of potential buyers. Presenting a price offer or price change in different ways is similar to the framing of purchase decisions. A decision frame refers to a decision maker's perception of the behaviors, outcomes, and contingencies associated with a particular choice. It is often possible to frame a particular choice in more than one way. Moreover, shifts of reference points can change a perception of value and thereby change preferences. For example, including an external reference price in a purchase offer allows the seller to *frame* the buyers' choices. Comparative price advertising or point-of-purchase tags giving the usual or regular price and the lower asking price (sale price) provide buyers with a price frame of reference. In the context of the argument sketched here, a price frame of reference enhances perceived acquisition value by increasing perceived transaction value (reducing the perceived sacrifice associated with the lower sale price).

Whether buyers process price information in an absolute or relative sense affects their perceptions of price changes (Grewal & Marmorstein, 1994; Heath, Chatterjee, & France, 1995). For example, buyers will perceive a $20 reduction on either a $100 jacket or a $400 television similarly if they process the price reduction information in an absolute way, for example, a $20 saving. However, if they process the price reduction information in a relative way, then the savings on the jacket (20%) would be perceived more favorable than the savings on the television (5%) (Chen, Monroe & Lou 1998). We would expect that the psychological satisfaction of saving a given amount of money would be related to the price of the product. Thus, an offer of 50% off an item priced at $1.00 would be perceived more favorably than an offer of $0.50 off. On the other hand, an offer of $1,000 off a $20,000 automobile would be perceived more favorably than an offer of 5% off. Thus, the relative attractiveness of a price promotion depends not only on the absolute amount of the monetary savings, but also on the price level of the promoted product. Similarly, the relative unattractiveness of a price increase will depend on the absolute amount of the price increase as well as the price level of the product.

SUMMARY OF THE PRICE-PERCEIVED VALUE RELATIONSHIP

Throughout this chapter we have been developing a behavioral explanation of how buyers perceive price and how these perceptions influence their perceptions of value. The concept of a reference price is based on adaptation-level theory. Adaptation-level theory indicates not only that there is a reference price but that it changes. Reference price is affected by contextual effects such as frequency of previous price changes, buyers' expectations about future prices, the order that price information is presented to buyers, the advertisement of prices, and the intensity of price promotion (Winer, 1986; Puto, 1987; Kalyanaram & Little, 1994).

Assimilation-contrast theory indicates that buyers have a latitude of acceptance of prices for products. This theory also suggests that the acceptable price range may be affected by the amount of price variation for a product category as perceived by buyers. Another implication derived from assimilation-contrast theory is that there is likely to be a range of prices around the reference price within which little change in demand is likely in response to a price change, that is, the price resulting from the price change may not be perceived as very different.

Finally, the psychological argument recognizes that people respond differently to perceived gains and perceived losses and suggests that buyers are more sensitive to price increases (perceived loss) than to price decreases (perceived gain). The concept of the range of acceptable prices (defined between the lowest acceptable price, PL, and the highest acceptable price, Pmax) indicates that there is likely to be less change in demand in response to a perceived small price change (difference) relative to the buyer's reference price. However, once the price difference (Pref $-$ P) is perceived to be important by the buyer, there is likely to be a more noticeable change in demand. These price differences can occur because of either a price increase or decrease, or because of comparative price advertising in which the seller provides an external reference price for comparison. Thus, relatively small price differences, whether due to a price change or to differences between perceived similar offerings, are less likely to produce significant demand responses.

A PERSONAL NOTE

It is indeed a personal pleasure to contribute to this volume honoring Dan Nimer, a true pioneer in pricing. During the years that I have known Dan I have learned from his wisdom and his wit. During 1999 and 2000, we conducted several pricing training programs together and I enjoyed developing the material with Dan and then watching and listening to him enthrall the participants with well-crafted presentations and exercises. His style is unique and the knowledge he imparts is profound and insightful. So, Dan, thank you for your contributions to pricing and marketing, but more than anything else thanks for your support and friendship.

Kent B. Monroe
January 2011

REFERENCES

Ahluwalia, R. (2002). How prevalent is the negativity effect in consumer environments. *Journal of Consumer Research, 29*(September), 270–279.

Bolton, L. E., Warlop, L., & Alba, J. W. (2003). Consumer perceptions of price (Un)fairness. *Journal of Consumer Research, 29*(March), 474–491.

Boulding, W., & Kirmani, A. (1993). A consumer-side experimental examination of signaling theory: Do consumers perceive warranties as signals of quality? *Journal of Consumer Research, 20*(June), 111–123.

Brucks, M., Zeithaml, V. A., & Naylor, G. (2000). Price and brand name as indicators of quality dimensions for consumer durables. *Journal of the Academy of Marketing Science, 28*(3), 359–374.

Campbell, M. C. (1999a). 'Why did you do that?' The important role of inferred motive in perceptions of price fairness. *Journal of Product & Brand Management Featuring Pricing Strategy & Practice, 8*(2), 145–152.

Campbell, M. C. (1999b). Perceptions of price unfairness: Antecedents and consequences. *Journal of Marketing Research, 36*(May), 187–199.

Campbell, M. C. (2007). Says who?! How the source of price information and affect influence perceived price (Un)fairness. *Journal of Marketing Research, 44*(May), 261–271.

Chen, S.-F. S., Monroe, K. B., & Lou, Y.-C. (1998). The effects of framing price promotion messages on consumers' perceptions and purchase intentions. *Journal of Retailing, 74*(3), 353–372.

Cooper, P. (1969). The begrudging index and the subjective value of money. In B. Taylor & G. Wills (Eds.), *Pricing strategy* (pp. 122–131). London: Staples Press.

Cox, J. L. (2001). Can differential prices be fair? *Journal of Product & Brand Management Featuring Pricing Strategy & Practice, 10*(5), 264–273.

Dodds, W. B., Monroe,, K. B., & Grewal, D. (1991). The effect of brand, price and store information on subjective product evaluations. *Journal of Marketing Research, 28* (August), 307–319.

Erickson, G. M., & Johansson, J. K. (1985). The role of price in multi-attribute product evaluations. *Journal of Consumer Research, 12*(September), 195–199.

Feinberg, F. M., Krishna, A., & Zhang, Z. J. (2002). Do we care what others get? A behaviorist approach to targeted promotions. *Journal of Marketing Research, 39*(August), 277–291.

Grewal, D., & Marmorstein, H. (1994). Market price variation, perceived price variation and consumers' price search decisions for durable goods. *Journal of Consumer Research, 21* (December 1994), 452–460.

Grewal, D., Gotlieb, J., & Marmorstein, H. (1994). The moderating effects of message framing and source credibility on the price-perceived risk relationship. *Journal of Consumer Research, 21*(June), 145–153.

Grewal, D., Monroe, K. B., & Krishnan, R. (1998). The effects of price-comparison advertising on buyers' perceptions of acquisition value, transaction value, and behavioral intentions. *Journal of Marketing, 62*(April), 46–59.

Hagerty, M. R. (1978). Model testing techniques and price-quality tradeoffs. *Journal of Consumer Research, 5*(December), 194–205.

Heath, T. B., Chatterjee, S., & France, K. R. (1995). Mental accounting and change in price: The frame dependence of preference dependence. *Journal of Consumer Research, 22* (June), 90–97.

Herr, P. M., Kardes, F., & Kim, J. (1991). Effects of word-of-mouth and product attribute information on persuasion: An accessibility-diagnosticity perspective. *Journal of Consumer Research, 17*(March), 454–462.

Kahneman, D., & Tversky, A. (1979). Prospect theory: An analysis of decision under risk. *Econometrica, 47*(March), 263–291.

Kahneman, D., Knetsch, J. L., & Thaler, R. (1986). Fairness as a constraint on profit seeking: Entitlements in the market. *The American Economic Review, 76*(4), 728–741.

Kalyanaram, G., & Little, J. D. C. (1994). An empirical analysis of latitude of price acceptance in consumer packaged goods. *Journal of Consumer Research, 21*(December), 408–418.

Krishnan, R. (1984). *An investigation of the price-perceived quality relationship*. Unpublished doctoral dissertation, Department of Marketing, Virginia Polytechnic Institute and State University, Blacksburg, VA.

Kukar-Kinney, M., Xia, L., & Monroe, K. B. (2007). Consumers' perceptions of the fairness of price-matching refund policies. *Journal of Retailing, 83*(August), 325–337.

Levin, I. P., & Johnson, R. D. (1984). Estimating price-quality tradeoffs using comparative judgments. *Journal of Consumer Research, 11*(June), 593–600.

Manning, K. C., & Sprott, D. E. (2009). Price endings, left-digit effects, and choice. *Journal of Consumer Research, 36*(2), 328–335.

Martins, M. (1993). Promoting product value through price fairness. *Pricing Strategy & Practice, 1*(2), 16–21.

Martins, M. (1995), *An experimental investigation of the effects of perceived price fairness on perceptions of sacrifice and value*. Unpublished doctoral dissertation, Department of Business Administration, University of Illinois, Champaign, IL.

Martins, M., & Monroe, K. B. (1994). Perceived price fairness: A new look at an old construct. In C. Allen & D. R. John (Eds.), *Advances in consumer research* (21, pp. 75–78). Provo, UT: Association for Consumer Research.

Maxwell, S., Nye, P., & Maxwell, N. (1999). Less pain, some gain: The effects of priming fairness in price negotiations. *Psychology & Marketing, 16*(7), 545–562.

Miyazaki, A. D., Grewal,, D., & Goodstein, R. C. (2005). The effect of multiple extrinsic cues on quality perceptions: A matter of consistency. *Journal of Consumer Research, 32*(1), 146–153.

Monroe, K. B. (2003). *Pricing: Making profitable decisions*. Burr Ridge, IL: McGraw-Hill/Irwin.

Monroe, K. B., & Chapman, J. D. (1987). Framing effects on buyers' subjective product evaluations. In M. Wallendorf & P. Anderson (Eds.), *Advances in consumer research* (14, pp. 193–197). Provo, UT: Association for Consumer Research.

Monroe, K. B., & Lee, A. Y. (1999). Remembering versus knowing: Issues in buyers' processing of price information. *Journal of the Academy of Marketing Science, 27*(2), 207–225.

Nimer, D. A. (1975). Pricing the profitable sale has a lot to do with perception. *Sales Management, 14*(10), 13–14.

Ofir, C., Raghubir, P., Brosh, G., Monroe, K. B., & Heiman, A. (2008). Memory-based store price judgments: The role of knowledge and shopping experience. *Journal of Retailing, 84*(December), 414–423.

Purohit, D., & Srivastava, J. (2001). Effect of manufacturer reputation, retailer reputation, and product warranty on consumer judgments of product quality: A cue diagnosticity framework. *Journal of Consumer Psychology, 10*(3), 123–134.

Puto, C. P. (1987). The framing of buying decisions. *Journal of Consumer Research, 14* (December), 301–315.

Rao, A. R., & Monroe, K. B. (1988). The moderating effect of prior knowledge on cue utilization in product evaluations. *Journal of Consumer Research, 15*(September), 253–264.

Richardson, P. S., Dick, A. S., & Jain, A. K. (1994). Extrinsic and intrinsic cue effects on perceptions of store brand quality. *Journal of Marketing, 58*(October), 28–36.

Skowronski, J. J., & Carlston, D. E. (1987). Social judgment and social memory: The role of cue diagnosticity in negativity, positivity, and extremity biases. *Journal of Personality and Social Psychology, 52*(4), 689–699.

Skowronski, J. J., & Carlston, D. E. (1989). Negativity and extremity biases in impression formation: A review of explanations. *Psychological Bulletin, 105*(1), 131–142.

Srivastava, J., & Mitra, A. (1998). Warranty as a signal of quality: The moderating effect of consumer knowledge on quality evaluations. *Marketing Letters, 9*(4), 327–336.

Suri, R., & Monroe, K. B. (2003). The effects of time constraints on consumers' judgments of prices and products. *Journal of Consumer Research, 30*(June), 92–104.

Teas, R. K., & Agarwal, S. (2000). The effects of extrinsic product cues on consumers' perceptions of quality, sacrifice, and value. *Journal of the Academy of Marketing Science, 28*(2), 278–290.

Thaler, R. (1985). Mental accounting and consumer choice. *Marketing Science, 4*(Summer), 199–214.

Thomas, M., & Morwitz, V. (2009). Heuristics in numerical cognition: Implications for pricing. In V. R. Rao (Ed.), *Handbook of pricing research in marketing* (pp. 132–149). Northampton, MA: Edward Elgar.

Thomas, M., Simon, D. H., & Kadiyali, V. (2010). The price precision effect: Evidence from laboratory and market data. *Marketing Science, 29*(1), 175–190.

Urbany, J. E., Bearden, W. O., Kaicker,, A., & Smith-de-Borrero, M. (1997). Transaction utility effects when quality is uncertain. *Journal of the Academy of Marketing Science, 25*(1), 45–55.

White, J. D., & Truly, E. L. (1989). Price-quality integration in warranty evaluation. *Journal of Business Research, 19*(September), 109–125.

Winer, R. S. (1986). A reference price model of brand choice for frequently purchased products. *Journal of Consumer Research, 13*(September), 250–257.

Xia, L., & Monroe, K. B. (2010). Is a good deal always fair? Examining the concepts of transaction value and price fairness. *Journal of Economic Psychology, 31*(December), 884–894.

Xia, L., Kukar-Kinney, M., & Monroe, K. B. (2010). Effects of consumers' efforts on price and promotion fairness perceptions. *Journal of Retailing, 86*(1), 1–10.

Xia, L., Monroe, K. B., & Cox, J. L. (2004). The price is unfair! A conceptual framework of price fairness perceptions. *Journal of Marketing, 68*(October), 1–15.

USING CASE ROI™ TO DETERMINE CUSTOMER AND SEGMENT VALUE IN THE BUSINESS-TO-BUSINESS ENVIRONMENT

Reed K. Holden

ABSTRACT

As pricing has evolved as a specialty over the past 20 years, there has been increased focus on the concept of value — what it is, how to measure it, and why it is important. Value is important not only for setting prices but for establishing product and negotiating strategies and tactics. This chapter first discusses the importance of value in the price-setting process. Second, it frames how to define and measure value. Last, it explains how value tools can help salespeople in their negotiations process. It will review the application of these value measures in a business-to-business (B2B) environment and report on a technique of value measurement called Case ROI™. This measurement is particularly useful because it calculates the value of new products, technologies, and

Visionary Pricing: Reflections and Advances in Honor of Dan Nimer
Advances in Business Marketing & Purchasing, Volume 19, 153–171
Copyright © 2012 by Emerald Group Publishing Limited
All rights of reproduction in any form reserved
ISSN: 1069-0964/doi:10.1108/S1069-0964(2012)0000019013

services at both the segment and the individual customer levels with a higher level of precision and relevance than other methods. It is based on a field-value-in-use technique that will be discussed in detail.

The intent is to show how a series of customer depth interviews can provide insights into a wide range of sources of value for customers. These insights can then be used to create a robust model of the value structure for a broader group of customers. The value model then can be applied to calculate value for a segment of customers to inform initial product development and subsequently as a sales support tool during the sales process with individual customers.

The area of study is a new process technology for hospital and independent medical laboratories. For reasons of client confidentiality, much of the specific data and detail is obscured or disguised. Despite deleting confidential details, this report has more than enough information for students and researchers to understand the process and results without revealing the true nature of the product. It contains a number of conclusions worthwhile for users of the technique in a wide range of business-to-business (B2B) applications.

THE IMPORTANCE OF VALUE

An important question for the business, marketing, and sales manager is "How is a price set?" While there are many ways and theories to support this activity (Smith, 2012), the method generally considered the best is based on the financial benefit that buyers and users experience from the product or service being considered (Nagle, Hogan, & Zale, 2011). In the case of a new process technology, such as the example used later in this report, value data is developed by comparing the product to current products or processes being used by the customer. Value data can also be developed by comparing the product to competitive offerings that are similar, though that is not the focus of this report.

Value-based methods have been compared and contrasted with approaches that use a number of other *less strategic* inputs to determine price. Less strategic because these other methods often focus on limited criteria that fail to evaluate the full range of inputs needed to develop a good pricing strategy and ultimate price. For example, cost-based methods ignore issues like customer perception of value and competitive pricing activities. Instead, they rely on internal calculations of cost and often fail to look at how those costs change with changes in volume. Pricing based on competition ignores the comparative value of different competitors. It assumes that all competitors are the same when often they are not (Provines, 2011). This approach also fails to recognize that competitors will change price as customers take them down the slippery slope of price negotiations. Finally, many *market-based* methods are really based on customer negotiations where the customer incentive is to obscure real value and try to obtain lower prices for high-value products (Holden & Burton, 2008).

Providing products and services to customers and the subsequent pricing of those activities are substantially an exchange of value. Thus, it only stands to reason that prices should reflect, in some manner, the value that customers get from the use of those products and services. Some measures of value, such as brand image and trust in the supplier are intangible, and in these cases, customers' perception of the trust and value of that brand has a direct impact on their willingness to pay. This is especially true for high-priced consumer luxury goods where the brand impacts the purchase decision for a wide range of products depending on subjective criteria, such as personal preference and product positioning.

The focus of this report is on value in a B2B environment. Here evaluation of vendors often goes far beyond brand image to how the specific features of the products and services can play a role in helping the customer reduce costs and enhance profits. Criteria such as quality go beyond the issue of image to the pragmatic analysis of how that quality impacts the successful operation of the supply system in which the product is introduced. Equally important is an evaluation of how that quality, or lack of it, impacts costs and the subsequent revenue and profits of a customer's business system.

This type of value analysis answers important questions for the vendor. If a failure shuts that system down, what are the implications of that shut down to the customer in lost revenues, profits, and increased costs? If there are certain features that increase the performance and subsequent throughput of the system, what are the cost, revenue, and profit implications of that? It is important to note that it also applies to the services wrapped around that system. If the service response is slower or faster than competitors, how does that performance impact costs, revenues, and profits?

Quantifying value in financial terms helps managers understand how to set price relative to competitors. After all, if the value of a like product is higher or lower than competitors, it only stands to reason that the subsequent prices should be higher or lower than those competitors. This applies to both the initial setting of pricing strategy, whether to be higher, lower, or the same as competitors (skim, penetration, or neutral), and how those prices get set and often subsequently lowered during intense customer negotiations.

This point is often missed in pricing theory. In a B2B environment, customers have considerable buying power because of the large quantity of materials and services they buy. They also purchase expensive systems made up of technologies, services, product – or a combination of all three. Their procurement function is expert and finely tuned to use tactics which seek to gain extra discounts from suppliers (Steinmetz & Brooks, 2005). The value of the products and services in use by customers provides suppliers caught up in this procurement process with a critical understanding of what a fair price is for their offerings.

Without knowledge of the value, the only other frame that suppliers have for answering the daunting question of *what is the right price?* is internal costs or the prices of competitors – neither is guaranteed to be close to what the real product value is for a specific customer. Understanding the value of the offering provides both suppliers and properly educated customers a reasonable frame for understanding what the final price should be.

MEASURES OF VALUE

Because value is important for successful price setting and discounting during customer negotiations, the next relevant question is: how does one measure value by customers? As one might expect, there are a wide range of thoughts on this subject. The most comprehensive work on this question was based on research with 80 industrial researchers and 20 market research firms (Anderson, Jain, & Chintagunta, 1993). The authors concluded that "focus-group value assessments and importance rates are the most widely used methods." This is noteworthy because at the time, importance rates were considered to be acceptable surrogate measures of value. As you will see in subsequent comments and research, more reliable measures of value are becoming increasingly popular. They further found that "conjoint analysis, though used less frequently, has the highest percentage of judged successful applications." This points to both the problems with traditional focus group and importance-based methods and the rising importance and success of more recent experimental techniques such as conjoint analysis.

In this case, it was the market research firms that led the way with 60 percent using conjoint analysis, versus only 28.8 percent of the industrial firms. Recent work by Dierick and Depril (2010) found that 44 percent of European firms use conjoint analysis, though it appears to be used significantly more in B2C than B2B research projects. These authors further found that 50 percent of the B2B firms use no research method at all to set price. Despite this finding, Orme (2009) estimates that over 14,000 conjoint studies are conducted per year. Clearly, it has become the dominant method of measuring value. This is true for B2C markets like automobiles and foodstuffs or B2B markets where products are purchased for use or resale in a business. It is especially true in consumer markets where common measures of value that come from attitudinal research, like the variety of forms of conjoint analysis, have grown increasingly popular; they are relatively easy to implement by marketing research firms (Dierick & Depril, 2010).

Conjoint analysis identifies relevant product/service attributes and compares their value to price with a weighted scale. It is an *attitudinal* measure of value in that respondents weight their perception of a feature's value relative to price and other features deemed important. It is fast and easy to implement and is fairly inexpensive. Conjoint results give the appearance of statistically significant precision, but this precision often misses important value drivers and the real financial impact of those value drivers on a business system. Also, conjoint permits the building of complex models that predict simulated market share moves given changes in price and feature sets for the product, though some point out that this is an improper application of the technique (Orme, 2009).

Conjoint analysis works well as a measure where respondents understand and have a lot of experience with a *complete* consumer product. By complete, we mean finished products, such as cars, DVD players, phones, and PC's. It works well when respondents can value individual features and that value has a direct impact on their decision to purchase and their willingness to pay. The results are relevant to retail sales organizations that don't have a lot of price negotiations or pricing flexibility.

Conjoint analysis doesn't work as well when one or more of the following conditions are present:

1. The product is part of a more complex product or system – since the focus is on the performance of the part and not how it impacts the broader system. This is particularly relevant when the cost of the product is quite small relative to the greater system, yet it still impacts the overall system's performance.

2. It is being sold through a field sales force that negotiates prices with customers – they will need to have a very specific understanding of the real mechanics of the value in use of the product or part. Conjoint analysis fails to provide this.
3. There is a likely competitor discount that will need to be matched. This would indicate that value may no longer be the relevant measure to investigate. Here, a more relevant technique would be scenario analysis that models the resulting competitive and subsequent customer response to a particular pricing approach.
4. The results will be used to convince a discount-oriented sales force and senior executives to stop their behavior of easily giving away margin.

You can see that many B2B products and services fall into these categories.

Therefore the question is: How do we determine value for B2B (and occasionally consumer) applications? At a pricing symposium in Europe, five methods were presented and evaluated (Dierick & Depril, 2010):

1. Conjoint Analysis which, in its different forms, asks respondents to compare and value different features, including price.
2. Van Westendorp Price Sensitivity Meter which asks respondents to identify prices that are too high, too low, or are acceptable for the product and then models the responses to estimate price sensitivity.
3. Gabor and Granger's Buy-Response Method which simply asks people if they would be willing to purchase a product at a particular price.
4. Brand versus Price Trade-off Studies which evaluates the respondents value of the brand relative to price.
5. Expert Judgment which uses a panel of expert judges to determine the price of a product.

The problem is that none of these techniques attempts to determine financial value that customers achieve from adopting a product or technology. The first four are extensions of earlier attitudinal measures of value using more sophisticated analytic techniques. Expert Judgment relies on the judgment of highly informed experts to determine the sources of customer value, but in our experience, and in the case we present here, they often miss important sources of customer value.

The Institute for the Study of Business Markets (ISBM) points to two primary methods to expose real value: internal engineering assessments *based on laboratory tests* and *field-value-in-use* assessments (Anderson et al., 1993). The focus of the ISBM paper is on calculating value, not developing the structure of systems that determines value for individual customers after the research is completed.

The depth interviewing technique has been proposed to accomplish an understanding of customer-specific value (Nagle et al., 2011). The depth interview method of insight collection is field-value-in-use methodology which is used to "determine a comprehensive listing of cost elements associated with the usage of a product offering compared with the incumbent product offering" (Anderson et al., 1993, p. 7). This technique has been called Economic Value Modeling, Value in Exchange (Smith & Thomas, 2005), and Economic Value Estimation (Nagle & Holden, 2002), to mention a few. Another method, Case ROI (Burton & Beram, 2011) uses a technique that permits a case-by-case assessment of the financial value that customers achieve by adopting the new technology. It evaluates the customer's likely return on investment for purchasing the technology or product.

In Case ROI, depth interviews are used to determine the field value in use. The data from the interviews form an understanding that becomes the basis to develop a mathematical model of value for an individual customer or a segment of customers. By focusing on building that structure, it permits subsequent use by a salesperson to determine a specific customer's estimated financial value for adopting the technology or new product. This is accomplished simply by having that salesperson ask the customer a battery of questions that input data into the Case ROI model. This complete process makes up the Case ROI technique.

Case ROI analysis includes conducting interviews with customers to see how the product has a direct impact on their business – in terms of increased profits and reduced costs. Both of these areas are included, because improvements in capacity of a production system through the adoption of a new machine or process technology can yield higher revenue and profits from the increased sales that the system can produce. This often makes cost reductions relatively small by comparison. The interviews with customers are exploratory and qualitative at the start of the process, but after surprisingly few interviews, the purpose evolves to confirmatory and quantitative. That is, they confirm what has been learned about the customer's operational structure or relevant business system and use those confirmations to build a quantitative model of how a customer firm's use of the product or service improves their throughput and profits and reduces costs.

The advantage of this method is that the resulting model fulfills two primary functions critical for the go-to-market strategy of any organization.

First, it provides an understanding of the product or service's value in order to set price. That understanding can be applied to the responding customer or used to make assumptions based on the range of responses from customers within a segment of customers to a broader segment of customers. Second, it becomes a selling tool that (a) supports the salesperson in asking the right questions with prospects, (b) subsequently shows what the specific value benefit is to each customer by plugging the answers into the sales tool which calculates the financial value in specific dollars and payback period, and (c) can be used to minimize the damage of price negotiations by providing a value frame rather than the *lower competitive price* frame that buyers often use.

THE CASE STUDY – AN ILLUSTRATION

Having described the Case ROI method, let's see how it worked in a case study for a global provider of medical equipment. The research was conducted in the spring of 2010 over a three-month period of time. The objective was to provide a quantifiable value proposition for a new process technology to support hospital and independent medical laboratories. Additional objectives included identifying how key attributes of the technology would enhance or inhibit the likelihood of adoption, to test a segment's payback on value at anticipated price points, and finally, to develop a model to test the financial returns to specific customers at these price points.

Initially, the client requested a conjoint study. Given that the new technology represented a significant change in the workflows with the existing technology, it was likely that the value structure was going to be quite different both for different customers and their respective segments. Further, there was a concern that there were hidden value drivers that were yet to be identified. Based on past experience, we knew that it might not be until the midpoint of the research before all sources of value fully materialized. Part of the Case ROI process is to validate existing value drivers and develop their operational structure in a business. Effective research techniques must also seek to uncover new drivers of value as well. That is the nature of the exploratory process. Given these criteria, the Case ROI method was deemed a more appropriate technique.

Initial exploratory work was done to hypothesize the probable value drivers in each segment and to model how those value drivers impacted the costs of the laboratory. Through existing workflow studies and exploratory focus group research, we determined that there were adequate insights to begin the interview process. For this project, we structured the questions based on expected value drivers with more granular detail questions for the interviewer to follow, if they were needed.

Forty-five supervising physicians and laboratory managers were interviewed in the United States and Europe. Interviewees were identified from supplier records and independent listings of medical laboratories. All respondents were screened based on their experience with the area of technology or in the diagnostic area targeted by the new technology. In some cases, respondents refused to cooperate, since they had advisory contracts with suppliers of competitive systems already in development.

The client had planned to provide an honorarium for respondents. It has long been an industry practice to provide a $400 incentive to get physicians to participate in vendor research. With that, they saw response percentages in the 10−20 percent range. This level of response appears to be consistent with that reported at a recent AMA conference where commercial research showed response rates of 20 percent, considerably lower than academic response rates which tended to run closer to 50 percent (AMA/SPSS Rountable, 2008). Other analysis that didn't distinguish between the source of the research found that average response rates were 38 percent (Manfreda, Bosnjak, Berzlelak, Haas, & Vehovar, 2008).

There was concern that an incentive would trivialize the effort, making it just another piece of research and that it could bias both the sample and the results. Further, experience showed that if the research was introduced with a point of interest to the respondents, and it was conducted to permit the respondent to focus on their specific areas of interest rather than those of the interviewer, they would be quite willing to both participate and provide good data without the honorarium.

Ultimately we decided to not use any type of payment. Instead, the interviewers used multiple telephone callbacks to obtain respondent participation and, in most cases, described the area of research, not the supplier. They achieved a response rate that exceeded 80 percent.

As previously mentioned, an internal review of prior focus group research had identified a battery of value drivers to validate in the interviews. Those value drivers were supplemented with expert judgment from company internal technical, sales, and marketing people. The objective was not to determine what specific value could be found for each laboratory, rather it was to identify the sources and structure of that value − the value model. This model looks at the operation of an entity, in this case the hospital laboratory or the entire hospital, and its current workflows for the particular test in focus. It also looks at the costs of those workflows. These sources were used to build an understanding of the structure of value for customers and create hypotheses about both the value and the structure of value during the interviews.

Once the current workflows and their subsequent cost structures were understood, the respondents were asked to validate those flows and the likely changes due to the adoption of the new technology. Data was collected on salaries and efficiencies in each of the operating areas, number of participants, costs of equipment, and physical and electronic storage costs to support the financial analysis.

Initial focus was to identify and interview people in the role of supervising physicians. These are the expert diagnosticians in the area of study and are also the senior management of the laboratories. In some cases, they are quite well informed on the workflows of the various elements of the lab. However, during the initial round of interviews, the team found that in roughly half of the interviews, they were not. Accordingly, we decided to interview the nonmedical laboratory managers who often managed the flow of work around the supervising physician. By including both functions during separate interviews, we obtained a good understanding of the workflow of each lab and interviewers were able to get respondent estimates of how the new technology would impact those workflows.

The interview method could be characterized as *semi structured*. Because the intent was to learn operating structure, efficiencies, and costs from the participants, the interview was intended to develop a *holistic point of view* from the respondents on how their laboratories operated. This is also often called qualitative depth interviewing (Berry, 1999).

The interview guide identified areas of focus to be tested and refined during the interview. These guides serve as more of a checklist to identify areas of relevance, concern, and expertise for the respondent. It is up to the interviewer to determine the topics of focus for each interview and probe deeper in both appropriate areas and areas where respondents had interest and high levels of expertise. Some interviews might focus on the efficiency of people involved in the workflow, while others might focus on the effectiveness and accuracy of those staff members. An important task was determining which of the target respondents had the information needed to build out the resulting value model. If the respondent did not have relevant information, the interviewers were able to quickly adjust the target respondents to include more appropriate respondents.

While some researchers might be concerned at the looseness of this approach, an in-depth approach has been shown to have high levels of predictive validity (Oliphant, Hansen, & Oliphant, 2008). In remarkably few interviews, interviewers usually achieve several important objectives. First, the value drivers that had been identified in the initial phases of the research were validated or rejected as being of little relevance to the respondent. For example, it was thought that the cost of handling, storage, and recovery of the physical test samples was going to be important to most of the respondents. Initial, top-of-mind responses seemed to confirm this hypothesis. However, once the interviewer probed for data on the actual costs, it was discovered to be of little importance to most of the respondents and their lab operations.

Second, the depth interview process discovered additional value drivers that may not have been identified in the initial phases. These value drivers had significant value for certain segments of laboratories. For example, efficient utilization of operating rooms and staff that have a fixed cost of thousands of dollars per hour was not in the initial hypotheses but was quickly identified as an important value driver for at least two of the segments. The new technology could dramatically speed up some surgeries, thus reducing the overhead and salary costs of the procedures. Also, for hospitals with capacity problems in their surgical units, it would help relieve some of those capacity constraints and save the need for costly surgical suite expansion.

Finally, the interview insights showed how the new technology would be viewed by adopting physicians and laboratory managers, what might enhance their adoption, and what might inhibit it. For example, because this was a new process technology, the assumption was that physicians who were newer to the field would have been exposed to the technology during their education and that exposure would have been a positive experience. During one of the interviews, one of the respondents, an assistant to a supervising physician, commented that she *hated* the new technology and would never adopt it. While surprised, the interviewer asked why. The assistant claimed that the quality of the technology was inadequate for good diagnosis. In probing deeper the interviewer found the assistant had been exposed to an older version of the technology and that the newer technologies were in fact quite good at providing not only adequate but superior results. This provided the interviewer valuable information for how the sales force needed to think about positioning the new technology with prospective adopters during the final product rollout.

Of the 45 interviews, 42 percent were conducted in person and 58 percent over the phone. The initial intent was to conduct only 30 interviews, all in person. The client asked that additional interviews be conducted in two of the focus segments and that the scope be expanded to include a number of international locations.

Conducting the interviews in person does provide for better data quality, and it permits an easy addition of other respondents from the same location. Often the discussion with a single respondent will get sufficiently involved that s/he will call in someone else to participate. At times the added interaction with an additional respondent can provide valuable insight. For example, the insight about the quality of the result never would have happened if we were conducting the interview over the phone. It should also be pointed out that the importance of reduced waiting time and costs of the operating room came from several of the phone interviews to remotely located respondents. Whatever the nature of the interaction, interviewing is an iterative process that refines insights in four important areas:

1. Customer value drivers;
2. How those value drivers interact in a system of cost and, in some cases, profits;
3. How new product, service, or technology impacts that system;
4. What the likely inhibitors and drivers of adoption will be and how all of this varies by segment.

When reviewing all of the results from all of the interviews, it becomes clear that value varied significantly on a customer-by-customer and segment-by-segment basis. Looking for segment-level ranges of value does help to identify higher-value segments; however, these ranges of value are of little use to salespeople and of no credibility to customers in the final sales process. Instead, customer-specific projections of value resulting from direct questioning by salespeople have high levels of credibility in the sales process.

Sometimes marketers will use glossy customer case studies to portray the value of new products and services, but those case studies can suffer from the same problems. They portray an example of how one customer achieves value. Since the amount of value a customer gets from new products and services varies considerably, it is unlikely that any other customer would achieve similar value. This makes case studies interesting stories that have little relevance in the actual selling and subsequent adoption of new products and services. The Case ROI tool becomes an effective sales mechanism, because the structure is determined and established via a simple spreadsheet or software tool. It helps salespeople prepare the right set of questions for a potential customer and determine the likely value on a real-time basis. It provides each salesperson and customer with a specific calculation of how that specific customer will reduce their costs or add profits — it provides the true value that they will achieve from adopting the new offering in a real, highly believable form.

When there is a lot at stake with new products and services — high revenue and profit opportunities — the best approach to determining value, price, and subsequent discounts is to invest the effort to build out a spreadsheet or model that contains the value drivers and how they interact in the customer organization to reduce costs, add revenue, and profits. A summary of the primary detail of the spreadsheet is shown in Fig. 1. The summary is set up to input the customer-specific information and provide the value and, in this case, a specific return on investment payback in terms of months required to pay back the equipment investment, which is an excellent selling tool to convince the customer to make the equipment investment.

Value Profile		
Prospect Profile	**Value Profile**	
Inputs:	**Savings**	**Per Case**

Inputs:	Small Hospital
Facility Type	Small Hospital
No. of Cases	10,000
Inefficiency Current System	20%
Physician Time/Case (Hrs.)	0.5
% Cases from OR	15%
% Cases Remote Sites	30%
Current External Diagnostics	10%
Fee for External Diagnostics	$142

Savings		Per Case
Physician Efficiency	$	3.50
Staff Efficiency	$	1.75
Operating Room Usage	$	6.10
Case Handling	$	1.40
Remote Sites	$	3.62
Total Savings	$	15.59
Revenue		
External Diagnostics	$	1.83
Costs		
Storage Costs	$	4.20
Equipment Costs	$	5.80
Net Financial Benefit	$	12.62
Equipment Payback		5.4 Months

Fig. 1. Customer-Specific Information and Value Profile.

The interviews provide the understanding needed to begin the process of identifying primary value drivers and how they vary by segment. For example, in the Support Lab segment, the following value drivers were identified:

1. Physician efficiency — Time spent performing, reporting on, and handling the documents and materials from the test.
2. Staff efficiency — Improvements in process flow of the laboratory reflected in higher utilization and reduced costs.
3. Operating room usage — Time currently spent waiting for test results, estimates of the reduced time, and the subsequent value of those time savings in capacity and costs of the operating room and attending staff.
4. Case handling — Time spent handling current cases, likely improvements in efficiencies, and the subsequent value of reduced costs and increased capacities.
5. Remote sites — Ability and cost efficiencies to handle remote sites more effectively.
6. External Diagnostics — Ability to improve efficiency of handling and volume of external work outside of the laboratory.
7. Storage Costs — The costs of storing test results on a short- and long-term basis. It detracts from the overall value of the new process in this case since the electronic storage of the data is higher than some of the physical storage costs of the lab samples which was negligible.
8. Equipment Costs — There will be a fixed cost for the new equipment which needs to be deducted from the value case for adopting the new technology.

After only a few interviews, the data revealed (a) the identity of the value drivers for a particular segment and (b) an understanding of how those value drivers connect to the cost and subsequent value structure for a laboratory. The beauty of this approach is that it doesn't need large sample sizes. Once convergence is achieved, that is, once all of the respondents agree on the value drivers and how they interact, there is enough information to begin building the model of how those value drivers interact. This conclusion is consistent with prior research on the subject (Silver & Thompson, 1991).

HOW CASE ROI HELPS SALESPEOPLE IN NEGOTIATIONS

This value research approach seeks to understand value structure and apply that understanding to segments in the initial product development, pricing and marketing process, and to individual customers in the actual selling process. Large sample sizes aren't needed to accomplish this task. What is needed is a tool to help the salespeople convince a customer that the prices established are based on that value and are fair. Case ROI takes an analysis of a specific customer's value and provides a case-by-case, customer-specific return on investment (Burton & Beram, 2011). The resulting and summarized version of the value calculator is shown in Fig. 1, which provides a value profile for a small regional hospital. In addition to summarizing the value calculation in a simple spreadsheet, the Case ROI also provides a tool for use in the product rollout by salespeople. The tool is useful. First, it provides a fairly simple set of questions for salespeople to ask of their target decision maker. Second, it provides an immediate value calculation, which can be presented to a potential customer for the adoption of the new technology. Finally, the resulting net value number is credible to the respondent, since they or their staff provided the data.

Once the important value drivers are understood for a customer segment and how these drivers create value, that information gets translated into the value profile spreadsheet. It takes segment inputs of current processes, estimates of improved or diminished performance, and calculates the likely financial values that a group of customers will receive by adopting the new product or technology. These spreadsheets may get quite sophisticated and complex. In many cases, researchers will focus on getting every last detail of cost to improve the accuracy of the process. While such efforts are impressive, they are often not needed. Instead, a rough estimate of ranges of value for a particular segment is more than adequate to develop pricing strategies and price matrixes. The specifics are needed during the actual sales process and those are best determined when salespeople interact directly with a prospective customer.

To support the analysis of individual customers and segments, a value waterfall can be developed to indicate graphically the specific value drivers, the importance of each and how they appear in total and comparative value for each other (see Fig. 2). To accomplish that, averages of the range of value driver performances can be estimated and plugged into discrete cells in the value calculator spreadsheet. This type of averaging, while risky to use in customer selling situations, is useful in developing the final pricing strategies for the product.

Once pricing is determined for the product, those estimates of value can be compared to the product costs and rough payback on the customer investment can be calculated as well. Since ROI paybacks are generally accepted by customers to be good indicators of the value of a purchase or equipment investment, they become excellent selling tools. Those ranges of

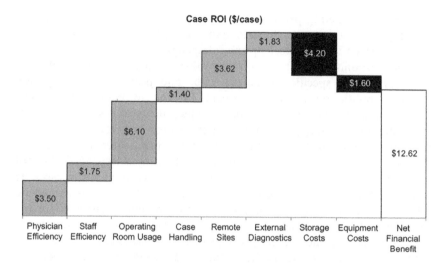

Fig. 2. Value Waterfall.

Table 1. Segment Value Analysis.

Net Financial Benefit (10-yr NPV)	$/Case		Payback (months)	
	Low	High	Low	High
Support Lab	$11.60	$13.42	4.5	3.5
Small Hospital	$10.27	$11.22	5.4	4.6
Top Diagnostic Ctr.	$7.15	$12.63	6.7	3.8
Large Lab	$0.83	$1.98	9.0	7.0

payback can be then used to initially identify target segments (see Table 1) – in this case, the Support Lab segment has the highest per-case value for adopting the technology – due primarily to the value of being able to handle remote surgical locations more cost effectively with the new technology.

CONCLUSIONS

Case ROI assessment, though more expensive to conduct than the more popular conjoint analysis in its various forms, has a number of distinct advantages:

1. It permits the development of a value framework that can be used to define segment-level ranges of value and customer-specific value.

2. It analyzes specific customer cost structures and measures of value and are far more accurate and relevant than traditional attitudinal methods usually conducted by marketing researchers.
3. The framework is easily converted into a sales tool to be used in the subsequent introduction of the product.
4. The data collection uses a method that is more respondent friendly; it is possible that honorariums, which add costs and bias, can be eliminated.
5. The area of research is often of interest to the respondent, thus response rates are dramatically higher than most other methods of data collection.

While not appropriate for every product or service in B2B markets, it certainly is a technique that adds considerable clarity and credibility to calculations of a product or service's value to a customer. For complex products and services that are expensive and take a long time to develop, Case ROI provides additional depth and insight into value. As such, it offers opportunities for improved performance in product development, pricing, and subsequent introduction.

It is clear that when there is a lot at stake in terms of revenue and profits, Case ROI puts backbone and confidence in the value analysis. This believability is proven during the sales process, because customers are directly involved with providing the data and assumptions necessary to populate the model and calculate the value. If they disagree with a piece of data or an assumption, it can be changed − the resulting numbers are more than believable; they are the customer's numbers.

Case ROI should be used for those offerings deemed sufficiently important to invest considerable research and development dollars into their creation. Many innovations that have received those research dollars fail. They fail not because the innovation is necessarily bad but more often than not, because the launch team does not effectively consider how it provides value for customers. The extra effort to perform a Case ROI on a new product or service can be viewed as the key to achieving a successful introduction. It enables researchers to target segments and customers that receive relatively high value from the product. It also helps identify specific positioning points with financial backup that will increase the likelihood of customer adoption. And finally, it helps salespeople close business with prospects, the most important step of all.

ON DAN NIMER

Recently, I had the pleasure of singing Happy Birthday to Dan Nimer who had just turned 90. Dan is the Father of modern pricing theory. He started talking about value before we understood the connection. Before that, pricing was the sub-bullet of finance and economics.

When Tom Nagle, the author of the first edition of *The Strategy and Tactics of Pricing*, was at University of Chicago, he decided to write the first graduate textbook on Pricing Strategy. To do that, he wanted to get better grounded in theory. He went and spent a day with Dan. Dan didn't charge for the day – he gave his time and ideas freely back then and now, over thirty years later. Tom is now at Monitor and still uses Dan's ideas, as we all do.

One of the greatest honors I have had was to present the third edition of the book to Dan – it was dedicated to him. It was just the two of us. He had dropped by a Professional Pricing Society conference in Chicago. The look on his face when he opened it and saw his name still brings tears to my eyes.

When I finished singing, Dan commented on the lousy tone but appreciated the words. Then he said "You know Reed, ideas are the children of the mind. Let them go and pretty soon the whole world knows." Yes, Dan, they are. So a belated written "Happy Birthday, my Friend, and thanks from all of us for your thoughts and words over the years."

REFERENCES

AMA/SPSS Rountable. (2008). Where have all the respondents gone? *Marketing Research*, (Winter), p. 22. Interview with Chuck Chakrapani, Ryerson University, Patrick Glaser, Council for Marketing and Opinion Research, Simon Chadwick, Cambiar, Colin Shearer, SPSS, Inc.

Anderson, J. C., Jain, D. C., & Chintagunta, P. K. (1993). *Customer value assessment in business markets: A state of the art practice*. Report 10-93, Institute for the Study of Business Markets, Pennsylvania State University, University Park, PA.

Berry, R. S. Y. (1999, September). *Collecting data by in-depth interviewing*. The British Educational Research Association Annual Conference, University of Sussex at Brighton, UK.

Burton, M. R., & Beram, A. (2011). The case ROI method: Versatile sales tool for defending price. *The Journal of Professional Pricing*, 20(4), pp. 26.

Dierick, K., & Depril, D. (2010). *Assessing the value of 5 pricing research methods*. suAzio Consulting: A white paper done in participation with the European Pricing Platform.

Holden, R. K., & Burton, M. R. (2008). *Pricing with confidence: 10 ways to stop leaving money on the table*. Hoboken, NJ: Wiley.

Manfreda, K. L., Bosnjak, M., Berzlelak, J., Haas, I., & Vehovar, V. (2008). Web surveys versus other survey modes: A meta-analysis comparing response rates. *International Journal of Market Research*, 50(1), 79.

Nagle, T. T., & Holden, R. K. (2002). *The strategy and tactics of pricing: A guide to profitable decision making*. Upper Saddle River, NJ: Pearson Education.

Nagle, T. T., Hogan, J., & Zale, J. (2011). *The strategy and tactics of pricing: A guide to growing more profitably*. Upper Saddle River, NJ: Pearson Education.

Oliphant, G. C., Hansen, K., & Oliphant, B. J. (2008). Predictive validity of behavioral interview technique. *Marketing Management Journal, 18*(2), 93–96.

Orme, B. K. (2009). *Getting started with conjoint analysis: Strategies for product design and pricing research* (2nd ed.). Madison, WI: Research Publishers.

Provines, C. D. (2011). Implementing value selling: 5 Key lessons from both sides of the table. *The Journal of Professional Pricing, 20*(1), 12.

Silver, J. A., & Thompson Jr., J. C. (1991). *Understanding customer needs: A systematic approach to the 'voice of the customer'*. Masters thesis. Sloan School of Management, Massachusetts Institute of Technology, Cambridge, MA.

Smith, G. E., & Thomas, T. N. (2005). A question of value. *Marketing Management, 14* (July/August), 38–43.

Smith, T. J. (2012). *Pricing strategy: Setting price levels, managing price discounts, & establishing price structures*. Mason, OH: South-Western Cengage Learning.

Steinmetz, L., & Brooks, W. T. (2005). *How to sell at margins higher than your competitors: Winning every sale at full price, rate, or fee*. Hoboken, NJ: Wiley Sons.

LEGAL TOOLS THAT SUPPORT VALUE PRICING

Eugene F. Zelek Jr.

ABSTRACT

"Price is what you pay. Value is what you get."

— Warren Buffett

Value pricing can be a successful means to maximize profit by pricing products and services based on their value to end users. Using this approach necessarily means that customers are segmented, with some receiving better prices than others. However, many companies mistakenly believe that U.S. law requires that all customers receive the same price or a "fair and equitable" price, an unrealistically high standard that is a self-imposed roadblock to value-based differentiation.

Not only is the law supportive of segmentation and the economic discrimination that goes with it, but, where resellers are involved, the law also permits value pricing to be facilitated and preserved through the use of non-price vertical restrictions and resale price setting. In addition, price signaling can be a lawful way to avoid sending wrong messages to the marketplace that jeopardize value pricing strategies.

Visionary Pricing: Reflections and Advances in Honor of Dan Nimer
Advances in Business Marketing & Purchasing, Volume 19, 173–194
Copyright © 2012 by Emerald Group Publishing Limited
All rights of reproduction in any form reserved
ISSN: 1069-0964/doi:10.1108/S1069-0964(2012)0000019014

Consistent with an unparalleled amount of pricing freedom under current law in the United States, there are four powerful and lawful tools that can help achieve and maintain prices based on value. The first is economic discrimination, which is useful in recognizing relative value, while the other three assist in facilitating segmentation or preserving value – non-price vertical restrictions, resale price setting and price signaling.[1] The last two often scare the daylights out of businesspeople and their lawyers who are not familiar with this area.

VALUE PRICING

For purposes of this chapter, value pricing will be defined as pricing services or products based on their value to end users. By looking at things from the end user's perspective, pricing opportunities can be readily identified, and a marketplace reality check is built into the process, as end users are willing to pay only so much. Of course, this focus does not mean that other factors should not be taken into account in determining prices, such as (1) the supplier's financial and other goals, (2) the competitive landscape, (3) regulatory parameters, (4) trade relations and end user relations issues, and (5) the sales path. The last consideration has significant implications for value pricing.

The Sales Path

To view value pricing in context, it is important to understand the relevant sales path. Services are typically provided directly by the supplier to end users. So, for example, Verizon is a supplier of cellular phone services, while Southwest Airlines provides air travel services. Sales and follow-on service may be furnished directly or through agents, such as Best Buy acting as an agent for Verizon. Agents usually work on a commission that is a percentage of the selling price, with the price generally determined by the supplier.

Like services, products may be sold and serviced directly by manufacturers to end users or through agents. But more importantly, products often are sold and serviced through resellers that take ownership to the products and resell them for their own accounts. Rather than a commission, resellers are compensated for the functions they perform on the difference between their buy price and the street price paid by the end user.[2] Depending on the industry, such resellers may be referred to as wholesalers, distributors, dealers, value-added resellers (VARs), or retailers. For example, Deere & Company sells agricultural equipment through dealers, while Kellogg sells food products to retailers and to foodservice distributors for resale, as well as providing industrial food products directly to other food processors.[3]

To apply value pricing analysis, the value to the end user (*e.g.*, in the examples just mentioned, the farmer, consumer, foodservice operator, or industrial user) must be ascertained, usually by asking, either directly or through formal marketing research. Then, the trick is to deliver the value, something that typically is easier in direct sales or through agents due to the degree of control inherent in the relationship.[4] The fact that resellers have more independence makes it somewhat more complicated to deliver value through them.

The Stakes

For the sale of services and the direct sale of goods, the value is simply the street price or what the end user is willing to pay. Fig. 1 shows sales made directly by a supplier of a single service or product. If all sales were made at list price, total revenue to the supplier would be $90 million. However,

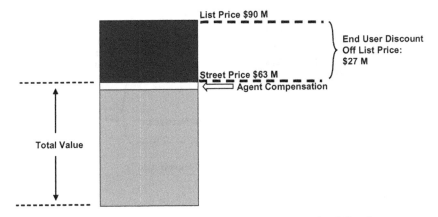

Fig. 1. The Stakes: Sale of Services and Direct Sale of Goods.

because the street price is less, revenue is $63 million, representing the aggregate value.[5]

It obviously is in the best interest of the supplier to increase the street price, as this result puts more money in its pocket. If an agent − like an independent sales representative or broker − is used, its commission or other compensation does not affect street price, but is paid by the supplier from its revenue.

When products are sold through resellers, the picture changes. In Fig. 2, the list price and street price are the same as the previous example. However, this time the manufacturer splits the value or street price with its resellers to compensate the latter for what they do, so the $63 million in value is divided between that received by the manufacturer ($33 million) and what the resellers get ($30 million).[6] If the manufacturer uses agents, their commissions still come off the manufacturer's share.

Often, manufacturers see their resellers as their customers and stop the analysis there. However, the real focus should be on the end users, because they ultimately determine the street price and value. Just as important, the price paid by each reseller allocates revenue and profit between the manufacturer and the reseller. Moving the reseller's buy price up or down changes the way the value pie is cut.

It also is possible to increase the aggregate street price (or the size of the pie) through value pricing, whether achieved by the manufacturer, the reseller or both. All other things being equal, if the manufacturer sees the reseller as its customer and isn't paying attention to the street price, any

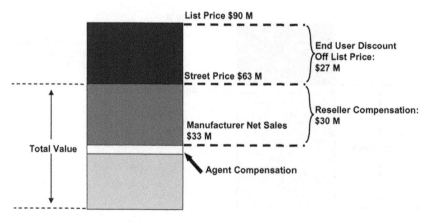

Fig. 2. The Stakes: Sale of Products Through Resellers.

increase in the street price is retained by the reseller. Any decrease in street price – perhaps due to real or imagined competitive pressure – often results in the reseller asking for price concessions from the manufacturer to maintain the reseller's margin. By ignoring the street price, the manufacturer cedes management of it to the resellers, and smart resellers take advantage of this position, as they should.

At a minimum, the smart manufacturer should monitor the street price and periodically adjust the reseller's buy price, if necessary, to maintain a split that provides the reseller with an appropriate margin to the cover the costs of what it is expected to do and its profit.[7] However, it is even better for the manufacturer to engage in value pricing by taking a direct role in managing both the street price and the split. Just as value pricing recognizes the different relative values that end users ascribe to the product, the manufacturer can reflect in its pricing to resellers the relative values they bring to the table that support end user value. In other words, recognizing and rewarding the value provided by the reseller can be used to help achieve value pricing to the end user.

Recognizing Value

Depending on how the supplier sells, optimizing street price necessarily involves value-based segmentation of end users, resellers, or both. As a result, there will be discrimination in price, as not all customers will pay the same. A common myth among U.S. businesspeople is that the law requires all customers to receive the identical price, with maybe a bit of leeway for higher-volume purchasers, something that is implicit in the common use of the term "fair and equitable" as a pricing parameter. The reality is far different under the federal law addressing economic discrimination, known as the "Robinson-Patman Act."[8]

First, this statute does not apply to the sale of services, just goods.[9] Moreover, only goods sold on a business-to-business (B2B) basis are relevant[10] So, for example, price discrimination among users of cellular phone services or air travel is not covered, nor are the different prices consumers pay for the identical vehicle at the same auto dealer.[11]

Second, when sales of products in the B2B context occur and Robinson-Patman applies, the law states that only competing customers need to be treated the same, unless there is a good reason to do otherwise.[12] In other words, customers that don't chase the same purchaser don't compete.[13] This lack of overlap may be naturally occurring, such as having one customer in New York and another in California that each resells only in its respective geographic area.

Alternatively, the divisions may be contractually imposed, using something called "non-price vertical restrictions," where the manufacturer lawfully tells the reseller to whom it may sell, where it may sell or what it may sell to control the degree of overlap and the channel conflict that goes with it.[14] The use of such restrictions can be an effective tool for establishing value-based segmentation by controlling who competes with whom to preserve such segmentation.[15]

Robinson–Patman prohibits certain forms of two types of economic discrimination – price discrimination and promotional discrimination – with somewhat different legal standards for each. The former is always associated with the initial sale (the left oval in Fig. 3) and includes things like volume discounts and extended payment terms. In contrast, promotional discrimination (right oval) is associated with resale activities only, such as the supplier's provision to the reseller of demonstrators, free display racks or financial incentives based on reseller sales loyalty.[16]

PRICE DISCRIMINATION

Under price discrimination rules, competing customers must receive essentially the same prices, unless at least one defense is available.[17] The first defense is *availability*. If the same price realistically is made available to competing customers, but not all of them choose to take advantage of it, there is no discrimination and the legal analysis ends, even though a price difference results.[18] A good example is a prompt-payment discount that is offered to all competing customers. Those that pay within terms receive a better price than those that don't.

The second defense is *cost justification*, where a disparity in price is permitted based on legitimate cost-to-serve differences. Some or all the cost savings can be passed on, but not a penny more.[19] For example, a typical

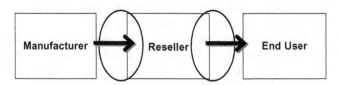

Fig. 3.   Buying versus Selling.

way to justify the lower price for a private label product that is identical to the branded version is where the latter bears substantially more marketing and sales expenses.[20]

The third defense is *functional discounts*, applying when a customer performs added services, such as warehousing, stocking, or delivery, that functionally distinguish it from other customers. So, for example, a price reduction to one reseller over another may be justified as a reasonable reimbursement to the former for the added value that it has provided to the supplier or end user.[21]

A fourth defense is *meeting competition*. Under the law, discrimination is permissible if it is based on a good faith belief that a discriminatory price is necessary to meet that of a competitor or to maintain a price difference. All competing customers do not have to be offered or receive the special price.[22]

The final defense to price discrimination is called *"changing conditions."* Where the supplier has perishable goods, which are about to go out of date or seasonal, obsolete, or distress merchandise, it may lawfully drop the price to clear them, even if, before doing so, the supplier sold to some competitive purchasers at full price.[23]

Promotional Discrimination

In many industries, the trend has been away from things like volume discounts, which focus on how a customer buys, to performance-based incentives that look at how the reseller sells and the value that it delivers. The latter is where promotional discrimination comes in. In some respects, its rules are more flexible than those for price discrimination.

Under Robinson-Patman promotional discrimination standards, discounts, allowances, and services must be functionally available on proportionally equal terms to competing customers, unless a variation is necessary to meet competition.[24] Because proportional equality is required (rather than the arithmetic equality implicit in the rules regarding price discrimination), flexibility for variation by competing customer is permitted.

Indeed, there are three ways to proportionalize benefits — based on (1) purchases, (2) cost, and (3) value.[25] Under the first method, those that buy more receive more promotional goodies (*e.g.*, a rebate of $5 per case purchased in exchange for displaying the product). The second approach, cost to the reseller, allows more to be paid if the cost of performance is higher (*e.g.*, the price of a full-page ad in a national magazine likely is greater than a full page in a local publication). Finally, the law allows pro-portionalization based on the value to the manufacturer, allowing it to place a price tag on particular performance. So, for example, a plumbing fixture manufacturer may determine that end users value seeing its pro-ducts displayed in a showroom, so it provides a two-percent rebate on pur-chases of the covered products to each of its dealers suitably displaying such products. This amount is not based on the dealer's showroom costs, but on the value to the manufacturer to encourage something that in turn is valued by the end user.

By the way, a frequently overlooked mechanism to insure that price concessions or promotional benefits are passed on to end users by resellers is mandatory pass-through, a practice that is subject to the rule of reason and generally lawful.[26]

PRESERVING VALUE

While U.S. law is supportive of recognizing value through economic dis-crimination, it also permits preserving value-based prices by allowing the manufacturer to set resale prices and to engage in price signaling.[27]

Lawfully Setting or Encouraging Resale Prices

If a supplier is selling directly or through an agent to the end user, the sup-plier determines the street price. However, where resellers take title and resell, they set the street price, which is, of course, the same as the resale price. Regardless whether manufacturers are engaged in value pricing, they often wish to control or influence the street price. Historically, this could be done with varying degrees of success by the manufacturer simply adjust-ing the reseller's buy price or selecting resellers carefully and ending rela-tionships with those that don't operate in a manner consistent with the manufacturer's goals. However, the U.S. Supreme Court has made it clear that the manufacturer can go beyond these steps to dictate resale prices, sometimes referred to as "resale price maintenance" or "vertical price fixing."

The first type of resale price in which manufacturers are interested is maximum prices, that is, placing an upper bound on what the reseller may charge. In the value pricing context, putting a ceiling on resale prices can prevent resellers from taking too much margin, and throwing off the manufacturer's value price structure. It also can be used for promotional resale price uniformity in order to permit nationally or regionally promoted prices.

The second type – minimum or exact resale prices – is far more common.[28] Establishing a price floor or exact price can insure sufficient margin for resellers to furnish the things end users or the manufacturer value, such as convenient locations, on-site inventory, and knowledgeable salespeople. Other common uses include protecting brand image, facilitating the introduction of new products, and leveling the playing field to permit different types of resellers to compete.[29] In some cases, building in a margin for resellers allows a manufacturer to enhance its own.

Until 1997, setting any type of resale price by agreement was illegal on its face. Then, the U.S. Supreme Court determined that agreeing on maximum resale prices is subject to the much more manufacturer-friendly rule of reason, the same standard that governs the rather common use of non-price vertical restrictions discussed earlier.[30] Ten years later, the Court extended this more lenient approach to minimum or exact resale price setting, so that, under current federal law, all agreements that establish a resale price are presumed to be lawful until they can be shown on balance to be unreasonably anticompetitive.[31] However, the decision to include minimum price agreements under the rule of reason umbrella was controversial, as various efforts have been made at the federal and state levels to go back to or enforce the previous standard, only some of which have been successful.[32]

However, there is another way to set resale prices that is unaffected by these efforts. Section 1 of the Sherman Act, which is the principal U.S. antitrust statute in this area, requires that a "contract, combination ... or conspiracy" be present for a violation, which means that there must be some sort of agreement.[33] Because of this requirement, the Supreme Court in 1919 ruled that a manufacturer could unilaterally announce a minimum resale price by policy (*i.e.*, without an agreement) and simply refuse to supply any reseller that didn't follow it.[34] Moreover, if a reseller adheres to the price in the policy, there is still no agreement.

After a long dormant period, use of minimum resale price policies blossomed with the rise of discount retailing in 1980s, then spread to B2B products and became even more prevalent for both consumer and business products due to the challenges brought by the growth of Internet sales and the expansion into other new distribution channels.[35] Such policies are used for luxury goods, consumer durables (particularly appliances, electronics, and sporting goods), and various industrial products (like foodservice equipment, premium tools, and test equipment).[36] They can be broad or narrow, covering some or all products or geographic areas. A policy violation can result in the loss of a single product, a product family, or all products. Finally, because a policy is unilateral, a reseller that violates it can be reinstated by the manufacturer anytime, as long as the latter is careful to avoid probation or any form of agreement on compliance.

Apart from using agreements or policies, another way to dictate a resale price is for the manufacturer to jump over the reseller and agree with the end user on the latter's buy price, something that can be referred to as "direct dealing." As long as there is no contractual or other legal impediment, one way to do this is for the manufacturer to make the end user a direct customer.[37] However, when the involvement of intermediaries is necessary for logistical or other reasons, the manufacturer can determine the resale price by offering one or more resellers the opportunity to resell to the end user at the price agreed between the manufacturer and the end user. If the reseller declines, the manufacturer finds someone else to serve the end user, but there otherwise is no penalty. If the reseller accepts, there is no agreement on resale price or, at most, an agreement subject to the rule of reason.[38]

Although not as potent as dictating a resale price, it is possible to encourage one through the use of financial or promotional incentives. Because reseller participation is voluntary, such incentive programs are judged under the rule of reason.[39] One example is a minimum advertised price (MAP) program, where the reseller receives a payment (such as a co-op advertising allowance) in return for adhering to a specified minimum price in the ads or Internet listings for which the allowance is paid.[40] However, if the reseller uses only its own funds, it can advertise at any price it wants, and, regardless whether it takes the manufacturer's money, it can always sell at any price it desires.[41]

Other examples of price encouragement include: (1) group or shared-price advertising – only those resellers that wish to participate are identified in ads that offer a special price; (2) target price rebates – based on point-of-sale (POS) data, resellers receive payments based on how close their actual selling prices are to the target prices; and (3) floating price allowances – resellers are offered a promotional allowance to reduce their shelf, catalog or Internet prices by a specified percentage during a designated promotional period.

Lawful Price Signaling

Another way to preserve value-based prices is to use price signaling to avoid competitive misinterpretation of pricing actions. While this term is rather pejorative, the fact is that every company signals all the time, as each intentional or unintentional act or failure to act sends a message or signal to the market. For example, a company that repeatedly refuses to price below a certain level communicates that it will not take business at any cost. This suggests to competitors that it will not undercut them, something that may lead to more price stability in the market. Similarly, the decision to follow or not to follow the lead of another may be intentional or inadvertent, but it too sends a message to the market.

Even if these steps were aimed at sending a signal, few would find them particularly risky, as the essence of competition is unilaterally deciding to lead, follow, or sit on the sidelines. Indeed, U.S. law supports this point, as it is clear that the practice of independently imitating or following competitors − known as "conscious parallelism" − is entirely lawful.[42]

When information flow is imperfect, customers and competitors plan their own moves through trying to read the market by looking at the signs, signals, tracks, and tea leaves to discern what others intend or are likely to do or why others did what they did. Indeed, price wars have been ignited when one company wrongly interprets another's actions and overreacts to the real situation (Baker, Marn, & Zawada, 2010). For example, an equipment manufacturer may drop all of its U.S. prices on a particular product in reaction to a price reduction by a competitor, unless it understands that the reduction was both limited and temporary in an effort to clear some excess inventory.

A concept that may be referred to as "strategic price management" seeks to formalize and manage the flow of information within a company along both offensive dimensions (outgoing signals) and defensive dimensions (responses to incoming messages) with the goals of consistency and clarity. At the same time, clarity may not be desired for all pricing moves, as a company may wish certain actions or inactions and their rationale to be clear, while others to remain murky.

Signaling is a subset of strategic price management. As such, it is the overt communication or explanation of future, contemporaneous or previous pricing actions (or other things of competitive significance) with an intent that competitors receive such communication. Signaling contrasts with the more subtle forms of communicating with the market − such as merely turning down certain business − and makes it easier for others to figure out what is going on.[43]

Adding price transparency could be one of these more subtle forms or could constitute price signaling. One real-life example of the latter is an elevator manufacturer creating a hypothetical "standard" product in an environment where each product is custom configured, then publishing both a description and a price for it. The standard product was then used as a vehicle to communicate changes in price for the custom products, where pricing is necessarily opaque.[44] In another situation, a seller added transparency to its contract pricing to blunt the fact that powerful buyers were playing the few sellers off each other because each price was separately negotiated and effectively invisible.

Sometimes signaling goes farther. Faced with some recurrent issues, a prominent company in a cyclical industry announced that, unlike its prior practice, the company would not add capacity during the then-current boom period, as such capacity was a drag on its financial performance during slow times. It also communicated a price increase. Within a short time, its two primary competitors independently made similar announcements. The effect was to improve industry pricing.[45]

From a legal point of view, the danger implicit in price signaling is that it may constitute or provide evidence of price fixing among competitors, sometimes referred to as "horizontal price fixing." This form of cartel action is almost always illegal on its face in the United States, and often is prosecuted criminally under the Sherman Act.[46] However, as is the case with vertical price fixing discussed earlier, the Sherman Act requires that an agreement be present in order for there to be a violation.[47] The problem from an enforcement perspective is that explicit price fixing language in a written contract or otherwise between or among competitors is rare.

As a result, the law has established a two-pronged test that allows an illegal agreement to be inferred when there is no smoking gun. The first element is proof of parallel business behavior or conscious parallelism. But, as was noted previously, this element alone is not illegal, as it is the essence of competition. So, conscious parallelism must be coupled with the second element — the presence of one or more "plus factors" that subject the circumstances under scrutiny to a smell test.

One of these factors is whether the parallel behavior is unlikely to have occurred absent an agreement, while a variant of this concept is whether the behavior is against individual self interest, but is consistent with a conspiracy.[48] Another plus factor is evidence of meetings or other direct communications among competitors, particularly if pricing was discussed by persons in a position to make pricing decisions. Incriminating statements made in documents, e-mail, or otherwise can also be a plus factor, as can a history of horizontal price fixing.

If both conscious parallelism and plus factors are present, there is a presumption of conspiracy that can be rebutted by various considerations.[49] For example, an oligopolistic industry or other market structure where pricing is interdependent can explain parallel behavior that may be suspect.[50] Other plausible, benign explanations for the conduct being examined also can undercut conspiracy arguments.[51]

In the leading case on price signaling, DuPont and other chemical manufacturers announced price increases well in advance of the notice periods in their supply agreements with industrial end users. The FTC determined that this practice was unlawful, as it facilitated price parallelism, but the appellate court disagreed, stating that consciously parallel pricing is not illegal unless it is collusive, predatory, coercive, or exclusionary – none of which was present.[52] Moreover, the court noted that, while signaling raises the possibility of collusion, it can have legitimate business purposes too, such as aiding buyers in planning for the future.[53]

If the following elements are in place, it is generally irrelevant that competitors receive the information conveyed and unilaterally act on it:

(1) *A legitimate interest to communicate with stakeholders.* The communication from the company should be relevant to its stakeholders, which may include actual and potential end users (regardless whether sold directly), resellers or other intermediaries, employees, investors, and investment analysts. In general, pricing-related matters meet this test due to the obvious effect on purchasing decisions and the supplier's earnings. Indeed, the fact that public companies are required to publicly disclose relevant information in timely fashion is helpful (*See* Steuer, Roberti, & Simala, 2011).

(2) *Communication directed at stakeholders.* The announcement or other communication should be directed at the stakeholders with an interest in it, rather than at competitors. It is preferable to do so out in the open, both to be up front about what is being conveyed and to make it easier for competitors to get the message.[54] Appropriate means to reach stakeholders include press releases, letters, or other written or electronic communications, postings on the company's website, speeches, presentations, public filings, and articles or interviews in the general or specialized press.

(3) *An appropriate message.* The signaling company should focus its comments on what it will do or has done, rather than referring to competitors or inviting them to follow.[55] While industry context may be relevant, it is the actions or inactions of the company that directly mesh with the interests of the stakeholders.

Without evidence of agreement, the signaling of pricing behavior, even if acted upon by competitors, is lawful. The key is focus on directing an appropriate message to stakeholders with a bona fide interest in it, while avoiding the plus factors (like direct communications with competitors on price) that tend to support the presence of a conspiracy. As long as competitors unilaterally act on such message, signaling is a lawful means to help preserve value pricing.

CONCLUSION

For some time, U.S. law has been increasingly more flexible regarding pricing matters. As part of this trend, tools like economic discrimination, non-price vertical restrictions, resale price setting, and price signaling help suppliers and resellers both achieve and maintain value pricing by (1) recognizing the value of products and services from the end user's perspective, (2) establishing prices that vary with perceived value, and (3) taking steps to preserve value-based prices. While the law is not black and white in the area of pricing (or in many others for that matter), there is considerable room to meet the challenges of enlightened pricing strategies.

A FEW WORDS ABOUT DAN NIMER

Because it is impossible, there is no point in trying to use only a few words to describe a pricing visionary like Dan Nimer, who has given so much to the field, especially in the area of value pricing. It has been a pleasure to call Dan a friend and to share and debate his endless ideas over many lunches and in other discussions. It is also a pleasure to be associated with the many pricing superstars who are honoring Dan with their contributions to this volume.[56] Dan, this one is for you.

NOTES

1. For convenience, this chapter is written primarily from the perspective of the service supplier or the manufacturer, but much of it is relevant to resellers that wish to engage in value pricing or wish to encourage manufacturers to do so. In addition, this chapter focuses on the parameters under the antitrust laws of the United States at the federal level. State law tends to be essentially the same, with some exceptions (*See, e.g.,* notes 9 and 32 *infra*). The laws of other countries vary, with those of Canada perhaps the closest to those in the United States. While competition law in the European Union has evolved to embrace certain standards

conceptually similar to those of the United States, it remains different in key respects, such as regarding resale price setting (*See, e.g.,* Determann & Batchelor, 2010).

2. Both the buy price and the street price are net prices, that is, after all discounts, allowances, rebates, free goods, credits, and the like. For consumer products and services, the street price is the retail price, but the term "street price" will be used throughout this chapter.

3. Of course, it is possible for a manufacturer to sell directly or through agents to some end users, while simultaneously using either agents or resellers or both to reach others. Alternatively or in addition, the manufacturer may use multiple layers of intermediaries before some or all end users are reached. This chapter assumes that there is either a direct manufacturer/end user relationship or a path that only uses one reselling intermediary between the manufacturer and the end user. However, the approach described here also can be applied to different or more complex sales paths.

4. Among other things, the supplier's employees and agents for legal purposes are considered to be part or an extension of the supplier. So, sales made by such employees and agents are deemed to be made by the supplier.

5. This example is based on a real-life situation. Note that this analysis could be done for different products, particular markets, competitive suppliers, the industry as a whole, or any combination. In many industries, manufacturers negotiate prices directly with end users or end user buying groups, effectively selling directly, even if one or more resellers handle the logistics (*See* note 38 *infra*).

6. In the event an intermediary (such as a wholesaler) sells to another reseller (like a retailer), the value is further divided.

7. If there is too much margin, the reseller frequently lowers the street price, something that puts the value-based price at risk. This behavior occurs because, once resellers are making a profit acceptable to them, they typically wish to gain ground on competitive resellers. At the same time, if the reseller does not have sufficient margin, it will cut back on what it provides (such as depth and breath of inventory and support), which may be the very things that the manufacturer wishes the reseller to offer in order to differentiate the manufacturer's products and provide the value the end user expects (*See* Henderson, 2011). For a description of this approach, see http://www.franklynn.com/resources/?t=2540&st=3875&sst=452.

8. 15 U.S.C. § 13. Section 2(a) deals with price discrimination, while Sections 2 (d) and 2(e) address promotional discrimination. *Id.* §§ 13(a), (d)-(e). In 1936, the Robinson-Patman Act amended the antidiscrimination provisions of the Clayton Act, and this area of the law has come to be referred to by the name of the amendment. "Fair and equitable" does not appear in the statute or, to the knowledge of the author, in any case. It seems to have evolved as shorthand for the obligations under law, but vastly overstates them. For a more detailed discussion of the operation of the Robinson-Patman Act, see Holmes and Mangiaracina (2011) and Zelek (2010). Although often overlooked, the Robinson-Patman Act also applies to sales by resellers made in interstate commerce.

9. *Metro Communications Co. v. Ameritech Mobile Communications, Inc.*, 984 F.2d 739, 745 (6th Cir. 1993). Actually, the term used in the statute is "commodities." 15 U.S.C. § 13(a). However, it should be noted that various states have

enacted antidiscrimination laws that apply to services, although they are rarely enforced (*See, e.g.,* Cal. Bus. & Prof. Code § 17045).

10. *Volvo Trucks N. Am. v. Reeder-Simco GMC, Inc.,* 546 U.S. 164, 169 (2006) (to support Robinson-Patman claim, plaintiff had to prove that the allegedly favored and disfavored customers were both businesses "contemporaneously competing to resell to the same retail customer"). For further discussion of the B2B nature of Robinson-Patman (*See* note 17 *infra*).

11. When there is a mixed offering, such as an industrial process control computer bundled with a software maintenance agreement, Robinson-Patman applies only if the "dominant nature" of the overall transaction is the sale of goods, that is, the value of the good is greater than that of the service (*See Metro Communications,* 984 F.2d at 745).

12. *Eastern Auto Distributors, Inc. v. Peugeot Motors of Am., Inc.,* 795 F.2d 329, 335 (4th Cir. 1986).

13. *Volvo Trucks,* 546 U.S. at 178-79. When a manufacturer sells to resellers, two or more of the latter compete if they pursue the same consumer or business end user. Where sales are made by a manufacturer directly to business end users, the question becomes whether the end users compete. For example, in the industrial context, end users often use or consume the product sold to them in the manufacturing process (such as cutting tools or work gloves) or they (sometimes referred to as "OEMs" or "original equipment manufacturers") incorporate the product into their own, so that the purchased good loses its separate identity. As an example of the latter, if a fastener manufacturer sells the same bolt assembly directly to Ford and Toyota for use in full-size pick-up trucks sold in the United States, such bolt assembly sales are to competitive customers and economic discrimination standards apply.

14. See *Continental T.V., Inc. v. GTE Sylvania Inc.,* 433 U.S. 36, 51-52 (1977). Non-price vertical restrictions are governed by a manufacturer-favorable standard known as the "rule of reason," where they are presumed to be lawful, unless they can be shown on balance to be unreasonably anticompetitive. Moreover, the Supreme Court has stated that the primary concern of the antitrust laws is *interbrand competition* (one manufacturer's brand versus that of another), so *intrabrand competition* (that occurring between two resellers of the same brand) can be restricted if interbrand competition is fostered (*See id.* at 52 n.19).

15. While common in B2B markets and consumer durables, non-price vertical restrictions generally are not used for consumer packaged goods, particularly where manufacturers seek intensive, rather than selective, distribution. In contrast, suppliers of luxury packaged goods often prefer selective distribution, making non-price vertical restrictions attractive.

16. As a result, manufacturers selling directly to business end users are subject to the rules regarding price discrimination, while those selling to resellers have to comply with price discrimination and promotional discrimination standards.

17. More specifically, the presence of each of five elements is required for a violation: (1) discrimination (*i.e.,* charging different prices to different customers), (2) on reasonably contemporaneous sales to two or more purchasers, (3) of goods, (4) of like grade and quality, (5) where there is a reasonable probability of competitive injury. 15 U.S.C. § 13 (a)-(b). The courts have interpreted the fifth element,

among other things, to require that only competing customers be treated alike. *Infusion Res., Inc. v. Minimid, Inc.*, 351 F.3d 688, 692 (5th Cir. 2003), *cert. denied*, 542 U.S. 920 (2004) (plaintiff must prove that "as the disfavored purchaser, it was engaged in actual competition with the favored purchaser as of the time of the price differential"). This standard applies to "secondary line" discrimination – the most frequently litigated type – where a disfavored reseller may pursue the manufacturer for the discrimination against it.

The law also recognizes "primary line" discrimination, which permits a manufacturer to sue a discriminating competitive manufacturer, but only if a rather high threshold is met: (1) the discriminatory price must be below the offending manufacturer's cost and (2) the market structure must be such that the offending manufacturer's losses can be recouped later. *Brooke Group v. Brown & Williamson Tobacco Corp.*, 509 U.S. 209, 222-24 (1993). "Tertiary line" discrimination cases, although rare, have been brought, where competitive customers of the favored and disfavored purchasers pursue the manufacturer. See *Texaco Inc. v. Hasbrouck*, 496 U.S. 543, 565-66 (1990).

The common denominator is the requirement of competition. It is because of this element that Robinson–Patman is a B2B statute, since consumers do not compete against each other. See *generally Feeney v. Chamberlin Mfg. Corp.*, 831 F.2d 93, 96 (5th Cir. 1987) (commissioned salesperson was not a competitor, so standing to sue for price discrimination was lacking).

18. *Shreve Equip., Inc. v. Clay Equip. Corp.*, 650 F.2d 101, 105-06 (6th Cir.), *cert. denied*, 454 U.S. 897 (1981).

19. *Empire Rayon Yarn Co. v. Am. Viscose Corp.*, 160 F. Supp. 334, 337 (S.D.N.Y. 1958).

20. However, an end user preference for a branded product over a physically identical private label offering does not itself justify a price difference. *FTC v. Borden Co.*, 383 U.S. 637, 639-41 (1966) (branded and private label evaporated milk).

21. See *Texaco*, 496 U.S. at 562. Unlike the precision required for an allowance dependant on the cost justification defense, a functional discount need only bear a reasonable relationship to the services provided. *See id.* at 561.

22. *Falls City Indus. v. Vanco Beverage, Inc.*, 460 U.S. 428, 445 (1983).

23. See, for example, *Comcoa Inc. v. NEC Tel., Inc.*, 931 F.2d 655, 659 (10th Cir. 1991) (obsolete products); *A.A. Poultry Farms v. Rose Acre Farms*, 683 F. Supp. 680, 691 (S.D. Ind. 1988), *aff'd on other grounds*, 881 F.2d 1396 (7th Cir. 1989) (fresh eggs).

24. *Comcoa*, 931 F.2d at 664-65. Promotional services include things like the provision of product demonstrations for the benefit of a reseller's customers.

25. The first two proportionalization methods are discussed in the *Guides for Advertising Allowances and Other Merchandising Payments and Services*, 16 C.F.R. § 240, a helpful, but nonbinding, discussion from the perspective of the Federal Trade Commission (FTC). *Id.* § 240.9. Support for the third is found in *Colonial Stores Inc. v. FTC*, 450 F.2d 733, 743-44 (5th Cir. 1971) and *In re Lever Bros. Co.*, 50 F.T.C. 494, 512 (1953). See *also FTC v. Simplicity Pattern Co.*, 360 U.S. 55, 61 n.4 (1959) (acknowledging *Lever Bros.* without specifically embracing or questioning it). In the last revision of the FTC Guides more than 20 years ago, the agency considered including value as a valid means of proportionalization, but stopped

short due to what it said was the possibility of abuse and the role of the Guides to encourage compliance. 53 Fed. Reg. 43,233 (October 26, 1988). Today, value is widely used to proportionalize.

26. See, e.g., *Acquaire v. Canada Dry Bottling Co.,* 24 F.3d 401, 410 (2d Cir. 1994); *Jack Walters & Sons Corp. v. Morton Building, Inc.,* 737 F.2d 698, 708 (7th Cir.), *cert. denied,* 469 U.S. 1018 (1984); *Lewis Service Center, Inc. v. Mack Trucks, Inc.,* 714 F.2d 842, 846 (8th Cir. 1983), *cert. denied,* 467 U.S. 1226 (1984); *AAA Liquors, Inc. v. Joseph E. Seagram & Sons, Inc.,* 705 F.2d 1203, 1206 (10th Cir. 1982), *cert. denied,* 461 U.S. 919 (1983).

27. As noted earlier, non-price vertical restrictions also may be useful in preserving value-based segmentation by controlling competitive overlap (*See* text accompanying notes 14-15 *supra*).

28. Relevant cases usually discuss minimum prices, but exact prices are analytically the same.

29. In many industries, there is considerable channel conflict between resellers with low costs (such as big-box retailers or those selling only over the Internet) and those with significantly higher costs (like traditional brick-and-mortar resellers). A manufacturer may wish to retain the higher-cost resellers to avoid becoming overly dependant on some resellers, serve market segments otherwise missed, or make sure valued services are provided. Setting a minimum resale price can help maintain the viability of such resellers.

30. *State Oil Co. v. Khan,* 522 U.S. 3, 17-18 (1997). The rule of reason is addressed in note 14 *supra*, and non-price vertical restrictions are discussed in the text accompanying that footnote and the following one.

31. *Leegin Creative Leather Prods., Inc. v. PSKS,* 551 U.S. 877, 886-87 (2007). Canada, through legislation, adopted a similar rule for resale price programs in 2009, repealing its criminal prohibitions on setting or influencing resale prices. Competition Act, R.S.C., ch. C 34 (1985), § 76.

32. Bills have been introduced in the last several sessions of Congress to overturn the *Leegin* decision, but none has passed. See S. 75, 112th Con. (2011); S.148, 111th Con. (2009); H.R. 3190, 111th Con. (2009); S. 2261, 110th Con. (2007). In 2009, Maryland enacted its own statute to make setting minimum prices by agreement illegal. Md. Commercial Law Code Ann. § 11-204(b) (2009). However, due to constitutional issues, this law likely applies only to sales wholly within that state's borders (*See* Blad & Killian, 2010). Other jurisdictions have claimed that their respective laws do not allow minimum resale price agreements. For example, California obtained a consent order from a cosmetics supplier to stop the latter's resale price efforts, but that state's view has yet to be tested in the courts post-*Leegin* (*See California v. Bioelements, Inc.,* Cal. Super. Ct., Riverside Cty., No. 10011659 (January 11, 2011)). New York brought a case against mattress supplier Tempur-Pedic that alleged illegal price setting under that state's law, but lost when the court determined that the statute upon which the state relied makes minimum resale price agreements unenforceable, but not unlawful. *People v. Tempur-Pedic Inter., Inc.,* 916 N.Y.S.2d 900, 909 (N.Y. 2011), *appeal filed* (N.Y. Sup. Ct. App. Div. Feb. 22, 2011). *Accord Worldhomecenter.com, Inc. v. Franke Consumer Prods., Inc.,* No. 10 Civ. 3205 (BSJ), 2011 U.S. Dist. LEXIS 67798, at **13-16 (S.D.N.Y. June 22, 2011) (under state law in New York, contracts that set resale prices are

unenforceable and the *Leegin* rule of reason standard applies to determine legality). See also *Worldhomecenter.com, Inc. v. KWC Am., Inc.*, No. 10 Civ. 7781, 2011 U.S. Dist. LEXIS, at *10 (S.D.N.Y. September 15, 2011).

33. See 15 U.S.C. § 1.

34. *United States v. Colgate & Co.*, 250 U.S. 300, 307 (1919). For a comprehensive discussion of the use of minimum resale price policies, see Henry and Zelek (2003) (written before *Leegin*, but still a useful guide).

35. Two Supreme Court cases in the 1980s helped by providing support for the use of minimum resale price policies. *Business Electronics Corp. v. Sharp Electronics Corp.*, 485 U.S. 717 (1988); *Monsanto Co. v. Spray-Rite Service Corp.*, 465 U.S. 752 (1984). Adding new channels increases the risk of channel conflict and corrosive price competition, particularly if the new channels have different cost structures than the incumbent ones.

36. Although the movement of consumer food products into mass merchandisers like Wal-Mart and Target set the stage for conflict with traditional grocery chains and others, as is the case with vertical non-price restrictions, minimum resale price setting typically is not employed for consumer packaged goods (including food), except in the luxury segment.

37. A manufacturer allocating an end user to itself is a customer restraint subject to the rule of reason as a non-price vertical restriction, a result that doesn't change even if the manufacturer, by taking an account directly, competes with the reseller, something called "dual distribution." *See Smalley & Co. v. Emerson & Cuming, Inc.*, 13 F.3d 366, 368 (10th Cir. 1993). At the same time, some state statutes may get in the way of selling directly. For example, as a legacy of Prohibition, producers in the alcoholic beverage industry generally cannot sell to retailers or consumers and must sell to wholesalers, which, in turn, sell to retailers. *See, e.g.*, Liquor Control Act of 1934, 235 ILCS 5/5-1, 5/6-4 (Illinois). In addition, some reseller protection laws of general or industry-specific applicability may inhibit a manufacturer from taking away a reseller's customer and going direct. *See, e.g.*, Wisconsin Fair Dealership Law, Wisc. Stat. § 135.03-.04 (prohibition in general applicability statute on substantially changing the reseller's "competitive circumstances" without good cause and an opportunity for cure).

38. *Metro Ford Truck Sales, Inc. v. Ford Motor Co.*, 145 F.3d 320, 325 (5th Cir. 1998), *cert. denied*, 525 U.S. 1068 (1999) (special wholesale discount program was unilateral action); *Wisconsin Music Network, Inc. v. Muzak Ltd. P'ship.*, 5 F.3d 218, 222 (7th Cir. 1993) (national account program subject to rule of reason); *Ohio-Sealy Mattress Mfg. Co. v. Sealy, Inc.*, 585 F.2d 821, 836-38 (7th Cir. 1978), *cert. denied*, 440 U.S. 930 (1979) (rule of reason treatment for national account program). Direct dealing is common in some industries (particularly when large end users or end user buying groups are involved) and generally takes one of two forms: (1) a manufacturer and an end user or buying group agree on the buy price, while the price for handling and delivery is separately negotiated between the reseller and the end user or buying group or (2) a delivered (or installed) price is agreed upon between a manufacturer and an end user or buying group.

39. See, e.g., *Lake Hill Motors, Inc. v. Jim Bennett Yacht Sales, Inc.*, 246 F.3d 752, 757 (5th Cir. 2001) (rule of reason treatment under the Sherman Act); 6 Trade Rep. Rep. (CCH) ¶ 39,057 at 41,728 (FTC May 21, 1987) (FTC announcement

that advertising price restrictions in promotional programs are subject to the rule of reason). While the FTC has no authority under the Sherman Act, application of the Federal Trade Commission Act, 15 U.S.C. § 45, to resale pricing uses the same Sherman Act analysis. *In re Russell Stover Candies, Inc.*, 100 F.T.C. 1, 1982 WL 608313, at *27 (FTC. Jul. 1, 1982), *rev'd on other grounds, Russell Stover Candies, Inc. v. FTC*, 718 F.2d 256 (8th Cir. 1983). The *Leegin* decision implicitly endorses the rule of reason for agreements that encourage resale price behavior, because, if it is lawful to *set* resale prices by agreement (unless such an agreement is unreasonably anticompetitive), the same must be true of the less restrictive *encouragement* of them by agreement. Alternatively, prices may be encouraged by unilateral policy, thereby avoiding the rule of reason and the risk, however modest, that goes with it. Keep in mind that the provision of financial or promotional incentives subjects such programs or policies to the requirements of the Robinson-Patman Act.

40. Somewhat confusing is the fact that sometimes any program dealing with resale pricing – including a policy that sets resale prices, rather than just advertised prices – is erroneously referred to as a "MAP program" (*See e.g.,* Pereira, 2008).

41. To further complicate matters, some companies (like certain foodservice equipment manufacturers) make the penalty for a MAP violation the loss of the offending reseller's ability buy the affected product in the future, a result more typical of a resale price policy. This approach likely evolved because the amount of co-op advertising or similar allowances at risk simply is not large enough to dissuade advertised price behavior that the manufacturer finds undesirable.

42. See, e.g., *Blomkest Fertilizer, Inc. v. Potash Corp. of Sask., Inc.*, 203 F.3d 1028, 1032-1033 (8th Cir.) (en banc), *cert. denied sub nom., Hahnaman Albrecht, Inc. v. Potash Corp. of Sask., Inc.*, 531 U.S. 815 (2000) ("Evidence that a business consciously met the pricing of its competitors does not prove a violation of the antitrust laws."); *In re Citric Acid Litig.*, 191 F.3d 1090, 1102 (9th Cir. 1999) ("A section 1 violation cannot...be inferred from parallel pricing alone,...nor from an industry's follow-the-leader pricing strategy."); *Wallace v. Bank of Bartlett*, 55 F.3d 1166 (6th Cir. 1995) ("Parallel pricing, without more, does not itself establish a violation of the Sherman Act.").

43. Influencing industry pricing in this fashion is part of one of the three levels of price management (*See* Marn, Roegner, & Zawada, 2004). The other two are at the transaction and the product/market strategy levels. *Id.* at 13-73.

44. *Id.* at 81.

45. The author worked with the signaling company in this example and in the previous one to structure and implement the approach used. There were no adverse legal consequences.

46. Since 2004, criminal violation of the Sherman Act is a felony punishable by: (1) a $100 million fine if the perpetrator is a corporation or other entity and (2) a $1 million fine or 10 years in prison or both if the violator is an individual. 15 U.S.C. § 1. Under the Comprehensive Crime Control Act and the Criminal Fine Improvements Acts, 18 U.S.C. §§ 3571-3572, the fine may be increased to twice the gain from the illegal conduct or twice the loss to the victims, while the Federal Sentencing Guidelines can also impact the penalties imposed (*See* United States Sentencing Commission, 2010 Sentencing Guidelines).

47. *See* text accompanying note 33 *supra*.

48. *See, e.g., American Tobacco Co. v. United States,* 328 U.S. 781, 805 (1946) (price increases despite surpluses that should have resulted in lower prices); *Interstate Circuit, Inc. v. United States,* 306 U.S. 208, 222 (1939) (price increases, although individual self interest to cut prices). The plus factors must tend to exclude the possibility of independent conduct. *In re Baby Food Antitrust Litig.,* 166 F.3d 112, 133 (3d Cir. 1999), *citing Monsanto Co. v. Spray-Rite Service Corp.,* 465 U.S. 752, 764 (1984).

49. *Todorov v. DCH Healthcare Authority,* 921 F.2d 1438, 1456 n.30 (11th Cir. 1991).

50. See *Baby Food,* 166 F.3d at 116, 121-22 (interdependent pricing of oligopoly defendants accounting for 98 percent of industry sales); *Reserve Supply Corp. v. Owens-Corning Fiberglas Corp.,* 971 F.2d 37, 39, 50-51 (7th Cir. 1992) (interdependent pricing in oligopolistic industry with defendants and third manufacturer collectively holding 85-90 percent market share). Ironically, it is in oligopolistic markets where price signaling can be the most effective.

51. See, e.g., *Baby Food,* 166 F.3d at 121-38 (failure to produce evidence of other than independent action in spite of some parallel behavior and low-level sharing of some information among salespeople). While the validity of the purported reasons for engaging in the behavior in question is a consideration, even a pretext for doing so does not alone establish a conspiracy. *See also Blomkest,* 203 F.2d at 1034 (mere opportunity to conspire not necessarily probative of price fixing).

52. *E. I. Du Pont de Nemours & Co. v. FTC,* 729 F.2d 128, 139-40 (2d Cir. 1984).

53. *Id.* at 134. See *Reserve Supply,* 971 F.2d at 54 (advance notice of price increases). See also *Catalano, Inc. v. Target Sales,* 446 U.S. 643, 647 (1980) (according to dictum in the per curiam opinion, "advance price announcements are perfectly lawful").

54. A good example of what not to do was a closed data collection and dissemination company jointly owned by eight airlines with a non-public computerized system that was used by each participant to communicate to the others fare changes and promotions in advance and permitted later modification or withdrawal of such announcements. Apparently taking the position that the airlines were effectively sitting in the same room and discussing prices, the Justice Department attacked this practice as horizontal price fixing. The defendants accepted consent decrees that ended it. *United States v. Airline Tariff Publishing Co.,* 1994-2 Trade Cas. (CCH) ¶ 70,686 (D.D.C. 1994) (all defendants, except United Air Lines, Inc. and USAir, Inc.); 836 F. Supp. 9 (D.C.C. 1993) (United and USAir).

55. Even when no agreement is reached on price, the FTC has obtained consent orders from signaling companies where they invite one or more competitors to follow or state that their pricing action is contingent on competitors playing ball. *In re U-Haul Int'l., Inc.,* 5 Trade Reg. Rep. (CCH) ¶ 16,461 (FTC July 20, 2010); *In re Valassis Communications, Inc.,* [2006-09 Transfer Binder] Trade Reg. Rep. (CCH) ¶ 15,860 (FTC April 28, 2006). Note that consent orders apply only to the accused parties that agree to them and do not otherwise carry the force of law. The FTC has attempted for some time to attack certain conduct where there is no conspiracy or agreement as "invitations to collude" or behavior that facilitates collusion (sometimes called "facilitating practices"). Although the agency has managed

to obtain these and other consent orders against unilateral behavior, this theory has never been endorsed by any court (*See* Alexis, 2009).

56. Special thanks to Jerry Smith, who readily agreed to edit this volume and, therefore, likes herding cats.

REFERENCES

Alexis, G. M. (2009). *Invitations to collude are the federal trade commission's new weapon to police unilateral activity.* 14 Antitrust 68 (Spring).

Baker, W. L., Marn, M. V., & Zawada, C. C. (2010). *The price advantage* (2nd ed., pp. 136–141). USA: Wiley.

Blad, L., & Killian, B. (2010, January). A civil conflict: Can the states overturn Leegin? *The CPI Antitrust Journal, 2*, 3–6.

Determann, L., & Batchelor, B. (2010, October 10). *Revised competition rules for online and offline distribution in European Union.* 99 Antitrust & Trade Reg. Rep. (BNA) 478, No. 2471.

Henderson, J. B. (2011, December 8). *Pricing strategy: How to design and implement effective channel pricing.* Frank Lynn & Associates, Inc. Workshop, Itasca, IL.

Henry, B. R., & Zelek, E. F., Jr. (2003). *Establishing and maintaining an effective minimum resale price policy: A Colgate how-to.* 17 Antitrust 8 (Summer).

Holmes, W. C., & Mangiaracina, M. H. (2011). *Antitrust law handbook* (11th ed., pp. 543–625). USA: Clark Boardman Callaghan.

Marn, M. V., Roegner, E. V., & Zawada, C. C. (2004). *The price advantage* (pp. 80–89). USA: Wiley.

Pereira, J. (2008). Group hits manufacturers' minimum pricing. *Wall Street Journal*, December 4.

Steuer, R. M., Roberti, J., & Simala, J. A. (2011, May 20). *Perils in disclosures: Making disclosures and reacting to competitors' disclosures.* 100 Antitrust & Trade Reg. Rep. (BNA) 566, No. 2500.

Zelek, E. F., Jr. (2010). The legal framework for pricing. In T. T. Nagle, J. E. Hogan, & J. Zale (Eds.), *The strategy and tactics of pricing* (5th ed., pp. 315–320).

UNDERSTANDING VALUE – BEYOND MERE METRICS

E. M. (Mick) Kolassa

ABSTRACT

The price of a product or service must reflect and capture the value delivered, but the bulk of attention paid to the area of value determination is to methods of calculating value. This approach ignores the less tangible but equally or more important aspects of value that often drive decision-making, aspects that don't lend themselves easily to the metrics many believe are essential to solving the pricing puzzle. Pricers, to be effective, must understand how to identify these nonmetric aspects of value and incorporate them into their pricing decisions. This chapter provides a foundation for determining the sources of value of a product or service, tools and models that can be used to determine and understand value, and commentary on ways to capture this value through pricing.

In recent decades, the fields of economics and marketing have become much less conceptual (or philosophical) and more technical in terms of both their study and their practice. Yadav (2010) recently noted and lamented this shift, while others warned of it before my birth. Although

Visionary Pricing: Reflections and Advances in Honor of Dan Nimer
Advances in Business Marketing & Purchasing, Volume 19, 195–212
Copyright © 2012 by Emerald Group Publishing Limited
All rights of reproduction in any form reserved
ISSN: 1069-0964/doi:10.1108/S1069-0964(2012)0000019015

quantitative models and mathematical manipulations do provide for a greater understanding of many phenomena and in many cases an unequalled method for performing what-if analysis, much can be lost when scholarship is reduced to quantitative methods and rules. As noted by Vannevar Bush in 1945:

> If scientific reasoning were limited to the logical processes of arithmetic, we should not get very far in our understanding of the physical world. One might as well attempt to grasp the game of poker entirely by the use of the mathematics of probability.

In my experience of over 30 years in the field, pricing, which is a child of both marketing and economics, has succumbed to the same forces as its parents, with many scholars and practitioners seeking solutions rather than understanding, metrics rather than concepts. As thought (if not practice) in the field has moved from cost-based or competition-based methods to value-based pricing, scholars and practitioners alike have sought ways to quantify the considerations and solve for a price, to calculate rather than deduce the appropriate price to charge. In doing so, they have missed many opportunities and made many pricing mistakes.

The idea of value-based pricing has been discussed and defined for years. Many have worked to codify the process of value-based pricing, and I believe that Nagle and Holden (2002) did this most succinctly and comprehensively with their guidance that the pricer must follow the process of comprehending the value that buyers seek, creating that value with the product, communicating that value to the buyer, convincing the buyer that the value is delivered, and then capturing some portion of that value with price. This is a very firm foundation for value-based pricing, and I do not intend to challenge or change it. I do believe, however, that our understanding or interpretation of value has been too narrow and is based on attitudes that are confined by economic orthodoxy.

In discussing value, I first wish to assert that value is not a simple monetization of the benefits of a product, but, in fact, encompasses much more. Value cannot be reflected totally in dollars and cents, despite what many may prefer or even claim. Attempts to calculate value solely in monetary terms ignore important aspects of human behavior, as well as the various ways price influences purchases, regardless of value. Many aspects of value defy monetization: no useful metric exists that can be applied directly to the happiness or emotional fulfillment that a buyer receives from certain purchases. This statement applies equally to consumer purchases as well as many B2B situations. Rather than attempting to measure precisely the value of a product or service and then set a price based on that information, we must first seek to identify and understand the sources and importance of the many facets of value, without economic blinders, and understand how that will enhance or support pricing decisions.

THE ROOT OF THE PROBLEM

Because prices play a central role in the field of economics (they are used to explain multiple economic phenomena and often serve as surrogate measures of both utility and value), many have come to rely on economic theory in price determination. But as economics has become more a quantitative endeavor and less a philosophical one, too many expect numeric solutions to pricing issues regardless of the more significant and meaningful market information that should inform pricing decisions. As Robert Heilbroner, Nobel Laureate in economics notes: "Mathematics has given economics rigor, but alas, also mortis." The economist or pricer who believes that value can be understood through mere mathematical calculation and the manipulation of sets of numbers misses the subtlety of value, and its many forms, by foregoing the rigor of investigation and relying on the mortis of metrics.

Many appear to conflate the concept of value with the economic concept of utility, which has been broadly defined as a measure of relative satisfaction with or from a purchase. This confusion is easy to understand because utility, as viewed from the classical economic perspective, has been measured indirectly in terms of a customer's willingness to pay (WTP) for nearly a century (Marshall, 1920), but many also use WTP as a revealed measure of worth or value (see Herriges, Kling & Azevedo, 1999). WTP has also been referred to as a fundamental economic concept of value. Thus, we have the classical economic and current marketing research connection that utility is found in the price, as reflected by a customer's WTP, which, by that thinking, makes utility (measured by WTP) an accurate measure of value.

WTP is often cited, even relied on, as a means of determining the price of a product or service. A customer's WTP is essentially the measure that is sought through choice modeling (including, e.g., conjoint analysis) and many other pricing research techniques. Because the WTP is believed to be a measure of what a customer is willing to give up in exchange for acquiring or using a good or service, many would accept that as a true measure of value. To bypass the circular argument that value, WTP, and utility are essentially the same, let me make this assertion: attempts to use WTP as a true representation of value are doomed to result in poor pricing. An individual's WTP is contingent on many factors that are unrelated to the actual value of a good. Willingness-to-pay is moderated by a potential buyer's:

- Source, amount, and accuracy of information about the product;
- Ability to understand adequately the benefits of some aspects of the good;
- Level of awareness of alternatives, their differences and prices;
- Lack of candor in revealing a true WTP;
- Lack of a context or appropriate price reference;
- Motivations for purchasing or not purchasing a product;
- Specific situation at the time the questions are posed;
- Lack of requirement to actually make a purchase.

Thus, WTP is at best a measure of a customer's perception of value, which has been moderated or distorted by the above factors. These moderating factors render any basic measure of WTP grossly inadequate and inaccurate if one is seeking to set a profitable price. Absent these moderators, we are still left with the issues that respondents are likely to either understate their WTP (knowingly or unknowingly) (see either Morrison, 1996 or Knetsch, 1989) or as Park and MacLachlan (2008) found overstate their WTP. To round out the problem, Lunander (1998) demonstrated that the amount of measured WTP depends on the ways in which the questions are presented. Such measures may not even be good reflections of perceived value. The argument is not that research and other market measurement should not be performed to inform pricing decisions, but that the results of any such investigation should never be accepted without caveats or accepted as true or precise measures of value or the optimal price. Believing that potential buyers can in some way reveal their actual WTP is, in essence, accepting an unspoken premise that customers are rational and have enough information about and understanding of a product at the time the research is conducted to make a reasoned assessment of its value *and* that they can and will provide truthful and accurate assessments of the price they would be willing to pay.

Many marketing theories, as well as most marketing research techniques and models, are based on the assumption that buyer preferences are fixed and marketers must respond to the predetermined structure of the market to be successful. Carpenter and Nakamoto (1989) argue that too often economic and marketing concepts are based on an assumption that consumer preferences are "fixed and exogenous — not the outcome of competition but the determinant of it." In broad terms, Carpenter and Nakamoto contend that many market models (and thus, much marketing research) ignore the idea that marketing activities change markets — that promotion and communications of value that help the customer to better understand how a product may be valuable are unnecessary and will not change behavior. This observation, which is argued quite persuasively, implies that contemporary marketing thought runs counter to one of the earliest assertions on price setting, laid out by Edwards in 1952, that, "It cannot be too strongly emphasized that the deciding factor in price fixing is the price which the consumer is willing, or can be induced, to pay." This 60-year-old statement demonstrates that our forbearers knew what we seem to have forgotten: WTP is not a static figure but is contingent on information (or inducement) and thus the value that may be reflected through WTP is subjective and can be altered. This situation renders the objective measurement of WTP potentially harmful in that overreliance on such measures can only lead to suboptimal pricing decisions.

Value, rather than being a singular measure or concept, is, in fact, multidimensional and dynamic. Simple unidimensional measurements or portrayals of value may be appealing to both pricing practitioners and theoretical economists, but they can hide the actual reasons for purchase behavior and heighten the risk of bad pricing. The problem is that value, like price, should be deduced, and not calculated. Instead of simply asking customers how much one should charge in a WTP study, the pricer must understand and convey the context and an appropriate frame of reference for a customer to be able to respond in any useful way. Several years ago Johnson and Johnson (J&J) launched a product called *Procrit*, which stimulated the production of red blood cells. Although the product has several uses, the one in which J&J was particularly interest was the treatment of the anemia, and the fatigue it causes, that is commonly cause by the administration of chemotherapy for cancer treatment. Oncologists were not particularly receptive to the clinical messages about the product because they saw no inherent value in boosting red blood cells to overcome fatigue; after all, the patient still had cancer. Many physicians voiced their belief that the product was too costly and that a substantial price reduction would be needed to gain use, especially when the economic models developed by J&J and others demonstrated conclusively that *Procrit* greatly increased the cost of care and had virtually no impact on survival. When J&J realized that the true value of the product was not in overcoming fatigue but by allowing the cancer patient to live a more normal and relatively active life they changed tactics, instead of trying to convince oncologists that fatigue was a problem worked with nurses to help the physicians understand that cancer patients could and should be able to enjoy a higher quality of life, or a more normal life, and *Procrit* enabled that. With that aspect of value firmly planted, many price objections simply fell away and the sales of the product grew rapidly. The key for J&J was in understanding that the actual value of *Procrit* need not, and indeed could not, be quantified in economic terms and instead was communicated in more humanitarian and emotional terms. Quantifying and monetizing value, although important in economic analysis, deprives the pricer of a true depth of understanding of the reasons for purchases (and non-purchases) and, in fact, distances pricing from its marketing roots by placing it firmly in the realm of quantitative economics.

Pricing Based on Value

Rather than being a purely quantitative exercise, pricing based on value is contextual and deductive. The different faces and types of value, as well as the different types of customers, prevent us from using a neat and clean formulaic approach to pricing — if we wish our prices to be the most profitable. Moreover, because several considerations beyond value, such as corporate or portfolio strategic needs, can and should affect the final price, it is naïve to believe that a mechanical approach could ever render appropriate prices.

In the end, when it comes to a product's value, there are several key questions that must be asked and answered:

- In lieu of or in addition to which other products will this one be used?
- What are the costs and value propositions of the current alternatives?
- What is the incremental benefit of this product?
- Are there segments where the product is more or less beneficial?
- Which value(s) should I focus on?
- Who receives value from this product?
- Finally, what problem does this product solve, and who owns that problem?

Every player in the market will assess the value of a product differently. In situations where a product offers significant incremental value over the current alternative, price is often a nonissue. In situations where a new product offers no discernible value over existing ones, sometimes a low price will generate sales. But often no price, however low, can salvage the product. How does value relate to price? The answer is that it helps move you closer to the final decision, but it doesn't get you all the way there.

The market in which I work the most, pharmaceuticals, provides a good canvas upon which to paint some of the problems of measuring value. Millions of dollars are spent each year on *technology assessment*, which is essentially an attempt to measure the economic value of medicines. Methods have been developed to measure *Quality of Life* using basic utility and WTP models, with a variety of techniques all considered acceptable — however, it is well established (Pathak and MacKeigan, 1992) that different techniques result in different valuations, which should render their results questionable, at the least. But outside the United States many nations accept these measures as the true value of a medicine, and several governments use them to set the price they will pay for a product. This approach is more a price control method than an objective evaluation — although that may reflect the fact that governments place less value on pharmaceuticals than they do on their ability to control budgets, but that is a narrow definition of value. Many in the pharmaceutical industry appear to accept this definition of value for their products without question, despite the fact that it is used as a price control mechanism. Rather than seeking to understand and communicate the actual value of a new medicine, many market participants simply accept the *plug and play* nature of *solving for a price* based on faulty economic methods and assumptions. Accepting a singular method for or approach to the valuations of all medicines leaves a great amount of untapped value, as was pointed out earlier in the discussion on *Procrit*. In some cases the difference in the actual value, in terms of the price that can be charged, and the value that is determined through simple economic measurement can be substantial. There are many medicines that command prices well above their economic value, but it is easy to dismiss the case of medicines because of their unique nature — but can the same principles apply in other markets? Most certainly, consider the many cases in which consumers and industrial buyers will pay premiums in the hopes of avoiding some risk; Kirimani and Rao (2000), in examining information asymmetry and quality cues, provide a number of examples in which WTP, or purchase, can be substantially increased through communications. Helping customers better understand what they actually receive and, in fact, how to evaluate a product, can result in prices that are substantially above those that are derived from simple WTP studies or basic economic analyses.

Some pharmaceutical products can literally give patients their lives back, while others may be perceived as imposing restrictions on a patient's life, which makes the measurement of value using a consistent method almost impossible. For instance, some drugs treat diseases that have no overt symptoms, such as high cholesterol, and patients soon view these drugs more as an imposition on their daily routine than as anything helpful — they don't feel it working and thus don't really value it. On the other hand, drugs that treat previously untreatable diseases that were once fatal in the short term, such as HIV and a host of rare disorders, provide immense value in economic, emotional, and Quality of Life terms. As Bonoma (1982) laid out, different players in the market, or members of the buying center, will value the medicines differently — a physician's assessment of the value of a medicine will be different from that of the patient, which will differ from that of the insurance company that may be paying for it. Understanding which player (or Buying Center member) has the most influence in the eventual purchase decision and the way in which that individual will comprehend the value of the medicine is essential for profit maximizing. But reliance on a single method of measuring only the economic value of a medicine can miss the true value of the product altogether. Moreover, because many fail to understand the nature of pharmaceuticals and similar products, there is an inherent downward bias in the way in which most in the market will value pharmaceuticals. This means that some aspects of value cannot be quantified, but some portion of that additional, subjective value can be captured through higher prices. The lack of quantifiable added value should not keep the pricer from adjusting prices upward — that, in fact, is a major part of the *game* of pricing as opposed to the science!

Unlike most products with which we are familiar, some products, including pharmaceuticals, are *negative goods*, that is, products that people would rather not buy. Pest control, tow trucks, and even gasoline are examples of other negative goods — you buy them because you need them, not because you want them (see Widrick & Fram, 1992). The motives for a customer to purchase (or prescribe) a negative good is to overcome or reduce the underlying problem, not to add pleasure or enhance their personal image. The difference in the reasons for the continued purchase of positive and negative goods can be summed up as follows: "[p]ositive reinforcement occurs when the subject's positive utility increases. For example, the purchase behavior of ice cream is reinforced by pleasant consumption. On the other hand, negative reinforcement causes an increased probability of a behavior through disutility reduction. The subject is under some pain or discomfort, and the action that reduces that discomfort is reinforced."

Because of this negative nature of these goods, the prices of most will always be considered *too high*, because people would rather not have to buy them in the first place – this holds true for any negative good, including tow trucks or auto insurance or disposable diapers. This poses a huge problem for the pharmaceutical company that looks at their new product as providing great new value, which their customers often fail to see. Without understanding the many facets of value beyond those that can be measured using simple economic concepts, the pricer is very likely to set prices that fail to capture or properly reflect the value of the product. To do this we need to leave the *clinical* or *functional* nature of basic economics behind and look to the basic premises of marketing, in which the value of a product is driven by the way it is communicated to the market and not simply a static attribute of the product itself.

In the dozens of times I've taught introductory marketing courses I have always found that the first challenge is to disabuse the students of the belief that marketing consists solely of advertising and promotion, opening the door for the teaching of the 4 Ps (product, promotion, price, place of distribution). It is thus somewhat ironical that the promotional and communicative aspects of marketing appear to be absent from most pricing discussions; we argue that pricing is one of the fundamental elements of marketing and that pricing should be based on value but choose to ignore the role that marketing activities can play in shaping the way value is interpreted by customers. In seeking to understand and capture value, pricers would be well served to review some of the seminal material in the advertising and promotional literature, which indirectly addresses value at its core (see especially McGarry, 1958 and Park, Jaworski & MacInnis, 1986) – pricers must realize that appropriately crafted marketing messages will enhance and increase a buyer's perception of the value of a product.

Value begins by filling some level of unmet need – known or unknown. MacInnis and Jaworski (1989) delineated two distinct types of needs: *utilitarian needs* and *expressive needs*. These differ in that a utilitarian need is defined as a requirement for a product that removes or avoids problems while an expressive need relates to products that provide social or aesthetic utility, just the type of thing that defies precise or useful economic measurement. These very different types of needs also require very different definitions and communications of value, because the needs being filled are so divergent. Similarly to Whan, Jaworski and MacInnis (1986) describe three types of brand image that are driven by specific types of need: functional, symbolic, and experiential. The image, they go on to say, is a "perception created by the marketer's management of the brand," in other words the communication of the brand influences (alters) the perception of the brand and its value. Here again we see fundamental marketing premises that undermine the static economic approach to value measurement.

Rather than approaching value as an objective construct based on physical properties that are fixed and measurable, the pricer should seek to understand all aspects of product values, including the intangible aspects that often drive purchase decisions.

An Alternative Way to Think About Value

The most important questions the pricer can ask are, "What problem does my product solve, and who owns that problem?" Answering those questions is the first step in understanding and clarifying value. For any new product or service, the value will be determined in the context of current options. I argue that value is comprised of multiple components, including both negative aspects of value (such as risk in use) and positive aspects (such as the incremental benefits of the product) that drive the value of the product. The dynamic between these positive and negative aspects and value is depicted in the Fig. 1, which I refer to as a general model of value.

The structure of this model is simple, in that overall value is composed of both positive and negative aspects, and each of those dimensions is composed of factors that are important in determining and communicating value. Put another way, value is determined by the interaction of the utility of the product (as defined in the model) moderated by the risk (also defined in the model) in using it; descriptions and discussions of my use of the terms *utility* and *risk* are in the following paragraphs. The implications of this relationship are fairly straightforward: increasing the utility of a product or decreasing the risk in its use can both result in increased value, which can translate into either a higher price or an enhanced value proposition in which the buyer understands that the price paid is far below the value received.

The individual components of the general model of value act together, in fact, they must be considered together if value is to be understood. The positive aspects (or sources) of value begin with a determination of the *need* for the product or service, which is driven, or moderated, by the

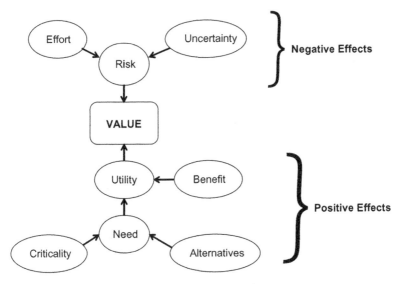

Fig. 1. General Model of Value.

criticality of the situation in which it is needed or used and the number and quality of *alternatives* that are available.

Criticality is the urgency of the need for the outcomes of the use of the product. This urgency is not strictly temporal but also captures the likelihood and severity of the negative consequences if the product is not used or acquired. Higher levels of criticality will positively affect the level of need. Criticality is moderated by a number of alternatives in that the level of criticality of the situation is a key driver of value, while the availability of alternatives can mitigate the level of need.

The higher the level of need for a solution, the lower the level of essential incremental benefit required to drive meaningful utility and thus more incremental value. In situations of relatively low or minor unmet need, however, significantly higher levels of incremental benefit are required to offer meaningful new utility. Generally speaking, a greater number of alternatives acts to reduce the level of need for any individual product in the consideration set, while the availability of fewer alternatives typically results in a higher level of need for a product.

In highly critical situations, such as the breakdown of a car or an essential piece of machinery or the case of a potentially deadly disease that progresses rapidly, the value of any alternative will be seen to be quite high.

In situations of less urgency, a purchaser can evaluate more options and make a more leisurely and less pressured decision, which would moderate the level of need for any product in the consideration set. The level of need in the market can best be thought of as a performance gap (Greer, 1988) between what current alternatives deliver and what the market (or customer) actually desires.

The better a product can fill a performance gap the greater its value. Incremental improvements such as a slightly faster operating speed for a computer or slightly higher cure rate for a new drug may have some additional value that offers pricing flexibility, depending on the amount of the performance gap that is filled and how meaningful those improvements are to the final outcome of the use of the product. Perhaps the most striking example of this phenomenon has been in the area of new drugs for the treatment of cancer; throughout much of human existences and, indeed, most of our own lifetimes, most cancers have been almost untreatable, or the treatments were often so toxic that they were closer to torture than to therapy. The performance gap for effective and safe cancer treatments was so large that new treatments, almost regardless of their effectiveness, have been able to command very high prices relative to other therapies. Now there are often several drugs available to treat a variety of cancers, such as chronic myelogenous leukemia (CML) and breast or prostate cancer. The performance gap in these areas has narrowed so much that new products need to show massive improvements to garner interest, and cannot sustain the price premiums that were once a *given* in the market.

Once the level of need, or performance gap, has been established, it is necessary to understand the degree to which the product under consideration can meet any unique need — to understand how much of the performance gap this product may fill or bridge. This is the point at which the question, "What problem does this product solve?" comes into play. Often a marketer bringing a new product to the market will focus on what the product does, failing to consider whether other products can deliver the same benefit. Just as important, even when marketers consider differences among products, they will often focus on what their product does better (e.g., operates faster or at a lower error rate) without providing customers with an understanding of why the difference matters (e.g., faster operating speeds mean faster turnaround and higher levels of customer service which can mean greater customer retention and higher profits). A helpful method for understanding why a specific benefit or physical feature of a product or service may be important and actually enhance value is to adapt an approach from root cause analysis (RCA) called the *five whys*, which is essentially portrayed within the final parentheses of the previous sentence. In asking why a specific benefit is important, one is able to delve more deeply into the realm of value. In the previous example, faster operating speed does not have the same level of value as higher profits. This approach to understanding value will be more fully discussed momentarily.

Understanding the specific benefits of the product over other alternatives — that is, the incremental benefit distinguishing the product from its competitors — provide a better understanding of the overall value of the product. To summarize what I refer to as the positive sources of value, the *utility* of a product is a function of the *need* for that product (or the performance gap), which is conditioned on the number of suitable *alternatives* and the *criticality* of the situation in which that need arises. This need then provides the basis for understanding the degree of incremental *benefit* over competitive alternatives that is needed to bring new and meaningful utility to the marketplace. This basic utility, however, comes with caveats, which I refer to as the negative sources of value for a product.

The negative sources of value are contained in the factor called *risk*, which can be thought of as the probability that the expected (or hoped for) outcome of product use will not be realized. In essence, risk is a composite of uncertainty and effort, combining the ambiguity or doubt over the eventual effects or utility of the product and the amount of additional work or new learning (effort) that goes into its use. Higher certainty of effect reduces risk. When a customer can be more confident that the desired effect of the product (or the outcome of its use) will be achieved, the product has more inherent value than alternatives that offer less certainty. Conversely, when there is less certainty that the desired effect will be achieved there is less inherent value.

Effort, or ease of use or acquisition, can drive value up or down. A product that is difficult to obtain could be either more or less valuable depending on whether the difficulty is caused by a lower level of availability relative to demand (in which case the value could increase) or because of obstacles to use (such as the need to go through several levels of permission or qualification to obtain the product). Effort can be driven by the strength of a habit, the need for new or extra behaviors relative to alternatives, such as the need to learn totally new methods or routines before using a new product, which reduces the inherent value of the product to potential users. Similarly, reducing the number of new behaviors or the degree of effort required to obtain or use a product can impart a great deal of incremental value.

Risk can be a huge value driver in that a reduction or increase in the risk for customers can greatly influence their assessment of value of the product. A product that eliminates a large portion of the current level of effort required for product use – either because it is simpler, more convenient to use or it is more easily attainable – will be appreciated and adopted more readily than products that are more difficult to acquire or use. A driver of value in pharmaceuticals is the reformulation of products to require fewer doses, such as reducing the daily dosing form three times per day to once daily. The simplification of dosing to once daily makes it easier for the patient to remember to take their medicine on time, which means less effort. Drugs dosed once daily can command higher prices than those dosed more frequently, even though arguments of additional economic value can be difficult to make, but patients and physicians prefer them. There are no hard and fast rules of pricing drugs dosed once daily versus those dosed more frequently (in fact, many firms elect to forego any premium and sell based on the incremental value of fewer doses), but the effort-sparing feature of fewer doses allows for much more pricing flexibility because many customers appreciate that value. When determining the value of a product or service, especially in regard to pricing decisions, this general model provides a construct that allows for an in-depth understanding of the structure of the value, the ways in which value can be altered as well as the ways in which it can be communicated. One must first understand the main source(s) of value; only then is it possible to have the real value reflected in the price. This statement does not imply that the general model of value leads directly to a pricing decision or that there is some formulaic relationship between value and price, only that once one truly understands the value provided, the pricing potential becomes much more apparent.

FELE Model of Value

A useful method for understanding and communicating the value of a product that is complementary to the general model of value is the FELE method, which is presented graphically in Fig. 2. FELE is the acronym for the four different types of value that can be derived from a product or service: functional, economic, lifestyle, and emotional. These elements can be thought of as parts of a continuum of value, ascending from the functional to the emotional. Each successive level of value is more difficult to communicate but is also more influential in customer decision-making and thus

Functional	Economic	Lifestyle (Work Style)	Emotional
• Speed • Efficiency • Effectiveness • Safety • Etc.	• Price • Savings • Cost/Outcome • Revenue enhancements • Impact on other costs • Productivity • Etc.	• Ease of use • Convenience • Stress reduction • Compatibility with current routines and processes • Etc.	• Self-perception • Peace of mind • Habit • Satisfaction/ Happiness • Preference • Other psychological impact

Fig. 2. FELE Model of Value.

more important to communicate. I was introduced to a variant of the FELE concept several years ago and have worked to further develop the concept, but I have been unable to identify any of its precursors in the literature or the originator of the concept, to whom much credit is due.

The FELE model helps to identify the relevant aspects of the value of a product based on the end result of its use. The model begins with the functional aspects of value, with each succeeding type of value derived from the previous and providing a higher level of value from a behavioral perspective. When the product offers improvements in functional areas (e.g., faster processing speed, clearer sound, better taste) there may be value because of those improvements, but the value will not be readily apparent. Functional value can be thought of broadly as the physical result or effect of the use of the product and how that differs from alternative products. The next level of value is economic, and it is at this level that much of the discussion of value in the realm of value-based pricing has confined itself.

Although the economic aspects of value can be quantified and monetized, and therefore used to help determine a price, there is often value beyond the calculated economic value that can be communicated to the customer and reflected and captured in the final price. The functional aspects of a product that result in economic savings or revenue enhancements brought about by preventing an equipment breakdown and work stoppage may be significant, but those same physical and economic types of value may also lend themselves to other types of value in that they can provide assurances of performance that may indirectly affect or result in workflow, job security, and eventual peace of mind. Although these additional factors are difficult to monetize (and impossible to do so with precision), they can be essential elements of a pricing and value communications strategy.

Lifestyle (and work style) value can be derived from a product because it enables a customer to live a better life or have a more rewarding or less stressful or complicated work experience. Products that provide lifestyle (or work style) value make a customer's life easier or better, regardless of the functional or economic aspects of the product itself, and therefore bring about a different type of value. This value is often much more important and meaningful to the customer than the economic value that can be calculated using standard techniques.

Emotional value, in this model, is derived from the ability of a product to bring about improvements in a customer's feelings of well-being. In this instance, emotional value is similar to but essentially different from the concept developed by Barlow and Maul (2000). Their concept focuses on customer service and addressing customers' emotions as a means of customer retention and increasing the organization's profitability. Whereas in this application, it is the intangible psychological benefit that is realized by a customer or user. Examples of emotional value come from products that can provide some level of peace of mind, such as a special memento as a gift for family members, or from those purchases that enhance perceptions of self-worth, items ranging from high fashion and luxury cars to the latest electronic gadgets. The Volvo® focus on safety, which leads directly to associations of peace of mind, and the Michelin® tagline, "Because so much is riding on your tires," are direct examples of high levels of emotional value that act to reduce price sensitivity — which means higher prices are made possible through this nonquantified value. Although it may be argued that different trade-off methods can be used to determine how high a premium might be charged based on this emotional value, it cannot be argued, given the previous discussion on WTP, that such measurement can have the precision that calculations of pure economic value can attain.

Although those who study and offer improvements to the field of pricing will acknowledge the behavioral issues that confound quantitative pricing approaches, many will return to those same quantitative approaches when the time for price determination arrives. The advances in our understanding of human behavior have enriched our discussions and presentations but don't often make much of a difference in the final pricing recommendation or decision. We acknowledge that pricing is a game to be played, but too often we treat it as a puzzle that must be solved. In attempting to monetize value to establish a price, even the best thinkers fall prey to the premise that every price must have a sound economic rationale — which is a wonderful theory that can lead to lower profits. As my brother notes: "There is no one silver bullet regarding pricing. There are more factors in the DNA of a pricing strategy than in the entire human genetic code." Mathematical models of the human genome may provide new and important insights into our makeup, but they cannot offer any help in really understanding how and why we behave as we do. Similarly, attempts to quantify the key aspects of value and pricing can provide important insights but cannot and should not be relied upon to provide the final decision.

When pricers fully understand the drivers of value, they have the confidence to push a little further, knowing that the price they have set truly reflects the value that the product provides. Failing to consider the aspects of value that cannot be quantified leads to prices that are lower, and thus less profitable, than those that can be achieved when the nonquantifiable aspects of value are understood.

TRIBUTE TO DAN NIMER

For over thirty years Dan Nimer has influenced every thought I have had on pricing. Over that time I have seen Dan absolutely wow audiences with his rock solid logic and engaging style and left all of us wanting more. As an apostle of value-based pricing Dan has no equal, but beyond that he is also one of the most generous people when it comes to sharing his thoughts on pricing — virtually every recognized thinker in the field has learned from Dan personally, and we cling to every word. He never misses an opportunity to teach you a pricing lesson or make an important point, even when handing out his business card (for a small fee!). All of us who work in the field of pricing strategy owe Dan Nimer a debt that can never be repaid. It continues to be an honor and great pleasure to interact with and learn from Dan, and I look forward to every opportunity to do so.

REFERENCES

Barlow, J., & Maul, D. (2000). *Emotional value: Taking customer service to a new level.* San Francisco, CA: Berret-Koehler.

Bonoma, T. V. (1982). Major sales: Who really does the buying? *Harvard Business Review, 60* (May/June), 111–119.

Bush, V. (1945). *As we may think, atlantic monthly.* 112–124. Retrieved from http://www.theatlantic.com/magazine/archive/1945/07/as-we-may-think/3881/. Accessed on July.

Carpenter, G. S., & Nakamoto, K. (1989). Consumer preference formation and pioneering advantage. *Journal of Marketing Research, 26*(August), 285–298.

Edwards, R. S. (1952). The pricing of manufactured products. *Economica, 19*(75), 298–307.

Greer, A. L. (1988). The state of the art versus the state of the science: The diffusion of new medical technologies in practice. *International Journal of Technology Assessment in Health Care, 4*, 5.

Herriges, J. A., Kling, C. L., & Azevedo, C. (1999). *Linking revealed and stated preferences to test external validity*. Annual Meetings of the American Agricultural Economics Association, Nashville, TN. Retrieved form http://agecon.lib.umn.edu/cgi-bin/pdf_view.pl?paperid=1308.

Knetsch, J. L. (1989). The endowment effect and evidence of non-reversible indifference curves. *American Economic Review, LXXIX*. 1277–84.

Kirimani, A., & Rao, A. R. (2000). No pain, no gain: A critical review of the literature on signaling unobservable product quality. *Journal of Marketing, 64*, 66–79.

Lunander, A. (1998). Inducing incentives to understate and to overstate willingness to pay within the open-ended and the dichotomous-choice elicitation formats: An experimental study. *Journal of Environmental Economics and Management, 35*(1), 88–102.

MacInnis, D. J., & Jaworski, B. J. (1989). Information processing from advertisements: Toward an integrative framework. *Journal of Marketing, 53*, 1–23.

Marshall, A. (1920). *Principles of economics: An introductory volume* (8th ed.). London: Macmillan.

McGarry, E. D. (1958). The propaganda function of marketing. *Journal of Marketing, 23* (October), 131–139.

Morrison, G. C. (1996). *Willingness to pay and willingness to accept: Some evidence of an endowment effect*. Discussion Paper 9646. Department of Economics, Southampton University.

Nagle, T. T., & Holden, R. K. (2002). *The strategy and tactics of pricing* (p. 280). Saddle River, NJ: Prentiss Hall.

Park, J. H., & MacLachlan, D. L. (2008). Estimating willingness to pay with exaggeration bias-corrected contingent valuation method. *Marketing Science, 27*(4), 691–698.

Park, C. W., Jaworski, B. J., & MacInnis, D. J. (1986). Strategic brand concept-image management. *Journal of Marketing, 50*(4), 135–145.

Pathak, D. S., & MacKeigan, L. D. (1992). Assessment of quality of life and health status: Selected observations. *Journal of Research in Pharmaceutical Economics, 4*(4), 31–52.

Widrick, S., & Fram, E. (1992). Identifying negative products: Do customers like to purchase your products? *The Journal of Product and Brand Management, 1*(1), 43–50.

Yadav, M. S. (2010). The decline of conceptual articles and implications for knowledge development. *Journal of Marketing, 74*, 1–19.

CREATING VALUE WITH SALES PROMOTION STRATEGIES THAT AVOID PRICE DISCOUNTING

Takaho Ueda

ABSTRACT

This paper introduces the development of a new type of sales promotion strategy to create more value for goods and to avoid price discounting. I use a psychological approach designed by creating consumer insight hypotheses based on in-depth interviews, which are then verified by web-motivation research and text-mining. This innovative sales promotion approach is a very hot topic as a new type of promotion development among large companies in Japan and is useful in avoiding price-discounting sales. This paper explains the concrete process used in this type of promotion and reveals the successful case of a large spice company in Japan. The process uses price sensitivity measurement (PSM) as a pricing technique. In the experiment, conducted in nine retail stores, the most successful sales promotion condition saw an increase of 900% in monetary sales without price discounting during the two weeks of the experiment, and 500% in the two weeks after that.

Visionary Pricing: Reflections and Advances in Honor of Dan Nimer
Advances in Business Marketing & Purchasing, Volume 19, 213–256
Copyright © 2012 by Emerald Group Publishing Limited
All rights of reproduction in any form reserved
ISSN: 1069-0964/doi:10.1108/S1069-0964(2012)0000019016

It is difficult to determine how pricing in the business world will be in the future. The fluctuation of pricing policies in Japan is presently quite intense. At the beginning of the year 2000, companies made efforts to bring their prices back up to an adequate reference level from the discounted price levels that emerged in the early 1990s because of fierce price competition; they almost succeeded. Then they encountered increases in the prices of oil and other raw materials, and were suddenly faced with the unexpected Lehman financial crisis in September 2008, causing them to resume price competition because consumers were less willing to buy and were more price sensitive. Even drugstores, who are famous discounters, had proclaimed that they were stopping deep discounting before the Lehman shock, but they quickly went back to a deep discounting policy. Though the General merchandizing store (GMS) founded a new-format discount supermarket (SM), they began to increase their prices gradually in 2011 because of the repeated increases in the prices of oil and other raw materials. It is evident that in a short period of time, there have been complex changes in the retail pricing climate.

In such situations, the polarization of the good retail chains is also evident (see Fig. 1). The horizontal axis represents the strategy (low-cost oriented or non-price values oriented), and the vertical axis represents the

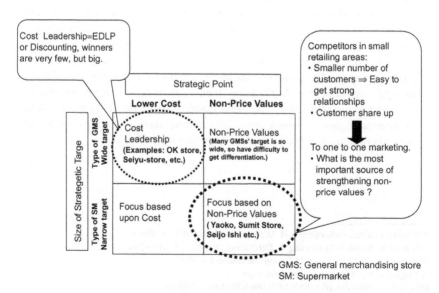

GMS: General merchandising store
SM: Supermarket

Fig. 1. Two Types of Current Supermarket Winners in Japan.

width of the target area. Successfully profitable retailers in Japan are shown in the upper-left and lower-right cells. The former use a cost-leadership strategy of being low-cost oriented with a wide target area, and the latter use a focus strategy based on non-price values and a narrow target. However, there are very few successful retailers in the former category, for example, OK-store and Seiyu (Walmart). They have to be particularly large or have an innovative low-cost system. The stance adopted by the latter in terms of focus strategy based on differentiation, which many successful retailers use, needs to be examined; for example, Yaoko, which offers a good lifestyle for customers through its merchandising. Such retailers create additional value for their customers.

In short, retailers using the focus strategy based on differentiation do not appeal much to the bargain hunters who are interested in discounting, but aim to keep their non-price-conscious customers who willingly pay more for good products.

Therefore, it is very important to determine how retailers can encourage their customers to buy their goods even though their goods are rather expensive. The important point is to determine how retailers can create sales promotions that add value to their goods in order to avoid price discounting. Concretely speaking, retailers must find the appeal points of their goods for the customers' unconscious and subconscious mind, so that customers want to buy goods without price discounting (see Fig. 2).

Nothing can appeal perfectly to a customer's subconscious or unconscious mind. In most cases, values remain hidden like a buried treasure. For example, consumers think of cream stew as a dinner food that makes them feel warmer in a cold winter; thus, most firms market the idea that

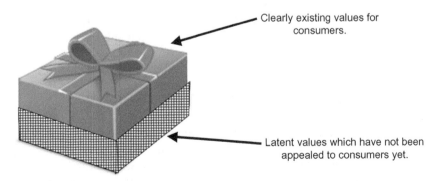

Clearly existing values for consumers.

Latent values which have not been appealed to consumers yet.

Fig. 2.   Latent Values of the Product.

such food warms people well. However, most parents feel strongly in their subconscious minds that they want their young children to eat enough vegetables for them to be healthy, even if they generally do not like vegetables. Once parents understand that their children will willingly eat vegetables in cream stew, the cream stew gains value as a food that gets children to eat vegetables. Thus, for food companies to take advantage of this aspect, it is very important for them to emphasize this aspect to those parents who are not yet aware of this. Such values are hidden in most cases, but once they emerge, they have the potential to be very attractive for demand expansion without price discounting. Companies require sales promotions that create more value for their products in order to avoid fierce price competition. Hereafter, this type of promotion is called the *sales promotion of creating more values (SPOCMV)*.

It can also be said that once these companies create an important value for their goods, they can acquire more long-term, loyal customers, which mitigates price competition. How can they do this through sales promotion? It is particularly significant to find the core purchase points in the customer's in-depth psychology, in addition to the designated values.

In the case of the cream stew, the core purchase point for mothers is that their children will willingly eat vegetables. Therefore, such a sales promotion could lead to good sales without price discounting, which is the result of in-depth customer research. These continuous efforts create strong bonds between companies and their customers. This stew case involves the House Foods Corporation brand. The firm produced an advertisement targeted at mothers, which promotes their cream stew as a way to get children to eat vegetables. It becomes the series of the so called sommelier of vegetables now[1].

After explaining the outline of this type of promotion, this paper will explain the newest case involving EBARA Foods Industry, Inc. The duration of the case study was one and a half years, and this period included retail store experiments.

THE NECESSITY OF THE SPOCMV

Companies encounter several problems, enumerated below, when they sell their products or goods with deep discounting. First, deep discounting destroys the brand image. In the case of retail stores, the brand is seen as just a discount store brand that sells cheap and low-quality goods. Second, deep discounting takes the customer's internal reference price down and makes them feel that products or goods at normal prices are expensive in comparison; therefore, they do not buy anything and do not visit the store in the absence of discounting. As a result, companies cannot achieve adequate profits. Third, deep discounting pre-loads customer demand. Customers buy more and keep more stock in their houses. When companies restore the price to the original level, the customers refrain from buying and companies cannot achieve reasonable profits.

Because of these problems, selling only with deep discounting leads to hard price competition by destroying companies' ability to create new ways to avoid price discounting. Similarly, price increases tend to create customer resistance unless value is added. This indicates that it is very important for customers' subconscious or unconscious minds to recognize value in goods or retail stores themselves.

The SPOCMV is an effective means to achieve this goal and increase brand loyalty or store loyalty.

Value Hierarchy and the SPOCMV: Four values of Goods and Services[2]

What are the values of goods and services, in other words, the brands? In order to create a strong identity, the brand has to ensure its functions and image are unique among other brands. If the brand does not have such uniqueness, it cannot easily be differentiated, which results in price competition. After consumers use the brand and feel it is good, they develop trust in it, then they become attached to it, and finally they have a strong bond with it. Companies have to practice this process. This process corresponds to the hierarchical structure displayed in Figure 3.[3]

Suyama and Umemoto (2000) demonstrate this process using the Kao Merit shampoo brand. First, the basic values are fundamental values, like washing hair well in this case. The functional values are the attributes that distinguish a brand from others; in this case, one example is to protect against dandruff and an itching scalp. The emotional values are the feelings that users have after using the product, like refreshment. Finally, the self-expression values lie at the top of this pyramid. They are the most important values and function as a symbol for consumers to show who they are. Further, they are values that allow brand users to belong to the class of people who own the product; they are brand symbols. This value for the Merit shampoo brand is the neatness to feel perfect not to give people discomfort as the self-defense, which is especially important in Japan in the case of meeting important people.[4]

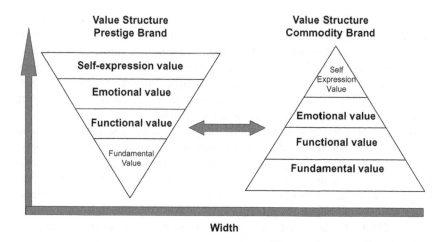

Fig. 3. Hierarchical Value Structures of the Commodity Brand and the Prestige Brand. *Source*: This figure was altered based on Tanaka (2002), p. 189, and Wada (2002), p. 19.

Therefore, in order to create high brand value for consumers, companies should construct brand structure well and practice good consumer communications based on the appropriate brand value pyramid. In brief, in order to create a strong bond between the company and the customer, that is, in order to obtain a loyal customer for the company rather than just a user, the company must create values beginning with the basic and moving up to the self-expression level of the value pyramid. Companies must extract these particularly important emotional values and self-expression values from the consumers' in-depth psychology, and then build up suitable sales promotions on this basis.

There are two types of pyramids in Figure 3; the one on the left is for prestige brands, and the one on the right is for commodity brands. The reverse-triangle structure of the prestige brands shows that the top values are much more important than the lower ones.[5] For example, BMW is a high-status brand among automobiles, and the value structure shape is the reverse triangle shown on the right of Figure 3. Its consumers are more interested in the self-expression value than the basic value. In this case, one of the self-expression values is probably the demonstration of success in society, which people can achieve by driving such a car. But the other three kinds of values have to be excellent, because they sustain the top value of the pyramid. Therefore, people are willing to pay more money for BMW than other standard cars, even if they feel the car price is relatively high. The company does not have to focus on price discounting, and rather should avoid it and focus on the upper values. The main means of doing this is to use the SPOCMV.

Outline of the SPOCMV

The starting point of this process is the pre-in-depth interview, with approximately five subjects, which is conducted prior to the normal in-depth interview used in motivation research, to screen research target points. The result of such an interview is similar to that of an in-depth interview. This pre-in-depth interview is valuable as a predictor of the results of the normal in-depth interview.

Next, the in-depth interview is conducted, and several hypotheses on appeal points are proposed after the records are interpreted. The in-depth interview is usually a process in which experts in psychoanalysis or clinical psychology interview a subject, record the answers in detail, and analyze the answers. They usually interview between twenty and thirty subjects, and take between one and two hours, or occasionally three hours. As a rule of thumb, it is usually sufficient to interview approximately around ten subjects for one theme. Hypotheses are developed after analyzing and examining these results. The record volume seems to be large, even with ten subjects. After these processes, web motivation research is conducted. In this process, questionnaire items are developed using traditional motivation research techniques, and subjects give free answers. After analyzing these answers using text-mining, the hypotheses are verified and more worthy findings are revealed.

According to these results, sales promotion plan ideas are developed, plans are completed, and store experiments are begun. Then, the sales results are measured, and sales promotion alternatives are evaluated. The company chooses the successful plans, develops them into more extensive areas, occasionally by modifying them, and produces advertisements for its brand if necessary.

This process is illustrated in Figure 4. The SPOCMV has four main parts. The details are explained subsequently, through the case of EBARA Foods Industry, Inc., but the measurement of the store experiments is explained here. This measurement comprises two analyses: the scanner data analysis and analysis of questionnaires from the volunteers visiting the stores. The latter analysis involves checking whether the volunteers'

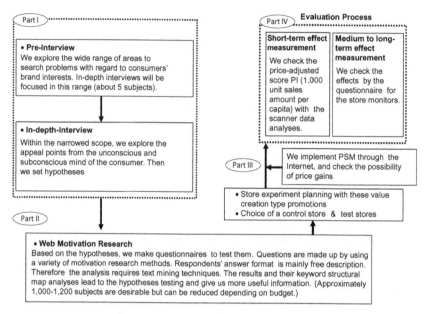

Fig. 4. The Process of the SPOCOMV.

interests in the sales promotions relate to actual purchases using the structural equation model (SEM).

The store experiments involved two types of stores: the experiment store, which used the planned sales promotion, and the control store, which had a simple volume display. The results from both experiments were compared with the scanner data analysis in order to measure the pure effects of the sales plans.

Price Sensitive Measurement (PSM) should be used to determine the price range that consumers will accept for the brand. PSM should be done between Part III and Part IV of the SPOCMV process. PSM can be used to evaluate sales promotions even during the process of mocking up display plans. The details will be explained later in the case of EBARA Foods Industry, Inc.

Importance of Appeal Points from the Perspective of Consumer Insights

Appeal points are extracted from the consumer insight (sub-conscious and unconscious) because many factors that create consumer price insensitivity hide there. According to Packard (1957)[6], the consumer has three kinds of senses: conscious, subconscious, and unconscious. The conscious sense allows people to understand their situation and can explain it well. The subconscious sense gives people a vague sense of the situation through their own five senses, but does not allow them to explain it clearly. In the unconscious sense people are not completely aware of their feelings about what they want. Additionally, according to Zaltman (2003), approximately 95% of human thinking and emotion are influenced by the subconscious and unconscious mind. Only 5% of thinking is controlled by the conscious mind.[7] These three senses are often compared to an iceberg. The conscious sense is compared to the first layer, which is the top part above the water; the subconscious mind is compared to the second layer beneath the surface of water; and the unconscious mind is compared to the bottom layer at deeper water depths. This means that the consumer knows something only within the conscious mind above the water, but is also much influenced by the other two senses under the water, although he or she does not understand the latter. Thus, it is important to understand and examine the senses under the water in detail. However, Figure 5 illustrates the three senses as a mandala, which is a more useful analogy than an iceberg. A

The state of mind is like Mandara.

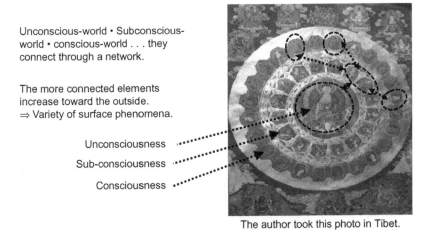

Unconscious-world · Subconscious-world · conscious-world . . . they connect through a network.

The more connected elements increase toward the outside.
⇒ Variety of surface phenomena.

Unconsciousness

Sub-consciousness

Consciousness

The author took this photo in Tibet.

Fig. 5. Why Should We Explore the Appeal Points from the Deep Psyche?
Note: "*Mandala*" is summarized as a representation of any religious worldview as a whole.

mandala is a Buddhist artwork that consists of three layers, like the iceberg. The biggest difference is that the elements of every layer of the mandala connect to the other elements of the other layers (see Figure 5). Thus, the mandala is a much better metaphor than the iceberg.

Motivation research, a traditional form of consumer insight research, aims to extract the consumer's hidden important needs from the subconscious and unconscious mind. According to Akuto (1994), the main characteristic of motivation research is that the expert interviews a few subjects; however, motivation research involves not only in-depth interviews, but also other techniques. According to Akuto (1994) and Packard (1957), motivation research involves in-depth interviews, association method, sentence completion test (SCT), thematic apperception test (TAT), cartoon completion, and the Szondi test.

An appropriate context is required to make the consumer feel better about the brand and raise the purchase value using the SPOCMV. The context has to be based on important appeal points extracted from the subconscious and unconscious mind of the consumer. Recently, a company used Internet motivation research to develop a new product. Though the details are secret, the example is the case of Suntory's Iemon brand. Suntory gained consumer insights that could not be obtained from the quantitative data through some unusual questions. For example, their questionnaire contained questions such as, "What kind of objection would you have if the Japanese government prohibited the nation from drinking Japanese tea?" and, "In what kind of situation do you feel strongly that you are Japanese?" These are typical motivation research questions, and aim at achieving insight into the subject by surprising them in the moment.

There is very little recent literature on motivation research aside from Zaltman (2003): only the final chapter of Akuto (1994) is relevant. However, relatively more research appeared between 1950 and 1960, including Dichter (1960), Packard (1957), Newman (1957), and Cheskin (1951).

Recently, Zaltman (2003) has contributed to brushing up the motivation research method. Zaltman's greatest contribution is the Zaltman Metaphor Elicitation Technique (ZMET), which functions in the following manner: First, ask the subject to bring between six and eight photos or pictures that depict something that makes the subject feel strongly about a theme. Then ask the subject one question after another, systematically, so the subject gradually starts telling the interviewer about his or her feelings that are difficult to express using metaphors. Use the metaphors as opportunities to analyze, ask more questions, and finally clarify the subject's feelings, way of thinking, and insight. The Proctor & Gamble Febreze brand case is an example[8]. However, this method is within the scope of traditional motivation research, as this does not include Web motivation research.

The Collage method is another insight-analysis method, and a business tool used by some advertising agencies. In this method, the researcher asks the subject to choose and place photos or pictures that they collected beforehand on a mat. Then, the researcher interviews the subject about his or her choices and placement reasons one after another. This method seems not to be so different from ZMET[9].

Supplementing Motivation Research with In-depth Interviews and Web Research

Motivation research is a psychological technique that describes the important consumer senses that are oppressed and remain in the sub-conscious or the unconscious mind; it is a projective technique. This projection is based on the idea of Jungian Psychology, in which people have an inclination not to consciously recognize something in their subconscious or unconscious mind. This projection is used to analyze the reaction or statements of the subject in order to find something in his or her subconscious or unconscious mind through something vague. The advantage of this is that the subject does not try to change the facts on purpose. On the contrary, the analysis is likely to contain subjective aspects, and may thus lose its objectiveness.[10] Therefore, this method is most appropriate for extracting hypotheses if there is a good method to verify them. This could include Web motivation research, which seems to be indispensable for standard motivation research, because the main problems of modern motivation research seem to be small samples and subjectivity of analysis. However, there these problems are not significant if motivation research is used to extract hypotheses. The point is that these hypotheses need to be verified at the same time. Modern and convenient business tools like Internet research and text-mining tools make this approach easier. The combination of these tools can produce the SPOCMV. Ueda and Shibata (2003) and Ueda and Hatai (2005) use a similar research method, the Web-laddering method, to identify consumer values; they handled 3,000 and 1,000 subjects' free answer data each from an Internet research tool and a text-mining tool, respectively. These approaches can overcome the small number of subjects by handling large subject data; at the same time, switching from qualitative analysis to quantitative analysis by text-mining the free answers can change the approach. The latter allows judgmental objectiveness. The SPOCMV is a fusion of both analyses, which will be a new stream of future research. An illustration of SPOCMV is given in the next section, which describes the case of EBARA Foods Industry, Inc.

THE CASE OF EBARA FOODS INDUSTRY, INC.'S "OHGON NO AJI" BARBEQUE SAUCE BRAND: GOLD TASTE

This case involves industry-academia joint research that was conducted over one and a half years from the beginning of 2009 to 2010; members of both Gakushuin Management School and EBARA Foods Industry Inc. participated in this project. The author was responsible for the administration of this project as headmaster of this management school. "Ohgon no aji" barbeque sauce brand was the object of this project. It has the largest share of the barbeque sauce market, but has been exposed to price competition, as have many commodities. The goal was to raise brand sales without price discounting and make a clean break from the commodities price war by finding and adding value from the consumer insight gained through the SPOCMV study.

Conducting the pre-in-depth interviews as a first step limited the range of the in-depth interviews, following the SPOCMV process.[11] The following were the screened items.

(1) Potential variations in the barbeque sauce as it is likely to get boring.

There seems to be potential of mixing other condiments and vegetables with this sauce. In particular, one famous brand of vegetables is identified for a special day. Parents can produce their own unique sauce taste in this manner, and reduce boredom through variations. As a result, their children become willing to eat vegetables.

(2) Meat potential of the barbeque sauce

Usually, people eat beef with a higher unit price on the weekend. In order to promote consumption of barbeque sauce even on weekdays, promoting pork meat is a good idea, as pork is healthy. How can "Ohgon no aji" be made appealing for use with pork?

(3) Casual cooking using barbeque sauce on weekdays

Using barbeque sauce in a pan has great potential to increase the opportunities for casual barbeque cooking on a weekday because of easier cleaning, as well as easier cooking.

(4) How should people use the surplus sauce?

As people think it is wasteful to dispose of surplus sauce after one-time use at dinner, there seems to be potential in finding a way to reuse it. People's eco-thinking about the bottle and plastic bottle also seems to have potential.

Hereafter, this paper will focus on the abovementioned aspects.

Outline of the In-depth Interview

The in-depth interview is a qualitative research method conducted in the personal interview format. This method has the advantage of making it easy to access the subject's deep psyche, of which he or she often seems to be unaware. Therefore, this technique can deeply delve into the topics and can deeply approach even private issues. During the introduction process, the interviewer has to get the subject to relax and start listening for vague images of the product. The purpose of such an interview is that the interviewer wants the respondent to get familiar with the interview format by creating a situation of easy-to-answer questions, thereby enabling the interviewer to access the respondent's insights in the subsequent interview. The respondent is initially unaware of these insights in the conscious mind, but is able to start telling the researcher something when given the opportunity to think and feel. Depending on the question, the respondent may be silent. In such a situation, the interviewer occasionally has to wait for a response. That is, the interviewer has to give the respondent enough time to consider the response. The interviewer also has to ask the next question according to the timing of the respondent's answer.

In order to clarify the respondent's subconscious/unconscious feelings during the interview, the interviewer should dig deeply into ambiguous words from the respondent. Feelings in the deep psyche are expressed using vague images in many cases. For example, if questions are asked about the subject's feelings at that time, and the answer obtained is that he or she felt nostalgic, then the respondent must be asked about the vague portions of this mood step-by-step in order to dig deeply and make the nostalgic mood concretely clear. It is difficult for a respondent to express his or her feelings from the deep psyche in concrete terms and within a limited time frame. Thus, the interviewer has to ask the respondent various types of questions. The conversation between the interviewer and the respondent should be recorded, and it should be summarized after the interview. However, since occasionally respondents provide information that cannot be expressed with words alone, caution must be exercised in this situation. For example, such information includes respondents' gestures and facial expressions during the interviews. The interviewer should record the respondent's non-verbal expressions during an interview. These non-verbal expressions can give rich information to record readers, who were not present in the interview, about the appearance of the respondents during the interview. This record also helps the interviewer recall the specific situation of the interview.

Question Items of the In-depth Interview

When creating in-depth interview question items, it is important to avoid detailed and excessive questions and make the interview flow based on the selected questions from the pre-in-depth interview. The reason why the detailed question items are not set is that there is great possibility to develop further questions one after another depending on the answers of the respondents. The regular process of the interview should proceed on the basis of the contents of the answers. Even if the interaction between an interviewer and a respondent deflects the right course slightly, the interviewer should not correct the path, and continue the interview along the conversational contents. This interview style could lead to new findings by making the respondent feel and speak freely, focusing on the flow of the conversation.

Although detailed questions should not be set beforehand, it is important to ask the subject some basic interview questions regarding the object product.

(1) The image of the object.

As already mentioned, the respondent was free to talk about the object product in the beginning of the interview. Then, the interviewer asked questions on the basis of the content extracted from the respondent's association, thereby extending the content.

(2) The basic information of the object.

The questions to the subject address frequency of use, recent ways using, and so forth. Common questions about the facts are relatively easy to answer, and become a chance to extract deep insights.

(3) The relationship with the object.

The questions address the subject's first contact with the object. For example, they address what and how the respondent felt and when he or she had an experience to use it. They also address memories of the respondent's childhood, for example, the best memory and the worst memory of using the product.

With regard to other question items, they are usually used to ascertain the stream of conversation with the respondent. However, the interviewers should limit questions using the personification approach, for example, "What kind of personality does it have, if you compare it to a human being?" and the projection approach, for example, "What kind of people are they, if they use it extremely frequently?" These questions make it easy to break the shell of consciousness by giving respondents a slight surprise and as a result drawing something useful from their subconscious and unconscious minds.

Though the question level at this time mainly deals with the product category, the interviewer must ask questions to differentiate the object brand from other brands for brand-level research.

Process Outline

The authors selected four housewives in each of the following three age categories: thirties, forties, and fifties; thus, the total number of respondents was twelve. Half of the housewives in their forties and fifties were full-time housewives, and all of those in their thirties were part-time housewives. The interview duration per person averaged approximately two hours, but occasionally it lasted more than three hours. In the personal interview format, the interviewer needs a long time for each interview, which limits the interview capabilities to a small group of people. Table 1 indicates a portion of all the records resulting from a typical sample. There were approximately 23 pages for each subject because most of the interviews lasted for over two hours; the authors chose these subjects because their records contain following two points.

From Table 1, it is clear that people may use a pan or a hot plate to cook easily. Casual cooking with a pan for barbeque increases the opportunities for barbeque, which also increases the demand for barbeque sauce. Such a convenience can be the added value for consumers. The second half of Table 1 also shows that respondents prepare several sauces. That is to say, in the case of barbeque meals may get boring with only a single sauce, but they can be more enjoyable with several sauces because they boost the value of barbecued meats. This table shows that the respondents use different types of purchased sauce, but they sometimes mix some grated daikon

Table 1. Housewife in her 30s.

[Question]: Which do you use when you cook BBQ at home, a hotplate or a pan? [Answer]:
Strictly speaking, I do not eat meats so much, though I like them. When I cook BBQ, we use
a hot plate with our family, and I make use of the leftovers for my husband's lunch the next
day. To your surprise, as a great story, I occasionally cook BBQ in the morning with a pan.
When I come back home late at night and feel hungry, I cook BBQ using a pan for myself,
just one person. When my child was small, I cooked BBQ for all of us using a pan. [Point]:
I do not eat meats so much, although I like them. I cook BBQ in the morning using a pan,
and when I come back home late at night and feel hungry, I cook BBQ using a pan if I have
a small child.

[Question]: How many types of BBQ sauce do you want to use at a BBQ dinner ? [Answer]:
Five types in bottles: standard sauce, salt sauce, Ponzu sauce (Japanese traditional vinegar
sauce), sesame sauce for shabu-shabu (thinly sliced meat boiled quickly with vegetables and
dipped in sauce), and ginger sauce. Apart from these, I occasionally use just salt. I am fond of
sauces, maybe (laughing slightly). [Point]: This respondent uses various kinds of sauces during
a BBQ dinner to avoid being bored. [Question]: Why do you use so many kinds of sauces?
[Answer]: Maybe to avoid getting tired of the taste. Moreover, I guess the various tastes of
sauces make meats delicious.

(Japanese radish) into the sauce; so mixing something into a sauce has
great possibility to add even more value. Considering the importance of
vegetables, which appear throughout the respondents' records, this method
of mixing some cut or grated vegetables into a sauce appears to be an
opportunity to create significant added value.

Summarizing all respondents' answers, the following aspects emerge as
the most important ones.

• *Insights for meat*

Meat is the source of energy and power. Eating too much meat is not
good for the health, so it is necessary to make it appealing to eat it with
enough vegetables, and pursuing a way of making pork (which has a
healthy image) delicious using some sauce will divert people from the negative image of meat. As a result, the frequency of eating meat will probably
increase.

• *Insights for vegetables*

Meat and vegetables are considered one set. We absolutely need to eat a
lot of vegetables to avoid eating excessive amounts of meat and to achieve
nutritional balance. If her children and husband are willing to eat vegetables it helps a housewife have peace of mind. The advantage of home
barbeque over outside barbeque is to be able to eat plenty of vegetables.

Thus, it is quite important for them to eat a lot of vegetables. That is to say, it is quite important to figure out how to encourage people to willingly eat vegetables.

• *Promoting and blocking factors for barbeque*

Barbeque is quite a popular menu item for both ease of cooking and being a family favorite dish, and is thus worth enjoying as part of a holiday dinner because of the symbolism of the happy family. On the other hand, methods are required to address the troublesomeness of tidying up, and the boredom of getting tired of the taste of barbeque.

• *Increase in value of barbeque sauce*

The barbeque sauce represented by EBARA Foods Industry Inc. has established the Japanese traditional home cooking style. On the other hand, because a barbeque sauce is so familiar, people are also likely to perceive it as outdated and slightly cheap. Barbeque sauce is indispensable for barbeque, but it is still just a supporting player. It therefore makes sense to reconsider the utility of barbeque sauce and increase its value by giving it better taste, more novelty, and an original style (for example, mixing with cut or grated vegetables).

The summary is shown in Figure 6. Firstly interviewers extracted the important points from the all respondents' records and wrote them down on post-it sheets. Then, these were classified into clusters using the KJ method, and the clusters grouped into one flow diagram. We call this the barbeque mandala. The mandala is a Buddhist visual schema of the enlightened mind, because of the similarity of the relationships among all the elements in which the core elements have relative elements in the secondary layer, the third layer, and more layers.

Web Motivation Research as the Verification Method for the Hypotheses[12]

The appeal points from the in-depth interview lead to the hypotheses, that is, what type of approaches awakens consumers' buying intentions at the store. As described above, time and cost constraints limit the number of subjects for the in-depth interviews, which also have the disadvantages of subjective interpretation of the results, though it is possible to extract deep psychological insights from under the consciousness relatively easily. Therefore, Web motivation research is required to gather much of the subject data, and also allows the handling of the amazingly large volume of

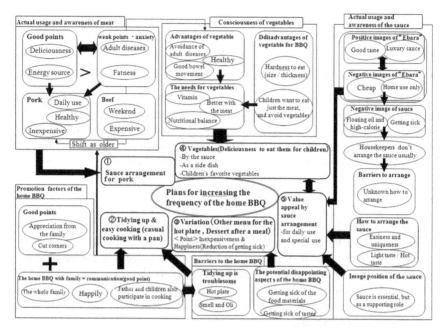

Fig. 6. Promotional Plan Policies from the Depth Interviews.

free answer data due to the text-mining. Hereafter, the authors try to verify these hypotheses with Web motivation research based on the projected methods from the quantitative approach to create some final sales promotion experimental ideas about barbeque sauce.

Creating Projection-type Questions Items for Web Motivation Research

The Internet interface required a minimum number of Japanese characters in the free answers, and respondents had to use more than the minimum number of characters, as we wanted high-quality answers. Furthermore, the questions evoked respondents' deep insights using the personification and projection approaches, which slightly surprised respondents. The criteria for sampling of respondents were as follows: They had to have a home barbeque and purchase barbeque sauce at least once every six months, and be in their thirties or forties or over 50, with 400 subjects in each age group for a total of 1,200 subjects in three prefectures of the Kanto area of Japan.

The questionnaire provided easy-to-answer introductory questions without the projective approach at first, which allowed a kind of warming up to the consecutively difficult questions to answer. As the questionnaire contained more than 30 questions in free-answer form, the researchers divided the respondents into three groups, and lessened the questions to 10 questions per respondent to reduce their answer load.

Due to the page constraints, only typical projective questions are introduced here. First, see the below Q7–Q9. Each individual respondent answers while watching the picture and each respondent should answer only one of these three questions. The purpose of these questions is to ask what kind of image the respondent has about the housewife in the picture, and to examine the differences that appear for table pan barbeque depending on the family structure at the table. The aim was to find promotion factors for home barbeque.

(1) Insights on table pan barbeque cooking

Q7. In this picture, housewife A lives with her husband. They decide to have a table pan barbeque at home one day. What kind of image do you have of the housewife? Please answer freely using more than 50 letters in Japanese. (Free answer) Figure 7

Q8. Housewife A lives with her husband and two children. In this picture, she and her children decided to have a table pan barbeque at home one day, as her husband would come home very late at night on that day.

Fig. 7.   Situation Shown: Housewife With Husband.

What kind of image do you have of her? Please answer freely using more than 50 letters. (Free answer) Figure 8

Q9. Housewife A lives with her husband and two children. In this picture, this family decided to have a table pan barbeque at home one day. What kind of image do you have of the housewife? Please answer freely using more than 50 letters. (Free answer) Figure 9

Fig. 8. Situation Shown: Housewife With Two Children, Husband Away.

Fig. 9. Situation Shown: Whole Family Present.

Next, respondents see a question that aims to derive both positive and negative images from the respondents' latent insights regarding the EBARA Ohgon no aji brand. This will be the basis for increasing the value of the brand.

(2) Positive and negative images from the conscious mind regarding EBARA Ohgon no aji.

Q18. Please imagine you are EBARA Ohgon no aji. You, as EBARA Ohgon no aji were jilted by your lover. At that time, he said, "EBARA Ohgon no aji, although I liked your (1), I did not like your (2) when we were dating."

What words do you think are appropriate in (1) and (2)? Please answer freely using more than 20 letters. (Free answer)

The third question aims at finding new styles of home barbeque by asking housewives about their own original barbeque images. These questions aim to identify factors to promote barbeque.

(3) The possibility of their own original barbeque style at home.

Q30. Housewife B said, "As I can cook my own style of barbeque at home, I prefer my home barbeque to those in restaurants." What kind of home barbeque is her own original one? Please answer freely using more than 30 letters. (Free answer)

The fourth question aims at finding concrete ways to get children to eat vegetables based on the hypothesis dealing with vegetables.

(4) The plans to get children to eat vegetables.

Q13. Housekeeper A grills vegetables and meats together, but her children tell her they don't want to eat the vegetables. She is worried about how to get them to eat vegetables. What advice would you give her to solve this problem? Please answer freely using more than 50 letters. (Free answer)

Analysis and Interpretation of Free answers from the
Web Motivation Research

The first stage of this analysis is to perform text-mining of the sentences in the answers, derive the keywords, and then check the link strength between them by counting the link frequency to understand the meaning of each keyword group in the sentences. The more *frequent* the connection between keywords, the stronger and more important the link between them seems to be. This analysis is called *co-occurrence analysis*. More detailed analysis is usually performed using the so-called frequency counting analysis, in which the occurrence ratio of quasi-synonym keyword groups is counted. Figure 10 shows an example. The first half of the Figure, part ① expresses the gathering of Japanese word co-occurrence over a certain frequency, and describes the typical original respondents' answers containing keywords into balloons for each group in order to facilitate the interpretation. The emergent percentage of the quasi-synonym keywords is shown in part ② of the figure. Since this figure was originally a Japanese illustration, some Japanese keyword descriptions remain. However, it is also explained in English in the balloons.

We next show the interpretations of the analyses for the answers using such approaches.

(1) The interpretation of the analyses of Q7–Q9: The insights for table pan cooking.

The question of Q7 is as follows: "In this picture, Housewife A lives with her husband. They decided to have a table pan barbeque at home

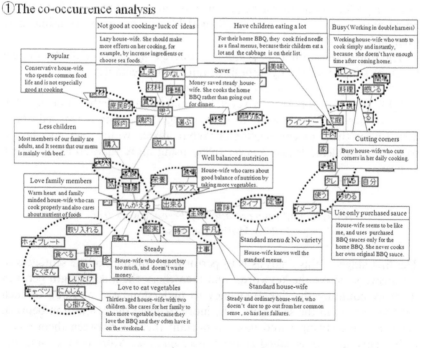

①The co-occurrence analysis

Fig. 10. How to Analyze the Answers with Text Data.

② Frequency count analysis based on co-occurrence analysis

Category (Q2)	Q2
Well balanced nutrition	36.3
Ordinary housewife	23.7
Love to eat vegetables	22.2
Love family menbers	18.8
Have children eating a lot	13.6
Saver	8.6
Lack of vegetables	7.9
Popular	6.9
Less children	6.7
Cutting corners	6.7
Standard menu & no variety	6.2
Use only purchased sauce	5.9
Busy (working in double harness)	5.2
Steady	4.9
Few repertoires of menu (stereotyped)	4.7
Smart	4.4
Not good at cooking - luck of ideas	4.2
Do not challenge	4.0
Rich	4.0
Efficient - good cooking	3.5
Poor side menus	3.5
Young housewife	3.0
Love to eat meat	2.5
Less kinds of meats	2.5
People who cook with a hot plate	2.5
Middle-aged and old Housewives	1.7
Good manager	1.7
On a diet	1.7
Standard housekeepers	1.5
Eating at home is better than eating outside	1.2
Cooking something other than the BBQ	0.5
Poorly balanced nutrition	0.2
Scheduled menu plans	0.0
Others	4.9

Format : multiple answers(MA) %

Fig. 10.   (Continued)

one day. What kind of image do you have of her? Please answer freely using more than 50 letters."

It is evident from Figure 11 that there are differences among family members in Q7, Q8, and Q9. The purpose is to determine how different the respondents' answers are. Generally, respondents had a positive image of a housekeeper who takes good care of her family and values its harmony. On the other hand, they had a negative image of the housewife as one who wanted to cut corners in housekeeping.

In the case of the couple only (Q7), the respondents most often said that the housewife wanted to enjoy the communication and dinner, but said second-most often that she wanted to cut corners because table pan cooking could reduce the labor of tidying up after dinner. In the case of four family members without the husband (Q8), the respondents felt that they wanted to be released temporarily from the stress of having to prepare the

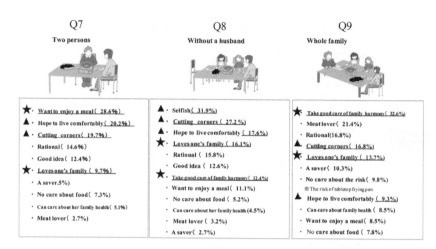

Fig. 11. Interpretation of the Analyses of Q7–Q9: The Insights of Table Pan
Cooking.

perfect dinner themselves. However, as most of the respondents seemed to
feel a sense of sin in feeling this way, they responded negatively to the question, saying that the housewife was egocentric or cutting corners. In the
final case of all four members of the family (Q9), the main association was
that the housewife took good care of her family and valued its harmony,
but approximately ten percent of respondents worried about whether the
children would be burned by the pan or the table gas range. The detailed
results of the frequency counting analysis are shown in Figure 11.

In any case, table pan cooking allows housewives to cut corners,
releases them form the stress of tidying up after dinner, and gives them a
feeling of enjoying home barbeque with their families, though respondents
do exhibit a sense of sin as they accuse her of corner cutting in the dinner
preparation. At this point the authors believed it was possible to increase
the frequency of casual-style home barbeque with table pan cooking, and
to increase the demand for Ohgon no aji barbeque sauce, but the house-
keepers' sense of sin had to be erased beforehand.

*(2) The interpretation of the analyses of Q18: The positive and negative
images of EBARA Ohgon no aji in the subconscious and unconscious mind.*

Q18 is stated in the following manner. Please imagine you are EBARA
Ohgon no aji. You, as EBARA Ohgon no aji were jilted by your lover. At
that time, he said, "EBARA Ohgon no aji, although I liked your (1), I did
not like your (2) when we were dating."

What words do you think are appropriate in place of (1) and (2)? Please answer freely using more than 20 letters. (Free answer)

As shown in Figure 12 the positive images of EBARA Ohgon no aji are mainly that it fits everyone, and that it has been unchanged through the ages. The negative images are mainly that respondents are getting tired of it, and that it has been unchanged through the ages. That is, the positive images and the negative images come from the same origins. It is clearly necessary to introduce something novel into the brand, while maintaining the unchanging reliability and quality. For example, mixing in cut or grated vegetables or other seasoning could be a good way to introduce novelty.

(3) The interpretation of the analyses of Q30: The possibility of an original housewife's barbeque taste.

Q30 is as follows. Housewife B said, "As I can cook barbeque at home in my own style, I prefer home barbeque to those in restaurants." What kind of home barbeque is her own original one? Please answer freely using more than 30 letters. (Free answer)

As evident from Table 2, respondents offered many comments about the barbeque sauce in terms of the original taste. The answer "An ingenious variation" constituted 20.4% of the responses, and there were many answers related to the sauce. On the other hand, there were many descriptions of vegetables, rather than the sauce. Therefore, there is a great possibility of devising a sauce using vegetables.

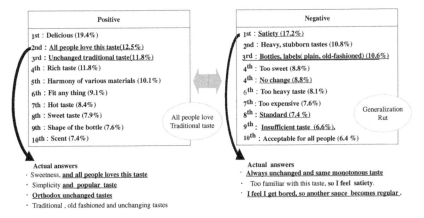

Fig. 12. Interpretation of the Analyses of Q18: The Positive and Negative Images of EBARA Ohgon no aji in the Subconscious and Unconscious Mind.

Table 2. Original Housewives' Barbeque Taste.

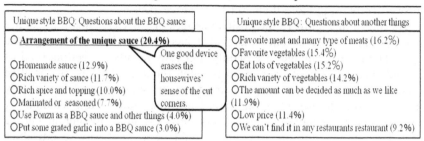

Unique style BBQ: Questions about the BBQ sauce	Unique style BBQ: Questions about another things
O **Arrangement of the unique sauce (20.4%)**	OFavorite meat and many type of meats (16.2%)
	OFavorite vegetables (15.4%)
	OEat lots of vegetables (15.2%)
OHomemade sauce (12.9%)	ORich variety of vegetables (14.2%)
ORich variety of sauce (11.7%)	OThe amount can be decided as much as we like
ORich spice and topping (10.0%)	(11.9%)
OMarinated or seasoned (7.7%)	
OUse Ponzu as a BBQ sauce and other things (4.0%)	OLow price (11.4%)
OPut some grated garlic into a BBQ sauce (3.0%)	OWe can't find it in any restaurants restaurant (9.2%)

(Callout box: One good device erases the housewives' sense of the cut corners.)

In addition, respondents were asked about devising a barbeque sauce in Q5: "What kind of barbeque sauce would you cook with for pork barbeque, if you could use magic? Please answer freely using more than 50 letters." (Free answer)

Respondents offered many ideas in response to this question. For example, respondents said: "We mix grated vegetables into the sauce," "We make a fruit-based sweet sauce," and "We mix some lemon juice or some Ponzu (Japanese sauce made primarily of soy sauce and citrus juice) into grated radish." Such innovations will eliminate housewives' sense of corner-cutting that accompanies the cooking easeof the barbeque.

(4) The interpretation of the analyses of Q13: Plans to get children to eat vegetables.

Q13 is stated in the following manner. Housekeeper A grills vegetables and meats together, but her children tell her they do not want to eat vegetables. She is worried about how to make them eat the vegetables. What advice would you give her to solve this problem? Please answer freely using more than 50 letters. (Free answer)

Respondents gave answers such as "shred the vegetables so the children cannot recognize their original shapes," and "cook vegetable soup," in addition to the device of a barbeque sauce. Although respondents gave fewer answers relating to changing the taste in order to match the children's favorite flavor, like "changing the sauce to a sweet taste," there were answers like "have variations in the sauce."

First, respondents gave the following answers in terms of ideas for vegetables.

- serve vegetables in a salad, or as sticks (9.7%)
- change their shapes, such as shredding vegetables so their original shapes are not recognizable, and grating (9.5%)

- cook vegetable soup (9.0%)
- mix grated vegetables into the sauce (7.5%)
- change their shapes into flowers or stars, etc. (6.1%)
- cook fried vegetables (4.9%)
- put some dressing on vegetables (4.6%)

Respondents also gave answers other than those listed above, most of which were regarding the use of barbeque sauce.

Examining Appeal Points of the Web Motivation Research and the Retail Store Experiment Plans

The authors considered retail store experiment plans to increase home barbeque opportunities on the basis of the results of both the in-depth interview and the Web motivation research containing the omitted parts not described in this chapter. The common theme of these plans could be the home barbeque as a means of facilitating family communication, particularly family communication with children's importance at its core. This result is derived from the projection-type question, "What would you do to obstruct a barbeque ban, if it were to be established?" and the many answers to it, such as "The home barbeque is the best communication means for a family, so a ban should not be established" (59%). Respondents also gave other answers, such as "Home barbeque gives us relaxation," and "We enjoy home barbeque very much."

The authors proposed the following four planning directions:

(1) The proposal for a full-course home barbeque.

This plan is appealing to shoppers because they can enjoy their own inexpensive barbeque menus, including unique ones, through which the authors aimed to pursue the superiority of the home barbeque. This plan includes various menus other than the usual barbeque menu. For example, it is possible to cook crepes as dessert with the same cooking tool of the barbeque.

(2) The proposal of table pan barbeque cooking as a home casual restaurant.

This plan is appealing to shoppers in that it can eliminate the negative image of the tediousness of tidying up after home barbeque, and allows them to cook and eat inexpensively and easily. The main targets are mothers, children, and married couples. In addition, this plan appeals to housewives because they can quickly join the family interaction after a quick tidy-up.

(3) The proposal of introducing various barbeque sauces in order to avoid boredom with a single barbeque sauce taste and to get children to eat vegetables willingly.

This plan is appealing to shoppers because it is very important for housewives to get their children to eat vegetables willingly because children usually hate eating vegetables. This plan also can eliminate housewives' sense of guilt about cutting corners, create their own inexpensive unique tastes for their families, and have some variations, that is to say, casual weekday barbeque or a gorgeous weekend one.

(4) The proposal of the healthy barbeque.

This plan is appealing to shoppers because they cook pork or chicken on weekdays and some beef on weekends, the former being inexpensive and very healthy. In both cases, shoppers are offered tasty menus using Ohgon no aji. This is because pork and chicken meats have a healthy and inexpensive image.

The authors produced four retail store experiment plans based on the above four planning directions by communicating with EBARA Foods industry Inc. and its in-house ad agency. However, plan (4) was excluded, and the other plans were adopted based on the company's policy. Two stores of a supermarket chain were used as experimental retail stores for each proposal, and one for the control store, in which there was no sales promotion, just a volume display. Therefore, tests were undertaken at a total of nine stores. The experiments took place at a supermarket chain whose headquarters are in the Kanto area and belongs to a large holding company of retail stores and restaurants. The main experimental period was the two weeks between February 17 (Wednesday) and March 2 (Tuesday) 2010, with slightly different time lags depending on the store. The experimental plans and pictures of the actual experiments in the stores are shown in the next several figures.

In Figures 13 and 14 Test Plan 1 chiefly portrays plan (1), and performs cross-merchandising, selling with children's favorite low-cost foods, such as Okonomiyaki (Japanese traditional pizza) mix powder, Monjayaki (Japanese traditional half-fried thin flour dough) mix powder, Okonomiyaki sauce, mayonnaise, pancake mix powder for barbeque dessert, and barbeque sauces.

In Figures 15 and 16 Test Plan 2 chiefly portrays the above plan (3), and offers variations in barbeque sauce. This plan's catchphrase was "home sauce collection 2010." This plan displays cooking ingredients (miniature vegetables, mayonnaise, box-type cut tomatoes, curry mix powder) to produce barbeque sauce variations by cutting, grating, and mixing them into

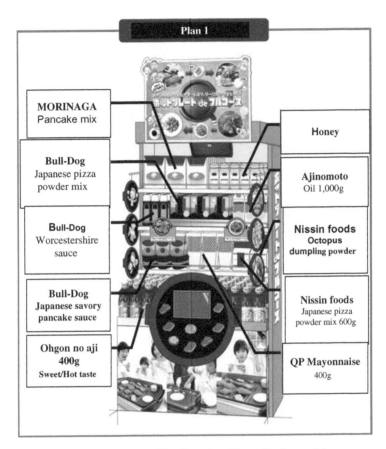

Fig. 13. Test Plan 1: The Complete Home Barbeque Menu.

the barbeque sauce. There is a special miniature stage like a fashion show in the center of these sales display stands, where the object brand Ohgon no aji looks like a fashion model.

As evident from Figure 17, the theme is the first home barbeque cooking plan for children. This test plan does not exactly express planning directions, but relates to the above plan (1), with ideas like children cooking a pancake. This plan's main appeal point is the children's first participation in cooking home barbeque with a hotplate, which would promote family communication. It is not too much to say that this plan has a common theme among test plans. This plan was performed based on the co-research company's strong wish. (Figure 18)

Fig. 14.   Test Plan 1: Pictures of the Store Experiments.

As illustrated in Figures 19 and 20, Test Plan 4 chiefly portrays the above plan (2), and suggests that an aristocratic housewife cooks home barbeque easily and quickly without the hassle of working in the kitchen even after coming home from a high-society evening. This display creates a slightly exaggerated expression, but appeals in that everyone can use it to cook easily. The goal is to get consumers who are passing near the sales stand to focus on the display because of the unreality of such an aristocratic housewife's appearance in the store. There is also cross-merchandising with products that are easy and quick to cook that are irrelevant to barbeque. The point-of-purchase (POP) signage describes housewives' wish to engage in easy and quick cooking.

Figure 21 presents a picture of the sales stand in the control store, where the object Ohgon no aji and other food products are piled high. This is a base case with which to compare the other experimental sales plans.

Measuring Short-term Effects for the SPOCMV Using the Scanner Data[13]

There are four possible sources for the sales growth during the sales promotion period in the store; these are presented below. (1) Increase in the category demand. People who seldom buy the target brand category start buying the target brand, taking advantage of the sales promotions. This

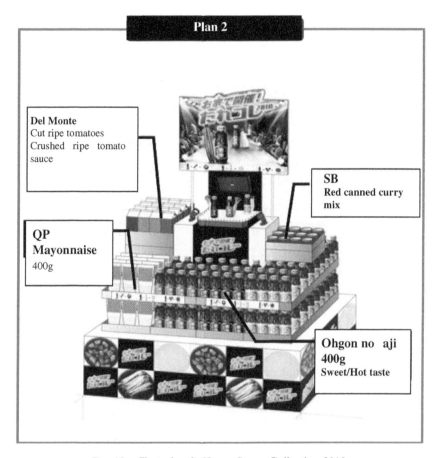

Fig. 15.   Test plan 2: Home Sauce Collection 2010.

increases the brand sales volume. (2) Brand switching. People who typically have purchased the non-target brand start buying the target brand due to the brand sales promotion. This increases the brand sales volume. (3) Stock piling of the target brand at home. People buy more than one of the target brand item, or they shorten their purchase interval due to the brand sales promotion. This increases the brand sales volume. (4) Store switching. People who typically have purchased the target brand at other stores start buying the target brand at the store with the brand sales promotion. This increases the brand sales volume.

Store N

Store E

Fig. 16.   Test plan 2: Pictures of the Store Experiments.

Brand sales growth that depends on price discounting is likely to lead to stockpiling, that is, creating demand in advance. As a result, such a promotion seldom leads to real increases in customers or long-term demand. Therefore, though the sales increase during the price-discount promotion period, they seem to drop sharply after the promotion ends.

As described above, the authors compare the performance of sales volume and the value-added promotion, that is, SPOCOMV by the experimental stores and just sales volume in the control store. Sales volume was used in the control store as a comparison to measure the correct performance as much as possible. The right figure in Figure 22 indicates the chronological expected performance of the sales volume in the control store. The control store's display itself offers no incentive such as hard price discounting to motivate purchase, so the expectation is that it will not create much demand in advance, but sales volume will drop a little after the experiment ends.

On the other hand, the SPOCOMV, which is a value-creation sales promotion, will be able to create sales growth that is not a result of creating demand in advance, but increasing the usage frequency of the brand as

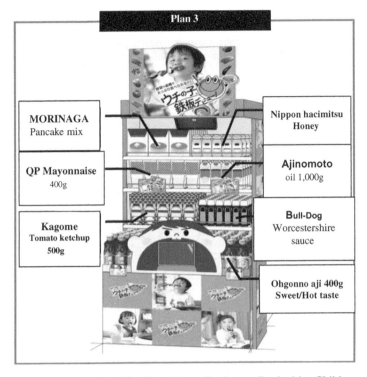

Fig. 17. Test Plan 3: The First Home Barbeque Cooked by Children.

Fig. 18. Test Plan 3: Pictures of the Store Experiments.

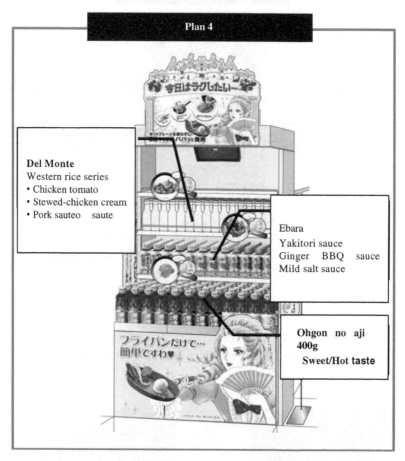

Fig. 19.   Test Plan 4: Quick and Easy Home Barbeque Cooking.

well as increasing the category demand and encouraging brand switching. Therefore, the expectation is that this will result in a demand increase not only during the sales promotional period, but also after the end of the sales promotion, which is called the *carry-over effect*. This is shown on the left side of Figure 22.

The following are the aspects to be checked for: (1) The differences between the sales increases during the sales promotion in the experiment stores and the control store. (2) The differences in the carry-over effects after the end of the sales promotions in the experiment stores and the

Fig. 20.   Test Plan 4: Pictures of the Store Experiments.

Fig. 21.   Picture of the Sales Stand in the Control Store.

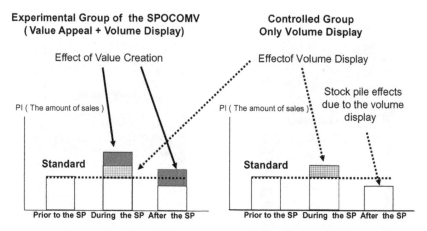

Fig. 22. The Hypothesis for the Scanner Data Analysis.

control store. (3) The plans' ranking, that is, which of the four plans is superior.

Scanner data provided by the retail stores was used to measure the performance of the plans. The monetary-based PI (Purchase Index) indicated the sales amount per 1,000 purchasers. Nine stores participated in the experiments, including one control store; they varied in terms of store scale, area characteristics, and the number of visitors, so monetary-based PI eliminated the influence of the visitor number from the total sales amount.

Monetary-based PI = sales amount ÷ number of purchasers × 1,000

It is difficult, however, to separate the pure performance of the sales promotion from the monetary-based PI. In order to address this issue, past average monetary-based PI provided a basis of comparison, so that the calculations could determine how much the sales promotion PI shifted from the past. This method shows the sales promotion's performance as a ratio:

Performance of sales promotion = monetary-based PI during the experiment ÷ past average monetary-based PI × 100

The object period for calculating the past average monetary-based PI is the same as the period of the experiment. Therefore, if no value-creation sales promotions like price discounting are performed, the calculated result for the above formula will probably surpass 100 by quite a lot, but the result after the end of the promotion will probably drop under 100 because of creating demand in advance. Thus, if the numerical result is over 100, the performance is positive, but if it is under 100, the performance is negative.

Table 3.   Promotion Effects.

	During the promotion experiment (Two weeks)	After the promotion experiment (Two weeks)
	Sales growth effects of this period	Carryover effects
value appeal + mass display (Test store)	①The amount of PI during the promotion period ÷ Average value PI × 100	③The amount of PI after the promotion period ÷ Average value PI × 100
Only mass display (Controlled store)	②The amount of PI during the promotion period ÷ Average value PI × 100	④The amount of PI after the promotion period ÷ Average value PI × 100

This verification of the SPOCOMV checks the sales increase effects during the experiments and the carry-over effects after the experiments. This verification requires checking the four effects in Table 3. For example, in the table a comparison of ① and ② reveals the sales increase effects during these experiments. If ① > ②, the SPOCMV had positive effects. Similarly, if ③ > ④, the carry-over effects are positive.

The following are the steps of concrete calculation. First, as scanner data was only available from the retail chain for a limited period, the authors calculated the daily scanner data for the two weeks before the experiments as the past average monetary-based PI. The calculating base periods are two weeks for each of the previous period, the experimental period, and the post-experimental period. During each period, the price was not necessarily fixed. As each PI value was theoretically influenced by the price variations, each PI value was adjusted to account for price discounting by converting into a fixed price calculated based on the price elasticity of each two-week period.

Analyzing the Results of the Experiments

Figure 23 presents the final results, in which it is evident that the best promotion was plan 2 (B in the figure). This proposal is the various barbeque sauces plan to avoid boredom with the single taste of barbeque sauce, and to get children to eat vegetables willingly. The index result of plan 2 was 911, that is, 9.11 times the previous sales PI, which was a fixed 100. This was a big success. In addition, the post-experiment effect was also good, with an index of 565, that is, 5.65 times the previous sales PI.

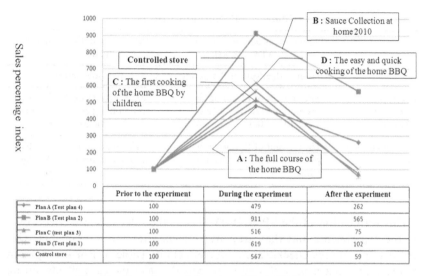

Fig. 23.   Experimental Results of Each SP Experiment.

Plan 4 (D in the figure) was the next-most successful plan, with an index of 619. This proposal is appealing to shoppers in that it can eliminate the negative image of tediousness for housewives in tidying up after home barbeque, and because they can cook and eat inexpensively and easily with table pan cooking. The result of the control store was also very good, with an experimental index of 567. However, during the post-experiment period, the experimental index dropped sharply to only 59 due to stockpiling at home. Compared to the high score of the control store result, the results of plan 1 (A in the figure: the full-course plan) and plan 3 (C in the figure: the child's debut plan) were not striking in spite of good performances, with indexes of 479 and 516, respectively. Even so, it is worth paying attention to the post-experiment results of plan 1, the full-course plan, because the index was relatively high at 262.

Table 4 presents the index compared with the control store result, which gives an easy performance image from the standpoint of the base value. Here the every duration index of the control store is represented as 100. A careful examination reveals that particularly after the experimental period, all the plans did better than the control store. This is because the control index was extremely low. The highest score was 955 (plan 2, the various barbeque sauces plan), and the second was 443 (plan 1, the full-course plan).

Table 4.   Compared with the Controlled Store (The bold and italic numbers are above the ones of the controlled store).

Plan	Prior to the experiment	During the experiment	After the experiment
Plan A (Test plan 4) The full course of the home BBQ	100	85	*443*
Plan B (Test plan 2) Sauce Collection at home 2010	100	*161*	*955*
Plan C (test plan 3) The first cooking of the home BBQ by children	100	91	*126*
Plan D (Test plan 1) The easy and quick cooking of the home BBQ	100	*109*	*173*
Controlled store	100	100	100

Note: Control store's index represented as 100.

Table 5 indicates that in terms of the cross-merchandising, which is the display of related items with Ohgon no aji barbeque sauce, the sales performances was also very high. The performances of plan 2 (the various barbeque sauces plan) and plan 1 (the full-course plan) were particularly high. These results suggest what types of cross-merchandising are profitable.

The Result of Applying PSM[14] to the SPOCOMV

Prior to this store experiment, the authors tested four PMS surveys with Web questionnaires and tried to examine consumers' acceptable price ranges.[15] The expected result was that the most acceptable plan would show the highest end points of the acceptable price range. The authors chose housewives in their thirties, forties, and over fifty in the Kanto area as the survey subjects, who had experience buying barbeque sauce by themselves at least once within six months. Each generation had an equal number of subjects, and there were 200 for each of the four plans described above. The price question items used were:

1. At what price do you begin to feel quality anxiety about this brand, as you feel it is too cheap?
2. At what price do you begin to feel this brand is cheap, though you don't feel quality anxiety?

Table 5. Cross-MD: Higher Growth Rate Items during the Experiments.

Plan	1st	2nd	3rd
Plan A (Test plan 4) The full course of the home BBQ	Cut ripe tomatoes (730)	Japanese pizza powder mix (460)	Crushed ripe tomatoes sauce (211)
Plan B (Test plan 2) Sauce Collection at home 2010	Cooking oil (715)	Crushed ripe tomatoes sauce (639)	Japanese pizza powder mix (393)
Plan C (test plan 3) The first cooking of the home BBQ by children	Crushed ripe tomatoes sauce (336)	Cut ripe tomatoes (224)	Japanese pizza powder mix (216)
Plan D (Test plan 1) The easy and quick cooking of the home BBQ	Crushed ripe tomatoes Sauce (429)	Chicken cream dona, mix powder (356)	Japanese pizza powder mix (293)
Controlled store	Crushed ripe tomatoes sauce (490)	Cut ripe tomatoes (309)	Japanese pizza powder mix (228)

Note: Numbers in parentheses are the experiment period PI index, which was expressed as 100 before the experiment.

3. At what price do you begin to feel that this brand is expensive, though you feel it to be worth buying for the quality?
4. At what price do you begin to feel it is not worth buying this brand in spite of its high quality, as you feel it to be too expensive?

Drawing a graph of the price points and extracting respondents' cumulative percentages from the answers determined consumers' acceptable price ranges. The result of the PSM analysis is in Figure 24. Next, through Web research, the authors showed the respondents brand pictures without value additions—that is, just the brand—and then the four experimental store plans, the pictures of which are described in Figures 13, 15, 17, and 19. The graph of the comparisons of these PSM results is shown in Figure 25.

The width of the arrow in this figure indicates the respondents' acceptable price range. The highest price and the lowest price are at both ends, and the ideal point and the compromised price exist at the middle of the range. Eventually, the acceptable price ranges for Ohgon no aji in the four plans showed the shift to the higher price, that is, to the right side, in comparison with the price of just the brand without value added. This result means the value-adding promotions are useful to raise the brand

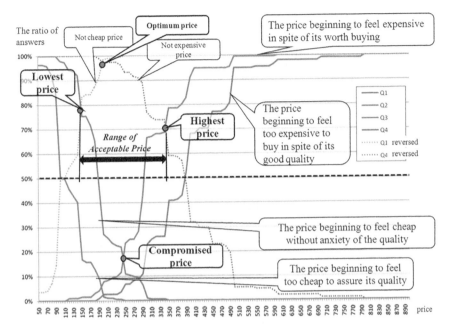

Fig. 24. The Result of PSM Analysis.

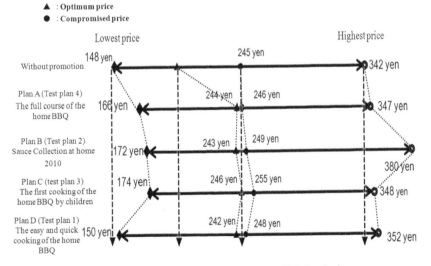

Fig. 25. Acceptable Price Ranges by PSM Analysis.

value. The upper limit price of plan 2, the home sauce collection 2010, was the top among these four plans, which is accepted at an 11.1% higher price than that of the just brand presentation. The second-highest upper limit price was that of plan 4, the easy and quick cooking home barbeque plan. The ranking was quite similar to that of the scanner data analysis.

These PSM results suggest that more experimental plans can be produced and narrowed down to the possible numbers prior to the actual store experiments. Conducting SPOCOMV with PSM prior to the actual store experiments will be extremely useful hereafter.

CONCLUSION

In conclusion, the most recommendable sales promotion of the SPOCOMV is the plan 2, the home sauce collection at home 2010. This plan attained nine times the sales amount in comparison with the prior sales with the same price during the store experiment, and five times still after the end of the experiment. This outcome is quite significant. The sales volumes of an oil brand, a box-type grated tomato brand, and a Japanese traditional pizza mix powder brand on the same stand at the same time increased approximately seven times, six times, and four times, respectively. This outcome implies that the SPOCOMV can be very effective as a cross-merchandising sales promotion technique.

If several sales promotions for barbeque sauce can be attempted at the same time, the best mix is to make the home sauce collection 2010 plan the core, and perform the second-best easy and quick home barbeque cooking plan in order to avoid wearing out the best plan, which aims at an instant increase. Then, the full-course home barbeque and the children's first home barbeque cooking plans, which aim at a long effect, should be introduced as reinforcements to popularize the brand.

The price variation influences are eliminated from these outcomes through the statistical analysis. Therefore, these results imply that even a no price discount-type sales promotion would be able to attain a large increase in sales and profit with a sufficient increase in value through the SPOCOMV. The results also suggest that producing the sales promotion from the analysis of the deep psyche analysis is important.

The sequential analyses included other questionnaire research for the store visitor, who observed the experiment at the store. In these analyses, the authors examined the correlations between the interest in the sales promotion and the actual purchases or store royalties with the covariance structure analysis, etc. However, these portions are omitted from this chapter because of lack of adequate verification due to a shortage of subjects.

ACKNOWLEDGEMENTS

The author appreciates Prof. Gerald Smith as an editor, Yoshihisa Kaneko and Hiromi Hoshino for their helpful comments on this paper.

NOTES

1. Ueda (2008), 6–7.
2. Ueda (2005), 64–68.
3. Tanaka (2002), 189 and Wada (2002), 19.
4. Suyama and Umemoto (2000), 60.
5. Wada (2002), 19.
6. Packard (1957), Japanese version 28.
7. Zaltman (2003), Japanese version 62.
8. Zaltman (2003), Japanese version 116.
9. http://www.dentsuresearch.co.jp/solution/approach/consumer6.html
10. http://koko15.hus.osaka-u.ac.jp/~mori/ensyu1-2.pdf
11. Hiromi Hoshino and Kaoru Okaze conducted this in-depth interview mainly under the supervision of Takaho Ueda.
12. Yoshihisa Kaneko conducted this Web motivation research mainly under the supervision of Takaho Ueda.
13. Kenji Mogami conducted this mesurement mainly under the supervision of Takaho Ueda.
14. Since this chapter does not focus on the PSM technique, please look for more information on this technique in the cited references.
15. Hiroko Yamanaka, a graduate student at the time, conducted this PSM research to write her master's thesis under the supervision of Takaho Ueda.

REFERENCES

Akuto, H. (Ed.). (1994). *Shouhisha Koudou No Shakai Shinrigaku [Psychology of consumer behavior]*. Tokyo, Japan: Fukumura Shuppan Inc.
Cheskin, L. (1951). *Color for profit*. Liverright publishing coTranslated by H. Oochi (1955), as Syougyou Shikisai Hand Book—Ri Wo Umu Shikisai [Commercial color handbook—Color for profit]. Tokyo, Japan: Hakuyosha Publishing Co.

Dichter, E. (1960). *The strategy of desire*. Doubleday and companyTranslated by A. Tago (1964), as Yokubou Wo Tsukuridasu Senryaku [The strategy of desire] Tokyo, Japan: DIAMOND, Inc.

Newman, J. W. (1957). *Motivation research and marketing management*. Boston, MA: Harvard UniversityTranslated by T. Matsuo, B. Kanehira, and S. Murakami (1963). Syouhisha No Shinri To Hanbai Kanri [Consumer psychology and sales management]. Tokyo, Japan: Seisinshobo.

Packard, V. (1957). *The hidden persuaders*. David Mackay CoTranslated by S. Hayashi (1958), as Kakureta Settokusya [The hidden persuaders]. Tokyo, Japan: DIAMOND, Inc.

Suyama, K., & Umemoto, H. (2000). *Nihon gata burando yuui senryaku [Japanese-type brand dominance strategy]*. Tokyo, Japan: DIAMOND, Inc.

Tanaka, H. (2002). *Kigyou wo takameru burando senryaku [Brand Strategy that enhances the company]*. Tokyo, Japan: KODANSHA.

Ueda, T. (2005). *Nippon ichi wakariyasui kakaku kettei senryaku [The most obvious pricing strategy in Japan]*. Tokyo, Japan: Asuka Shuppan Inc.

Ueda, T., & Hatai, S. (2005). Ruiji kachi taikei segumento hakken no webu radaringu chousa—Tekisuto mainingu no katsuyou [Web laddering research to discover segments based on similar value systems]. *Japan Marketing Journal, 96*, 4–17.

Wada, M. (2002). *Burando kachi kyousou [Brand value co-creation—Brand planning and brand building]*. Tokyo, Japan: DOBUNKAN SHUPPAN Co., Ltd.

Zaltman, G. (2003). *How customers think*. Harvard Business School PressTranslated by Y. Fujikawa, & S. Akutsu (2005), as Shinnou Marketing [Brain and heart marketing]. Tokyo, Japan: DIAMOND, Inc.

SECTION 4
PRICING CAPABILITY AND
PRICING INNOVATION

PRICING: FROM GOOD TO WORLD CLASS

Craig Zawada and Mike Marn

ABSTRACT

Many companies have made progress in pricing — instituting pricing rules, creating pricing organizations, and getting high-level visibility on pricing performance. Few, however, have truly turned pricing into a competitive advantage. Unfortunately, the growing complexity of pricing demands that companies take their pricing capabilities to the next level of performance. This chapter outlines some of the ways that companies can take their pricing capabilities to a higher level of performance. Managers should look at these ideas and identify one or two areas where they will take their capabilities not just to good but to a level of world class. Those that do will increasingly be able to outperform their competitors and drive significant value to the company's bottom line.

GROWING PRICING COMPLEXITY

After decades of advising companies about how to use pricing to their advantage, we have recently observed dramatic changes in the pricing

Visionary Pricing: Reflections and Advances in Honor of Dan Nimer
Advances in Business Marketing & Purchasing, Volume 19, 259–273
Copyright © 2012 by Emerald Group Publishing Limited
ISSN: 1069-0964/doi:10.1108/S1069-0964(2012)0000019017

environment that suggest that companies today need to make a step change in their pricing capabilities. Many companies have made progress in pricing – instituting pricing rules, creating pricing organizations, and getting high-level visibility on pricing performance. Few however, have truly turned pricing into a competitive advantage. Unfortunately, the growing complexity of pricing demands that companies take their pricing capabilities to the next level of performance. Those that do will increasingly be able to outperform their competitors.

To understand the changes occurring, it is helpful to break down pricing into four basic categories: (1) market strategy, (2) customer value, (3) transactions, and (4) pricing infrastructure (Fig. 1). In this chapter, we will examine the major changes in each of these categories that are shaping pricing practices today and then explain potential areas where companies can manage these forces to their competitive advantage.

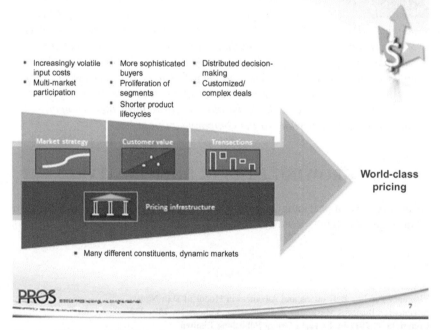

Fig. 1. Heightened Pricing Complexity at Each Level. *Source*: Walter L. Baker, Michael V. Marn, Craig C. Zawada *The Price Advantage*, Wiley Finance, 2010.

Market Strategy: Cost Volatility Increasing Amid Multiple Market Dynamics

The *market strategy* level is all about understanding how broad microeconomic components – like market demand, supply, input costs, and regulation – influence overall industry price levels. At the marketing strategy level, we've seen a dramatic increase in volatility for input costs across all industries. In the last 10 years, according to our research, there's been a 40% increase in price volatility and many companies simply don't have the systems or tools to identify and keep up with input cost fluctuations let alone respond appropriately (Fig. 2). For example, many companies that are dependent on petroleum or metals-based raw material inputs are finding that they increasingly have to deal with widely fluctuating cost inputs. Analysis needs to be constantly done on internal economics, such as how much will my costs go up or down and on which products?

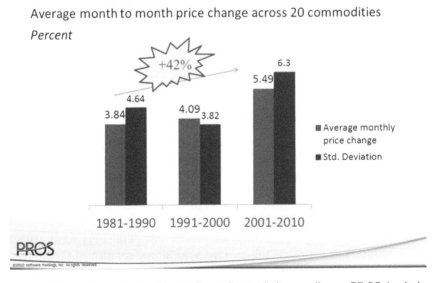

Fig. 2. Increased Volatility of Input Costs. *Source*: indexmundi.com, PROS Analysis.

Moreover, companies increasingly have to make strategic pricing decisions on if, when, and where to adjust prices given the new realities of profit risk and reward. For example, for which customers are we locked into fixed contracts? Which customers are more or less profitable? How are competitors dealing with the microeconomic changes? The bottom line is that strategic pricing decisions need to be made in a much more dynamic fashion and companies need to build the systems, organizations, and processes to be able to make these decisions.

The power to manage input cost volatility, however, can make a significant difference. For example, a computer server company faced a major challenge when an earthquake in Taiwan destroyed a key component supplier's factory. Because the server company knew the components were going to increase in costs, they responded immediately to increase their prices while their competitors lagged more than a month behind them. This server company was able to make an additional $20 million in profit from that ability to respond more quickly to cost changes.

The fragmentation of markets has also become a significant factor in pricing at the market strategy level. Our research indicates that the market dynamics of two different city locations in the same European country, for example, can show wide variations in competition, perceived value, and therefore sales success and profitability *for the exact same product*. Most companies today, however, are not equipped to identify and take advantage of geographic market differences through pricing segmentation. The result is lost opportunities to improve margins and profitability.

Customer Value: More Sophisticated Buyers, More Segments, Shorter Cycles

At the *customer value* level, the key issue is determining − within each segment that a business serves − the list price levels that best position a company's products relative to those of their competitors. So, against the market context set at the market strategy, companies strive at the customer value level to assure that they receive a fair premium for the superior product/service benefits that they deliver to customers. Another significant trend in pricing today stems from the power that purchasers have gained over producers in the marketplace. Last year alone, companies spent more than $3 billion to purchase e-procurement software to gain an advantage in negotiations (Fig. 3). This technology allows buyers to gain great insight and control over their suppliers (for example, insight into purchase trends

Spend on software tools – ($ Millions)

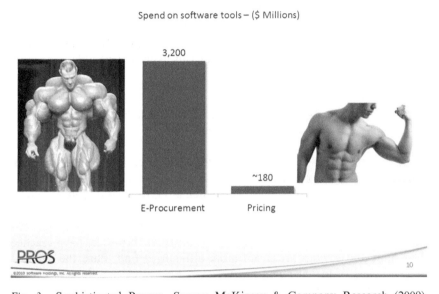

Fig. 3. Sophisticated Buyers. *Source*: McKinsey & Company Research (2009), Gartner Research (2010).

and costs to identify spend items to renegotiate, processes for receiving and reviewing competitive quotes, and access to competitive pricing information. Sellers that are not similarly prepared prior to negotiations and quoting (such as understanding customer profitability, competitive pricing, or transaction history) will find that they will lack the confidence and rationale to support their price levels.

At the same time, we've seen an explosion in the number of product segments as consumers *and businesses* want products and services that are customized to their wants and needs. This creates an enormous challenge for pricing, and makes a cost-plus approach obsolete. The conventional approach of juggling mounds of figures on spreadsheets simply can't keep pace with the frequency and complexity of various customer segments and requirements for customization and deal negotiation.

Shorter product life cycles complicate the challenge further. Products that once took years to develop are now introduced in a matter of months. From a pricing standpoint, companies need the ability to price right from the very beginning since there is no longer any margin for error. For example, when computer tablets first came out, there were some companies that tried to match or come just under the price of the Apple iPad. Buyers did not see the discount as significant enough to account for the perceived lower benefits, and sales were very poor. While these *attackers* responded by lowering the price, they had already fallen significantly behind in gaining a strong foothold in the market and will likely not be able to recover from this error.

Transactions: Pricing Decisions Widely Distributed; Deals
Grow in Complexity

The *transaction level* is the most detailed level price level where the challenge is deciding the exact price to assign to every customer transaction — from the list price set at the customer value level, to what discounts, allowances, and rebates to apply to each and every customer transaction. Much of the profit increases over the last few years have come from reducing variable and fixed costs. These cost cutting measures, however, have reached their limit and savings are much more difficult to find. Plus, the elimination of layers of management has typically pushed pricing decisions much lower in the organization. Some companies now have hundreds or even thousands of people involved in making pricing decisions. The result is an explosion of complexity as pricing involves more people in highly complicated negotiations with buyers juggling a myriad of discounts and promotions.

We have also seen that transaction pricing has become more complex because of the explosion of custom deals. For most B2B companies 15 years ago, 80% of customer deals fell under standard discounts, terms and conditions and 20% were custom negotiated deals. Today, the opposite is true for most sellers. They must contend with an enormous amount of special terms, conditions and discount structures — and most do not have the tools to manage this.

Pricing Infrastructure: More Pricing Professionals, More
Sophisticated Pricing Tools

The critical question at the *pricing infrastructure* level is what organizational structure, processes, incentives, tools, and support are needed to ensure sustainable pricing excellence? Given the changes described above, it's not surprising that we are seeing the growth of pricing departments and professionals devoted strictly to pricing within many organizations. And, to manage the complexity of all the pricing variables involved, these professionals are relying on enhanced pricing tools to help capture, process and disseminate pricing guidance when and where it is needed. That means using pricing tools to help analyze margins and develop strategies as well as equipping sales people in the field with information needed during the process of negotiating prices.

Harnessing Your Pricing Power: From Good to World Class!

For companies who have cut costs as far as they can, boosting profits further demands they explore their potential pricing power (Fig. 4). Yet, far too many companies today are stopping short — and not taking their pricing capabilities to the level required to manage the complexity of today's

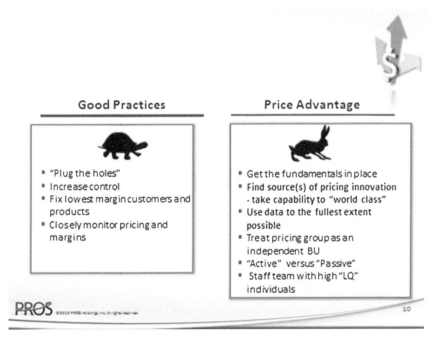

Fig. 4. The "Price Advantage" Mindset.

pricing environment. They don't possess what we call an *institutional memory of pricing*. That is, the collective wisdom of pricing in the organization is not brought to each and every deal. This often leaves their sales people isolated and on their own when negotiating with increasingly powerful customers. Companies today need to capture and bring the *collective pricing experience, wisdom and memory of all corporate staff and sales people* to bear to every transaction (Fig. 5).

The good news is that customer and pricing data has become much more readily available in the past few years. Data on customers and transactions are much more available through ERP systems, while storage and computing costs are far less. Most important, pricing tools have evolved to take advantage of this data and find the nuggets of margin upside by applying sophisticated science to finding those opportunities.

Warren Buffet was recently quoted as saying the number one thing he looks for in a company is pricing power. Some companies can exercise pricing power at will; for example, they have an overwhelming customer

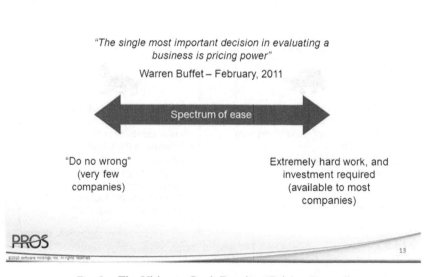

Fig. 5. The Ultimate Goal: Develop "Pricing Power."

preference, because of a technological or brand advantage, or due to control of limited supply. However, most companies have more pricing power than they realize, but this pricing power is hidden in small pockets. For example, many companies will have a large number of customers that generate adequate profitability for the company. Pricing initiatives will often target the very low profit products or customers. However, these companies miss this group of customers *in the middle* that, due to the customer segment, buying history, or cost to serve, should and will accept slightly higher prices. Finding these types of pockets of opportunity are very difficult and requires lots of detailed analyses. However, the pricing opportunity almost always *exceeds* just cutting off the bottom profit customers. Therefore, companies can achieve significant pricing power by investing in the time, effort and tools to extract these types of opportunities.

MOVING PRICING FROM GOOD TO WORLD CLASS

So in making the move from good to world class pricing, where should companies focus? We have described below several broad improvement levers that companies should consider. This is not intended to be an exhaustive list of pricing improvement levers, but rather ones that have been proven most impactful for so many businesses. Companies trying to make the jump to world class pricing should focus their attention on the one or two of these levers that address their largest gaps in pricing execution.

Gain Speed and Agility at the Market Strategy level

Coping with the forces of input cost volatility and significant local market differences requires speed and agility in pricing. Many companies use simple rules and logically group local market areas when setting their overall pricing levels. For example, an equipment rental company set their price zones based on geographic proximity under the assumption that competitive environments would be roughly similar, and that customers may cross-shop different branches. The facts told a different story however. The market and competitive environment were very different even between branches in a large metropolitan area (due to different construction activity, and the proximity of other competitors). Moreover, by analyzing the call center data, there was very little cross-shopping between branches. As a result, the company gained substantial profits by taking a more finely segmented approach to its local market price zones. They analyzed the transaction history (for example, the realized price levels on similar equipment, the amount of discounting, the current equipment utilization) to identify specific branches where prices could be adjusted upwards given the market context of that particular branch.

At the same time, given the increased volatility of input costs, companies need to go from yearly or monthly manual evaluations of cost inputs to making price adjustments in a much shorter timeframe. For some companies that can even be a matter of daily, or even hourly adjustments – so that prices accurately and immediately reflect the fluctuations of input costs when the market will bear a price change. For one distributor, we have seen this flexibility improve margins by over 100 basis points alone across an entire product line. Figure 6 highlights technology's advantages that can take companies from good to world class pricing practices.

Fig. 6. Market Strategy: From "Good to Great."

In today's dynamic markets, competitive price and product moves are more frequent than ever — requiring better and faster competitive intelligence to price well. For example, an electronics component manufacturer recently received feedback from the field that its major competitor was lowering prices on an entire class of products. This price drop was confirmed from multiple competitive bid situations, and the company was preparing to match those lower prices. However, deeper intelligence revealed in fact that the competitor was actually *exiting* that class of products and simply lowering prices to empty out its existing inventory. With this more complete competitive intelligence, the company instead immediately raised the price of the entire class of products by 5−7%.

Find and Exploit Key Variables in Customer Value

While many companies do a good job of making list price adjustments based on category-level analysis of pricing opportunities, they struggle with getting much more visibility into key differences among individual products. For example, a construction equipment company used to adjust its prices at a product category level. All hydraulic fittings would get the same price increase every year. However, they were missing the unique *DNA* of each SKU even by this category-level action. Some of the fittings were low volume and difficult to find alternatives, whereas others were easily replaceable with off the shelf parts at a local supplier. In addition, some were already much higher priced than competitors, and others still had room for increases while remaining below competitive alternatives. As a result, the company was under and over-pricing many of its hydraulic fittings. Pricing tools can deliver a granular level of analysis that makes individual product pricing not only possible but a competitive necessity.

Pricing software tools allow companies to set list prices for individual products based on a sophisticated analysis of each product's pricing history as well as comparisons with other products in similar categories. For example, these tools can look at the amount and trend of discounting on the product, the price spread, the typical share of wallet or invoice the product represents of customer purchases, competitive price trends, and availability to ascertain the product's price elasticity. This capability enables companies to quickly and easily identify underpriced products, and calculate the trade-off of margin to sales for specific list prices (Fig. 7).

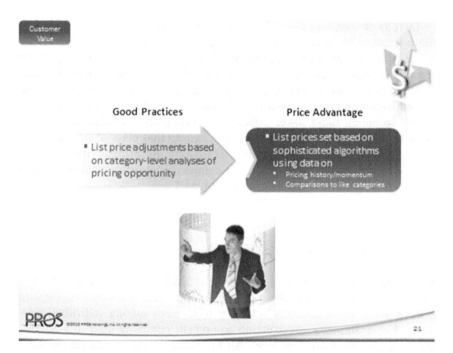

Fig. 7. Customer Value: From "Good to Great."

Provide Measurement and Guidance for Every Transaction

Despite the wealth of information generated by customer management systems, many companies are hard pressed to utilize this information fully when developing price guidelines and decision rules for setting and negotiating prices. Pricing tools technology provides a much more in-depth understanding of a customer's transactions and behavior so that underperformers can be identified and the biggest margin opportunities can be acted upon. Just as important, pricing tools can provide ongoing access to an account's transaction profitability (taking into account all of the special terms and conditions and costs to serve) and compare it to other like customers to find potential improvement opportunities.

Our experience has revealed, for example, that sophisticated transaction analysis often shows the most potential for margin improvement exists among customers in the middle range of the profitability distribution. Many companies have taken tactical measures to find the extremely low or negative profit customers. Few have applied the science to identify average profit customers that could do a little better when comparing them to other like customers. This is where scientific segmentation improves the negotiating confidence of the sales force in pushing for increases in prices and margins when it makes sense. Pricing tools can provide more accurate floor, target, and stretch price guidance at the point of negotiation and empower the sales force while enforcing accountability (Fig. 8).

Build Best Practice Performance Measures into Your Pricing Infrastructure

To fully exploit the power of pricing requires a company's pricing infra-structure be able to provide the right pricing insight to multiple levels of decision makers in the company. Unfortunately, most companies report pricing at too general a level to provide real insight on potential areas for improvement. For example, two salespeople might generate the same gross

Fig. 8. Transactions: From "Good to Great."

margins, but they could be widely different in their pricing capabilities because product or customer mix hides their true relative performance. Companies need to move from the usual categories of sales reporting and incentive structures (based on sales volume, or gross margins) to the use of true peer comparisons when comparing sales and regional pricing performance (by accounting for the sales reps unique product and customer mix differences). When a foodservice company ranked the salespeople in a particular region, they would take into account if a salesperson sold to more smaller, specialty restaurants and specialty items (which should have generated higher than average margins), than a salesperson that was selling more commodity items to large and mid-sized chain restaurants. Thus, a salesperson would know that their margin performance represented a fair comparison to other salespeople that were selling a similar customer and product mix. This transparency created a healthy tension and peer pressure for the salespeople to focus on their pricing performance in the future.

Fig. 9. Infrastructure: From "Good to Great."

With the increase in pricing departments and the number of professionals dedicated to pricing, and the phenomenal growth of available customer data, most organizations are poised to utilize their pricing power with readily available pricing analysis tools (Fig. 9).

CONCLUSION

To deliver on the promise of pricing, companies need to take a critical look at their capabilities across the market strategy, customer value, transaction, and infrastructure levels of pricing. While improvement can be made in any of these areas by better management discipline, it requires focused and significant investment to take capabilities to the level of world class. Unfortunately, too few companies are leveraging the data that they already have to the fullest extent possible − to make better pricing decisions and in motivating the organization to continue to focus on pricing. Given the increased market complexities, this type of focus will become increasingly important as a way of protecting and increasing profits, and for creating a competitive advantage in the market.

TRIBUTE TO DAN NIMER

Dan Nimer has made an indelible mark as a pioneer of the pricing profession. He is a unique individual who sees the world through a finely polished value and pricing lens. He is pricing's *great communicator*, bringing the most complex concepts of pricing and value to life with countless real-world examples − examples that are around all of us but that only Dan sees (and communicates) with such absolute clarity.

PRICING SOFTWARE: TEN PREDICTIONS FOR THE FUTURE

Allan Gray, Michael Lucaccioni, Jamie Rapperport and Elliott Yama

ABSTRACT

Recent years have seen explosive growth in the use of enterprise pricing software. Pricing software contributes to business returns by improving pricing decision-making, and by providing monitoring and process control for pricing processes across the corporation. This software has developed in a number of significant ways over the past decade and continues to evolve in terms of sophistication and ability to contribute to both top- and bottom-line growth. In this paper, the authors present a brief historical context for the role that pricing software fulfills in a typical B2B corporation, and a set of predictions of future capabilities based on emerging trends.

INTRODUCTION

Pricing, or the process of setting and (if necessary) negotiating price, used to be thought of as more art than science. Nowhere was this clearer than in the contrast with procurement, pricing's counterpart on the *buy side*

Visionary Pricing: Reflections and Advances in Honor of Dan Nimer
Advances in Business Marketing & Purchasing, Volume 19, 275–297
ISSN: 1069-0964/doi:10.1108/S1069-0964(2012)0000019018

of the corporation. Many corporations undertook major initiatives to strengthen their procurement functions by installing better data systems, aligning procurement policies with business strategies, and insisting on rigorous analysis prior to making purchasing decisions. By contrast, sales departments were left to rely on anecdotal information and personal experience to guide price setting and negotiation with customers.

Emergence of the Price Waterfall Framework

This picture began to change in the 1990s, when the *pocket price waterfall* emerged as a popular framework providing a graphical view of the pricing process and the resulting margin implications (Marn & Rosiello, 1992). In the pocket price waterfall, or price waterfall for short, the list price is shown as a baseline, with each subsequent adjustment to the price, both positive and negative, shown as one follows the waterfall from left to right (Fig. 1). Also included are customer-specific service costs, such as freight, which are effectively negative price adjustments. The waterfall culminates

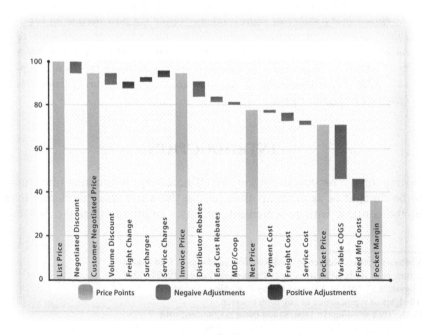

Fig. 1. Pocket Price Waterfall.

in a *pocket price*, or the price net of all adjustments, including on- and off-invoice elements, which is available to put in your pocket. A *pocket margin*, similar to a gross margin, is calculated based on pocket price less the cost of goods sold.

The price waterfall proved to be instrumental in moving pricing from an art to a data-driven decision process. The framework provides a number of benefits for analyzing pricing practices. Foremost among these benefits is the shift from viewing profitability on gross margin basis to viewing it on a pocket margin basis, where pocket margin is considered more accurate because it is based on pocket price less the service costs allocated to an individual transaction. The price waterfall also provides a means to perform comparisons of price and margin performance between peer customers or within product families. Peer comparisons allow a company to understand the attractiveness, or lack thereof, of each sale both on an absolute basis, including rebates, incentives, and service costs, and on a relative basis when compared to similar customers buying similar goods. Further still, the price waterfall unpacks or disaggregates price-related adjustments, such as freight charges, included on a customer invoice. This level of visibility allows managers to view the impact of these adjustments on margin performance and, if necessary, take action to control them.

Obstacles to Implementation

The price waterfall was, and remains, an enormously important tool for profitably managing pricing. However, when companies tried to implement the waterfall concept as a part of their regular business operations, they ran into three practical obstacles. The first obstacle was that gathering the data necessary to construct the price waterfall proved to be rather difficult because the data was spread across multiple functions in the corporation. For instance, production departments were the owners of cost-of-goods-sold data, logistics departments captured freight data, and sales or invoicing systems contained customer, revenue, and volume data. Moreover, rebate data, because it is not commonly associated with a customer's invoice, and frequently accrues over time following a sale, was typically available only to sales management teams and finance groups. As a result, gathering the information needed for comprehensive pricing and margin management was no small undertaking. Furthermore, much of the data existed at an aggregate level and had to be allocated in an appropriate manner to customers and/or products before it could be used for decision-making.

The second obstacle was the specialized expertise required to drive improvements. The price waterfall itself, and related concepts such as price segmentation, trade-off analysis, price-band management, discount-to-rebate ratio analysis, and value-based pricing, to name just a few, was very much the domain of specialists. The need for expertise, together with the sizable effort required to gather and analyze the data, meant that driving pricing improvement often required significant engagements with consulting organizations. Despite the difficulties involved, these early pricing initiatives often proved to be highly successful, achieving on average a 1–3 percent, and in some cases upward of 10 percent, incremental return on sales – which translated to 10–30 percent increase in profits. But these early successes often ran into the third obstacle: sustainability. Data gathering and analysis were often one-time exercises that lost relevance over time with changes in the market. As a result a large percentage of these initiatives, and the resulting profitability improvements, were costly and difficult to sustain. The result was a diminution in effectiveness over time characterized in the chart below (Fig. 2).

Development of Pricing Software

Sustainability was a problem, but the genie was out of the bottle. Corporations were now aware of the leverage associated with ongoing price

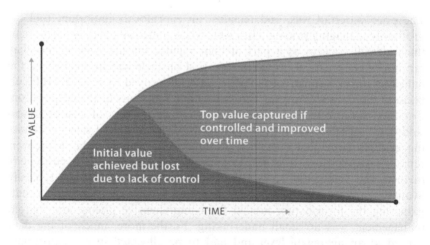

Fig. 2. One-off Project Impact vs. Sustained Price and Margin Management.

management initiatives and began working to achieve sustainable results. These early-adopters realized that the key to reaping these benefits was the definition of pricing processes in enterprise software and software's ability to embed expertise in the organization. Thus, *software* held the potential to overcome all three of the obstacles described above. It could automate the time-consuming and error-prone tasks of data gathering and analysis. It could incorporate much of the required expertise. And perhaps most importantly of all, it could make new pricing practices sustainable – by making them so straightforward that there was no longer any incentive to revert back to old habits.

Many of the early attempts to use software to drive and sustain pricing improvements used home grown, custom-built solutions which lacked the ability to keep pace with changes in the business environment. These systems successfully leveraged pricing expertise but struggled to scale with increasing amounts of data and organizational change. This led to the emergence of specialized pricing software vendors, who could build true enterprise-class pricing software and spread the R&D costs over many customers. Today's corporate pricing software features the price waterfall as a central, organizing theme and allows near-real-time analysis of an array of data needed for comprehensive price and margin management. In addition, these solutions embed and codify best-practice pricing strategies; they provide detailed views at the transaction line-item level, and they allow users to aggregate along any dimension of the business – for example, by customer, by product, by region, by business unit, or by segment. The software retains knowledge across geographies, functions, and time, thereby allowing the company's personnel to continually identify, address, and sustain price and margin improvements.

A LOOK FORWARD

The continuing evolution of pricing software is being driven by three trends that are common to most enterprise-class applications. These trends are

1. a shift in focus from automation to action;
2. the harvesting of vast troves of corporate data to extract key insights for decision-making; and
3. delivering these insights to the right people at the right time in an easy-to-use format.

What has the onset of these trends meant for today's pricing software? The shift in focus from automation to action has allowed companies to leverage software to quickly analyze and understand how changes in the marketplace affect top- and bottom-line performance, and to accelerate the implementation of corrective action plans. For example, when volatility in energy sectors results in raw material cost increases, companies leverage today's pricing software to quickly analyze the effects on margins across their product portfolio and implement the appropriate list and contract price increases. Further still, the software tracks the effectiveness of these increases, identifying the percentage of the target increase that actually sticks at the customer and product levels to ensure that customers were not able to negotiate exemptions to the increase.

Those same energy cost increases also affect expenses associated with delivery to the customer, sometimes known as *cost to serve*. Today's pricing systems link cost-to-serve information, derived from logistics systems, to the customer's charges for freight and delivery in the sales transaction system. This integration allows calculation of the percentage of freight cost recovered by the supplier at a transaction level, customer level, and overall company basis.

Further enhancing action and results, today's pricing systems are able to proactively alert sales representatives and management when freight cost recovery achievement falls below a target level, say 80 percent, for a customer, and reminds the sales representative to renegotiate prices or apply surcharges on future orders. To ensure action is taken in an appropriate timeframe, these alerts are sent via an e-mail, which contains a hyperlink to the deal-level information in the pricing system. These features make it easy and convenient to quickly update the pricing and terms and conditions for that customer's contract.

Today's pricing systems are also becoming increasingly flexible, in response to the rapidly changing pricing models seen in some industries. For example, many industries are moving from volume pricing (where discounts are based on anticipated volumes) toward volume rebates (where discounts are based on actual volumes). Other examples are the addition of surcharges for volatile cost elements (such as diesel fuel), the trend toward monetizing services rather than simply bundling these with products, and the proliferation of price points across channels. These shifts often occur within the time taken for a traditional enterprise software implementation project. In response, software vendors are making their offerings configurable, so that support for new pricing models can be rapidly added to existing systems.

What is in store for future development in pricing software? The follow-ing 10 predictions are based on the continuation of current trends in data-analysis and decision-to-action capabilities. (Note that a few of the capabilities listed below already may be available in some form from some vendors. However, these capabilities have not yet been fully adopted in the marketplace.)

(1) Pricing Software Will Take an Increasingly Holistic View of the Corporation

To date, pricing software has largely focused on capturing and analyzing transaction data. As we saw above, simply capturing all of the transactional data elements needed to populate the price waterfall and calculate pocket margin was a major advance. As pricing software evolves, however, transac-tion data will be supplemented by many other kinds of data in order to pro-vide an increasingly holistic view of pricing decisions in the corporation.

Deal Data
First to be added − if not already included − will be *deal* data. By deal data we mean the terms of proposed or agreed deals with customers, as opposed to the attributes of individual purchase orders that draw on those deals. For example, we may offer to sell an estimated 100 units of Product X to Customer Y over the course of 6 months at a price of $100 per unit. Those terms constitute deal data. Then, over the life of the agreement, the customer places 12 purchase orders, each for a different quantity and a dif-ferent requested delivery date. There are 12 transactions, but only 1 deal. Why is deal data so important? The key reason is that transaction data by definition only applies to *the deals that you won* − since deals that were lost do not lead to any transactions. As a result, transaction data almost always constitutes a biased sample. This is known as sampling on the dependent variable. This can lead to mistaken inferences about pricing. For example, suppose that historical transaction data for a certain segment shows pocket margins averaging 20 percent, but going as high as 50 per-cent (Fig. 3a). Based on this data it is tempting to tell the salesforce to aim for 50 percent margins, since that level of profitability has been achieved in the past. Now suppose the deal data shows that we have in fact previ-ously priced many deals at a 50 percent margin, but lost 98 percent of them (Fig. 3b). Suddenly 50 percent margins no longer look like such a good idea.

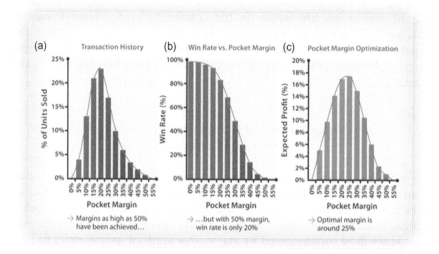

Fig. 3.   Use of Deal Data for Price Optimization.

This example illustrates another reason why deal data is so powerful: it can provide an excellent foundation for price optimization in certain kinds of business-to-business (B2B) settings. Look again at Fig. 3b. What is the optimal profit margin? If we multiply the margin by the win rate, we get an expected profit curve (Fig. 3c). This clearly shows the profit-maximizing margin, which is the margin that strikes the best balance between winning deals and earning profit on each deal. In the future, then, pricing software will capture the terms of all deals, won *or lost*, and will use this data for richer context and for optimization.

Cost Data
The next category of data that will soon be included in pricing software is cost data — not only *current* cost data, but also *projected* costs, especially for raw materials. The best of today's pricing software allows companies to react swiftly to changing costs; better still would be to anticipate them. Incorporating good cost projections will be particularly important for companies that are heavy users of volatile commodities, such as firms in the chemical industry. Correctly managing price during turning points in costs can be the difference between profit and loss in such industries.

Customer Data

Another category of data that will be added to pricing software is customer data. Note that we say customer data rather than simply market data — after all, firms negotiate with specific customers, not with the market as a whole. Examples of customer data that before long will be found in pricing software include the following:

- Total customer spend by product category (allowing a firm to calculate its share of the customer's purchases — a key metric)
- Other suppliers who compete for the customer's business
- Customer's business strategy
- Customer's switching costs

Imagine the negotiating effectiveness of a salesperson armed with this kind of data, compared to one who only knows the segment transaction history.

Competitive Data

Most pricing decisions today are made with only a hazy idea of competitors' prices. To address this deficiency, the pricing software of the future will properly capture and organize the competitive intelligence that is already gathered in an informal manner by any good sales force. It will integrate this with syndicated data from third parties such as Dun & Bradstreet, Moody's, and similar competitive vendors. The resulting data set will still rarely have 100 percent coverage, but there is scope for advanced analytics to fill in the gaps by smart interpolation. The competitive data captured by pricing software will extend beyond competitive prices. Examples of other data that are highly relevant to pricing are capacity utilization; plant openings, closings, and expansions; new or discontinued products; and promotional activity.

Salesforce Data

An intriguing possibility is to include data about the salesforce in pricing systems, because the composition, skill level, and tenure of the salesforce undeniably have an impact on pricing performance. There is evidence, for example, that the discounts offered to a given customer are related to the length of time that a sales representative has dealt with that customer (see, e.g., Ellison, Zimmerman, & Forelle, 2005). Interestingly, the correlation is not in the direction that one might hope for — a longer relationship leads to higher discounts and lower prices.

Pricing Metadata
Finally, future pricing software will mine *the pricing process itself* in search
of useful data. For example, suppose we have a workflow-management
system that escalates any deal to VP level if the proposed price is below a
defined approval level. The system can monitor the results of these escala-
tions, and draw appropriate inferences. If the VP waves through 20 out of
20 escalated deals in a certain segment, then one might reasonably infer
that pricing power in that segment is relatively low, at least in the opinion
of that VP, since she has not seen fit to push back on any of the escalated
deals. The system could then use this information to automatically recalibrate the approval levels and guidance prices for the segment in question.

(2) The Predictive Power of Pricing Software Will Increase Over Time

Software vendors love to boast that their systems enable what-if analyses.
Often these provide little more than the automation of basic arithmetic,
such as calculating the impact on profits of a price increase, assuming no
offsetting impact on volume. In the not-too distant future, however, we
will see the emergence of genuinely sophisticated predictive capabilities in
pricing software. These capabilities will be of three types of inquiry:

1. What will happen if we take a certain action (or no action at all)?
2. What will happen if competitors take a certain action?
3. What will happen if certain external events (e.g., recession, natural
   disaster, exchange rate change, commodity price spike) occur?

The point to note about these what-ifs is that they all depend on having
constructed some kind of *response model* that maps pricing and external
events to response variables such as volume, market share, revenue, and
win rate (for a good survey, see Hanssens, Parsons, & Schultz, 2003). It is
the existence of a response model that distinguishes these new, more powerful what-ifs from the purely arithmetical ones common in today's software. A key challenge here will be the extent to which reliable response
models can be automatically created and maintained by the software without intervention by skilled statisticians. Multivariable regression analysis,
for example, can be enormously powerful, but is also notorious for producing misleading conclusions if the regression output is not interpreted
correctly. As a result, considerable effort will be devoted to developing
response models that are relatively robust in the face of common problems,
such as outliers in the data and mis-specification errors.

From Point *Predictions to* Range *Predictions*

The preceding discussion implicitly assumed that the predictions being made by software are point or best guess predictions. However, as modeling sophistication increases, these point predictions will evolve into *ranges* that express the full spectrum of potential outcomes. Ranges are important because people often make different decisions when shown the range of possible outcomes stemming from an action, as opposed to just the average outcome. (This is an example of *loss aversion* in which a decision-maker prefers avoiding potential losses to acquiring similar-sized potential gains. This behavioral insight is part of prospect theory; see Kahneman & Tversky, 1979). For example, suppose we ask our pricing system to predict the impact on sales volume of a 10 percent price increase, and it replies that we can expect a 7 percent volume decline. This makes the price increase appear quite attractive, since the price elasticity is evidently well below 1.0, profits should increase, other things being equal.

Now suppose the system tells you to expect a 7 percent volume decline *on average*, but also tells you that there is 10 percent chance of the loss in volume exceeding 30 percent. A 30 percent loss of volume would be considered catastrophic in many companies, and would quite likely lead to the manager responsible being relieved of his duties. Is it worth taking a 1-in-10 chance of being fired in order to secure a useful but not transformative increase in profits? Many managers would answer a resounding *no*.

Incorporation of Competitive Reactions

The predictive power of pricing software will also increase by incorporating likely competitive responses. Pricing software will be able to analyze the structure of the competitive game in each segment, and to extract patterns that can be used to predict how a given price move will play out over time. For example, the software might detect that we are price leaders and our competitors are fast followers in a certain segment, and hence that a price cut in that segment would generate only a fleeting increase in sales volume before being neutralized by competitors.

(3) Segmentation Will Become More Sophisticated

Cube versus Tree Segmentation

To date, most pricing software has managed segments using a cube structure in which there is one segment for every possible combination of attributes. For example, a segmentation model for a company with 20 product lines, 10 regions, and 20 end-use applications could be viewed as a 20 × 10 × 20 cube, with 4,000 segments. Management generally chooses the segmentation dimensions intuitively (product line, region, and application in this example), based on their beliefs about the key drivers of pricing behavior. Cube segmentation has the virtue of simplicity, but also has some severe drawbacks.

First, cube segmentation can generally only handle two or three segmentation dimensions, otherwise the number of segments becomes completely unmanageable. This is unfortunate because there can easily be more than three factors that are important drivers of pricing behavior. Second, even with just two or three dimensions, the number of segments can still be excessive. It is difficult to keep track of 4,000 segments, even with the best pricing software. Finally, and most important, segmentation done as a cube generally leads to most of the segments being empty, or at least lacking enough data points to make statistically meaningful comparisons.

To surmount these problems, we are beginning to see the use of segmentation models that are structured as a tree rather than as a cube (Fig. 4). The key is to draw the branches of the tree in such a way that some chosen metric (like percent discount from list price) is as different as possible between segments, and as similar as possible within segments. This has the

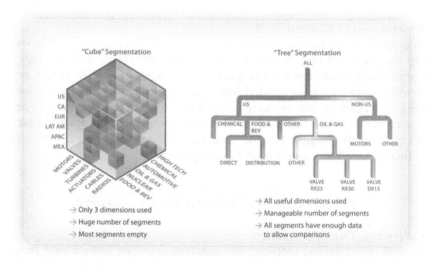

Fig. 4.   "Cube" vs. "Tree" Segmentation.

effect of minimizing the number of segments required to capture the key differences in pricing behavior, and helps overcome the deficiencies of cube-based segmentation.

First, since there is no requirement that the tree branch on the same dimension at each level in the tree, many more than two or three dimensions, can be used. For example, *All Transactions* might be split first into *North America* and *Rest of the World* (a geographical split). At level two, *North America* might by split by distribution channel, whereas *Rest of the World* might be split by product type. Thus, any given segment may be defined by only a handful of dimensions, but the tree as a whole can use as many dimensions as prove to be useful. Segmentation trees using ten to fifteen dimensions are quite common, whereas a fifteen dimensional hypercube with just ten attribute values on each dimension would have 10^{15} segments.

Second, the tree-based approach cures the problem of there being too many segments, most of which are empty or underpopulated. Tree-based segmentations are generated by repeatedly splitting larger parent segments into sub-segments. If there are insufficient data points in a parent segment to be sure that pricing behavior really is different between sub-segments, then branching will cease; the parent segment will not be split. So, by definition, no segments are created that are too small, and the segments that are created are drawn in such a way that they capture the biggest differences in pricing behavior.

(4) Pricing Software Will Guide Users Toward Opportunities in an Increasingly Intelligent Way

The first generation of pricing software enabled skilled users to uncover opportunities for better pricing. By contrast, the next generation of pricing of software will *uncover pricing opportunities for users*. This may sound like a subtle shift, but it will revolutionize the value realized by customers of enterprise pricing systems. To see this, let us compare the life of a pricing manager in 2010 to that of his successor in 2020. The pricing manager in 2010 is armed with a software infrastructure that would make his predecessors from the year 2000 envious. At the touch of a button he can see the complete price waterfall for his company; with a few mouse clicks he can drill down to individual product lines or customers. If a certain product line has become unprofitable because of unrecovered cost-to-serve elements, he can see it. If a new deal has been reached with an established customer at an unusually high discount, he can see it. If win rates in a certain segment have collapsed to below 30 percent, he can see it.

None of these facts were even visible to his predecessor in the year 2000, and all of them represent an opportunity for improved pricing in 2010. But — and here is the rub — the pricing manger of 2010 still needs to look for those opportunities. The system makes them visible, but he still has to find them. This takes time; it takes a certain amount of skill; and it takes a degree of discipline that is hard to sustain in a business world full of tight deadlines and constant interruptions.

Life will be different for the pricing manager of 2020. He arrives at work on a Monday morning to find a prioritized to-do list of pricing actions that have been automatically ranked based on urgency and the economic value at stake. He clicks on the first item in the list and the system takes him directly to a graph showing how a sudden doubling in freight costs from China is about to decimate profitability of a key product line. He clicks on the second item and it takes him directly to an analysis showing that despite a historic win rate of 70 percent, we have now lost eight consecutive deals with an important customer. He may still have five deadlines to juggle and still may be interrupted 20 times during the day, but he will observe and take action on those top two opportunities in the first hour of his workday.

Value Pricing Example: The shift identified above — from making opportunities visible to automatically finding and ranking them — will become even more pronounced as computing power continues to increase. This is because computers can uncover opportunities so deeply buried in the data that humans would almost certainly miss them. The partial automation of value pricing provides a good example.

Recent years have seen a surge of interest in value pricing — the practice of setting prices based on the value a product or service creates for customers, as opposed to a markup on costs. The logic behind value pricing is straightforward. Simply applying a standard markup to costs leaves excess value on the table where some customers in some situations would be willing to pay more. Equally, the standard markup may drive away customers who would have been profitable at lower markups.

Despite these advantages, value pricing has been less widely adopted than one might expect. This is largely because the time and effort required are often seen as being impractical for all but the most strategic products.

The gold standard way of implementing value pricing requires investing considerable time and resources to understand precisely, for each type of customer, how they use the product; the available competitive products or substitute solutions; how customers' costs and revenues are impacted by the differential value of each competitive alternative; and so on. This data is not easy to come by. Ideally it requires an in-depth consulting engagement with many different kinds of users, in which the economics underlying customer choices are painstakingly modeled. Modern market research techniques such as conjoint analysis can sometimes help the estimation process. But even these exercises typically involve an outlay approaching $100,000 and require weeks or months of effort for a single product category in a single channel. As a result most companies limit their use to a small fraction of the product portfolio.

The pricing software of the future will help to break this impasse. The key is to realize that much of what a firm needs to establish value-based pricing is already available in its data. Hidden in the data are hundreds or thousands of clues that point to untapped value. These clues lie in questions such as:

• How have prices been structured and distributed across similar deals in the past?
• How have realized prices responded to changes in list prices?
• When are win rates increasing or decreasing?

Answering these questions is repetitive, computationally-intensive, and exceptionally dull. In other words, it is a task unlikely to be done well by human pricing analysts but perfectly suited to the application of computing power.

Future pricing software will automatically comb through hundreds or thousands of segments, on a weekly or even daily basis, methodically asking and answering questions such as these, in search of opportunities for aligning price with value. The biggest opportunities will show up right at the top of pricing managers' automated to-do lists. This technology will not replace the traditional approaches to value pricing, but will greatly extend its reach.

(5) Lower Barriers Between Pricing Insight and Taking Pricing Action

We discussed above how pricing software will increasingly point users toward the most important and urgent pricing-related tasks, culminating in an automatically generated to-do list. But as we all know, making a list of tasks to do is one thing; actually doing them is quite another. Once again, pricing software will come to the rescue by seamlessly guiding users to take appropriate action based on the nature of the opportunity it has identified. For example, suppose the software alerts the pricing manager to a sudden increase in discounting behavior by the southeast regional sales office, unaccompanied by any increase in market share. The pricing manager clicks on the alert, and is shown two analyses that together help explain the apparent discrepancy. First, a time chart shows that the increase in discounting behavior began almost exactly at the moment that several experienced sales representatives retired and were replaced by new hires. Second, an analysis of competitive activity shows that we are the price leader in the southeast, and competitors are fast followers. Clearly, the inexperienced sales representatives have been attempting to buy volume through increased discounting in a market where competitive dynamics render that strategy ineffective.

To convert this insight into action, the software now presents the pricing manager with two options for taking action. One option is to temporarily reduce discount empowerment levels in the southeast. If the pricing manager has the required authority, he will be taken to the screen where these empowerment levels are set, provided with suggested changes to the settings, and guided through the process of executing them. A second option is to provide training for the new hires, focused on diagnosing patterns of competitive reactions and using this to inform bid strategies. Since the pricing manager probably lacks the authority to mandate such training, the software guides him through the process of making a training request, attaching the supporting analyses and routing the request to the necessary approvers in human resources and the divisional sales operations. To ensure that this request is not ignored, a ticket is created and tracked until the training either takes place or is formally rejected by management. In both cases, the pricing software of the future has not merely made a problem visible, but has proactively brought it to attention of the relevant managers, guided them through the process of taking action, and tracked execution until the action is either completed or knowingly halted. The contrast with today's ad hoc spreadsheets and endless e-mail chains could not be starker.

(6) Pricing Software Will Become Increasingly Supply-Aware

In most companies, pricing is managed quite separately from the supply chain. Yet there are compelling reasons to think that they should be managed jointly, and pricing software will increasingly enable that to occur. To see this, think about how supply chain costs can impact pricing decisions, and vice versa. Marketers often regard unit costs as fixed for the purposes of setting prices, but in reality costs are often a function of volume, and hence of price. For example, lower prices will lead to higher volumes, which in the long-run may lead to lower unit costs, either through economies of scale or through experience curve effects, in which unit costs are driven down by cumulative volumes. In the short run, however, the effect can be reversed: higher volumes may require costly overtime and expediting, thereby increasing unit costs. Optimal pricing over time therefore requires thinking about cost and price as being jointly determined, rather than as sequentially determined (Fig. 5).

Which indicators of the state of the supply chain will pricing software capture in the future? The answer depends on whether the business in question operates in a make-to-stock or make-to-order fashion.

Make-to-Stock Businesses
For make-to-stock businesses, which build finished goods based on forecasted demand, the key supply chain indicators captured by pricing software will be current inventory levels, the pipeline of incoming supply, and the demand forecast over the replenishment lead time. Suppose first that there is no way of securing additional supply within lead time. As soon as

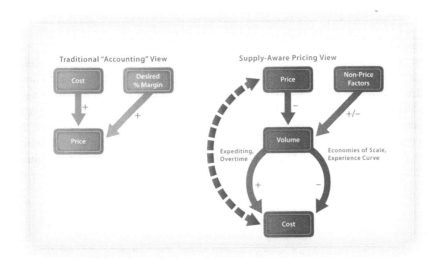

Fig. 5.   Traditional vs. Supply-Aware Views of the Cost-Price Relationship.

stockouts are projected within the lead time, pricing software will use a demand model to calculate by how much to raise prices to bring demand back into line with the available supply.

Now suppose that additional supply can in fact be made available within lead time, at a known cost (based on air freight schedules, penalties paid to suppliers for late order changes, over time rates). Now we have a three-way choice: use price to bring demand into line with supply, incur additional costs to bring supply into line with demand, or use some blend of the two approaches. In the future, pricing software will be able to rec-ommend which of these three paths to pursue. It will also be capable of automatically executing the required price changes, and making any neces-sary expedite requests to the supply chain systems.

Of course, the opposite case can also occur, in which inventories are pro-jected to increase to excessive levels. In that case it may − or may not − be appropriate to reduce prices to stimulate demand. Given a demand model, we can estimate the rate at which a given price reduction would bleed off these excess inventories. This needs to be balanced against the cost of the excess inventory. Often the cost of holding inventory is actually quite low; where inventory gets expensive is when its value erodes rapidly over time, due to short shelf lives (e.g., milk) or technological obsolescence (e.g., elec-tronics). The pricing software of the future will be capable of calculating whether inventory holding costs are so high as to justify price reductions, and, if so, what path those price reductions should take over time.

Make-to-Order Businesses

For make-to-order businesses that build finished goods only upon receipt of a purchase order, the key supply chain metrics tracked by pricing soft-ware will be production capacity and the lead times quoted to customers. In these businesses, demand is a function not only of price but also of lead time. If demand exceeds capacity, it may be better to ration demand by increasing prices rather than by subjecting customers to long lead times; the pricing software of the future will be able to orchestrate the required price changes.

(7) Deal Collaboration Will Become Progressively Easier

Correctly structuring and pricing a deal is often a collaborative affair. Var-ious levels of approval may be required; comparisons to previous similar deals are often requested; and some measure of discussion, be it live or virtual, may be needed. The pricing software of the future will streamline and simplify these various forms of collaboration. Ironically, the first contribution of software to better collaboration will be to exercise judgment about whether or not collaboration is actually necessary. Where collaboration is not required, the need for it will be eliminated. For example, there is no need to escalate a deal through an approval hierarchy whose terms are so manifestly attractive that any right-minded approver would agree to it without hesitation.

When collaboration is required, software will involve the right people, in the right order, and will show them the right information. Some of this workflow capability is already available in existing systems, but it will become more sensitive to context. For example, to whom should a deal be sent for review? Existing systems allow this to be determined on the basis of factors such as deal size and discount level. But there are clearly many other contextual factors that might influence an optimal set of deal reviewers. Perhaps a deal should be made visible to other salespeople who have had more experience with the customer and/or product in question. Perhaps the escalation path should be a function of managerial availability — the chief financial officer may want to see 10 percent of deals in normal times, but only 5 percent during the annual budgeting process. Perhaps the stage of the product lifecycle matters: Product managers may have more to contribute to pricing decisions early in a product's life than when it has reached maturity.

For some pricing decisions, the information presented by the system will not be sufficient and a free-form discussion is necessary. The pricing software of the future will enable these discussions through a variety of different media. For example, instant messaging or chat has already proven to be a useful supplement to e-mail in many companies, and is a natural addition to deal-management systems. On-demand video conferencing is another possibility, especially in corporate cultures that value face-to-face interactions. Even wikis, where multiple experts contribute their individual knowledge to a shared document, may prove to be a useful forum for certain kinds of deal collaboration.

(8) The Scope of Price Optimization Will Broaden Beyond Generating an Optimal Price

Pricing managers tend to assume that the objective of price optimization is simply to find the optimal price for each product, usually meaning the most profitable price. Indeed, this seems so obvious as to be tautological. But as pricing software develops, this assumption will be increasingly questioned and modified, in several ways.

Price Optimization for Negotiated B2B

Consider, for example, the whole domain of negotiated B2B pricing – meaning pricing in B2B settings where prices are set by negotiation. The whole concept of an optimized price sits uneasily in this context. After all, the point of a negotiation is to *arrive* at a price; price is the *output* of a negotiation, not an input. A better way to think about the role of pricing software in negotiations is that the software should generate an optimized *deal envelope* that provides data-based guidance to the negotiator, but does not presume to prejudge the outcome of the negotiation. Typically the deal envelope would include:

- a reference price that provides a suggested starting point for negotiation;
- a target price that provides guidance as to where the negotiation might be expected to end up, on average;
- a set of approval levels that drive escalation to progressively higher levels of management for progressively lower proposed prices; and
- a price floor equivalent to a walk-away price.

Sophisticated analytics can be applied to each of the points in the deal envelope. At what price, for example, should a proposed deal be escalated to a pricing manager for approval, or to the vice president of sales, or to the division president? Various factors play into this calculation. Clearly, one important factor is where the proposed deal lies relative to the history of similar deals in the past: if someone proposes the lowest-ever price in a certain segment, then that deal should generally be escalated to fairly senior levels. But this logic can be modified by knowledge of pricing power, and of the amount of business at stake. If pricing power is known to be very low, and the deal only represents a very small portion of annual revenues, then the deal is probably not worthy of escalation to an executive level, regardless of price.

Optimizing the Use of Managerial Time

The above discussion gives us another way to think about price optimization: *optimal allocation of scarce senior management time*. Often an executive will allocate a certain amount of his or her time to pricing matters; say 10 percent. The challenge is then to determine which deals to escalate to the executive in order to observe the 10 percent time constraint while maximizing the value added by the executive. Again, price relative to segment history, pricing power, and the amount at stake all play into this calculation.

Optimizing Bundling Strategies
Another potential role for pricing software is to optimize bundling strategies. Which items should be sold together in a bundle? At what price? Modern data-mining techniques can shed light on that question, by analyzing attach rates and detecting patterns in purchasing behavior. Pricing software will increasingly incorporate such capabilities.

(9) Pricing Software Will Increasingly Become Available on Mobile Platforms

Software vendors have traditionally thought of their users as working on a desktop PC, or perhaps on a laptop computer in a hotel or conference room. However, two forces are about to upend this paradigm. First, the availability of mobile platforms capable of doing serious computing is exploding. At the time of writing, sales of smartphones, tablets, and non-PC netbooks were expected to outstrip those of PCs during the course of 2011 (see Deloitte 2011). This will greatly expand the range of situations in which users expect to be able to do useful work, including work on pricing. Second, users are increasingly conscious of the cost of delay in pricing-related business processes, especially deal approval and execution. A salesperson who has to wait days for approval of a deal is at a considerable disadvantage relative to one who is able to confirm terms within hours or minutes.

The convergence of these two forces will drive vendors of pricing software to make their products available on mobile platforms in the near future. However, this will not be simply a matter of porting existing software wholesale onto new operating systems. The different form factors and use cases for mobile devices will force user interfaces to be redesigned, along with careful choices about what subset of functionality to make available to mobile users. For example, a key design imperative for smartphones is to minimize the number of clicks required to perform given task, since navigation and selection are more difficult on small screens.

(10) Pricing Software Will Support Deliberate, Structured, Experimentation

The best implementations of pricing software are eventually confronted by a paradox: The software is so successful at controlling prices that it begins to undermine the basis of its own success. The problem is that finding opportunities for improved pricing usually relies on there being a certain amount of variation − opportunities for *natural experiments* − in the data. Pricing software makes use of these natural experiments to establish relationships between price and response variables such as volumes and win rates. At most companies − prior to installing pricing software − there is no shortage of natural experiments, because pricing discipline is so lax that a large range of prices and responses have been observed. However, as the software imposes greater discipline, not only is harmful variation squeezed out, but so are the natural experiments that we formerly relied upon to measure price responses. In the extreme case, all prices have been set at the optimal level, and there is no variation left with which to recalibrate the price optimization models.

In the future, therefore, pricing software will proactively introduce just enough deliberate, structured price variation to measure price responses, while still eliminating harmful variation. This can be thought of as an instance of the exploration versus exploitation dilemma that has been widely studied in the machine learning literature. For example, suppose we have what we believe to be a profit-maximizing price, but there is an X percent probability that the true profit-maximizing price has changed. To find out if this is the case, we need to experiment with higher and lower prices. However, this comes at a cost, because $1 - X$ percent of the time the experimental prices will be suboptimal and therefore less profitable than the existing price. On the other hand, if the existing price is not optimal, this is costly too. There is therefore a tension between exploiting a known good price, and experimenting to see if a better price can be found. The software will invest just enough in experimentation to discover whether optimal price has changed, but not so much that the experimentation itself causes prices to depart substantially from optimality.

SUMMARY

Corporate pricing software has come a long way in its first decade. But as this paper has argued, the next decade holds the prospect for remarkable further advances. Pricing software was initially developed as a response to the need to institutionalize innovations such as the pocket price waterfall, and as such it largely automated the best practices of its day. But as we look to the future, it is clear that the role of pricing software will expand dramatically. The vast reservoirs of data now held by companies will be mined as never before, and the resulting insights translated into swift action by making the right choices available to the right users in the right place at the right time. It promises to be an immensely exciting journey, and one that we invite readers to join us in taking.

TRIBUTE TO DAN NIMER

We first got to know Dan Nimer in 1998 through his associations and friendships with those involved in Pricex. Dan has had a profound impact on the field of pricing. We are all indebted to him for his many forward-thinking ideas, and for the good humor he maintained while dispensing them to us.

REFERENCES

Deloitte (2011). *Technology, media, and telecommunications (TMT) predictions for 2011.* Available at http://www.deloitte.com/view/en_GX/global/industries/technology-media-telecommunications/tmt-predictions-2011/index.htm

Ellison, S., Zimmerman, A., & Forelle, C. (2005). P&G's gillette edge: The playbook it honed at wal-mart. *Wall Street Journal Online*, February 2, 2005.

Hanssens, D. M., Parsons, L. J., & Schultz, R. L. (2003). *Market response models: Econometric and time series analysis.* Boston, MA: Kluwer.

Kahneman, D., & Tversky, A. (1979). Prospect theory: An analysis of decision under risk. *Econometrica, 47*, 263–291.

Marn, M. V., & Rosiello, R. L. (1992). Managing price, gaining profit. *Harvard Business Review, 70*, 84–93.

CAPTURING THE VALUE OF PRICING ANALYTICS

Chuck Davenport, John Norkus and Michael Simonetto

ABSTRACT

When linked to human behavior and executed effectively, value-based pricing represents the most effective lever that a company has at its disposal to maximize profitability. The ability to integrate sophisticated analytics and market research in order to sell a customer the right product (and value) at the right price will drive profitability far more effectively and sustainably than other business initiatives (Marn & Rosiello, 1992, p. 84). This chapter addresses the use of analytics to determine where value resides and how to turn that analysis into an effective platform for pricing decisions. Organization-wide involvement in pricing is essential. A company must provide those persons responsible for pricing — including finance and sales persons — with information regarding the levers they can pull in the product transaction execution. Statistical business analytical software enables companies to apply microeconometrics (analytical and statistical capabilities) for the pricing and selling of products. The pricing waterfall helps companies understand where they can increase profits by using the pocket price and

Visionary Pricing: Reflections and Advances in Honor of Dan Nimer
Advances in Business Marketing & Purchasing, Volume 19, 299–333
ISSN: 1069-0964/doi:10.1108/S1069-0964(2012)0000019019

pocket margin to gain insights into which customer relationships can be more profitable than others. By examining the transaction structure, behavioral segmentation, and price optimization (three dimensions of the Analytics Triad), a company can conceive the full value proposition for groups of customers. An effective process and technology infrastructure that enables granular data development and analysis will help enable accurate and timely pricing decisions.

"One of the first rules of the analytics revolution is that years of experience are no substitute for rigorous analysis and the opposite is equally true. That rigorous analysis is no substitute for years of experience. We will have to use both," according to Robert Cross, Chairman and CEO of Revenue Analytics (Garrow & Ferguson, 2008, p. 4).

BUILDING VALUE

Warren Buffett stated that "the single most important decision in evaluating a business is pricing power," in his interview with the Financial Crisis Inquiry Commission (2011). His comment was intended to describe the characteristics of the company due to past brand building or monopolistic market positions. However, his reasoning was fundamental. Pricing is the most powerful profit lever available to managers. Even without premium market positioning, managers can significantly improve shareholder value through effective pricing.

A successful company creates value for all parties: the customer, employee, shareholder, partner, and supplier. To build that value, executives utilize their resources for greatest effectiveness by making organizational, process, tactical, and practical moves. Value can be measured in qualitative and quantitative measures such as profitability, revenues, customer and employee satisfaction, and shareholder confidence. In the words of one of the most admired chief executives in recent history, Roberto Goizueta, who led The Coca-Cola Company for two decades, "the mission of any business is to create value for its owners" (Goizueta, 1996). A company builds that value – economic value – through the economic profitability of each business transaction that a business undertakes.

Business leaders and academics have argued widely that pricing represents the strongest and most effective lever to maximize economic profitability. "Improvements in price typically have three to four times the effect on profitability as proportionate increases in volume" (Marn & Rosiello, 1992, p. 84). The authors continue: "many ... managers shy away from initiatives to improve price for fear that they will alienate or lose customers."

Some managers counter-argue that, dollar for dollar, they achieve the same transactional profit leverage by reducing variable costs, which requires no risk of customer loss or effort in appeasing unhappy buyers. While true, managers choosing not to address pricing leave a significant amount of shareholder value unclaimed, thereby reducing the effectiveness of the company's mission. To fulfill their obligations to shareholders, companies must choose to excel at pricing.

KEY INSIGHTS INTO VALUE PRICING

Companies use different approaches to determine prices. As a common path, companies choose cost-plus pricing to ensure they will make money. Contrary to general belief, however, this approach fails to consider market forces in the pricing equation. Two extreme cases serve to illustrate this problem.

In the first case, a company develops a fictional product that changes the chemistry of ordinary food to deliver the nutritional equivalent of organic food. The company spent over $10 million in research dollars to develop the product, a machine that costs $15,000 to manufacture. Because company management believes that about 2,000 households will be inclined to buy the product, management sets the price at $22,000, representing breakeven cost plus 10 percent (calculated as Price = [Fixed Cost + Variable Cost × Units Sold + 10% × Total Cost] ÷ Units Sold). The machine comes to market with much buzz, but no sales. Why? The target consumers recognize they can buy years of organic food for the price of the machine, without facing technology or breakdown risk. In short, the target market has no incentive to buy this product. Without a market, the strategy to build profits fails.

In the second extreme case, a company designed a doll collection consisting of grotesque foam caricatures of U.S. presidents. Created from molded foam, each doll costs about $1.50 to manufacture at a Chinese factory. To ensure significant profits, the company triples the unit cost to arrive at the manufacturer's suggested retail price and doubles the unit cost to arrive at the wholesale price. Given public displeasure with government, the entire first run of dolls sells out within a month, and the public clamors for more. However, the Chinese factory needs several weeks to manufacture and ship the next run. By then, the fad may have cooled. The company made money on the first run, but the CFO questions how much profit was left on the table.

These two fictitious examples illustrate the folly of cost-plus pricing. Although cost-plus represents a concrete, simple framework for pricing, the likelihood of maximizing economic profit with this approach remains small. How should companies consider pricing? "The purpose of price is not to recover costs but to capture the perceived value of the product in the mind of the customer," a statement attributed widely to pricing guru Dan Nimer. "If the customer's perception of your product's value is worth considering at all (as it most certainly is), why ignore it when it comes to price, which is precisely what perceived value is measured against by the customer" (Nimer, 1971, p. 32).

Value pricing takes into consideration what motivates the customer by addressing core questions like these:

- What is the customer willing to pay for the perceived value and utility of the product?
- How can the company extract the maximum value from the overall relationship with the customer, rather than from the individual transaction?

"The key to creating value-based policies is to understand every way in which your product or service might add more value to the customer than the product or service of a competitor, and every way that a change in a customer's behavior could add more value to you..." (Nagle, Hogan, and Zale, 2010, p. 104). An effective pricing strategy "starts with a rigorous analysis of the relevant facts — information about customers, competitive factors, market dynamics, and more. These facts can then be used to develop an integrated strategic framework to both guide an organization's internal behavior and communicate actions to an external market," (Manning and Laird, 2008, p. 2).

In the book, *Microeconometrics — Methods and Applications* (2005, p. 3), the authors Cameron and Trivedi provide an "analysis of individual-level data on the economic behavior of individuals and firms." They cite the work of Ernst Engel, among the "earliest quantitative investigators of household budgets." Engel put forth a proposition in 1857 to understand the relationship of the price elasticity of a good considering and overall household budget. That early research spawned extensive thought and investigation about how pricing in the marketplace affects behavior and consumption. Historically, the pricing and behavior relationship has been the exclusive realm of academic economists. Business lacked two things to make econometrics applicable: data availability and practical models to enable day-to-day application.

ONSET OF DATA AVAILABILITY

Although individual companies started to understand and examine value pricing as early as the 1970s and 1980s, the information infrastructure necessary to operationalize the concept was not yet in place. Pricing ideas without data were at best impotent and at worst destructive. Through the 1980s and early 1990s, the infrastructure caught up to the ideas with the development of the personal computer, local networking, distributed computing, and scalable enterprise computing (servers). These hardware technologies, together with comparable advances in software, such as production enterprise resource planning (as opposed to custom development) and client-server and distributed applications, created an incubating environment for data-driven management, including pricing (Fig. 1).

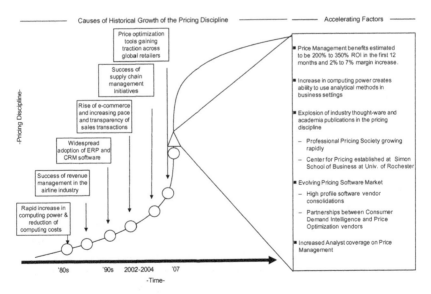

Fig. 1. Historical Growth of the Pricing Discipline and Accelerating Factors. *Source*: Deloitte Development, 2009.

The threat of Y2K in 2000 significantly motivated companies to implement ERP systems to fix failing legacy systems. Company leaders felt a responsibility to their customers, employees, and shareholders to make sure their systems and processes would not implode. Although the Y2K threat did not materialize, the surrounding hysteria drove the development of significantly improved company infrastructures. Major changes and upgrades yielded far superior electronic infrastructures and richer data sets that theoretically were available in near real time.

After the turn of the millennium, the information environment for pricing continued to mature at a rapid pace. Software companies began to develop products to exploit pricing as a powerful profit lever. Increasingly sophisticated statistical software from these companies began to move econometrics out of academia and into the real business world.

FACT FINDING AND VALUE REALIZATION

Lack of practical constructs for use in day-to-day business represented the second gap in the ability to apply econometrics. In their early article, Marn and Rosiello describe the value of the price waterfall and the pocket price band (1992, p. 84): "Reduced to their essentials, these concepts show companies where their products' prices erode between invoice price and actual transaction price, and they help companies capture untapped opportunities at that level." These concepts provided analytical models to help companies understand the true source of their transaction-level economic profitability as the base driver of company value.

Given all the structural pieces, tools, and models available today for managing pricing, management teams have few obstacles should they choose to pursue data-driven value pricing as a key plank in their profit-enhancement strategies. Not to deploy value pricing may undermine the mission to drive shareholder value. However, choosing a starting point is not always straightforward. How does a company develop the capability to deploy its understanding of all that goes into pricing, coupled with advanced and sophisticated analytics, e.g., conjoint analysis, ongoing micro-market segmentation, price optimization? How does a company make the right choices on an ongoing, sustainable basis? Unfortunately, no simple answers exist. Because of its complexity, pricing requires a simultaneous focus on six key areas (Meehan, Simonetto, Montan, & Goodin, 2011, p. 12): pricing strategy, pricing analytics, price execution,

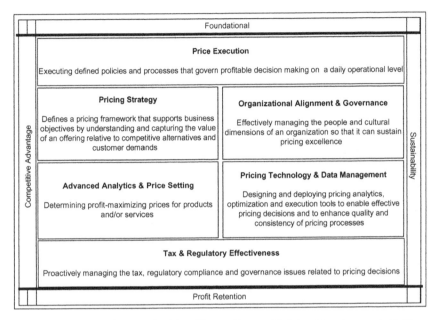

Fig. 2. Six Key Areas of Pricing Focus. *Source*: Deloitte Development, 2009.

organization alignment and pricing governance, pricing technology and data management, and regulatory effectiveness (Fig. 2).

FOCUSING ON DAY-TO-DAY PRICING OPERATIONS

While the six-box model is a comprehensive view of the pricing discipline, our focus is capturing the value of pricing analytics. To that end, the remainder of this chapter examines three areas that represent day-to-day pricing operations: (1) *pricing analytics* to guide decision-making, (2) *price execution* to implement determined actions, and (3) *organization and pricing governance* to provide the proper authority, motivation, and environment for efficient and effective execution.

Pricing Analytics to Guide Decision-Making

A company must ground its pricing choices in facts, not in gut feel or company wisdom and lore. A detailed, analytical view of three primary market considerations provides the grounding: *transaction-level patterns* of profitability, *customer segmentation* based on buying behavior, and advanced *statistical analysis of price targets*. The analysis of data required to support the Analytics Triad delivers the insights necessary to maintain the health of the market-facing profit engine of the company. A company should perform all three market analyses concurrently for two reasons:

1. The three analyses largely use the same data set, providing significant leverage for the extraction and cleansing effort.
2. The insights gained from one of the three analyses enhance what is learned from the other two analyses (Fig. 3).

Transaction profitability has been a subject of great discussion since as early as 1937, when Ronald Coase made the argument that "certain costs of making each contract will be avoided" by writing longer-term contracts (Coase 1937, p. 391). Today, however, transaction profitability has become recognized as far more complex, requiring management control of such varied issues as list price, segment asking price, sales price, transaction terms, and cost to serve. The pricing waterfall model illustrates the complexity of transaction profitability (Fig. 4).

The pricing waterfall represents the analytical structure of the fundamental value-creating unit of a particular enterprise, that is, the transaction. While each waterfall may share common elements with others, each

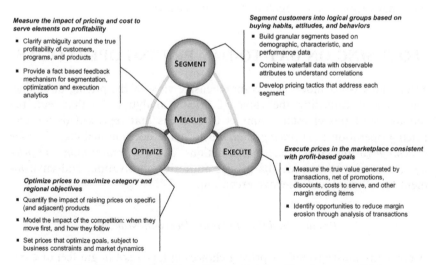

Fig. 3.   The Analytics Triad. *Source*: Deloitte Development, 2011.

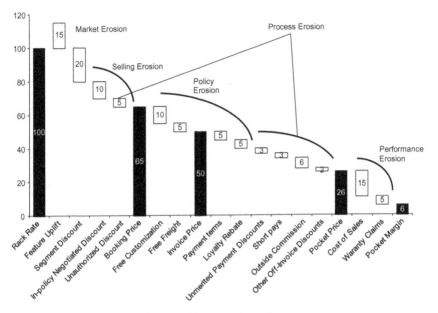

Fig. 4. The Price Waterfall.

organization has a unique waterfall. That organization may be a company, a business unit, or a smaller entity if the way it transacts business differs fundamentally from other units.

In addition to uniqueness, two principles help ensure accurate waterfall analysis:

1. *Controllable profit levers*: The waterfall represents profit levers that the team can control and attribute specifically to a transaction. Few allocations of fixed cost should be allowed, although some allocations of activity may be needed. The waterfall rarely includes unaltered accounting data.
2. *Lowest level of granularity*: As a key objective, the team should pursue insights into pricing at the lowest level of granularity, that is, the line-item on the invoice. At that level, all variations can be viewed, analyzed, and characterized by SKU/unique service identifier, customer, channel, region, salesperson, or other dimensions deemed important.

What information needs and insights may warrant organizing and analyzing millions of transactions at the line-item level? Why should a company invest in such an exercise? Most importantly, a company can identify and manage patterns of behavior and transactions that drive outlier profit performance. A company or unit with below-average profits should eliminate causative behaviors unless they provide some intangible value that can be measured elsewhere. Often, the team can characterize and trace below-average transactions to a specific customer, product, service, salesperson, channel, or geography. Then team members can take action to improve or eliminate the unprofitable behavior. Two examples lend insights into the value of the Analytics Triad:

1. *Flooring manufacturer example:* Having served its largest, most valuable customer for over a decade, a large flooring manufacturer would do anything to address the needs of this customer. However, the manufacturer analyzed that relationship through the lens of a transactional profitability analysis. Using its pricing waterfall as a basis for analysis, the flooring manufacturer realized that this customer was destroying value. In fact, the manufacturer likely had never made money on a single transaction with this customer. Growth in the account contributed to shrinking profits for the manufacturer. After deliberation, the company decided to let go of its largest customer and to focus only on valuable customers — those that contribute to business profitability. (The section below on pricing execution describes how to take action based on insights gained from analytics.)

2. *Specialty chemicals manufacturer example:* A specialty chemicals manufacturer identified a way to reduce per-unit transportation cost by providing pricing incentives to customers who ordered full-pallet quantities. Although the mixed pallet discount seemed like a good idea, it was not. Upon examining the detailed transaction economics, the manufacturer found that customers filled pallets with low-profit, low-priced products to get a steep discount on one or two bags of the expensive and (formerly) profitable product. Perhaps even more interesting, some customers returned bags of product, thereby making money on the return and on the discount. In understanding this hole in its discounting policy, the manufacturer plugged the leakage and offered the discount only on orders that merited it. That fix provided over $300,000 in annual cash profit in the United States alone.

The Pricing Waterfall: Illustrated and Explained

Although no standard structure exists for the pricing waterfall, certain conventions guide waterfall construction to deliver specific insights to management. For example, organizing the waterfall to show related buckets of profit erosion can help identify processes, policies, and procedures that represent prime opportunities for improvement. Companies commonly employ divisions such as market erosion, selling erosion, policy erosion, process erosion, and performance erosion.

The left side of the pricing waterfall details the revenue side of the transaction, which comprises two divisions: market erosion and selling erosion (Fig. 4). *Market erosion* encompasses all pricing erosions from the top-level price, such as an international reference price or another pinnacle price controlled by external forces. Driving forces for price erosion may include changes and mismatches in supply and demand, the entrance or exit of competitors, new product introductions that may cannibalize a market, severe changes in competitor pricing, or undifferentiated products (commoditization). The price optimization section of this chapter examines market erosion in more detail.

Selling erosion occurs in two forms: *systematic price discrimination* through categorization and segmentation, and *transaction leakage*. Systematic price discrimination involves any structured form of price differentiation based on customer characteristics. Often this discrimination takes the form of segmentation based on size or type, such as customer industry or end-use characterization.

As an example of systematic price discrimination, in the industrial gas business a company may sell containerized oxygen from the same production line to a medical supply company (as medical oxygen for therapy) and to a construction supply company (for welding). The medical supply company requires a product with a high purity level of oxygen, while the construction industry does not require that same purity level. However, given no capacity constraints, the industrial gas company will increase its efficiency by producing and selling one grade of gas to both buyers. Given the specific customer requirements, the product may require different quality assurance and packaging to meet the buyers' expectation levels. A higher price for the product to the medical company reflects additional value to the buyer. Moreover, such differences in end-use requirements drive the medical industry into a distinctly different value segment than the construction industry, necessitating different list prices and discounting rules.

Transaction leakage, the second type of selling erosion, stems from the company's negotiating process with an individual customer. To draw a distinction with process erosion, transaction leakage is defined as discounting offered to a customer within the bounds of current policies and procedures. In the absence of specific policies, all explicitly negotiated leakages reside in the category of transaction leakage. However, in progressive companies, the pricing guardrails (a target price and a floor price) established by policy tend to differ by customer segment because of such factors as value in use, competitive rivalry, switching costs, and customer value. Does the use of guardrails require all transactions to be executed at the floor price, which may represent the path of least resistance for the sales force? The answer should be *no* if the sales force receives proper motivation and oversight, which is discussed in the section on organization and pricing governance.

Policy erosion represents a unique section of the waterfall because it may or may not affect the invoice price of the good or service. Because policy erosion, a type of profit leakage, results from deliberate sales and customer service policies, this too is within bounds for the sales force. Such policies often result from industry norms or real/perceived customer needs and competitive threats. As an example of a normative expectation within the process chemicals industry, the sales price is a landed price with freight included. The customer expectation for free freight puts a significant burden on the supplier to determine the most efficient shipping route to the customer. For the smaller player, such a market expectation may limit geographic expansion because moving a bulky, commoditized product may make little sense from a profit perspective.

Continuing with the freight example, some distributors may collect revenue for freight in the form of a fixed delivery fee per order. This helps motivate the customer to order in a way that is economically feasible for the distributor. However, like free freight, fixed freight in the form of a delivery fee puts the burden on the distributor to be operationally efficient. If delivery costs for a transaction exceed the delivery fee, as they often do, the excess costs become a profit leakage against the invoiced revenue.

Other contributors to policy erosion may include payment terms, early payment discounts, cumulative purchase rebates, free samples, no-charge packaging and labeling, and credit for returns of expired or obsolete product. Illustrative examples include: credit for returns of expired/stale packaged bakery products (such as bread); consumer packaged goods companies providing free product for sampling events at retail stores; volume rebates that suppliers pay distributors for pushing specific products or brands; and pricing exceptions that flow through proper channels and approvals. Although the policies are the same, profit leakages tied to policy erosion can differ markedly customer by customer and even salesperson by salesperson.

All discounts and leakages discussed thus far have been within policy, that is, within the pricing boundaries set forth by a management team.

However, in many cases, companies may execute transactions outside of the stated and official boundaries. In such cases, leakages are indicative of process erosion: transactional profit reductions caused by lack of adherence to policies and procedures. Fully executed exceptions without approvals reveal process and governance flaws in a company's pricing capability. In addition to obvious exceptions of noncompliant contracts, many exceptions result from misalignment or poor information flow between sales processes and financial processes, such as within the accounts receivable process. Of course, sometimes internal stakeholders may drive misalignments deliberately. The sales force, for example, may find ways to work around process controls. Other misalignments result from deliberate or accidental inaccuracies in customer payments, such as short pays tied to unmerited early payment discounts or unpaid payment terms penalties. Regardless of the source of process erosion, patching such process holes before addressing other issues will help retain upstream profit opportunities.

Performance erosion, the final category, details the return of realized revenue and profit because of performance failures. Typical elements include credits and returns, uncompensated service or training, warranty claims, non-performance penalties, unwarranted free freight, and excessive selling costs. While the sales force may not control many elements directly in performance erosion, the ability to characterize and analyze those elements may provide forensic evidence of systematic flaws or abuses in customer management and perhaps even sales processes. For example, a provider of lawn chemicals selling directly to end users, landscape maintenance service providers, and so on, relies largely on a size-based customer segmentation scheme. Larger customers receive larger discounts. The lawn chemicals company's transaction profitability analysis (TFA) revealed that many large customers had purchased volumes that qualified them for this segment. Yet, these customers also had significant product returns that net-net reduced them to the status of medium-sized customers. However, the returns never affected the segment or the resulting discount.

Identifying Actionable Opportunities: The Analytics Triad

Although understanding the transaction structure provides management with a valuable perspective, producing and examining the waterfall will not put anything of value in the company's coffers. The Analytics Triad helps companies identify actionable opportunities across all divisions of the pricing waterfall. The three analyses represented by the triad include (a) TFA, (b) qualitative resolution, and (c) price optimization. Although distinct from one another, the three analyses require roughly the same data to employ them. Moreover, investing in one aspect without completing the triad represents a lost opportunity. Taken together, the three analyses may drive exponentially greater value than marginal cost.

Transaction Profitability Analysis

To manage economic profit effectively, a company ultimately must identify patterns of behavior that drive profit enhancement or profit leakage. An analysis of the pricing waterfall data lends insight into the behavioral symptoms for a given customer, product, channel, geography, salesperson, or combination thereof. Although data might be indicative of a problem, the underlying root cause cannot be found quantitatively. The TPA requires a qualitative-quantitative-qualitative approach to opportunity identification.

Given the mountain of data required to characterize profit at a line-item, invoice level, diving into data analysis immediately may prove fruitless. "The TPA process must be hypothesis driven" (Meehan et al., 2011, p. 143). Accessing the wisdom and insight that already resides in an organization, although perhaps fragmented, will reduce the effort of a TPA significantly, while increasing the likely value. Since pricing and profitability touch nearly every company function (and vice versa), the ability to cast a wide net of interviews prior to data analysis will yield a broad set of hypotheses about opportunities in each division of the waterfall.

Even with hypothesis-driven prioritization, the team will find the quantitative task daunting. However, each scenario does not require analysis. Moreover, the objective to speed toward significant benefit should drive prioritization. The ability to identify and analyze the areas of greatest leverage ensures an efficient use of the analytical resources deployed in the TPA. Three high-level questions and the respective sample analytical constructs will drive insights (Fig. 5): Where should the team focus? Where are the outliers? What leakages currently drive profit deficiencies?

Qualitative Resolution

The three high-level quantitative questions reveal focused and precise areas of opportunity, but they do not reveal why the opportunities exist. To create value and enact change, the team must determine the root causes so they can work to alter human behavior of internal stakeholders or customers. An in-depth review of pricing processes, policies, procedures,

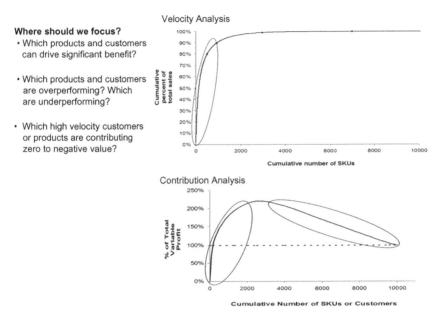

Fig. 5. Three High-Level Questions and Accompanying Analytical Constructs. *Source*: Deloitte Development, 2011.

controls, and information availability will reveal what strengths and weaknesses in a company's pricing capabilities allow outliers to exist. Such a review will uncover significant improvement opportunities.

The ability to understand what types of customers buy and pay, and also to infer the value those customers derive from a product, will provide high value. Customer segmentation, the second leg of the analytics triad, provides the insights necessary to develop a profitable and cohesive market approach. "Some business-to-business companies slice their markets by industry; others by size of business. The problem with such segmentation schemes is that they are static. Customers' buying behaviors change far more often than their demographics, psychographics or attitudes." (Christensen, Scott, Berstell, & Nitterhouse, 2007, p. 38). In addition, without actionable and dynamic segmentation, price discrimination and rational customer investments are at best approximately accurate at the time they are developed and are often maintained based on common wisdom and company lore. Precision is nearly impossible.

What are our outliers?

• Which products have the greatest variation in pricing and profitability?

• Which product families consistently garner high pocket prices?

• What price band drives the greatest volume in each customer segment?

• Is there a discernable pattern in unmerited low-priced transactions in low-value customer segments? In high-priced transactions in high-value segments?

• Which customers are receiving unwarranted discounts based on volume?

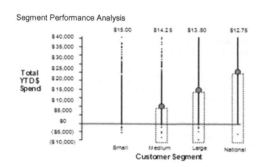

Segment Performance Analysis

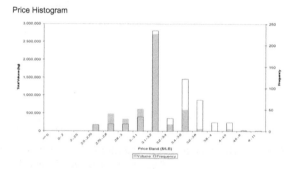

Price Histogram

Fig. 5. (*Continued*)

Why is segmentation so critical? "It is better to serve different market segments with separate price points, rather than serve the entire market with one price point." (Nagle and Holden, p. 228). A company can capture the value of those customers willing to pay higher prices without giving up the volume of customers that are not. At some level, the customer's industry, the end use of the product, and the customer's size can partially explain buying behavior. The static nature of these characteristics makes them easily knowable and manageable. However, a deeper level of insight into customer behavior will enhance the profit potential of each customer significantly. Additionally, understanding why a customer will buy at a particular price point provides two benefits.

First, with that understanding about the customer, the company can tailor an offer and a marketing approach to entice the buyer in the most economically advantageous way. The company should design offers to include the proper service model to avoid overserving the customer (leading to excess costs) or underserving the customer (leading to competitive

What leakages are driving profit deficiencies?
- Given a specific outlier, what are the critical drivers of low or high profitability?

- Given a specific customer, segment, product, or channel, what are the critical drivers of profitability?

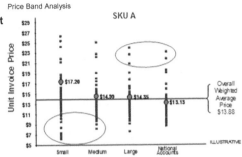

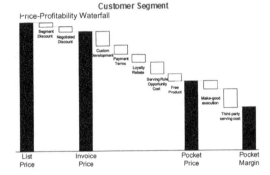

Fig. 5. (Continued)

exposure). Offers also should include fences, that is, elements that remove attractive elements/features for this customer at lower price points, thereby preventing cannibalization by lower-priced offers. The classic example of a price fence is the Saturday night stay-over requirement to qualify for a discounted airfare. The airlines deployed this pricing technique to extract premium fares from business flyers, while allowing more affordable fares for leisure flyers that usually stayed over a weekend.

Second, in understanding why a customer buys, the seller derives a basis for characterizing other customers for whom the company may not have as much information. The company gains significant competitive advantage by drawing a composite picture and creating a taxonomy of customer buying behavior so that groups of customers can be managed together to create profit enhancement strategies. Ideally, all stakeholders within a company would be so aligned to profit production that every customer could exist as its own segment. However, the ideal profit is impossible to determine. Because the sales team generally sets profit expectations by performance comparisons, one-customer segments remain impractical. Practically speaking, segments granular enough to allow relevant differences in market treatment will help the seller realize the vast majority of theoretical discrimination value by informing decisions such as customer investment, sales force deployment, service channel choices, and pricing guidelines. Such granular segmentation also helps the seller address each segment of a customer, including frequency and value of purchases and payments, motivation for buying, perceived value of the product, level and frequency of service demanded, and difficulty in cost of selling and characterizing customers.

Ultimately, segmentation helps companies make the right offer to the right customer at the right time through the right channel at the right price. This is critical to continuing revenue growth as a company expands its focus to a broader customer base. Once a customer's interest is captured, the price can seal the deal. However, companies must take care in sealing the deal with price, as pricing has a lasting effect beyond the initial sale. Dan Ariely, in his book *Predictably Irrational*, provides research-based insights into how people make decisions, including what influences their choices in buying products or services. Ariely questions the assumption that supply and demand are "independent and that together they produce the market price." Based on his research, "... instead of consumers' willingness to pay influencing market prices, the causality is somewhat reversed and it is market prices themselves that influence consumers' willingness to pay. What this means is that demand is not, in fact, a completely separate force from supply" (Ariely 2009, p. 47). Moreover, Ariely underscores the role of anchor or reference prices in the buying process − the first price the consumer/customer identifies with a product as they "contemplate buying a product or service at that particular price ....
Thus the first anchor influences not only the immediate buying decision but many others that follow" (p. 32).

Price Optimization
Because the nature of customer buying behavior continues to change, the effectiveness of the final leg of the Analytics Triad increases when treated as an ongoing process rather than a single analysis. Price optimization can be defined generally as "evaluating multiple options on how to sell your product and to whom to sell your product" (Cross 1997, p. 178). The process, however, can be daunting, especially in complex, highly competitive markets. Yet, each step in the optimization process provides insights that assist in refining other market treatments, including customer segment

construction and makeup, the product lifecycle stage, requirements for new products or product enhancements, offer construction, and targeted requirements for cost basis.

The essence of price optimization embodies the relationship of supply, demand, and price in the context of customer segments. Employing statistical techniques to derive correlative relationships between variables is not new. However, in the realm of pricing, the stakes remain high – particularly the cost of being significantly wrong. Therefore, careful model construction must be a priority. The following five considerations help keep optimization processes on track.

1. If using historical data, cleanse the data thoroughly and normalize as necessary. Unexplained outliers not representative of normal conditions can alter the validity and accuracy of a model significantly.
2. Recognize demand modeling as more than a mathematical exercise. Apply business context in developing independent variables. Also keep in mind that correlative relationships are not necessarily causative.
3. Externalities such as competitive response, threat of new entrants, economic conditions in customer markets, and changing technology will affect the validity of models. For that reason, approach optimization is more than a one-time exercise.
4. Simple, valid models perform better than models tied to historical market or transaction anomalies. "The analysis should begin with a simple model that includes the most important predictor variables and excludes unnecessary or synthetic ones" (Meehan et al., 2011, p. 173). The models predict the future, although they do not describe the past with great accuracy.
5. Define business constraints carefully, considering the needs of operations as the drivers of profitability. For instance, a chemicals manufacturer considers two price points, both on the efficient horizon where they deliver equal gross profit for the company. However, the higher price point would drive lower volume, require less efficient order quantities, and not allow the production plant to run at optimal capacity. When considering these operational constraints, the lower price would deliver higher overall profits to the company.

Demand modeling/forecasting works closely with price optimization. In fact, price optimization cannot be done without demand modeling. However, some companies stop after completing demand models because they believe they need volume forecasts only. Unfortunately, stopping at forecasting tends to leave significant profit on the table. "Forecasting suggests what customers are likely to do. Optimization suggests what you should do about it" (Cross, 1997, p. 178). Optimization determines solid guidelines for pricing, given certain market conditions and constraints. Despite limitations, including the ongoing effort required, applying optimization often results in the capture of significant profit opportunities.

The Analytics Triad can deliver significant benefits to any company employing it. Taken together, the ability to understand transaction-level profitability, the levers that affect it, how customers differ in their buying behavior, and how to deliver the right price for the right product to the right customer at the right time served through the right channel create a complete picture of the economics of transactions. Undoubtedly, this effort will help a company identify shortcomings in performance and opportunities to improve profits. However, a company will find the most significant value by instituting these capabilities and moving them from ad hoc efforts to ongoing processes. Such an approach requires deliberate focus and effort to build the infrastructure that will deliver valuable insights to those who can act on them, and then to shape the organization, process, policies, and procedures to guide and govern the actions highlighted through analytics.

Price Execution

Price execution provides the foundation for pricing competency. Without effective execution, the company's pricing capability has no value. The pricing strategy is worthless without the ability to turn it into action. Pricing technology achieves nothing without the proper processes in place to make productive use of it. A pricing organization becomes a waste of time if a lack of rigorous process allows its work and recommendations to be undermined.

As a case in point, a large manufacturer of enterprise hardware systems had a well-defined price creation process. The company's centralized pricing group filled requests to price complex, multi-product/service packages for customers, using corporate guidelines for customer segment pricing and bid size. Arguably, the transaction was profitable when conceived by the pricing group. However, the process and oversight ended there, prior to final negotiations, which were left in the hands of the sales force. Upon examination, the final transactions failed to match profitability expectations. Even the product/service mix was different. Clearly, following the initial bid, the sales force relied on an informal process to do as it pleased.

Execution defines (1) the ability to deliver an idea to the market, including a price change, a product/bundles offer, pricing or channel service policy, or any other customer-facing treatment, and (2) the capacity to make it a reality with accuracy, consistency, and validity. Effective execution requires defined, controlled, and enforced processes, policies, and procedures, which together help deliver new prices and guardrail policies to the field and support the ongoing monitoring of activity to maintain proper compliance and management of pricing exceptions.

Much like the waterfall, a pricing execution environment is unique to a company. However, the building blocks of that environment, common to any company with advanced capabilities, include communication, competitive and market assessment, deal/contract development, exception management, and measurement and performance management. Details about these five building blocks for an effective pricing execution environment follow.

Communication

While effective communication seems basic to any business process, the criticality of synchronization among various internal stakeholders and the need to communicate on multiple levels with widely varied stakeholders, both internal and external, creates complexity in pricing communications that does not exist in other disciplines.

The struggle of a medical device manufacturer helps illustrate the issues with synchronization. For this manufacturer, a steady increase in short-paid invoices from customers highlighted an internal communication issue. When Accounts Receivable followed up, customers pointed to incorrect unit prices on their invoices. For Accounts Receivable, this finding raised questions because the invoice unit price matched the price in the system. Upon investigation, the company determined that the customers were correct. Although the new price was updated in the system, a delay occurred in getting that revised pricing information to the field sales organization. During the lag time, the sales team executed transactions at the old price. Accounts Receivable produced the invoice based on the new price. This deficiency in internal price communication resulted in a cost to the company of hundreds of thousands of dollars per year. That cost included lost profit due to short pays, as well as the cost of employees hired by the Accounts Receivable department to identify issues and collect on short-paid invoices. In addition, the company had compromised its relationship with the customers, which would take time to mend.

Companies continue to face price communication issues. In the example described, the issue of price communication was particularly critical because this company used discrete pricing regularly rather than customized or bundled pricing. However, changes to pricing guardrails and other policies that affect transaction profitability cause similar issues if the company does not align changes across functions.

To control such difficulties, companies often implement specific procedures to govern price management and administration. Although communication content will vary based on unique company needs, such communication typically may include timing specifics, pricing and program changes, promotions, changes to exception procedures, and briefings on broader market-based communications programs.

Equally important, the company must plan and execute external communications on multiple levels. In any market, a company must communicate with at least two primary groups: customers and competitors. Public companies should add stakeholders in the financial markets too. Under U.S. antitrust law, price communication directed at competitors is illegal and could be considered collusion. However, "communications with a justifiable commercial purpose are generally appropriate" (Baker, Marn, & Zawada, 2010, p. 144). Among legitimate business purposes, communication provides awareness of and commentary about price changes. For example, cost increases for commodities might be an accepted reason for price increases. Communicating the existence of excess inventory might serve to put the customer on notice not to reset reference prices, because the discount is temporary due to a short-term operational and financial concern. This communication might also help protect against a price war, rather than serve as a competitive grab at market share for the long term. As perhaps the core benefit of broad communication of price moves, the sales force has air cover under which to work.

While internal communications among functions and external communications on a macro and micro level represent separate efforts, their synchronization in terms of timing and message will enhance a company's ability to execute prices by aligning expectations and creating an environment for rational discussion.

Competitive and Market Assessment

All companies collect competitive and market data on some level. The company needs that data to discuss market position, competitive and market strategy, and target market sizing. Unfortunately, many companies make mistakes in how they gather, store, and use these data. Some companies treat competitive and market assessment as a series of discrete efforts. They perform assessments in conjunction with major events, such as new product development, market entry, major price changes, and so on. This approach leaves significant holes in their understanding of their markets and the minor shifts and changes that may present significant profit opportunities. On the other end of the spectrum, a company may gather market and competitive information on a continuing basis, but informally through the sales force and other market-facing channels, such as customer service representatives and partners. This approach may provide context for the short term or even a specific transaction, but it cannot drive organizational learning and wisdom because the company never collects and codifies data in a way that can be studied.

A company manages effective market assessment as a continuous process managed like other processes through definition, documentation, role assignment, and measurement. All market-facing stakeholders have an important role in this process. Together with their managers, they measure their activities and outcomes in two ways: collecting and using informal information and undertaking discrete efforts in circumstances described above. As the information engine of execution, such disciplined market/competitive data collection enables a company to manage profit results in any macro- or microeconomic situation.

Deal/Contract Development

The core activity of every sales force is deal development. Effective salespeople spend the vast majority of their time courting and closing deals with customers. This distribution of independent activity creates difficulty in control of deal parameters. Certainly, the measurement and compensation scheme for the salespeople helps maintain desired performance. Generally, however, performance measurement feedback describes historical actions. Leading practices in pricing require in-process controls during deal/contract development. Companies can implement controls in various ways. Often, leading companies use a combination of techniques to cover a broader spectrum of situations. Such techniques include self-management, the deal desk, and deal management software.

Self-Management
The least expensive and least intrusive method for a company to control deal parameters is to establish guardrails – essentially a system of rules

within which the sales force uses discretion for deal development. To ensure effectiveness, the company uses the following criteria to develop these parameters: pricing strategy; probable economic profit, which will encompass customer segment; individual customer/customer segment strategy, in which the penetration objective may have different profit rules than the maintenance objective; strategic importance of the deal; and competitive activity.

Deal Desk

For more complex product/service environments, many companies use a centralized deal desk to standardize the pricing approach, which also relieves the sales force of the analytical burden of deal analysis. Two scenarios illustrate common design trade-offs for the deal desk.

Scenario 1 (Early involvement and hand off to sales force). The deal desk gets involved early in the sales cycle. Once structured, the deal moves into the hands of the sales force to negotiate, adjust, and close. That hand off to sales provides the benefit of offloading deal analytics without giving up flexibility and control at the point of impact with the customer. However, while the deal desk completes the upfront analytical work in a standard fashion, and sets pricing within acceptable parameters, the deal desk price rarely holds. In fact, the sales force often restructures the deal itself (different product/service mix, different volume), so that the potential collateral benefit of the deal desk cannot be achieved. For example, the supply chain organization desires order information as early as possible in the deal cycle. However, with the high likelihood of significant deal changes, the information from the deal desk becomes unreliable. Moreover, this approach places the pre-deal control very early in the sales cycle with no additional recourse. If one subscribes to the philosophy that control provides more effectiveness before the deal than after, then this approach is insufficient without other measures in place, such as profit-aligned compensation schemes.

Scenario 2 (Early involvement and continuing role). Involved early in the sales cycle, the deal desk offloads the analytics burden from the sales force. The deal desk then continues to have a role until the deal closing. This continuing role for the deal desk takes many forms, ranging from absolute central pricing control, to continuous reporting on deal variance, and to guidelines and profit improvement recommendations as the deal evolves. A balanced role for the deal desk may include designing an absolute deal envelope that provides the range of pricing variance and volumes allowed without additional approval. This deal envelope involves deal-specific guardrails, analogous to overall guardrails in place for the sales force. In practice, a company wants this level of specificity for its most valuable deals only. The labor intensity of such a function for all deals would be cost prohibitive.

Deal Management Software
A growing number of companies use pricing point solution software to manage their pricing processes. These software packages generally include a module that supports the development and negotiation of deals using company-defined deal parameters. Putting this technology directly in the hands of the sales force provides specific benefits and some risks. On the benefit side, the sales force can operate largely autonomously. The software performs much of the function of the deal desk, as it provides an environment for scenario analysis and helps the salesperson craft the most profitable deal within the customer's specifications. Guidelines and guardrails are built in. If the salesperson needs to go outside of standard guidelines, the software includes built-in workflow for exception processing. Two specific risks exist.

1. The sales force may spend too much time in deal development and lose focus on the customer. Training can help mitigate this risk, although time misallocation must be managed proactively.
2. The risk of disuse exists always. The sales force must support the implementation in order to drive value.

Exception Management

If a particular deal needs to fall outside of specified parameters, the company and its sales force need recourse to enable and control such an exception. The salesperson has the closest contact with and most detailed understanding of the customer needs. With proper alignment of objectives (not a foregone conclusion), the salesperson should be in the best position to manage the deal parameters. Yet perfect alignment does not exist and people's biases may affect judgment. Therefore, an exception approval process allows a company to offer flexibility at the customer impact point while still maintaining standard decision criteria and congruent assessment of transactional profitability and importance across the enterprise. Companies commonly manage the exception process through successive tiers of approvals, depending on the magnitude of variance from allowed pricing parameters. Exceptions can be approved for a number of reasons ranging from discounting, to getting a foot in the door of a new account, to protecting an account from competitive assault.

Measurement and Performance Management

In times past, when sole proprietorships and traveling salespeople were the rule, the sales person (typically the proprietor) set and negotiated the pricing. His or her personal wealth and capacity to support a family were contingent on the ability to obtain the best price for the product − tied directly to a person's ability to execute a profitable transaction. In modern companies, the relationship between the transaction profitability and the salesperson's personal wealth are often disconnected. Management measures sales performance and pays salespeople according to proxy measures designed to promote value growth through sales transactions. The management team crafts these proxy measures for ease of tracking and consistency across all transactions. Such measures include net revenue, gross margin, and cost-plus.

Net Revenue
As the most common measure, net revenue represents the total invoice price garnered through customer purchases over a given period of time. Companies use this base metric in multiple ways, such as an absolute measure against a target, or as a growth metric against a previous period. A simple assumption leads companies to use the net revenue measure, that is, more sales will yield more value. In order to grow, every company (no matter what business) must motivate its growth engine to seek more revenue. However, revenue measures alone may motivate unprofitable behavior in salespeople. Motivated by revenue targets alone, the sales force considers any sale a good sale.

Gross Margin and Cost-Plus Pricing
Recognizing the need to measure the quality of revenue, companies attempt to control revenue quality using gross margin and cost-plus pricing − two sides of the same coin managed from different perspectives. Gross margin represents quality management at a transaction level. The sales force and support players manage the quality of transactions based on target gross margins − at either the line-item level or in aggregate.

As a price-setting philosophy, cost-plus ensures the profitability of unit transactions by starting with the cost of an item and adding a premium. This control provides financial and company management with illusory comfort knowing that sales will grow the bottom line. This is false comfort because there is no guarantee that the cost-plus price is market-relevant. As part of the accounting function, gross margin is easy to measure and report. Nagle, Hogan, and Zale (2010 p. 2) observe that, "cost-plus pricing is, historically, the most common pricing procedure because it carries an aura of financial prudence. Financial prudence, according to this view, is achieved by pricing every product or service to yield a fair return over all costs, fully and fairly allocated. In theory, it is a simple guide to profitability; in practice, it is a blueprint for mediocre financial performance." Both gross margin and cost-plus pricing represent potential problems because assurance of profitability considers only costs that are arbitrarily attributed to a product according to accounting conventions. As has been demonstrated, transaction costs go far beyond accounting product costs. At best, gross margin provides a rough estimation of profitability. At worst, gross margin acts as a red herring, leading salespeople and financial managers astray of their real goal, to generate value for the organization.

ORGANIZATION AND PRICING GOVERNANCE: WHO OWNS PRICING?

Clearly, pricing is a powerful instrument for controlling and enhancing profitability. However, like any business activity, if a company does not create the proper environment and structure for pricing excellence to take root, the focus on value will wane, resulting in the loss of significant competitive advantage. Organization and pricing governance requires changes in three key areas: process governance, performance management, and sales force effectiveness.

"Functional integration is essential to balance revenue, profitability, and growth objectives" (Garrow & Ferguson, 2008, p. 4). Organization-wide involvement in value-based pricing must include finance, marketing, and sales. Performance measures must be carefully designed to align with economic benefit. The key is to understand the economic profit of a transaction and to motivate the sales force to support the expectations of the economic stakeholders. To do this effectively, companies must have real-time analytics at hand that measure economic profitability.

In many companies the pricing process is a fragmented and fractional-ized task; everyone owns pricing – and as an unintended consequence, no one owns pricing. Finance, sales, marketing, production, supply chain, and information technology all touch pricing. However, in trying to manage many people to undertake the same task, the company inevitably finds that the task gets done differently by all. Personal interpretations intervene. Pricing as a discipline becomes fractionalized and broken up into many parts handled by different people, each seeking to optimize the system under which they are measured and assessed.

As a case example, consider how price-setting was handled in the elec-tronic measurement equipment industry (think laboratory voltage meters, oscilloscopes, signal generators, etc.). These products were designed by a product engineering process, and measured by technical superiority. Fur-ther, company leadership emerged from the ranks of the best engineers, so that organizational mindset skewed toward rewarding the technically ele-gant. Pricing for decades was left unchecked as the engineers continually improved the technical capabilities with little regard to the potential mar-ket and with limited attention to what the customer thought about the price. Although the market respected the quality of the new products, they balked at paying more for products than they have paid in the past. Instead, the customers chose to pay far lower prices (even half) for a prod-uct from that company or another that simply meets their needs. In fact, a secondary market emerged where salvaged parts from old products were reassembled into products that were "good enough" to avoid buying brand new equipment.

Purpose, Motivation, and Feedback

When undertaking this type of work, clients always ask the question: How do we get the rest of the organization to buy into it? Author Daniel Pink (2009, p. 223) examines what motivates people, with a particular focus on autonomy, mastery, and purpose. Relevant here is Pink's focus on the alignment of profit maximization with purpose maximization:

> In Motivation 3.0, purpose maximization is taking its place alongside profit maximiza-tion as an aspiration and a guiding principle. Within organizations, this new "purpose motive" is expressing itself in three ways: in goals that use profit to reach purpose; in words that emphasize more than self-interest; and in policies that allow people to pur-sue purpose on their own terms. This move to accompany profit maximization with

purpose maximization has the potential to rejuvenate our businesses and remake our world. (Pink, 2009, p. 208)

A case study provides insights into the motivation of individual workers comprising the local salespeople. A country's leading manufacturer of a bottled beverage wanted to increase its marketplace effectiveness. For some areas of the country, the objective was to achieve greater profitability with limited volume increase. Other areas required greater penetration with no profitability improvement, while some areas wanted greater volume and associated profitability. Interviews revealed that the local salespeople selling the beverage on a day-to-day basis did not understand the basis of their compensation. To align their individual sales approaches with the regional goals, three motivators were provided to the local sellers:

1. Each seller was given a tool to suggest sales offers that worked best to meet the goals of that territory.
2. Each seller learned how his own selling behavior would directly affect personal success. A direct link was put in place to match individual sales behaviors to personal profitability in wages.
3. All sellers learned how the selling behavior of each local distributor directly affects the ability for the national manufacturer to achieve its overall goals. Every seller has the ability to impact the manufacturer's goals.

An immediate feedback loop was put in place in the form of weekly reviews about personal performance. Performance and resulting compensation were no longer a "black box." Instead, highly visible motivators were put in place, including personal performance "dashboards" (spreadsheets), individual territory coaching (addressing how particular offers may be made to specific customers), and public acknowledgment of successful behaviors. For example, a photograph was taken of each seller receiving a compensation check from the distributor's general manager.

Previously, the small local distributors thought they worked for a large regional distributor. Now they understood that they worked for the number one beverage manufacturer in the country − a national icon. Individual spreadsheets provided to each distributor let them understand the profitability of their own customers. They were further given training relating to three tools to help them expand the marketplace − knowledge about and use of discounts, rebates, and trade loans to help their local mom-and-pop account sell more products.

This granular analysis showed that different combinations of tools or offerings were effective for each region, segment, customer type, and strategic intent. The analysis also showed how much should be offered (optimal) and how much was too much (guardrails). Rebates worked better in some regions, and discounts in other regions. The more profitability provided to the parent company, the more money earned by the local distributors. Spreadsheets provided immediate feedback, and meetings were held for local distributors so that each salesperson could understand how they were performing against the new guidelines. As surprising evidence that the program was working, salespersons, who as a species avoid performance reviews, began to demand management review sessions to demonstrate how well they were doing against their goals.

The concept of personal drive or motivation is important in this context. It also supports the reasons to use granular analysis to illustrate (using spreadsheets) how the salespeople are performing against their goals. In other words, "I cannot manage what I cannot see." It makes sense to put these kinds of tools into place at all levels – even at the most simplistic levels – to make visible the real behaviors that are occurring. "Let me help you see how you are doing" is an important approach from strategic, operational, and technological perspectives. Such measures provide a way to set a baseline and measure the organization's performance. Measurement moves from a "finger in the wind" approach down to a level where action can be taken. The question "How do I know what good is?" can be answered through a granular approach to understand what behaviors are translating into actual numbers. A baseline can be drawn and measures can be set in place to understand where the team members started, where they are going, and how they are doing. All of this behavioral change is driven by the granular analysis. Without it, the tools (spreadsheets), the metrics, the baseline, and the measurement approach and the feedback loop are not possible.

Starting the measurement process at gross margin is a common mistake. While good as a shorthand metric, gross margin is the aggregation of so many uncontrollable forces that it is not specific enough to use as a metric for effective management.

A *granular analysis approach* brings greater meaning into the lives of the marketing and salespeople by providing immediate feedback to their behaviors through a baseline and measurement process. If people can behave in ways that align with goals like profitability, then ultimately the company will run better. A direct tie exists from behaviors in the marketplace to results in the marketplace. Finance cannot have one set of metrics and sales another set of metrics. That leads to a set of unhealthy tensions. Instead, this approach provides a set of metrics that all have agreed to, which link from the strategic objectives all the way to behaviors that make individuals more successful.

From a salesperson working with mom-and-pop stores to an account manager working with a big-box retailer, a set of simple rules (for example, discount guardrails) can be generated to manage the overall objectives of each channel, customer group, geography, category, etc. The marketing team understands where they will take profit, and the salespersons understand that they have permission to and will be compensated for walking away from business that do not meet particular criteria. In any case, all involved agree that the guardrails set will provide better performance (such as greater profitability, better penetration, greater volume) not only for the organization and greater reward for the individual. That said, when the supply chain takes a hit to volume, the team will consider that acceptable because the sales and marketing persons have been part of the planning and can adjust their output accordingly. By performing this way, the company and the individuals all profit and agree that the behaviors are in alignment. The stockholders will see a better-managed company and benefit from the greater controls in place.

Involve all members of the value chain. The objective is to make value pricing real by making it granular applies across the entire value chain. The methods and examples defined above are effective when applied to a particular company seeking to gain a value exchange with an end consumer. However, consider how effective these methods are when many players are involved, such as manufacturers selling through distributors or retailers.

The ability to make these concepts work requires all members of the value chain to participate. Historically, the relationship between manufacturers and distributors/retailers was adversarial at best (Hansen, 2009, p. 227). In more recent times, the growing trend is for all parties throughout the value chain to cooperate. This is partly influenced by the increasing power of the data that they hold together, as well as the deeper understanding of the value exchange that can be generated when they cooperate. Wal-Mart's use of Retail Link® serves as a good example of this trend. Wal-Mart requires all product suppliers to participate in Retail Link®. By providing transaction data to their suppliers, Wal-Mart has developed ways to provide greater value to its customers and to the entire business community in the form of greater efficiencies, increased volumes, and ultimately greater profitability. Because Wal-Mart's "vendors are integrated into its systems, and have access to some of the same data, Wal-Mart's decisions to push one product or pull back on another are transparent to the vendor. This transparency drives operational efficiency for the vendor/supplier and gives Wal-Mart great leverage during vendor negotiations" (Ehring, 2006, p. 3).

Such an approach can be applied to consumer services, business-to-business endeavors, and industrial products. In considering aircraft engines, for example, no value exists until the airplane starts to move. The value is in delivering up-time versus maintenance time. Yet with airplane engines too, the focus is about value that can be shared, modeled, and linked to the associated behaviors all the way back through the value chain. For packaged goods, the objective is to ensure that the right products get in the hands of the persons who will value the products most. Consequently, companies must understand what value they deliver to the marketplace. Not only should a company be concerned with the dollar value, it must also understand why and how its product differs from competitors' products. What is the company's value proposition to the market? How can that value be measured with the downstream consumer or the end consumer, depending on the structure?

Collaboration and Competition Along the Value Chain

Many of the internal aspects of the pricing structure and opportunities described can also be considered from downstream and upstream perspectives. The more a company understands the various pieces of the provider-supplier process along the value chain, the greater the probability that the company can align and optimize cost and value in a way that can make a significant difference for the organization.

A successful integrated waterfall requires an *economic picture of the total value chain*. In the automobile industry, that chain ranges from the workers who dig metal out of the ground through the smelting process to rolled aluminum and on to the process that integrates the aluminum into a structural product that becomes part of an automobile and ultimately to the consumer who purchases the automobile. In such a process, the seller must understand where there are leakages that can be controlled. The joint business planning dimension of the value chain looks at how to reduce those leakages so that more money can be made by all involved along the value chain. The ability to optimize where a company fits somewhere in the middle of the value chain is important to profitability and growth.

Historically, companies have focused on controlling the interface with suppliers and customers. Yet they have not been as successful at driving profit for their own organizations. Nor do most companies understand what is important to help drive profit for their customers.

Trends in collaborative planning for the supply chain have been understood for a long time, typically from the perspective of a customer looking backward from the supply chain. However, a company in the middle of the supply chain has an incentive to look in both directions to identify ways to make the process more efficient. Through greater efficiencies, a company has the prospect of extracting a higher premium from value-added services. Value chain cooperation can help optimize the whole chain while enabling the players to compete for their pieces along the chain. If one customer is not willing to cooperate in that way, it may be time to reduce the role of that customer or offer services to another customer instead. Significant negotiation is essential as companies compete for larger shares of pieces of the value chain.

DRIVING FORWARD

"Only a true comprehensive approach to pricing and profitability management will drive the desired results in today's complex market *and* help sustain them over the long term" (Meehan et al., 2011, p. 300). As described in this chapter, disciplined decisions about pricing, and full implementation organization-wide, take on even greater urgency in the current economic environment to help a company maximize performance and profitability. To capture the full value of analytics, stay focused on the following:

- *Customer value proposition*: Drive profitability by selling the right solutions to the right customers;
- *Power of pricing*: Capture the full value of pricing analytics, price execution, and organization and pricing governance;
- *Right structure*: Ensure excellence in process governance, performance management, and sales force effectiveness;
- *Buy-in throughout the organization*: Ensure shared purpose, strong motivation, and ongoing feedback across the organization and beyond.

"Carrots and sticks are so last century. *Drive* says for 21st century work, we need to upgrade to autonomy, mastery and purpose" (Pink, 2009, p. 218).

TRIBUTE TO DAN NIMER

This chapter is in celebration of the achievements and career of Dan Nimer: As with all truly great innovations, his brilliant insights into pricing for value preceded the capability of most companies to systematically take advantage of them. Now that information and technology are nearly sufficient for effective value pricing, we have had several decades to prepare. Thanks Dan, for creating a discipline that always challenges all of us. We can only hope to stand on the shoulders of a pricing giant and continue to reach higher.

REFERENCES

Ariely, D. (2009). *Predictably irrational, the hidden forces that shape our decisions.* New York, NY: Harper-Collins.

Baker, W. L., Marn, M. V., & Zawada, C. C. (2010). *The price advantage.* Hoboken, NJ: Wiley.

Cameron, A. C., & Trivedi, P. K. (2005). *Microeconometrics – methods and applications.* Cambridge, UK: Cambridge University Press.

Christensen, C. M., Anthony, S. D., Berstell, G., & Nitterhouse, D. (2007). Finding the right job for your product. *MIT Sloan Management Review, 48*(3), 38–47.

Coase, R.H. (1937). The nature of the firm. Reprinted in *Economica,* 4(16), 386–405, November 1937. Reprinted in Wiley Online Library, 2007.

Cross, R. G. (1997). *Revenue management: Hard-Core tactics for market domination.* New York, NY: Broadway Books. p. 178.

Ehring, D., (2006). The Wal-Mart model: Mortgage lenders could learn a lot from the king of retail efficiency Wal-Mart, Mortgage Banking, October 2006, 3.

Financial Crisis Inquiry Commission. (2011), Transcript of interview of Warren Buffet, February 11, 2011.

Garrow, L. A., & Ferguson, M. E. (2008). Revenue management and the analytics explosion: Perspectives from industry experts. *Journal of Revenue and Pricing Management, 7*(2), 219–229.

Goizueta, R. (1996). You are tomorrow's leaders, Speech at Emory University, May 13, 1996. Retrieved from http://www.goizueta.emory.edu/aboutgoizueta/quotes/calling_full.html

Hansen, J. M. (2009). The evolution of buyer-supplier relationships: An historical industry approach. *Journal of Business and Industrial Marketing, 24*(3/4), 227–236. Retrieved from http://www.emeraldinsight.com/journals.htm?articleid = 1784425

Manning, P. S., & M. Laird (2008). *Burden of proof: A skeptic's guide to the value of strategic pricing.* Deloitte. Retrieved from http://www.deloitte.com/us/pricing

Marn, M. V., & Rosiello, R. L. (1992). Managing price, gaining profit. *Harvard Business Review, 70*(5), 84–93.

Meehan, J. M., Simonetto, M. G., Montan, L., Jr., & Goodin, C. A (2011). *Pricing and profitability management: A practical guide for business leaders.* Singapore: Wiley.

Nagle, T. T., Hogan, J. E., & Zale, J. (2010). *The strategy and tactics of pricing (Fifth Edition)*. New York, NY: Pearson Education.

Nagle, T. T., & Holden, R. K. (1995). *The strategy and tactics of pricing* (2nd ed.). Upper Saddle River, NJ: Prentice Hall.

Nimer, D. A. (1971). There's more to pricing than most companies think. *Innovations* (August). Reprinted in Vernor, I. R., & Lamb, C. W. (Eds.). (1976). *The pricing function* (pp. 19–33). Lexington, MA: Lexington Books, D.C. Heath & Co.

Pink, D. H. (2009). *Drive*. New York, NY: Riverhead Books, Wal-Mart. Retrieved from walmartstores.com/suppliers/248.aspx

PREPARE YOUR PRICING OPERATIONS FOR CHANGE

Navdeep S. Sodhi

ABSTRACT

This chapter makes the case for companies to improve pricing operations that enable pricing strategies in any given set of market conditions by taking certain steps before embarking on large initiatives that can affect prices, such as mergers or acquisitions, continuous improvement efforts, breakthrough changes (e.g., business process redesign or new technology implementation), or large-scale reorganization. Starting with pricing-related challenges, we draw attention to the importance of pricing operations by clarifying how pricing operations differ from pricing strategy and also how they directly impact profitability. Companies should follow a four-step approach to precede any major initiative affecting pricing, including Assessment *of their pricing processes,* Analysis *of these pricing operations before bringing about sustained changes, then making and implementing* Recommendations *that should include* Training *of functional teams, in short, through AART. We discuss how companies can implement AART with illustrative examples.*

Visionary Pricing: Reflections and Advances in Honor of Dan Nimer
Advances in Business Marketing & Purchasing, Volume 19, 335–355
ISSN: 1069-0964/doi:10.1108/S1069-0964(2012)0000019020

INTRODUCTION

Pricing operations can be a key resource for profitability when companies face major change in the form of disruption in their market environment or opt for innovation as an avenue for growth. When companies embark on large initiatives that can affect prices, such as mergers and acquisitions, continuous improvement efforts, breakthrough changes (such as new technology implementation), or large-scale reorganizations, inefficient pricing operations can be a serious hurdle. But instead of yielding price control, companies can prepare to protect revenues and profits by following a four-step approach – *Assess*, *Analyze*, *Recommend*, and *Train* (or *AART*) – which should precede any major company initiative.

Contrary to common perceptions, a company's profitability is not dependent only on market conditions or other external causes, but also on the firm's internal operations. In this chapter we clarify the differences between pricing operations and pricing strategy and why the distinction is a key missing piece in our understanding of profitable pricing. We also elucidate problems that are related to the company's pricing operations and why it is important to look at internal processes to improve realized prices and to stem revenue leaks. We discuss the common failure modes for pricing to explain why internal support for pricing cannot be taken as a given. Finally, we outline the *AART* steps to prepare for change. We begin with *Common Pricing Problems*, followed by *Pricing Operations versus Pricing Strategy* to differentiate between these two important aspects of pricing. Then we discuss *How to Improve Pricing Operations*, which includes a detailed discussion on common failure modes for pricing. Finally, with *Preparing for Change*, we provide by a detailed treatment with examples for each step – *Assess*, *Analyze*, *Recommend*, and *Train*.

COMMON PRICING PROBLEMS

Whenever pricing gets attention in the boardroom it is in a strategic context usually during times of competitive upheaval or an equally significant market opportunity. Frequently, the *market* is blamed for a steep sales decline or severe margin erosion. Senior executives react to or agree with commonly voiced reasons such as competitors' irrational and aggressive pricing behavior, overly demanding customers or channel partners, out of control cost inflation, or excessive delays in pricing decisions. A closer look inside companies reveals the interesting texture as to how a given set of problems is perceived differently by different stakeholders within an organization. An internal focus group at one company troubled by declining profits and flat sales (adapted from Sodhi & Sodhi, 2008, pp. 142–144) evoked some of these common pricing concerns in a corporate environment. A group of 20 individuals from sales, manufacturing, finance, product management, and pricing personnel noted their concerns as follows:

Regarding the price approval process:

1. Too many handoffs in the discount approval process.
2. Too much time taken by pricing analysts to approve.
3. The discount process is very manual, needs to be automated.
4. Too much time taken up in creating and analyzing facts.
5. Sales do not provide required information, wastes time in the process.
6. Quotes are not at market price initially, provoking ongoing debate.
7. Competitive analysis is weak.
8. Where is the competitive pricing data?
9. Discount decisions are based on manufacturing cost not market price.
10. Sales group has poor visibility of cost data – need it early in process.
11. Sales reps give in price demands too quickly.

Regarding organizational and inter-functional issues:

1. Disconnect between incentives and decisions.
2. Too many silos – not enough delegation.
3. Multiple owners in the approval process.
4. No clear owner. Lack of defined roles.
5. Too many decision makers.
6. Manufacturing is not included in pricing decisions.
7. Sales force is not trained in price negotiation.
8. Limited product management involvement in approving concessions.

Other general issues:

1. Pricing metrics are nonexistent.
2. Discount goals not linked to business goals.
3. Transfer pricing is not clear.
4. Variation in the pricing process is high.
5. No price reviews, no win-loss analysis.
6. Uneven handling of quantity discount factors.
7. There are price negotiations internal and external to the company.
8. What is the appropriate way to use pricing as a tool to balance factory load?

9. No consideration to channel conflict.
10. Competitive data is not collected systematically.
11. How do we position pricing strategy relative to price/volume/share?

Clearly, such issues reflect limitations in the company's internal operations but also suggest that this company's profitability is not dependent only on the market conditions or state of the economy. Although in a tough economy there is likely to be added pressure to meet top-line goals, which only exacerbates the company's existing operational issues. Companies often try to *take control* of the marketplace by lowering prices, which often proves disastrous for the bottom line. Another perhaps better option is to control prices refers not just to the marketplace but also to the internal processes that result in the final realized price paid by a customer. Hence, companies should look at internal processes to improve realized prices and to stem revenue leaks.

PRICING OPERATIONS VERSUS PRICING STRATEGY

Prices are set at different levels in a company by several stakeholders. We need to differentiate between them in order to clarify the meaning of the term *pricing operations* and how it differs from *pricing strategy*. At one level is pricing strategy that concerns the positioning of the company's products in the price and value spectrum alongside competitive products in the market. At a different level is setting the discount off the list price for a specific transaction with a particular customer. There can be many processes at and in between these two levels (Table 1).

Table 1. Different Pricing Levels.

Pricing Level		Organizational Level	Frequency of review/ decision-making
Strategy		Senior management	Annual (Quarterly, sometimes ad hoc)
Operational	Tactical planning	Middle management	Monthly/Quaterly
	Execution	Middle management, Pricing analysts Customer service representatives	Daily (or continually)

Source: Sodhi and Sodhi (2008, p. 63).

At the *strategic* level, a company's senior leadership may desire, for instance, to grow sales or market share to a certain level, improve profitability to a stretch goal, expand the company's global footprint, or choose a market position as the high-price-high-value player. Such strategies would have a relatively longer-term decision span of several months to several years and are subject to change. For instance, a company may choose a high-price-high-value position just as Apple, Inc. did with the launch of the first iPhone. However, in 2011, Apple seems to have chosen to maintain its lead in the mobile phone at the top end of design and quality without raising price levels for iPhone 4S (Dignan, 2011).

These strategies engender, or at least should engender, *tactical* goals for the medium- and short-term over a few months to a year. These goals require multiple functions to work with one another and therefore create many projects and workflows within each function wherein the pricing function may lead or just participate as a minor player. On a day-to-day or weekly basis, the *execution* of transactions and contracts is or should be guided by medium- and short-term objectives. Execution involves sales personnel, information technology (IT), marketing, and legal among others who carry out specific steps or tasks critical for a successful execution.

The key point is that these three levels of pricing are, or should be, organizationally hierarchical. Decisions at one level should guide those at the lower level and in turn be informed by their outcomes, ideally, in a closed loop. Success eventually lies in operational workflows, otherwise flaws related to execution would limit a perfectly good strategy. In the reverse direction, the absence of a strategy or having an inherently poor strategy will limit the results of successful execution relative to the bottom line.

Pricing operations entail two types of processes to ensure operationalizing and adhering to pricing strategy. These are:

1. *Modification processes* involving list modifications in response to changes in the market environment (but not changes to strategy). For instance, the oil shock in 2005 caused airlines to tag special fees as a way to increase realized prices: such decisions are operational because they may have a decision horizon of a few months at the most. Modifying price guidelines is also an operational process. Since oil prices have stayed at high levels, airlines continue modifying ticket (Grossman, 2005) prices and various surcharges to reflect further increases. Similarly, communicating the list price changes to customers and internal operations (such as updating ERP or another system) is also part of such operations.

2. *Control processes* to ensure and track adherence to price guidelines. The purpose of these processes is to ensure high levels of realized prices relative to list prices, the latter being the embodiment of pricing strategy. Control processes can also track whether a price promotion was effective in getting the hoped-for incremental sales and profits.

List price changes are not as frequent as setting prices for individual transactions. Still, tighter operational processes for setting list prices also make this process of modifying list prices easier. Similarly, good processes also ensure that once list prices are modified, they can be implemented in the tens of thousands or millions of transactions that follow.

Pricing operations entail processes that face both the world outside and inside the company. Like pricing strategy, pricing operations may face the market, but, unlike strategy, operations work closely with internal processes linked with execution. For example, pricing operations include observing changes in the market, say, the penetration pricing used by Korean companies like Samsung and LG (Hagerty & Tita, 2011) in the US white goods market, or sharp increases in supply costs like that of copper or steel. Pricing operations also translate these external changes to more restrictive or more lenient discounting guidelines and then ensure adherence to the updated guidelines.

Whether market facing or internally focused, these processes require all levels of people in marketing, sales, finance, customer service, IT, inventory management, and legal to work together in producing intended results in executing to strategy (Fig. 1). Most of the activities or process steps at this level are internal to the company and therefore, at least theoretically, within the company's control.

If operational weaknesses are not fixed or remain undiscovered, a company can suffer in many ways that ultimately impact profits and even sales. For example, when a service company fails to turn on or switch-off certain offerings already agreed with its customers, the ensuing billing disputes can potentially reduce the company's bargaining power in future negotiations, increase the customer's interest for competitive products, delay payments and possibly waste hundreds of man-hours in dispute resolution. Such problems are realistic and surprisingly pervasive throughout commercial operations in many companies. Another example is how a company tracks, analyzes, and makes decisions based on price exceptions. An industrial manufacturer of premium products allowed concessions based on the guideline that all discounted prices would have to be at least 3% higher than the closest competitive bid. When the discount process eventually

Pricing Process/ Stakeholder	Strategic (S) or Operational (O)?	Divisional Head	Barnd Director	Finance Manager/ Analyst	Director Marketing	Marketing Communications	Legal	Global Account Manager	Sales Rep	Customer Service Manager/ Rep	Product Manager	Sales VP /Director	Country/ Territory Manager	IT Manager/ Analyst	Sales Manager	Pricing Director	National Pricing/ Contacts Manager	Pricing/Contracts Analyst
Standard List Price Change	S & O	■		■	■	■			■	■	■	■	■	■	■	■	■	■
Price Promotions	O					■	■			■	■	■	■	■	■	■	■	■
Price Communication to Customers	O				■	■	■	■	■	■	■	■		■		■	■	■
New Product Launch Pricing	S & O	■				■			■		■	■		■	■	■	■	■
Multi-Brand Pricing	S & O		■		■					■	■	■	■	■	■	■	■	■
Market Segment Pricing	S & O				■			■		■	■	■	■	■	■	■	■	■
Custom Product Pricing	O				■				■	■	■	■	■		■	■	■	■
Volume Incentive Programs and Rebates	O	■						■	■	■		■	■		■	■	■	■
Multi-Channel Pricing	S & O	■					■			■	■	■	■	■	■	■	■	■
Global Contracts	S & O	■				■	■			■	■	■	■	■	■	■	■	■
National or Regional Contracts	O					■	■		■		■	■	■	■	■	■	■	■
Competitive Transactional Pricing Intelligence	O								■	■	■		■		■	■	■	■
Analysis, Tracking and Reporting	O			■								■	■	■	■	■	■	■
Product Life Cycle Pricing	S & O										■	■		■		■	■	■
Discounts and Concessions Approval	O							■	■							■	■	■
Scorecards and Price Reviews	O			■												■	■	■

Fig. 1. Various Pricing Processes and Internal Stakeholders. *Source*: Sodhi and Sodhi (p. 73).

came under scrutiny and the relative frequency of reason codes was reviewed, management realized how the reason code *competitive match*, along with the notation *3% higher than competitor A or B* − for thousands of transactions was misleading. Furthermore, the resulting transactional price-points were all over the board hence providing no meaningful insight into competitive behavior.

HOW TO IMPROVE PRICING OPERATIONS

CEOs want to bring continuous improvement to functions beyond manufacturing and purchasing (Lee, 2011), so why not to pricing? Lean manufacturing, for instance, received worldwide acceptance with its simple features, such as, teamwork among line workers, simple but comprehensive information display systems, and total commitment across the organization to bring quality improvement to the shop floor. Similarly, Six Sigma methods, with their five-step DMAIC (Define, Measure, Analyze, Improve, and Control) has helped many organizations ensure that their product (or service) does not deviate from the design each time the product is made (or the service is rendered). Most pricing operations are repetitive just like manufacturing processes and hence similarly receptive to gains from quality methods. As such, we have proposed Six Sigma pricing (Sodhi & Sodhi, 2005, 2008).

However, in our own experience of implementing Six Sigma pricing, there are contextual differences between applying continuous improvement to pricing versus manufacturing or other services, such as:

1. *Lack of senior management support to projects*: In particular, weak or inconsistent support by senior managers can be a major cause for a failed initiative.
2. *Poor team dynamics*: Team dynamics can derail any project, but pricing-related projects representing diverse functions and reporting relationships are especially vulnerable. When input or representation from key stakeholders such as sales or customer service is not taken into account, it may weaken their support to recommended solutions.
3. *The pressure to undo even successful projects*: What goes up may come down again − if the average realized price improves then there may be calls from sales to removing price restrictions or adding flexibility in price negotiations that eventually result in prices coming down.
4. *Leaving pricing to pricing personnel*: Just as a failure mode for Six Sigma projects is to leave *quality* to the quality department thus leaving other stakeholders and implementers uninvolved, a problem for pricing projects is to leave these projects to pricing personnel while others figure out ways to undo any project's success.

What are the underlying causes that make it difficult to directly implement continuous improvement in pricing? In our experience there are four fundamental factors:

Inter-functional divergence: Pricing spans multiple functions and is therefore subject to inter-functional conflict, which may be rooted in differences in compensation structure, roles and responsibilities, and even individual needs for status and self-importance. Usually processes within a single function or even two functions are effective but several pricing processes involve marketing, finance, sales, product management who may not share the same perceptions or objectives. For instance, sales people who are typically compensated on sales volume want flexibility in pricing so they can increase volume at every opportunity. Marketing people are considered brand builders guiding the value of the product. This may put them at odds with sales who might believe that list price (or a proposed contract price) is too high to bring in large volume. Pricing personnel may use analysis from transactions of existing customers to present a view that the proposed price is low. Finance people may raise questions regarding why the proposed prices cannot be higher than those of existing customers.

The customer-is-always-right: Customers want quick turnaround on pricing decisions and there is no reason why it should not be so. However, excessive emphasis on rapid customer response rather than genuine customer focus allows some company personnel to sidestep internal consensus building and analysis. When a company does not have reliable processes, its personnel tend give in easily and too quickly for a single transaction, or worse, over many transactions by improving contract terms. We have to remain mindful that rigid processes and bureaucratic controls also do not help either the company or its customers. Still, even well established corporations can take several weeks to respond to a request for proposal for an existing customer.

For example, a division of a US-based firm precipitated an issue with their number one auto customer. The purchasing department at the auto company demanded a significant price cut during recent recession as a mandatory cost control measure. Rather than start an internal discussion to find a reasonable solution, the account manager withheld the information almost till the deadline thinking that time pressure would help him secure an instant discount approval. Pricing balked given the size of discount while each team blamed each other one for the prolonged back and forth. Meanwhile, the customer grew impatient and voiced their dissatisfaction to the division president who not only had to apologize to the customer but also authorize the lower prices demanded by the customer. He also severely admonished both teams for their lack of teamwork. System glitches, changes in people in-charge at the customer or vendor location, changes in product, or possible miscommunication are all problems known to exist in any business environment. Sometimes a customer learns of another customer receiving a lower price from a vendor or there is a problem but the sales rep is not sure of the problem source. Either scenario spurs an internal discussion around dropping price in the interest of keeping the customer happy.

Dynamic nature of change: Pricing is complex also because of its sensitivity to the continual changes in the internal and external environment.

Internally, a company may have seen turnover or may have brought in new leadership, resulting in new policies. Every new policy may require changes in related pricing process but the company fails to train everyone in the new process. Externally, economic cycles or massive changes like petroleum shocks change customer needs and drive a company's price response. External events like mergers and acquisitions also have internal impacts. For instance, existing IT systems and legacy processes with specific customer accounts or products (owing to a merger with another company) make controls difficult due to integration-related challenges. Even in stable environments, when companies make changes in processes and organizational structure, one has to watch for undesirable changes in the output of these processes, particularly for pricing.

Management-by-gut-feel: Managers often make pricing decisions based on intuition and mental demand curves that assume price drops always lead to increased (unit) sales and therefore (dollar) profits. Such thinking is not basically wrong but the devil is in the details of the execution: how sensitive is the *market* to price changes in one particular transaction? Staring down a customer's bluster on prices using one's gut-feel is one thing. It is quite another to be prepared by digging up information about the customer's business, their geography, and existing discount levels. Likewise, simply challenging the sales force to hold off on offering discounts to customers in tough times is one thing. It is quite another to estimate and communicate the impact on profitability based on the sales with lower prices versus the likelihood of losing such sales. Recall the example of the industrial manufacturer that instituted the rule to always price three percent higher than competition. Since no one was being held accountable and there weren't any adequate process checks to monitor effectiveness of the guideline *3% higher than competition* became an excuse for almost every price exception.

PREPARING FOR CHANGE

The hurdles in deploying continuous improvement to pricing apply to any other type of change or improvement (business process reengineering, for instance). As such, some of the fundamental issues must be uncovered before we start doing continuous improvement or technology-led business process redesign or reengineering. Hence, we propose a four-stage approach (Fig. 2) which must *precede* any major internal change or even in

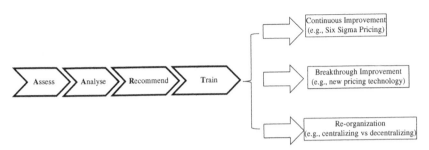

Fig. 2. Four-Stage AART Should Precede Any Major Pricing Initiative.

anticipation of changes in the external environment whether or not led by technology. The four steps follow a phased approach to apply learning from one phase to guide the next:

I. *Assess*: The key purpose of this step is to gain an understanding of organization, product, and logistic infrastructure in the context of pricing as well as identify challenges and understand gaps in perceptions across different stakeholder functions in all aspects of pricing. The tools used in this step typically may include high level mapping of existing pricing processes (as is) for chosen product-line/s and gathering qualitative data through interviews and surveys to ascertain, for instance, how price was set for a specific product-line or list prevalent myths or hypotheses, such as, small customers should receive the low prices offered to large customers.

II. *Analyze*: The purpose of this step is to uncover gaps and articulate possible reasons for process failures, as well as identify the source and size of challenges. The choice of tools depends on nature of the problems as well as access and quality of data. The qualitative information collected in Assess step comes in handy for quantitative analysis. Process analysis (including root cause analysis), analysis of transactional data, for example, analyzing discount as a function of explanatory variables) with statistical methods proves quite insightful in sizing problems and in framing recommendations.

III. *Recommend*: This step provides direction for change based on findings from Assess and Analyse steps in the context of internal pricing capabilities. Tools such as pay-off matrix prove handy in prioritizing remedial steps and developing a roadmap to start capturing benefits.

IV. *Train*: The purpose of this step is to create a shared appreciation of pricing at large and of possible solutions to fix problems. This can be

achieved by engaging internal teams involved in specific pricing processes or a special project through training on the critical need for
change as well as the possible benefits from successful execution.
Hence this step is critical in building a common definition and discipline which leads to a desired consistency in pricing communication
inside and outside the company.

Once these steps are carried out to create a shared understanding of
problems as well as possible solutions, then a company can proceed with
self assurance into initiatives such as Six Sigma pricing, new technology
implementation or organization changes. While every organization is
unique, we suggest that the entire AART process flow be no longer than,
say, ten weeks otherwise valuable momentum would be lost even before a
major initiative can get started. The first three steps — Assess, Analyze,
and Recommend — were applied in a consulting engagement for a manufacturer of playground equipment taking four weeks for completion.
Training was added later when the company experienced initial bottlenecks
in implementing the recommendations. Several individuals from different
functions provided enthusiastic feedback and some explained that their initial reluctance to adopt the recommendations was mainly due to a lack of
understanding of the purpose and context of the changes rather their lack
of support for any other reason.

ASSESSING PRICING OPERATIONS

A product or service price entails more than a single number that appears
at the end of a conversation between the customer and a salesperson. The
term price itself is broad-sweeping implying many levels of prices, for
instance, list price or MSRP (maximum selling retail price), contract price,
and the invoiced price. Companies manage various kinds of discounts,
coupons, concessions, rebates, and promotional rates to calculate invoiced
price. For instance, one data storage company manages guidelines for net-,
net-net-, and net-net-net-prices that are derived from applying different
levels of discounts to the list price in a way that is considered complex and
confusing within the company as well as by its customers. Managers must
identify and separate various pricing processes or steps that require
improvement and to facilitate being able to apply remedial efforts with
greater precision.

Identifying Pricing Processes

The number of key pricing activities and underlying processes is not immediately apparent in most companies and should not be taken for granted. Even companies with standard operating procedures (SOP) and documented role definitions find that the once-standard procedures have morphed and ad hoc practices have crept in over time. As a result, not everyone in the company is familiar with all the price-related steps. This is why workshops and surveys among cross-functional stakeholders are quite useful to identify all pricing processes and understand how their effectiveness is perceived by individuals in different functions — senior management, pricing, sales, marketing, finance, and legal, and so on.

Workshops with cross-functional teams prove quite insightful when identifying steps underlying various pricing activities. Sometimes the perceptions can be so conflicting that such meetings tend to regress into defensive behavior or finger pointing. Rather than precipitate conflict or suppress perceptions, it is better to elicit data specific to perceptions of pricing effectiveness using in-house surveys that assure some degree of confidentiality to the participants. For instance, internal stakeholders in an electronic equipment manufacturing firm participated in a workshop to identify key pricing activities and related steps while also assigning known functional roles to them. Based on feedback from finance, marketing, IT, pricing, customer service, sales, legal and manufacturing people, there were seven key activities that had (known) functional roles associated with them. The activities were broadly classified as (1) pricing new products, (2) annual price increases, (3) competitive price intelligence, (4) contract management, (5) discounts and concessions, (6) price-related financial analysis, and (7) fulfilling customer needs.

Each activity class then was supported by discrete steps, which were also identified. There was agreement that each activity or step may require the expertise from several individuals in different functions. For example, *pricing new products* entailed: (a) analyzing costs, primarily done by finance; (b) estimating and articulating differential value vis-à-vis the competition, an effort typically led by Marketing; (c) updating various internal IT systems with product information guided by Product Management and executed by IT, and (d) training frontline employees on how to articulate benefits of key product features to customers led by product managers. Other pricing activities required similar collaboration among cross-functional teams within the company.

Confidential surveys tend to draw out raw comments that point to genuine problems. For example, the in-house survey at the electronics manufacturer was administered to 113 people in 8 functional groups out of which 95 responded to the survey such that each functional team was well represented. The survey was structured around basic questions to better understand roles and responsibilities and to elicit perceptions about each major pricing activity and underlying step. The general survey questions included:

• What is your (functional) role in the company? (Choose from 8 functional roles)
• How would you rate the effectiveness of a certain activity/task (on a scale of 1 to 5, where 5 is most effective)?
• Do you have a direct responsibility in accomplishing that step? (Y or N)
• If yes, what is your responsibility in the process?
• Do you have any comments about the effectiveness of the process/step?

Gap Analysis of Pricing Operations
Analysis of results from such a survey reveals perception gaps in at least two aspects. First, it shows if there is a clear understanding of roles and responsibilities and if each process is adequately covered by individuals with direct-line responsibility. Second, the variation in scores reflects the extent of perception gaps for a given process. However, while gap analysis suggests which activities or processes may underpin known pricing challenges, perception data should not be taken for granted without verifying them in follow-up interviews with key stakeholders.

For example, the survey at the electronics equipment manufacturer revealed that at an aggregated level most processes scored between 2 and 3 (out of possible 5) and hence the overall operations capability of the company relative to pricing was acknowledged to be mediocre at best. However, at a functional level there were gaps in perception that potentially pointed out opportunities for improving pricing operations. Consider this: the sales group rated the discount approval process at 4.4 (out of possible 5) whereas product managers rated the same process at 2.7 (Fig. 3). Given that sales were responsible primarily for volume while product managers were accountable for profitability, sales preferred the existing flexibility in making discount decisions whereas the product teams wanted to take it away. Such analysis is quite helpful in updating organizational roles and responsibilities that may have become out of date and hence less effective, as well as preparing for impending changes.

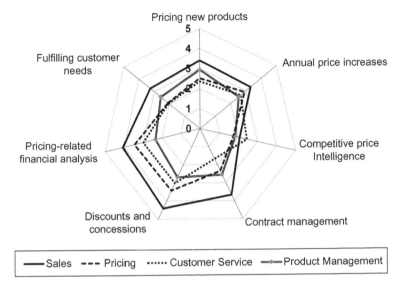

Fig. 3. Illustration of Variance in Ratings by Different Stakeholders as Part of Gap Analysis.

The survey also revealed that several critical tasks that were agreed upon in the original list were done in an ad hoc way and were not a part of anyone's direct responsibility. For instance, the steps underlying Contract Management, such as *pursuing compliance on contract terms like price escalation clausesand late fees,* or *follow-up to ensure sale-volume commitments were met* had no one directly responsible for them. Additionally, comments in the survey, such as *I respond to RFPs but have no visibility to competitive pricing* added insight to help frame questions for individual interviews when taking a more in-depth look at some processes.

ANALYZING PRICING OPERATIONS

Interviews with internal stakeholders – selected based on their input, high or low ratings or specific comments – can point to processes that may be falling short of expectation. Such qualitative feedback can often be handily verified with easily available data or existing reports. For instance, analysis of the annual price increase process at the electronics equipment manufacturer led to a review of contract templates and financial reports, which yielded evidence of several price leaks:

- Based on standard contract agreement, new customers did not get price increases within the first 12 months of signing a contract. But there was no control in place to include customers on the price increase schedule after one year. Data analysis verified that several customers did not get price increases even during their second or third year with the company.
- The contract language template did not include a standard price escalation clause. As a result, the company faced tough resistance from many customers. This also explained customers' low acceptance of price increases.
- There was no standard measurement of realized price increases, actual versus budget, or a mechanism to track exceptions. Hence, temporary price exceptions could become permanent and, moreover, customers could request further discounts and there still would not be a documented explanation in the order processing system.
- Price increases were waived if customers signed a long-term (three or more years) contract. Since there was no standard method or control, we found many short-term customers enjoying the same waiver. Incidentally, some long-term contract customers were forced into untimely increase prices, making some important customers quite unhappy.

Further enquiries revealed that the company was not well prepared to cover cost inflation even for precious commodities such as gold because of inadequate internal processes. For instance, the company had a process that failed to incorporate data from global metal exchanges for timely analyses of internal raw material cost impact. It subsequently failed to communicate the need for surcharges or price increases to internal stakeholders, let alone to important customers prior to announcing an increase. In the absence of a clear justification or standard communication guidelines, the frontline teams struggled with price increases and found it easier to retain customers by offering bigger discounts.

The survey and interviews also revealed gaps in how discounts and concessions were approved. The analysis of transactional data showed wide and inexplicable variation in discounts across all customer segments. For instance, the variation in transactional discounts (shown as a fraction of list price) for one SKU (a popular and high volume product among thousands of SKUs) was presented in two views, as shown in Figs. 4 and 5.

Fig. 4 reflects a wide variation in discounts − from 5% to 90% − that were offered to customers. In Fig. 5, the discount variation is presented

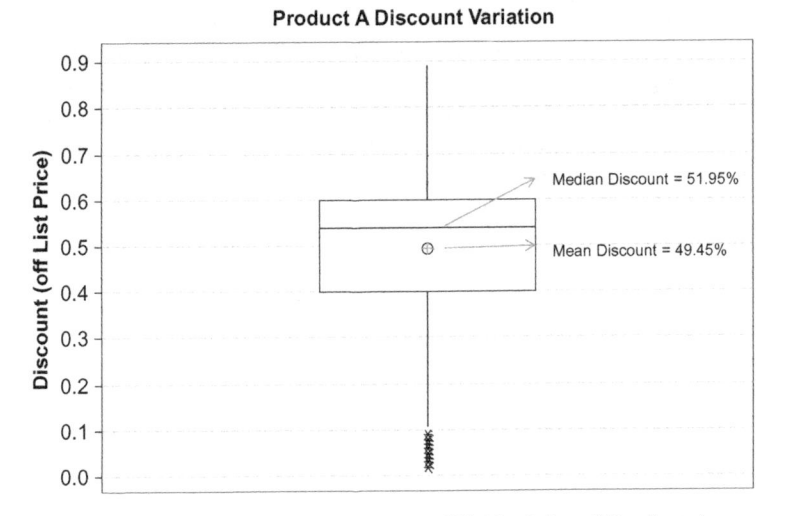

Fig. 4. Wide Variation in Discounts Within Sales of Product A.

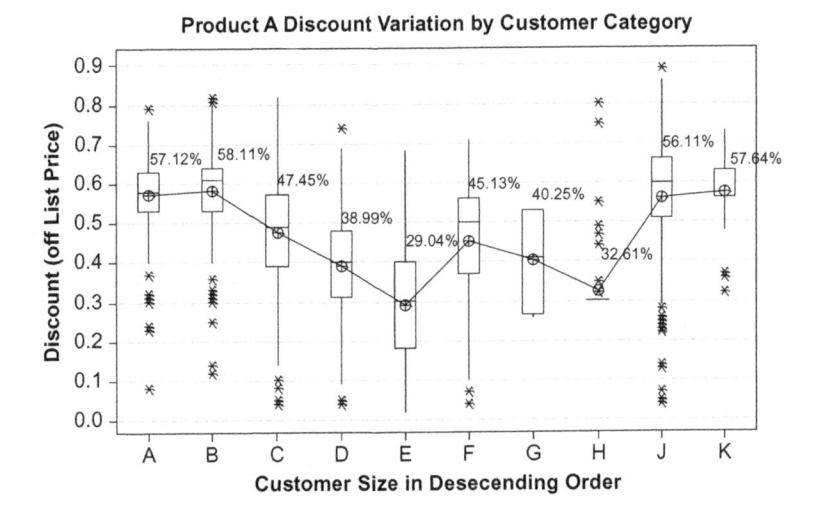

Fig. 5. Wide Variation in Discounts Within Sales of Product A Despite Customer Segment. *Note*: Percentages represent mean discount.

according to size of customer (*Size A customers* were largest based on annual sales revenue and *Size K* were the smallest). The wide variation in discounts suggested that large or small customers could get the same discounts. This also explained why some large customers complained of opportunistic pricing and demanded lower prices when they discovered that a much smaller customer was receiving richer discounts. Although high level and pertaining to a single SKU, this analysis helped senior managers appreciate that variability was a serious problem and also symptomatic of pricing process issues (Fig. 6).

Recommendations

After assessment and analysis, it can be relatively easy to point out areas requiring attention. But recommendations are meaningful only if there is a shared understanding why a company needs to improve pricing operations and an agreement on what steps to pursue and in which order. Moderated

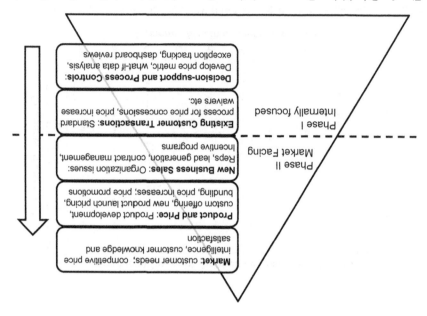

Fig. 6. Prioritizing Recommendations: Improving Internal Operations Precedes Improving Market Facing Activities.

discussions can help functional teams to agree on a methodology for prioritizing pricing issues. For example, one division of an outsourced services company developed 36 recommendations through a qualitative assessment of processes as well as quantitative analysis of data related to various pricing activities. Based on a guided discussion, the teams developed a priority matrix based on three criteria, *revenue growth*, *urgency*, and *time to value* by rating (on a 1–5 scale, 5 being the most important) each criterion for every recommendation. The tabulated scores for each recommendation ranked in descending order delivered the priority list that that met general agreement. Apparently, half the recommendations were relatively quick fixes and had therefore received higher prioritization. Other recommendations following the same logic were classified in a two-phased approach for follow-up and implementation.

Phase I initiatives were primarily internally focused and process-related whereas Phase II actions were mostly market facing and strategic in nature. Senior management set a 5-week deadline for completion of Phase I activities. This period also allowed the internal teams time for preparation to better understand and plan for Phase II activities. The Phase I recommendations not only received attention and a solid response in one division but were also shared with other divisions to encourage discussion on price improvement.

TRAINING

Pricing initiatives are particularly vulnerable to failure, even hostility, if the manner of the initial training is unclear. This is because people, say in finance, may question why some process improvement work pertaining to pricing should apply to them when they already have their hands full. One can find numerous examples of enterprise-wide deployment of major initiatives when everyone is forced to go through training without convincing them of the motivation and expected results. Therefore, the goals for training are three-fold:

1. Explaining the need for pricing assessment and gap analysis to succeed in a major initiative.
2. Sharing knowledge of perception gaps and evidence from data analysis to build broad-based organizational support.
3. Sharing the recommendations as well as expected entitlement from implementation.

The senior management at the electronics equipment manufacturer cited earlier set the work in motion by tasking a team comprising of a product manager, sales manager, and pricing manager to develop an internal training and communications plan. This team developed a playbook based on learning from the perception gaps and began explaining the recommendations to key stakeholders. Pricing and Product Marketing conducted training via phone and web meetings and followed up on any issues or objections that needed to be addressed. In doing so, it became clear that with the exception of reluctance around a few minor issues, there was general support throughout the organization.

CONCLUSION

Disruptions and changes in the internal and external environment are inevitable and companies will always strive to find opportunities and solutions in their veritable journey. Pricing improvement is part of that journey with its share of oncoming surprises and diversions from internal and external changes despite having planned milestones. The pressure to act can push companies into strategic initiatives without adequate planning for operations capability, only to realize that price execution becomes a bottleneck. Therefore, we emphasize that the steps entailed in AART, namely, Assess, Analyze, Recommend and Train, are not the end of the pricing journey but rather an important preparation phase that must precede all large projects directly or indirectly impacting pricing of a company.

HONORING DAN

I first met Dan in the summer of 2008 at the PRICEX, Chicago, where he gave an insightful and thought provoking talk. I asked for his business card, a 3 × 5 index card with his contact information at one narrow end and ample room on either side for writing notes. Handing it to me, he said, "This card has utility beyond this moment which differentiates it from all other business cards." And then he asked me for a dollar for it. He was joking at the time but Dan is always serious about adding and capturing value in everything he does. Like many others who know Dan as a friend and mentor, I sincerely thank him for defining value in pricing and for paving the way for the rest of us.

REFERENCES

Dignan, L. (2011). *Apple's iPhone 4S is swell, but pricing is the real killer app.* ZDNet, October 4. Retrieved from http://www.zdnet.com/blog/btl/apples-iphone-4s-is-swell-but-pricing-is-the-real-killer-app/59761

Hagerty, J. and Tita, B. (2011). Whirlpool accuses Samsung, LG of Dumping washers. *Wall Street Journal*, December 31. Retrieved from http://online.wsj.com/article/SB100014 24052970204632204577130483950517346.html

Grossman, D. (2005). A la carte: The future of airline pricing.*USA Today*, August 8. Retrieved from http://www.usatoday.com/travel/columnist/grossman/2005-08-26-grossman_x.htm

Lee, W. (2011). Angeion's latest boss aims to end turmoil, boost stock. *Star Tribune*, September 17. Retrieved from http://www.startribune.com/business/129981973.html

Sodhi, M. S., & Sodhi, N. S. (2005, May). Six sigma pricing. *Harvard Business Review, 83*, 135–142.

Sodhi, M. S., & Sodhi, N. S. (2008). *Six sigma pricing: Improving pricing operations to increase profits* (pp. 142–144). Upper Saddle River, NJ: Financial Times Press.

ABOUT THE AUTHORS

George E. Cressman, Jr. is President and Founder of World Class Pricing, Inc. George spent 30 years in industry, and has been consulting in marketing strategy, competitive strategy, and pricing for 15 years. George provides marketing and pricing solutions for global business-to-business and business-to-consumer firms. George has been named Marketer of the Year by the American Marketing Association, and is a frequent speaker in management education programs.

Chuck Davenport is a Senior Manager in the Atlanta Office of Deloitte Consulting LLP, and cofounder of Deloitte's Pricing Practice. He has more than 10 years of experience helping companies identify and realize profit improvements through innovative pricing strategies, practical process and organization design and effective implementation. Chuck has an MBA degree from the Goizueta Business School, Atlanta, and an undergraduate degree in electrical engineering from Georgia Institute of Technology in Atlanta. He currently lives in Roswell, outside of Atlanta, with his wife, Ronda, and their five children.

Allan Gray is a member of Vendavo's Pricing Science team. Allan has a wealth of experience designing and deploying supply chain and marketing analytics. Allan began his career at Procter & Gamble, where he introduced econometric forecasting techniques to Procter & Gamble Europe. He subsequently led a number of pan-European projects in supply chain management and purchasing as a consultant with McKinsey & Company. Allan holds an M.Eng. degree in engineering, economics and management from Oxford University and an MBA from Stanford's Graduate School of Business. He also held a Kennedy Scholarship at MIT, where he studied in the Department of Electrical Engineering, the Sloan School of Management and the Operations Research Center.

Reed K. Holden, world-class pricing expert and Holden Advisors founder, works with clients from a broad range of industries to build go-to-market strategies that drive price leadership and profitable growth He pioneered the Value Discipline^{SM}, a process to tune and sustain pricing power even in the most competitive markets. His most recent work focuses on successfully dealing with discount-oriented procurement departments through better product positioning, selling tactics and negotiation techniques. As a change agent, he helps business leaders translate these strategies into action by instilling pricing confidence across their organizations and within the executive ranks. Dr. Holden's latest book – *Pricing with Confidence: 10 Ways to Stop Leaving Money on the Table* – provides a practical framework and compelling examples for his presentations and keynotes. The book gives sales, marketing, finance, and pricing leaders an actionable road map for working together to outperform the competition.

E. M. (Mick) Kolassa, MBA, Ph.D., is Chairman and Managing Partner of Medical Marketing Economics, and is recognized internationally as the leading expert on pharmaceutical pricing and value-based strategies. He is Adjunct Professor of pharmacy administration in the School of Pharmacy and former Associate Professor of pharmacy administration and marketing in the School of Business at the University of Mississippi. Dr. Kolassa is the author of several articles and book chapters on pharmaceutical marketing and pricing issues, coauthor of the book *Pharmaceutical Marketing: Principles, Environment, and Practice*, and author of *Elements of Pharmaceutical Pricing* (1997) and *The Strategic Pricing of Pharmaceuticals* (2009).

Michael Lucaccioni is Director, Value Realization at Vendavo. Michael's team of value realization consultants are responsible for ensuring customers achieve and exceed their price management initiative's ROI by identifying, quantifying and capturing price efficiency and price effectiveness opportunities. Prior to joining Vendavo Michael was a pricing domain expert at a strategy consulting firm focused on analyzing and recommending end-user pricing strategies and channel compensation systems. Prior to consulting Michael spent 12 years in various sales and marketing roles, marketing commodity, specialty and new, patented products both direct and through distribution. Michael has a Bachelor of Science degree in mechanical engineering from the University of Illinois and an MBA from Northwestern's Kellogg School of Management.

Mike Marn is one of the world's leading and most recognized experts in pricing. Until his retirement in 2009, he built and led the McKinsey & Company's worldwide Pricing Practice over 25 years. He has developed many of the most widely used approaches for identifying and capturing opportunities in pricing. He has written a variety of articles on pricing appearing in *The Wall Street Journal, The New York Times, The Harvard Business Review, Boardroom Reports,* and *Sales and Marketing Management.* He has been quoted on issues of price management in *Business Week, Fortune, Investors' Business Daily, Financial Times,* and *USA Today.* He is also a coauthor of both the first and second editions of *The Price Advantage* and has been named to *Consulting Magazine's* list of the world's top 25 most influential consultants.

Kent B. Monroe is a pioneer of research on the information value of price and author of the classic text, *Pricing: Making Profitable Decisions.* He is the J. M. Jones Distinguished Professor of marketing Emeritus, University of Illinois at Urbana-Champaign, USA, and Distinguished Visiting Scholar, University of Richmond, Virginia, USA. He teaches pricing strategy and tactics, marketing management, and research methods among other areas. His research on buyers' perception of price information has been groundbreaking. Professor Monroe's papers have been published in the topmost journals in marketing and management. He has also served as the editor of the *Journal of Consumer Research* and *Pricing Strategy & Practice.* He is a recipient of "Pricer of the Year" award (Pricing Institute), Marketing Pioneer Award, the American Marketing Association/Irwin/ McGraw-Hill Distinguished Marketing Educator Award, and the Converse Award. He has conducted executive training programs for business firms, nonprofit organizations, and universities in North and South America, Europe, Asia, Australia, and Africa.

Thomas Nagle is Senior Advisor at The Monitor Group. Before his quasi-retirement, he was a Senior Partner at Monitor, the founder and CEO of The Strategic Pricing Group (acquired by Monitor in 2005), and the author or coauthor of five editions of *The Strategy and Tactics of Pricing* (Prentice Hall) beginning with the first edition in 1985.

Dan Nimer is founder and President of The DNA Group, Inc., a consulting firm specializing in the development of value-driven pricing marketing and planning strategies in both domestic and international markets. Prior to forming his own organization, he was Vice President, Corporate Planning, and Market Development for a major ITT subsidiary, and Assistant to the President of the former Zenith Radio Corporation. He developed a systematic and logical approach to the formulation of pricing objectives, strategies, and tactics that has been presented to most of the Fortune 500 companies in the United States and to more than 2,000 senior management executives of some of the largest companies in Canada, Europe, and Mexico. He has spoken for a number of organizations representing industries in banking, health care, and telecommunications, along with private organizations such as the YPO, The Executive Committee, and a number of international symposiums. The U.S. State Department sponsored a conference in Sweden conducted by Mr. Nimer on the subjects of international marketing and corporate planning.

His major marketing thrusts for his clients involve the use of the 3C's: Creating, Communicating, and Capturing Value through each element of the marketing mix. For his pricing efforts over the past 30 years, he was given the *Pricer of the Year* award a few years ago; it was then renamed the Dan Nimer Award. His consulting assignments have included the pricing of new products and services, developing pricing policy guidelines, creating a mechanism for establishing prices on a worldwide basis, and augmenting the skills of sales forces in capturing value through pricing tactics.

John Norkus is Principal at Deloitte Consulting LLP specializing in pricing and profitability management across a number of industries most recently leading the consumer business sector globally. His pricing experience includes strategy, execution, advanced analytics, technology, and process/ organization design. In John's 23 years with Deloitte, he has served as the national leader for the revenue enhancement set of services, led Deloitte's largest client, and was a charter member of Deloitte's Global Customer Relationship Management (CRM) practice. He was one of the conceiving authors of the Deloitte ValueMap^{TM}, which links operations levers directly to company shareholder value. John holds a bachelor's degree in aeronautical engineering and a master of business administration degree, both from the University of Illinois. He currently lives in Lake Forest, outside of Chicago, with his wife Robin and their three children.

Jamie Rapperport is Founder & EVP Marketing and Business Development at Vendavo and brings an impressive record of entrepreneurial success to Vendavo. Prior to Vendavo, he served as a founder and vice president of marketing and sales at VXtreme, a leading streaming video technology provider which he helped lead to its category-leading position and subsequent acquisition by Microsoft. Mr. Rapperport's 20 years of experience in the technology sector also includes senior management, product management, marketing, and business development positions with Lotus, Sun Microsystems, and WebTV Networks. Mr. Rapperport holds a Bachelor of Arts degree from Harvard and an MBA from the Stanford Graduate School of Business.

Hermann Simon is the founder and Chairman of Simon-Kucher & Partners Strategy & Marketing Consultants. He is a well-known speaker at business conferences all over the world and has published over 30 books in 25 languages. Simon was a member of the editorial boards of numerous business journals, including the *International Journal of Research in Marketing, Management Science, Recherche et Applications en Marketing, Décisions Marketing, European Management Journal*, as well as several German journals. As a board member of numerous corporations and boards of trustees, Professor Simon has gained substantial experience in the area of corporate governance. Before founding today's leading pricing consultancy Simon-Kucher & Partners, he was a professor of business administration and marketing at the Universities of Mainz (1989–1995) and Bielefeld (1979–1989). He was also a visiting professor at various international universities: Harvard Business School, Stanford, London Business School, INSEAD, Keio University in Tokyo and the Massachusetts Institute of Technology. He has received honorary doctorates from the University of Siegen, from IEDC, Business School of Bled, Slovenia, Kozminski University, Warsaw, and is an honorary professor at the University of International Business and Economics in Beijing. In German-speaking countries Simon is ranked as the most influential management thinker after the late Peter Drucker.

Michael Simonetto is Principal with Deloitte Consulting LLP and founder and leader of Deloitte's Global Pricing and Profitability Management Practice. Mike has also been the Chief Operating Officer of a leading pricing software firm. He holds a bachelor's degree from Indiana University and a master of business administration degree from the University of North Carolina – Chapel Hill, where he also currently serves as an Adjunct Professor in the Executive MBA Program. Mike is also a member of the President's Advisory Board for Oglethorpe University, and sits on the Advisory Board for the Professional Pricing Society. When not working, he splits his time between Cashiers, NC and Atlanta, with his wife of 31 years, Theresa.

Navdeep S. Sodhi is Managing Director at Sodhi Pricing. He has helped companies improve earnings and revenues through pricing strategy and execution for over 16 years. His experience, as practitioner and consultant, spans several global industries: Airlines, Medical Devices, B2B manufacturing, Electronics, Chemicals, Outsourced Services, and Building products. Navdeep's approach to improving price is presented in his book *Six Sigma Pricing: Improving Pricing Operations to Increase Profits* (Financial Times Press, 2008) and was first introduced in his seminal Harvard Business Review article (2005) with the same title. He has published other articles on pricing strategy and execution in reputed publications such as Oxford Press, Journal of Pricing, and Quality Digest. He is a recipient of *Professional Pricing Society Award of Excellence* and has also received several employee awards for his outstanding work in pricing. Navdeep teaches price management at the University of St Thomas and is a frequent speaker at pricing conferences and company meets. Navdeep has an MBA from Georgetown University and is based in Minneapolis.

Lisa Thompson is Senior Partner and a Director at The Monitor Group. She has nearly two decades of experience helping B2B and Life Sciences companies manage pricing and value communication in ways that enable them to grow more profitably.

Takaho Ueda is Professor on the Economics Faculty at Gakushuin University in Tokyo, where he teaches courses in marketing, pricing strategy, and global marketing. He is an expert in pricing, marketing and promotion strategy. He is author or coauthor of seven pricing books, including most recently *Pricing and Promotion Strategy* and *Case Studies and Theories of Pricing Strategies in Japan*, and another 21 books in information strategies and technologies, marketing research, financial marketing, and international marketing. He has been a visiting scholar at UCLA, and held positions at Tonen General Sekiyu k.k. of Tokyo.

Elliott Yama is Director, Education at Vendavo. He is an expert in pricing competency development in B2B organizations. He possesses a wealth of experience as a consultant on pricing strategy in a broad range of industry settings. Elliott has over 12 years of experience as an instructor for global B2B companies. At Vendavo, Elliott holds the title of Director of Education and leads Vendavo University. Prior to joining Vendavo, Elliott was a partner at Strategic Pricing Group/Monitor, a global consultancy. Elliott is a recognized member of the pricing community and is a member of the faculty of the Professional Pricing Society as well as the Institute for the Study of Business Marketing (ISBM) at Penn State. Elliott holds an MBA from Boston University.

Craig Zawada serves as Senior Vice President, Pricing Excellence, at PROS Pricing, the world's leading provider of price management and optimization software. Prior to joining PROS in 2010, Zawada was a partner and coleader of the North American Pricing Practice at McKinsey & Company gaining experience across a wide range of B2B and consumer products. He is a widely published author on the subject of pricing strategy, with articles featured in the *Harvard Business Review*, *Mergers and Acquisitions*, and the *McKinsey Quarterly*. He has been interviewed and quoted in *Fortune Magazine*, *CFO Magazine*, *Canadian Business*, and *Business 2.0*. Zawada is coauthor of both the first and second editions of *The Price Advantage*, recognized as one of the most pragmatic books on pricing strategy available.

Eugene F. Zelek, Jr. practices marketing-related law and chairs the Antitrust and Trade Regulation Group at the law firm of Freeborn & Peters LLP. The author thanks his colleagues William C. Holmes and Hillary P. Krantz for their assistance.